POLYNESIA
IN EARLY HISTORIC TIMES

DOUGLAS OLIVER

THE BESS PRESS

3565 Harding Ave. Honolulu, Hawai'i 96816
808/ 734-7159   www.besspress.com

In memory of Peter Buck and Raymond Firth, for their different but equally peerless ethnographic achievements

Design: Carol Colbath

Index: Lee S. Motteler

Cover art: Tahitian war canoes. George Tobin. Reproduced with permission of the Mitchell Library, State Library of New South Wales, and Bernard Smith, Rudiger Joppien, and Oxford University Press Australia from Smith and Joppien, *The Art of Captain Cook's Voyages*, vols. 1–3, 1987, now out of print, © Oxford University Press, www.oup.com.au.

Library of Congress Cataloging-in-Publication Data

Oliver, Douglas.
    Polynesia in Early Historic Times /
Douglas Oliver.
        p. cm.
    Includes bibliography, index,
illustrations.
    ISBN 1-57306-125-5
    1. Polynesia - History.
2. Polynesians. I. Title.
DU510.O45 2002   919.6-dc20

Printed in the United States of America

POLYNESIA
IN EARLY HISTORIC TIMES

Other books by Douglas Oliver

The Pacific Islands

A Solomon Island Society

Bougainville: A Personal History

Ancient Tahitian Society

Two Tahitian Villages: A Study in Comparisons

Return to Tahiti: Bligh's Second Breadfruit Voyage

Oceania: Native Cultures of Australia and the Pacific Islands

# Contents

Fig. 1.1. Culture areas of the Pacific

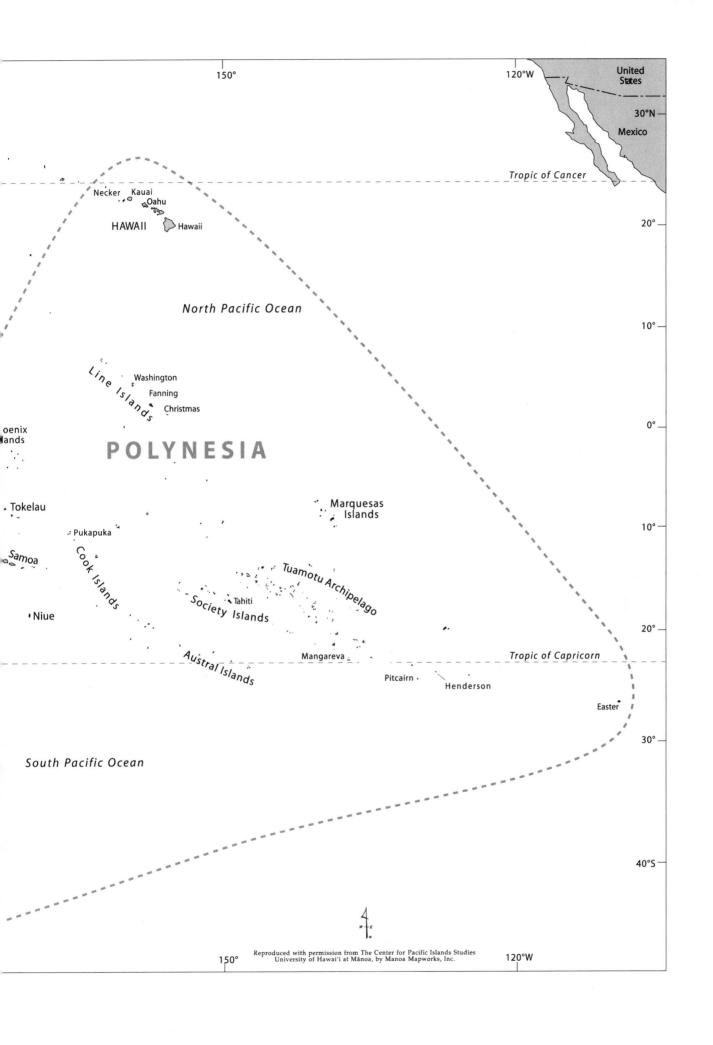

150°   120°W

United States

30°N

Mexico

Tropic of Cancer

Necker Kauai
     Oahu
HAWAII   Hawaii

20°

North Pacific Ocean

10°

Line Islands
    Washington
    Fanning
    Christmas

0°

oenix
lands

POLYNESIA

Tokelau

Marquesas
Islands

10°

Pukapuka

Samoa

Cook Islands

Tuamotu Archipelago

Niue

Tahiti
Society Islands

20°

Austral Islands

Mangareva

Tropic of Capricorn

Pitcairn ·
      Henderson

Easter

30°

South Pacific Ocean

40°S

W   E

Reproduced with permission from The Center for Pacific Islands Studies
University of Hawai'i at Mānoa, by Manoa Mapworks, Inc.

150°   120°W

ACKNOWLEDGMENTS

The sources of most of the descriptions and conclusions contained in the text are referenced and are identified in the Bibliography—although some of them come from my own experiences during decades of travels and sojourns in Polynesia. More specifically, I wish to acknowledge with special thanks those individuals whose writings or whose comments on the text have been especially helpful or influential in my writing of the text, mainly Atholl Anderson, Angela Ballard, Ernest and Pearl Beaglehole, Peter Buck (Te Rangi Hiroa), Edwin Burrows, Ross Cordy, Janet Davidson, Richard Feinberg, Ben Finney, Raymond Firth, Irving Goldman, Roger Green, E. S. C. Handy, F. A. Hanson, Alan Howard, Adrienne Kaeppler, Michael King, Patrick Kirch, Robert Kiste, Katherine Luamala, Joan Metge, Paul Ottino, A. K. Pawley, Michael Pietrusewsky, Marshall Sahlins, Anne Salmond, D. R. Simmons, D. G. Sutton, A. P. Vayda, and Douglas Yen.

Illustration sources are listed under that heading, but I wish to acknowledge with special thanks the individuals and institutions whose permissions or publications have been especially helpful in assembling the illustrations, mainly Tricia Allen, Ben Finney, Raymond Firth, S. R. Fischer, Richard Hey, Helen Leach and Nancy Tichborne, Lois Johnson, the British Library, the National Library of Australia, the State Library of New South Wales, Rudiger Joppien, Bernard Smith, the Oxford University Press (Melbourne), and most of all, Robert Kiste, the Center for Pacific Islands Studies at the University of Hawai'i-Mānoa, and Manoa Mapworks.

ILLUSTRATIONS

Parkinson (1773). Reproduced with permission of Bernard Smith, Rudiger Joppien, and Oxford University Press Australia from Smith and Joppien, *The Art of Captain Cook's Voyages*, vols. 1–3, 1987, now out of print, © Oxford University Press, www.oup.com.au.

15.9   A Hawaiian dancer holding a gourd rattle. Engraving by John Webber, 1784. Courtesy of Bishop Museum.

16.1   Weapons of various Polynesian peoples. Drawing by Lois Johnson in Oliver (1989b).

16.2   A Marquesan warrior with club. In Krusenstern.

16.3   Tahitian war canoe. Drawing by William Hodges. Reproduced with permission of the Mitchell Library, State Library of New South Wales, and Bernard Smith, Rudiger Joppien, and Oxford University Press Australia from Smith and Joppien, *The Art of Captain Cook's Voyages*, vols. 1–3, 1987, now out of print, © Oxford University Press, www.oup.com.au.

17.1   The body of a Tahitian chief as preserved after death. Drawing by John Webber. Reproduced with permission of Dixson Library, State Library of New South Wales, and Bernard Smith, Rudiger Joppien, and Oxford University Press Australia from Smith and Joppien, *The Art of Captain Cook's Voyages*, vols. 1–3, 1987, now out of print, © Oxford University Press, www.oup.com.au.

17.2   A chief mourner of Tahiti (on left) beside the bier of an embalmed high-rank man. Drawing by John Webber in Cook (1777) Reproduced with permission of Bernard Smith, Rudiger Joppien, and Oxford University Press Australia from Smith and Joppien, *The Art of Captain Cook's Voyages*, vols. 1–3, 1987, now out of print, © Oxford University Press, www.oup.com.au.

17.3   Close-up of a Tahitian chief mourner in mourning dress. Drawing by John Webber in Cook (1777). Reproduced with permission of Bernard Smith, Rudiger Joppien, and Oxford University Press Australia from Smith

and Joppien, *The Art of Captain Cook's Voyages*, vols. 1–3, 1987, now out of print, © Oxford University Press, www.oup.com.au.

17.4   Chiefly burial pyramid at Tongatabu. Drawing by James Wilson in James Wilson (1799).

17.5   The Tongan Ha'mongaamaui monument. Courtesy of Bishop Museum.

18.1   Hamlet scene in Hawai'i. Drawing by John Webber in Cook and King.

21.1   Portrait of the Tahitian chief Pomare. Drawing by William Hodges. National Library of Australia R 755. By permission of the National Library of Australia, Bernard Smith, Rudiger Joppien, and Oxford University Press Australia from Smith and Joppien, *The Art of Captain Cook's Voyages*, vols. 1–3, 1987, now out of print, © Oxford University Press, www.oup.com.au.

21.2   A chief of Hawai'i leading his party to battle. Nan Kivell collection, National Library of Australia. By permission of National Library of Australia, Bernard Smith, Rudiger Joppien, and Oxford University Press Australia from Smith and Joppien, *The Art of Captain Cook's Voyages*, vols. 1–3, 1987, now out of print, © Oxford University Press, www.oup.com.au.

21.3   Portrait of a Marquesan chief. Engraving of a drawing by William Hodges in Cook (1777).

21.4   Portrait of the Tongan "king." Engraving of a drawing by John Webber. In Cook and King (1784).

21.5   A young woman of Tahiti wearing presents of barkcloth and gorgets. Drawing by John Webber. Reproduced with permission of Dixson Library, State Library of New South Wales, and Bernard Smith, Rudiger Joppien, and Oxford University Press Australia from Smith and Joppien, *The Art of Captain Cook's Voyages*, vols. 1–3, 1987, now out of print, © Oxford University Press, www.oup.com.au.

23.1   Wooden carving of Easter Island Birdman. In Wardwell. Courtesy American Museum of Natural History Library.

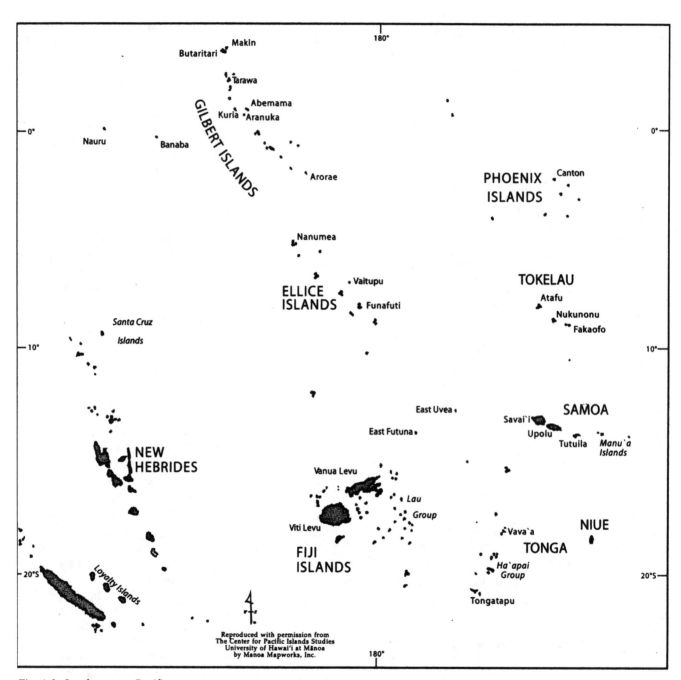

Fig. 1.2. Southwestern Pacific

1

INTRODUCTION

About 3,300 years ago one or more canoe-loads of Pacific Islanders, males and females, set out in an easterly direction from southern Melanesia (either from the Santa Cruz or New Hebrides or Loyalty islands) in search of new homelands. The reasons for their expeditions are not known: perhaps defeat in warfare, perhaps food shortage through overpopulation or natural disaster, perhaps hope for more fruitful lands—or perhaps adventurous curiosity for what lay beyond the sunrise horizon. Even a forced departure need not have been darkened by unmitigated despair: from the remembered experiences of some of their forebears—who had been migrating eastward out of Island Southeast Asia for centuries—there had always been islands not far ahead, whether visible or not from their current settlements. Moreover, throughout their migrations those forebears had found most of the islands they had landed on to be habitable, and populated, wholly or partly, by earlier settlers—earlier in some places by thousands of years.

Such expectations were, however, not to be realized by our particular voyagers. Their landfall(s) turned out to be one or another island in the Fiji Archipelago, at least 575 (statute) miles distant from their point(s) of departure[1]—twice the distance of any previous successful voyage along their forebears' migration routes. Moreover, neither their own landfall(s) nor any other island beyond was or had ever been inhabited by humans.

Skeptics have argued that all or most of the successful long voyages of Pacific Islanders—i.e., distances more than about 375 miles—had been accidental: that they had been made by offshore fishing parties or interisland trade missions, blown off course and surviving miraculously until cast up on a far distant island. Undoubtedly, islanders had experienced scores of such accidents in the course of their longtime presence in Pacific waters, including a few from which some of their crews had survived to form settlements on previously uninhabited islands. However, the voyage(s) of these particular islanders were clearly for intentional colonization—i.e., they included females; offshore fishing parties and lengthy trading voyages did not normally include females. Moreover, their canoes evidently, and purposefully, carried enough food to keep them alive for what could be a two- or three-week voyage, along with enough other supplies (e.g., tools, planting stock, and animal breeding stock) to found a new settlement. Also, the survivors of the voyage(s) must have included at least enough reproductively capable males and females to ensure the colony's endurance and proliferation.

During that "first wave" era more than one canoe, or fleet of canoes, may have accomplished such a voyage, from southern Melanesia to Fiji, all or most of whose passengers spoke the same language and carried the same kinds of edible plants, domesticated animals, portable artifacts—and many similar genes. However, after a few decades or centuries those first-wave crossings evidently ceased. Then, after scores of years another set of similar crossings began again, but this time carrying people with a somewhat different language, some slightly different kinds of ideas and portable artifacts, and genes producing darker-pigmented skins. Before that, however, their first-wave predecessors had proliferated and spread, fairly rapidly, not only throughout the Fiji and Lau islands, but to Tonga and possibly Samoa as well. In time the second wave of migrants interbred their genes and intermixed their artifacts, ideas and practices with those of the lighter-skinned first-wave pioneers remaining in Fiji and Lau, but experienced only occasional contacts with those first-wavers who had settled farther east, and who were the ancestors of the peoples now labeled "Polynesians."

1

"Polynesia" is a European word, derived from Greek *poly* (many) and *nesia* (island). It was coined by the French scholar Charles de Brosses and first used by him in his *Histoire des Navigation aux Terres Australes* (published in 1756) to label the region containing all islands in the Pacific east of Australia and of the Philippine and Malay archipelagoes. Subsequently that label was restricted to those islands whose peoples—according to one of Captain James Cook's officers—resembled one another closely in language and "in their religious ceremonies, their arts and their manners" (James King, second lieutenant of Resolution, quoted in Beaglehole 1967, 1392).

Meanwhile, all other Pacific Islanders became classified by Westerners, more geographically than culturally, as either "Melanesians" ("black-skinned islanders": the natives of New Guinea, the Solomons, New Hebrides, New Caledonia and Fiji—including their adjacent islands); or "Micronesians" (natives of the "small-islands": those of the Mariana, Palau, Caroline, Marshall and Gilbert archipelagoes, along with the isolated islands of Banaba [Ocean Island] and Nauru). Of these three labels only "Polynesia" is fully justifiable on ethnic[2] grounds. "Micronesia" contains at least six widely different ethnic units, and has no monopoly on islands of small size. And as for "Melanesia," it contains hundreds of distinct ethnic units, and only those natives of the northern Solomons are truly black—all other so-called Melanesians ranging in skin color from light to dark brown. Nevertheless, the ethnically misleading labels of "Melanesia" and "Micronesia" remain infixed in most writings and maps about Pacific Islanders (including several earlier publications of my own!).[3]

Reverting to the truly valid ethnic category "Polynesian," the special interests of Westerners (i.e., persons of European descent) in such peoples commenced centuries ago, and for a number of reasons. One was the observation that islanders so much alike in physical features and in languages and other customs were scattered over an ocean area of millions of square miles, thereby evidencing extraordinary capabilities in boat building and seamanship. Another reason for Westerners' fascination with—and attraction toward—Polynesians in general was what was perceived to be their hierarchically organized societies—which contrasted sharply with what seemed to be the "savage anarchy" of most Melanesian peoples. And, of course, the relatively lighter skins, straighter hair, and more European facial features of most Polynesians—especially of young females—was reason enough for many Western seamen and traders to prefer them to Melanesians. "Micronesia" also contained several Polynesia-like polities (as well as a majority of individuals of lighter skin and straighter hair than most Melanesians), but the Micronesians, with their many interisland differences in language and other cultural features, attracted less intellectual interest than did the Polynesians. Also, except for Guam, the islands of Micronesia were less frequently visited by Westerners than those of Polynesia—and were virtually closed to Westerners after their seizure by Japan from Germany in World War I.

For those and other reasons several scholarly (and many more unscholarly!) books have been written about the peoples of Polynesia as a whole. Why, then, add another to the list?

My warrant for doing so is, first, that all of the scholarly English-language, Polynesia-wide books now in print focus on only one or two aspects of peoples' cultures (e.g., on their remote prehistories, or on their social institutions, or subsistence technologies, or crafts, or religions, or arts, or mythologies, etc.).[4] Moreover, even those are either partly outdated (as a result of a recently increasing flurry of archaeological and archival research), or are written mainly for specialists—and therefore in language uncomfortably technical for nonspecialists. The present book is written for the nonspecialist reader in search of a more comprehensive, less technical, but nevertheless (I hope) nonsimplistic introduction to the subject. Its plan is as follows:

Part One is an account, based on archaeology and linguistics, of the origins of the peoples who came to be known as Polynesians, and of what is known, or reasonably inferred, about the beliefs, artifacts, and practices they brought with them, or came to develop and consolidate, in their new central Pacific (i.e., west Polynesia) homeland. Following that is an account, still very tentative, of the dispersal of some of those "ancestral" Polynesians into other parts of the Pacific.

Parts Two and Three, the main body of the book, are an introduction to the cultures of the descendants of those ancestral Polynesians as they were at or soon after first *recorded* contacts with

Westerners and before those and subsequent contacts had begun to initiate major changes in those cultures,[5] Part Two being devoted to those peoples located on islands in the tropics and subtropics, Part Three to those in New Zealand (and their offshoots in the Chatham Islands)—a division called for by New Zealand's significantly larger size and colder climates.

To reconstruct the cultures as they were "at or soon after" Western contacts is at least the aim of Parts Two and Three—an aim that is, however, difficult if not impossible to achieve in some instances, inasmuch as some of the cultures were competently studied only decades after contact. Nevertheless, the book's title is intended to represent the fact that its focus is (as just said) on the behaviors and the credible memories of Polynesians at and soon after the times when Westerners first observed and competently recorded them. Several publications about indigenous, "pre-European" Polynesian cultures have been titled "ancient" this or that, without specifying how "ancient" their time-span focuses were— "ancient" in such cases being an alluring but imprecise term for localized cultures that had been changing for hundreds or even thousands of years.

PART ONE

2

FOREBEARS OF THE "POLYNESIANS"

The distinctive combination of physical types and cultural traits (including languages) now labeled "Polynesian" was developed in Tonga and Samoa and a few smaller nearby islands between about 1000 B.C. and A.D. 500 (Davidson 1989; Irwin 1992). Components of that combination, including all of its domesticated animals, most of its food crops, many of its tools and crafts, some of its social patterns and religious ideas and, of course, the genes producing the human physical types, had evolved earlier and elsewhere. But the combination also included many cultural innovations made locally, partly in adaptation to the peculiarities of the area's pristine physical environments, partly as a result of the immigrants' isolation from all other peoples, and partly because—as with all other humans—some of their beliefs and practices had inevitably changed over time. What is known about that distinctive combination will be summarized in the next chapter; the question now is, Who were those immigrants who became the first, i.e., ancestral, Polynesians?

To begin with, it can be answered with solid reassurance who they were not. They were not a mixture of Mesopotamians and (India) Indians, driven from South Asia by later Vedic-era peoples—as was proposed by one early "authority" (Abraham Fornander, in 1878). Furthermore, they were not Egyptians, nor "Caucasians," nor Japanese, nor British-Columbian Indians—as proposed by other nineteenth-century scholars and summarized in an informative study by Alan Howard (1967). Nor were they Peruvian Indians—as proposed by Thor Heyerdahl, and as allegedly substantiated by him and his well-publicized 1947 drift voyage from Peru to the Tuamotus aboard the now-famous raft *Kon Tiki*. A fuller answer to the question awaits more archaeological research, but enough has been discovered during recent decades to provide many positive and credible clues. Moreover, those clues

point to the relevance—to this specific question—of the prehistory of the western Pacific in general. That prehistory goes back a very long time; and while it also concerns some peoples unrelated, or only remotely related, to the Polynesians' forebears, it serves to point up the cultural and physical distinctiveness of the latter.

Skulls and skull fragments of hominid (humanlike) primates have been found in Island Southeast Asia, specifically Java, in deposits dating as early as 1.9 million years ago.[6] These skulls differ from those of modern mankind (*Homo sapiens*, "man wise") in being thicker, heavier browed and more prognathous, and in having smaller and more recessive chins, larger teeth and smaller brains (i.e., capacities of 46 to 67 cubic inches, compared with modern humans' 73 to 110). Nevertheless, from the position of the *foramen magnum* ("great hole," the large orifice in the back of the skull through which passes the spinal cord) it is inferred that those hominids stood almost fully erect, from which characteristic they have been labeled *Homo erectus* ("man erect"). Nothing like them, in shape or in antiquity, has been found in New Guinea or Australia, which, as will be described, have been separated by wide ocean gaps from Island Southeast Asia for millions of years.

The oldest remains of *Homo sapiens* so far found in Island Southeast Asia were located at sites dating no earlier than about forty thousand years ago, but they must have been present there long before then, as evidenced by the discovery, in New Guinea and Australia, of manmade artifacts at least as old. Experts disagree concerning the origins of those Southeast Asian *Homo sapiens*—whether they evolved *in situ* from the older *Homo erectines* or were immigrants from the Asian mainland (who, it is argued, either supplanted the *erectines* altogether or absorbed them into their own populations).[7] In any case, I will refer to them as Sundanoids (after Sunda, the [dry] land that made up their periodically interlinked islands), and characterize them, positively, as having had larger brains, smaller teeth and jaws and more prominent chins than the predecessor *erectines*. (And, since all their presumptive descendants have dark skins and curly to woolly hair, it is probable that the Sundanoids had the same.) Also, it is highly likely that, up to about ten thousand years ago, they obtained all or most of their food by hunting, gathering wild plant food and fishing.

At this point in the narrative it is necessary to add a few words about that penultimate geological epoch, the Pleistocene.

Beginning about one million years ago the Earth's atmosphere cooled enough year-round to diminish the summertime melting of wintertime ice and snow, thereby impounding in glaciers and huge ice sheets what ordinarily melted in summertime and flowed back into the oceans: circumstances that resulted in lower sea levels globally—low enough to narrow or even eliminate ocean gaps between land masses everywhere. During the last million years the Earth has experienced four major and several minor occurrences of such Ice Ages, separated by "interglacial" periods of warming—the last of the Ice Ages having peaked and begun to end about eleven thousand years ago.

The relevance of the above to the subject matter of this chapter is that during certain periods within the documented presence of humans or humanlike beings in Island Southeast Asia, most of those islands west of about longitude 130 degrees west were joined one with another and with the Asia mainland by dry land—as was Australia with New Guinea (the former land aggregate labeled "Sunda," the latter "Sahul") (fig. 2.1). However, it should be emphasized that at no time during the span of modern human (i.e., *Homo sapiens*) existence in the area was the sea level low enough to bridge all of the ocean gaps between Sunda and Sahul. At times the islands in that area were either joined or brought closer together, but any human attempting a crossing between Sunda and Sahul would have had to swim or boat at least 36 nautical miles (i.e., 41.4 statute miles).

Beginning no later than about forty thousand to fifty thousand years ago some Sundanoids did however cross those gaps,[8] some of them doubt-

2.1. Sunda and Sahul (shaded areas now submerged)

less encouraged by the periodic narrowing of the gaps, others compelled to do so by the periodic dwindling of their lands, resulting from alternating rises in sea level. Speculation is that the migrants did so on rafts or in small boats (rather than by swimming with or without log supports), that crossings took place along several different routes (via successions of intervisible islands), and that the final landings took place at several different places along a two-thousand–mile Sahul shoreline that extended from the northwestern capes of New Guinea to Australia's adjacent dry land.

Such crossings doubtless continued for thousands of years, and the descendants of the migrants constituted, eventually, two separate major streams—the one having peopled Australia and Tasmania, the other New Guinea and its nearby archipelagoes to the north, east and southeast, as far as the southern Solomons. Australia's southwest corner was reached about thirty-eight thousand years ago, the northern Solomons by about ten thousand years later. (The land shelf linking New Guinea and Australia was finally inundated at the end of the Pleistocene about nine thousand years ago—by which time their respective inhabitants had become, and were to remain, profoundly different, genetically and culturally.)

Meanwhile, the inhabitants of New Guinea and their offshoots in the Bismarck and Solomon archipelagoes had themselves become fragmented into numerous small and geographically separate populations that varied widely both in physical characteristics and in culture. For example, by time of Western contact their peoples ranged in skin color from light brown to jet black and in stature from tall to pygmoid. As for their languages, they reveal no historical relationships with any others in the world. And although they have been labeled "Papuan," linguists are still debating whether they are all interrelated.

Beginning about three to four thousand years ago four momentous innovations entered this area from the west and became established, first in the Bismarck Islands and then in New Guinea and the Solomons, a region that the archaeologist Roger Green has aptly labeled "Near Oceania" to distinguish it from "Remote Oceania," the islands north, east and south of there (1991). Those four innovations were (1) some languages of the far-flung Austronesian family; (2) some peoples who were more "Mongoloid" than "Sundanoid" in physical type; (3) terrestrial subsistence systems based mainly on gardening—accompanied by more integral domestication of pigs, and in some cases of dogs and chickens; and (4) marked advances (over Sundanoid practices) in the construction and operation of watercraft. While gene-based human physical types and cultural traits (including language) have not always "migrated" together—as witnessed, for example, by the spreads of sub-Saharan physical types and the speaking of English—these four "momentous" innovations do appear to have been or become joined together upon reaching the Bismarck Archipelago, and in some cases to have "migrated" from there eastward and southward together as a "bundle." In addition, there were some other less "momentous" but nevertheless novel kinds of cultural traits that were or came to be associated with all or some of those four, including new kinds of tools, the making of pottery, and (inferentially but not demonstrably) more hierarchic forms of social organization and more pantheistic religious ideas.

Regarding the Austronesian ("southern islands," often abbreviated AN) languages, the linguists claim that the speakers of that family of languages first lived on what is now Taiwan or its adjacent mainland (which during some lowered–sea-level periods of the Pleistocene were connected) and propose that the hypothetical "ancestor" of that family of languages, proto-Austronesian, began to branch and differentiate about six thousand years ago. (Eventually, Chinese supplanted its mainland branch[es], so that today the oldest surviving Austronesian languages are those spoken in northern Taiwan.) The first major differentiations from the "homeland" Austronesian language(s) are said to have taken place when some of their speakers migrated southward, thereby diversifying their languages, eventually, into the subfamily now known—somewhat illogically—as Malayo-Polynesian. Subsequent migrations of some Malayo-Polynesian speakers resulted in the further branching of their languages, as shown on figure 2.2. (While not directly relevant to our present concern with the antecedents of the languages labeled "Polynesian," it is interesting to note that some other Austronesian speakers ended up in very distant Madagascar.)

Focusing on that branch of Malayo-Polynesian labeled "Central Eastern," its speakers either supplanted the earlier (and as yet unknown) languages of the earlier indigenes of those areas—by eliminating or mixing with and dominating their speakers—or they settled in places previously uninhabited. In any case, more directly relevant to the subject matter of this book are the ramifications of the Oceanic (sub-sub) branch of Austronesian, which itself began to differentiate from other Malayo-Polynesian languages about five thousand years ago, and whose subsequent branches are shown on figure 2.3.

(In case readers are surprised by the speed with which all this branching and sub-branching took place, it should be recalled that we are dealing here with languages that were not written—that once a group of speakers moved away from and lost touch with its "parent" speech community, a process that seems to have occurred quite frequently among these mobile Insulars, the changes that took place, inevitably, in their day-to-day speech were not slowed by common written texts.)

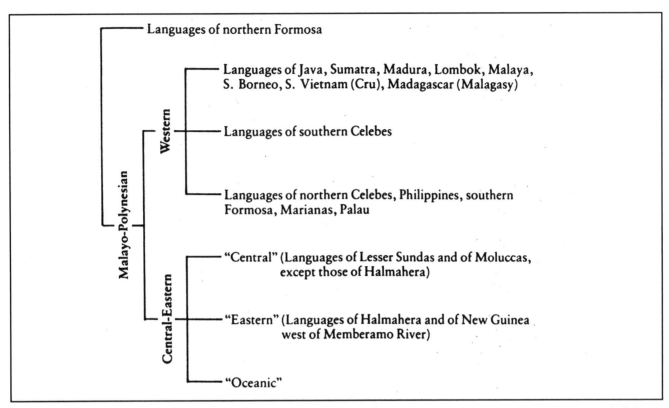

2.2. Major divisions of the Austronesian language family. This classification is based on the studies of Blust (1978), which have built on the work of Otto Dempwolff, George Grace (1966), William Milke (1958), and others.

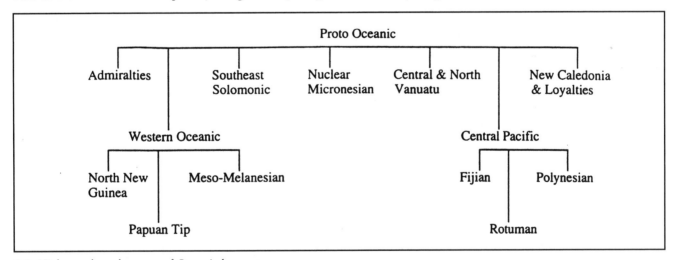

2.3. Higher-order subgroups of Oceanic languages

Up to about thirty-three hundred years ago, speakers of one or another Oceanic language had spread from the Admiralties eastward and southward down the Melanesian archipelagoes to New Caledonia and had colonized some coastal spots on New Guinea as well. En route, as far south as the Santa Cruz Islands, they had encountered many Sundanoid peoples, speaking one or another "Papuan" language, and had either mixed with them, linguistically and genetically, or remained more or less separate (as for example on New Britain and Bougainville, where the Austronesian-speaking settlers remained on or near the coasts and the Papuan speakers in the interiors).[9] It was from one or more of those separate coastal enclaves in the New Hebrides or Santa Cruz or Loyalty islands that the immediate forebears of our Polynesians ventured eastward and ended up, initially, in Fiji.[10]

Turning now to the second of the "momentous" innovations to enter Inner Oceania three to four thousand years ago, i.e., people who were more "Mongoloid" than "Sundanoid" in physical type, it will be useful first to point out how scholars now study and classify what used to be called "races" (a term currently avoided by some scholars as being "politically incorrect").

Until fairly recently "racial" classifications of humans were based mainly on directly visible characteristics—such as stature, head shape, skin and eye color, and color and form of hair—which resulted in classifying individuals into broad physical types such as "Caucasian," "Negroid," "Mongoloid" and "Australoid." According to such criteria, the people I label "Sundanoids" were more or less "Negroid" in skin color and in color and shape of hair—although different from similarly colored peoples of sub-Saharan Africa in many other physical respects. And according to such criteria, peoples generally labeled "Mongoloids" differ from their Pacific predecessors, the "Sundanoids," in having lighter-pigmented skin, straighter hair, and flatter browridges—to list their more conspicuous physical features.

In recent decades the study of genes has served to discover less visible but more fundamental "racial" relationships and differences based on the sharing or nonsharing of one or more genes. However, the results of such studies concerning the origins of the "original" speakers of Polynesian languages are still inconclusive. Four of those studies, based on mtDNA data, support the linguists' Taiwan hypothesis (Sykes et al. 1995; Melton et al. 1995; Redd et al. 1995; Melton et al. 1998), while another study points to eastern Indonesia (Richards et al. 1998). Most recently, however, studies based on Y chromosome data (Bing Su et al. 2000) propose a primordial "racial" origin of both Polynesians (and Micronesians) and Taiwanese in mainland Southeast Asia—and argue against any significant mixture with Sundanoids of the Polynesian samples studied (mainly Samoans and Kapingamarangans). (The study did not include samples of certain "Outlier" Polynesian populations, such as the Tikopians. Had it done so it would doubtless have revealed the presence among them of some Sundanoid genes, in view of their known or presumed contact with nearby peoples of Melanesia.) Genetic studies of Polynesians (i.e., of those few

not yet possessing Caucasian or other non-Polynesian genes) do indeed offer some insights into their physical relationships with other Pacific and Asian peoples, but as the author of the last one cited notes: "[The] debate continues and other plausible scenarios are being examined as well."

The third "momentous" innovation to enter Near Oceania about three to four thousand years ago was subsistence systems based mainly on gardening and the domestication of pigs, dogs and chickens—fishing having been no "innovation," since it was also practiced by their predecessor Sundanoids. The key word in the above statement is "mainly," archaeologists having discovered indirect signs of gardening and pig keeping in the Central Highlands of New Guinea dated as early as nine thousand years ago. Also, some food plants cultivated within Near Oceania in recent millennia are known to have had local natural origins; among the most widely used of them were sago (*Metroxylon*), sugarcane (*Saccharum*), some root crops (*Araceae* and *Dioscorea*) and the nut-bearing canarium tree (*Canarium harveyi*). Moreover, there is the possibility, even probability, that ideas about cultivating food plants, in contrast to gathering them from the wild, diffused into Near Oceania from the west prior to the arrival of the "mainly" horticultural Austronesian-speaking immigrants—or may even have originated among Near Oceania Sundanoids themselves. Nevertheless, it was the arrival of the Austronesian speakers that provided the added stimulus—including many of the horticultural materials and practices—that eventually led most of the Sundanoid peoples of Near Oceania to adopt gardening as their "main" form of subsistence as well.[11]

The fourth "momentous" innovation to enter Near Oceania some three to four thousand years ago—the "marked improvements in the construction and operation of watercraft"—refers to the attachment of one or more outriggers or, somewhat later, a second hull, to canoes (for added stability or capacity) and the widespread use of one or more sails (for reducing paddling effort and for increasing speed). During the previous millennia the Sundanoids had doubtless made improvements—in size, seaworthiness, etc.—over the craft that had carried the first bands of them from Sunda to Sahul. Also, here and there they may have added a sail. But the markedly superior features listed above, plus the widespread use of sails, were most likely introduced by Austronesian speakers themselves.

Other important innovations linked with the four just listed were new and better tools and the making of pottery; however, mention must be made of the views held by some scholars that the above innovations, "momentous" and otherwise, did not necessarily constitute a unified "bundle" introduced initially into New Guinea waters by a single set of Southeast Asians—i.e., that components of them might have entered the region initially over a period of some centuries, some having been carried by actual migrants, others, possibly, by less cohesive diffusion of objects and ideas. There was, however, at least one more or less cohesive "bundle" of innovations that at some point traveled together: namely, people who shared mostly Mongoloid genes; who spoke a single Austronesian language (or set of closely related ones); whose subsistence economy included gardening, animal domestication and fishing; who made and used large canoes capable of traveling—including sailing—relatively swiftly over long distances; and—highly important for the archaeological purpose of identification—made pottery of a very distinctive kind. Indeed, archaeological traces of such a people, or a closely related set of peoples, have been discovered in numerous islands of Near Oceania—all of them on or near shorelines. Moreover, it is safe to assume that they (i.e., several succeeding generations of them) moved from northwest to south and east, settling temporarily or permanently on some islands and bypassing others—in some cases on uninhabited islands, or parts of islands, in others near enough to earlier inhabitants to mix genes and cultural traits with them. What is less certain is the location of their immediate, formative "homeland": whether they originated as a single genetic-cultural bundle in, say, the Moluccas, or became such further east (say, in the Bismarck Archipelago) through adaptation to local conditions—environmental, cultural and genetic.

The most conspicuous identifiable component of that bundle is a type of pottery that was first found decades ago in New Caledonia at a site named La Pita—from which the pottery and, eventually, the whole bundle, has received its label. And therein lies an assumption that may or may not be proven sound, namely, that all of the people who made such pottery were alike in those other cultural and genetic features wherever they lived.[12]

In any case, those people who began arriving in previously uninhabited Fiji about 3,200 to 3,300 years ago did make such pots, did carry Mongoloid genes,[13] did speak an Austronesian language, did feed themselves by gardening and fishing, did keep pigs and dogs and chickens and, inferentially, did possess large and seaworthy canoes—all of which warrants labeling them "Lapitans" (for lack of a more suitable name). In time some of those Lapitans spread to Tonga and Samoa and a few nearby islands, where after several generations of successful adaptation and of proliferation they became what have come to be known as "Polynesians."

3

THE ANCESTRAL POLYNESIANS

The Lapitan forebears of the Polynesians first landed in previously uninhabited Fiji about 3,300 years ago. Other Lapitans from southern Melanesia were to follow them for a century or more, but after that such migrations became infrequent or ceased. Then, about 2,000 years ago, migrations to Fiji from the west were resumed, but by people with darker skins, a different kind of pottery and a language, which though closely related, differed somewhat from that of their Lapitan predecessors. Long before that, however, some of the Lapitans had pushed on farther eastward, and within a few "centuries or decades or even months or years" (Burley and Dickenson 2001), had colonized Tonga, Samoa, Niuatoputapu, East Uvea and East Futuna—and after a few more centuries had "become" Polynesians—i.e., ancestral Polynesians.[14]

The cultural side of the transformation, from Lapitan to Polynesian, was shaped by—among other influences—the physical environments of the various islands on which the Lapitans had settled. Those environments differed one from another in some respects (i.e., in size, in topography—"high" [i.e., mountainous] or "low" [atolls or raised coral (makatea) islands: see below], in quality of soils, etc.), but they all differed from Fiji and from their temporary Melanesia homelands in having had fewer kinds of terrestrial plants and animals and fewer kinds of stone for fabricating tools. However, the various new colonies eventually made up for some of their local deficiencies in natural resources through interisland exchanges—an activity that they and other Lapitans were well practiced in and that doubtless helped also to preserve many traits of their common heritage. But even so, each colony developed some distinctive cultural features over time, through relative isolation and adjustment to its own local environmental constraints and opportunities. Notwithstanding those differences it has been established archaeo-

logically that the various branch colonies of Lapitans-becoming-Polynesians shared several practices, including their locations (all of their settlements having been located on or near a shoreline of ocean or lagoon), and in their subsistence economies. Regarding the latter, the colonists everywhere practiced a mixed one consisting of gardening, animal husbandry (pigs or dogs or chickens or a combination), arboriculture and fishing. Evidence of animal husbandry is represented archaeologically by numbers of bones, and of fishing by fishhooks, parts of octopus lures and deposits of mollusk shells—the latter having been especially numerous in earlier deposit layers, indicating that the colonists had depended heavily on marine food while the food plants brought with them were multiplying. The only direct archaeological evidence of gardening or arboriculture is a piece of carbonized coconut shell, but indirect evidence abounds: for example, in the presence of types of tools (which at time of Western contact were those used to peel tubers and breadfruit and to crack coconut shells), in the remains of pits (which in later eras were used for storing and fermenting breadfruit), and in the remains of certain tiny snails (which are found only in garden soils).

An entirely different kind of evidence used by scholars to reconstruct a people's past is based on historical linguistics. By use of this method linguists have reconstructed the past relationships, if any, among present-day languages, and in doing so the vocabulary of the hypothetical (i.e., "proto") languages that were ancestral to related present-day ones. Thus, proto-Polynesian (often abbreviated PPN)—the reconstructed language from which all Polynesian contact-era languages are said to have "descended," and which is assumed to have been spoken by the Lapitans who colonized ancestral Polynesia—contained words for pig (*puraka) (note: the asterisk preceding a reconstructed word is the linguists' sign for characterizing it as "proto"), dog (*kuli'i), and domestic fowl (*moa), in addition to several words for food plants and gardening, e.g., Colocasia-type taro (*talo), Alocasia-type taro (*kape), yam (*'ufi), breadfruit (*kulu), banana (*futi), Tahitian chestnut (*ifi), to plant (*to'o), to harvest (*utu), and a garden (*ma'ala). The reconstructed hypothetical proto-language of the ancestral Polynesians also contained words for the archaeologically attested—and at Western contact times widespread—practices of fermenting breadfruit and of baking food in earth ovens. And harking back to the archaeologically attested practice of fishing, the PPN vocabulary also contained words for to fish (*fa'angota), to fish at night with help of torches (*rama), fish trap (*fi'inaki), net (*kupenge), and fishhook (*ma(a)ta'u).[15]

Not surprisingly, proto-Polynesian also contained words for house (*fale) and canoe shed (*falau), as well as for archaeologically attested adzes (*toki) and cooking pots (*kulo). Regarding the latter, it will be recalled that pottery vessels—of high-quality fabrication and distinctive designs—have served archaeologists as the earmark of the cultures from which that of the Polynesians (among other Lapitans) derived, and our ancestral Polynesians continued to manufacture and use those so-called Lapita pots—of various shapes and sizes—for more than a millennium after settling in the ancestral Tongan, etc., colonies. During that time, however, there is archaeological evidence of diminishing craftsmanship, fewer pot types, and less decoration, so that after about 500 B.C. the pots so far discovered were of crude fabrication, and none of them decorated—which has earned them the label of "Polynesian plain ware." Then, around A.D. 0 pottery making ceased altogether—not because of lack of clay, but likely because of deliberate and area-wide conversion to wooden and plaitware containers, of which, however, no "ancestral" specimens have survived the ravages of time. This has also been the fate of the barkcloth (*tapa), mats (*fala) and baskets (*kete), which, according to linguistic reconstruction, also were fabricated during the ancestral era.

The only positive archaeological clues to social relations among the ancestral Polynesians had to do with the size and layout of their settlements—namely, hamlet-sized clusters of spatially separated multiunit households (a pattern that also prevailed in most Polynesian societies centuries later, at times of Western contact). The reconstructed proto-Polynesian vocabulary also contains the word *ariki, which itself (or cognates of it) meant one or another type of "chief" in most Polynesian societies at their times of Western contact. It may also have had the same meaning among the ancestral Polynesians, but if so the archaeological evidence contains no further clues concerning persons of that status—i.e., no larger-than-average households nor richer-than-average burials. The same may be said of the reconstructed proto-Polynesian words *tufunga (expert), *toa (warrior) and *tautai (seaman-navigator), although those words, or cognates of them, did have such meanings in most Polynesian languages in contact times—and may have referred to corresponding statuses among the ancestral Polynesians.[16] A similar conclusion may be drawn concerning reconstructed proto-Polynesian sibling kin terms: *tuakana (a male's elder brother, a female's elder sister), *t(a or e)hina (a male's younger brother, a female's younger sister), *tuanga'ane (a female's brother), and *tuafatine (a male's sister).

In my opinion, however, less certitude attaches to the reconstructed meaning of *kainanga (glossed by some linguists as "corporate landholding descent group") and *kainga (glossed as "minimal descent group with land"). Those two words, or cognates of them, did exist in many contact-era vocabularies, but not in all cases with precisely the same meanings.

Turning now to the religious beliefs and practices of the ancestral Polynesians: although there are no archaeological clues concerning them—i.e., no material remains identifiable as, for example, temples or shrines or godly images, linguists have plausibly reconstructed proto-Polynesian terms for some such beliefs and practices, to wit: *atua (deity), *'anga'anga (spirit, soul, corpse), *fai (to perform rites) and *mori (offering, act of worship, to remove taboo). Less plausible are the meanings of "sacred" and "prohibited" attributed to the reconstructed word *tapu. And it is my opinion that to translate the reconstructed word *mana as "supernatural power" is in one sense too general and in another sense too limited—as will be argued in chapter 8.

Related to the above are three other words of more plausible reconstruction: *kawa, *taano'a and *renga. *Kawa is translated as kava, *Piper mythysticum*, a domesticated plant from whose root was infused a widely imbibed narcotic drink, and *taano'a as the bowl in which the root was shredded and infused. Understandably, no remains have been found of the plant in ancestral Polynesian sites, but it is reasonable to assume that the plant and its ceremonial usage did exist during that era. Indeed, it is likely that the plant was grown and similarly used by the Polynesians' Lapitan forebears even before they migrated to Fiji. As for the word *renga, it was the name of the saffron-colored stain extracted from turmeric, the root of the ginger plant *Curcuma domestica*. The plant and that usage of it was common throughout contact-era Polynesia, and in many parts of southern and southeastern Asia as well; it can be assumed to have been carried by the Lapitans to Fiji and beyond—and therefore grown and used by the ancestral Polynesians as well.[17]

By now some readers may be wondering what were the physical characteristics of the ancestral Polynesians: how did they differ from the Sundanoid peoples who had preceded them, by many millennia, throughout Near Oceania, and with whom many of their own precursive Lapitans had mingled and interbred?

Statements in chapter 2 assert that the peoples who entered Near Oceania about three thousand to four thousand years ago were more "Mongoloid" than "Sundanoid" in genetic composition—that the latter were, for example, dark skinned and woolly haired, the former lighter pig-mented and curly-to-straight haired. It should be noted however that those statements are based on assumption rather than on direct evidence; i.e., on the physical appearance of recent peoples (who are assumed to be their respective descendants) rather than on archaeological evidence—which in any case would not reveal a specimen's pigmentation and hair form. In fact, up to the writing of this chapter, very few human skeletal remains have been found in sites datable to the ancestral Polynesian era (Kelly 1996; Pietrusewsky 1996). Nevertheless, in the absence of contrary evidence, it is sensible to assume that the ancestral Polynesians were not widely different in physical appearance from their contact-era descendants (i.e., before the latter had begun to interbreed with Western and Asian outsiders). The physical characteristics of those descendants will be summarized in chapter 6 and depicted in illustrations throughout the book.

At various times after colonizing ancestral Polynesia, single canoeloads or fleets of their inhabitants set out eastward, northward and northwestward in purposeful searches for new homes, and by about A.D. 500 they or their descendants had reached, and either tarried or permanently settled on, nearly every habitable island in the vast triangle outlined by Hawai'i, Easter Island and New Zealand—plus several islands west of that triangle, thereby accomplishing (in the words of one writer) "the greatest purposeful dispersal in human history" (Kirch 1984, 71)—a topic to which we next turn.

4

DISPERSAL

By about A.D. 1600 Polynesians had colonized every habitable island within the vast triangle defined by Hawai'i, Easter Island and New Zealand,[18] along with several west of the triangle—which are known as the "Polynesian Outliers." Questions arise as to why they did so, how they did so, and when.[19]

Some colonizations may have occurred by accident—by canoeloads headed for known destinations but blown off course. Or some may have been necessitated by defeat in war or by food shortages caused by overpopulation or natural disaster. Or some may have been undertaken by a younger brother and his dependents and supporters, because of operation of the Polynesian principle of primogeniture, whereby an eldest son inherited the lion's share of his family's goods and privileges. In addition, myths and legends abound with voyages of discovery and colonization undertaken through adventurous curiosity, strengthened by ancestral memories of there always having been more islands ahead. And finally, some colonizations may have been undertaken based on information about discoveries accidentally gained and brought home by deep-sea fishermen or by parties of intentional explorers—who, however, without women would themselves have been unable to establish lasting colonies.

Turning next to "how": it is important at the outset to distinguish between the directions in which most of those expeditions traveled—i.e., either westward or eastward. Westward would have presented no great difficulty, since the more prevalent winds of the region blew from the east; and as will be described, canoeloads from western Polynesia—of Tongans, Samoans, Tuvaluans, etc.—colonized numerous islands west and northwest of there. However, except for Hawai'i, what were to become the largest colonies in tropical and subtropical Polynesia were to windward; therefore it is necessary to consider how that was possible, given the kind of watercraft used.

It is safe to assume that those watercraft were large canoes, either single outrigger or, more probably, double-hulled ones, and that they were propelled mainly by sail—because of the slow speed of paddling and the prohibitively large amount of energy, hence of food, that paddling would have required. (Recent experiments with a forty-two-foot–long double-hulled canoe showed it could be paddled about one knot an hour against even a slight current and a twenty-knot headwind [Finney 1977, 150]). However, because of their lack of keel, such canoes were subject to wide leeway and were unable to point close to the wind. Thus, on an upwind course, they would have had to travel, by tacking, about four miles for every one mile gained in the direction of the wind (Finney 1994, 127).[20] Moreover, upwind travel in heavily laden canoes—such as those of colonizing voyages—would have been extremely hazardous, in terms of the canoe's construction and its passengers' endurance.

In other words, eastward-traveling migrants may have chosen to travel during periods of more favorable, i.e., westerly, winds—which did in fact occur even in the region of prevailing easterly trades. For, in that region, "prevailing" does not mean ceaseless: during the Austral summer (December to April) westerly winds often replace the easterlies for days or weeks at a time, and even during that region's winters the same sometimes occur. In addition to their seasonal variations, the winds of that region sometimes blow westerly in response to the occasional disturbances, in wind direction and ocean current, known as El Niño. As far as is known, Polynesians were unable to predict particular occurrences of El Niño disturbances, but their year-round calendar systems would have enabled them to count on regular seasonal changes in winds, and their knowledge of weather signs equipped them to make shorter-term forecasts as well.

In contrast, according to some credibly reported episodes, some overseas expeditions, both exploratory and colonizing, appear to have set out deliberately upwind, with the option of turning around and running home when food supplies began to run low.

Mention was made above of voyages of "exploration." Reference here is to the possibility that in some cases intentional migrations—i.e., those consisting of large numbers of persons together with supplies large enough to found a colony—were preceded by the sending of one or more lightly manned and less heavily provisioned canoes to discover a suitable place and then return home with information about its suitability and with directions about getting there.

The first comprehensive and more or less scholarly book to deal with Polynesian voyaging was *Vikings of the Sunrise* (published in 1938 and reissued in 1959 as *Vikings of the Pacific*). Its author was the part-Polynesian New Zealander Peter Buck (Maori name: Te Rangi Hiroa), a physician turned ethnologist. Before becoming director of Hawai'i's famed Bishop Museum, in 1936, he carried out research in several Polynesian societies, facilitated by his fluency in Maori, which enabled him to master quickly other Polynesian languages. *Vikings*, in his own words, was "an attempt to make known to the general public some of the romance associated with the settlement of Polynesia by a Stone Age people who deserve to rank among the world's great navigators" (1959, v). In pursuing that objective Buck depended mainly on oral evidence—archaeological data having been virtually nonexistent at the time. And while he attributed great depth to the memories of natives trained in such matters, he himself distinguished between their "myths"— their accounts of creation—and their "legends and traditions," recognizing the former to be colorful fabrications but attributing to the latter a certain amount of historical verisimilitude, especially with respect to accounts about colonization and subsequent interisland voyaging. Regarding the latter he expressed belief in there having been fairly frequent two-way contacts between some purported homelands and their far-flung colonies, including Tahiti with Hawai'i and New Zealand, for centuries after settlement.

When Westerners first encountered them, most Polynesians were keeping to their home waters or traveling only to islands nearby. Influenced by that situation, most anthropologists of Peter Buck's generation were skeptical of Buck's views about the facility and frequency of Polynesian long voyaging, but the first broadside attack on those views was authored by Andrew Sharp, a retired New Zealand civil servant whose monograph *Ancient Voyagers in the Pacific*, published in 1956, dismissed views like Buck's as romantic fiction and contended that Polynesians, even in their heyday, were capable of making intentional two-way open-sea voyages of no more than about 350 miles each way, and that their longer voyages—say, to Hawai'i or New Zealand—must have been "accidental," i.e., the result of drifting after being blown off an intentional course. Moreover, he argued, after being cast up, accidentally, on an island more than about 350 miles distant, the castaways would not have had sufficient oceanographic and astronomical knowledge, or navigational skill, to enable them to accomplish an intentional voyage home. (For a discussion of Sharp's views see Golson 1962.)

Sharp's well-publicized judgment about Polynesian seamanship provoked many reactions—pro, con and querying. One such was a prodigious, computerized study of ocean drift, which the authors defined as follows: "[to] go with the wind and current, resulting in a track not influenced by consciously prescribed and enacted alternatives, which would be navigation. Navigation implies setting a course or sequence of courses and is a conscious activity directed to some goal, whether the goal is a known landfall or the search for possible homelands across a stretch of unknown ocean. In the drift situation the mariner is passive, being active only to keep the craft seaworthy" (Levinson et al. 1973, 13). The simulation model used in that inquiry dealt with "as many as possible of the parameters which affect the course and survival of a small vessel and its crew when drifting at sea without motor power," namely, "temporal and spatial changes in wind direction and force; current (or surface drift) direction and speed; the course steered; the sailing qualities of the vessel; the location of reefs, islands, and coasts; the crew's survival chances; and the seaworthiness of the vessel" (Ibid.). The

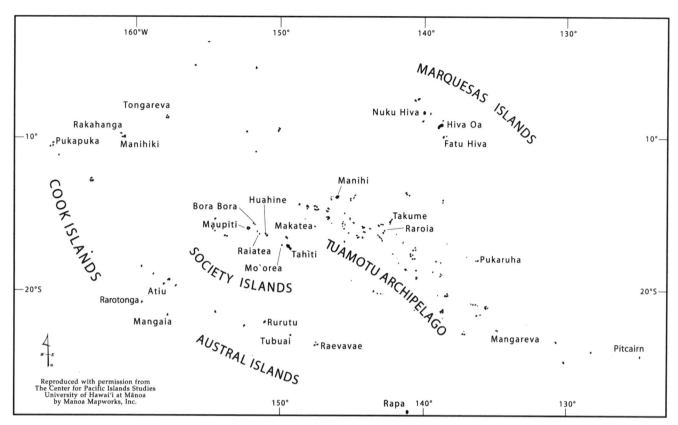

4.1. East-Central Polynesia

study concluded that the initial crossings from the New Hebrides or Solomons to Fiji, and from Samoa-Tonga to the islands east of there, were unlikely to have been reached by drift. And even more unlikely could uncontrolled drifting have enabled canoes from east-central Polynesia (e.g., Tahiti and the Marquesas) to reach Hawai'i, Easter Island or New Zealand. In other words, according to this study the discovery and eventual settlement of most islands within the Triangle may have been "accidental" in that the discoverers had no way of knowing where they were, but in their search for new homelands they must have expected them to be in certain directions and have purposefully navigated their canoes in one or another of those directions.

Another, more realistic, set of experiments undertaken to test the long-voyaging capabilities of Polynesian canoes and seamanship was initiated by the anthropologist Ben Finney, in the early 1960s. First, as described earlier, he planned and supervised the construction of a forty-two-foot–long eighteenth-century–style Hawaiian double-hulled canoe and measured its performance, in Hawaiian waters, by paddling and by sail. Then he and other boating experts built a sixty-foot–long double-hulled canoe, christened *Hōkūle'a* (Hawaiian for Arcturus, the bright star that passes directly over Hawai'i) and modeled on drawings made by draftsmen and artists accompanying Cook and other eighteenth-century explorers of Polynesia—with the intention of voyaging in it from Hawai'i to Tahiti without the aid of modern navigational instruments. From among Hawai'i's numerous canoe paddlers the organizers were able to put together a highly experienced crew, but finding someone capable of navigating, without instruments, the three thousand miles (crow-fly miles; the intended sailing course was several hundred miles longer) of ocean between Hawai'i and Tahiti was another matter. No Hawaiian—indeed, no Polynesian—was known to possess such expertise, so that in the end the search turned to the Caroline Islands of Micronesia, where long, open-sea, noninstrumented voyaging still survived. The man selected was Pius ("Mau") Piailug, a master "traditional" navigator of Satawal Atoll; and while the Satawal methods of navigating differed somewhat from what was known about those of precontact Polynesia, and while the waters and skies between Hawai'i and Tahiti differed from those of the

4.2. The experimental canoe *Hōkūleʻa*

Carolines—in wind direction and celestial "geography"—it was expected that Mau, after learning about the location of Tahiti and the intervening waters and heavens, would be capable of adjusting to the difference and guide *Hōkūleʻa* safely to Tahiti. And so he did, after thirty-two days at sea, guided mainly by stars, winds, ocean currents and swells (Finney 1979).

After returning to Hawaiʻi, *Hōkūleʻa* made a second round-trip to Tahiti and a round-trip to New Zealand, via Tahiti and the Cook Islands, these having been navigated by a young Hawaiian, Nainoa Thompson, who learned his craft from Mau Piailug (Finney 1994b).

The voyages of *Hōkūleʻa* demonstrated that eighteenth-century–type canoes were capable of long sea voyages under navigation, and not just drift. They also demonstrated that such voyages could have been guided by means of natural signs. And although those experimental voyages of 1975–1995 do not necessarily prove that the canoes and navigational methods of pre-Western times did the same, it seems more than likely that they could have done so.

As for colonizations westward from western Polynesia (i.e., Tonga, Samoa, East Futuna, East Uvea, and Tuvalu), some were doubtless intentional and others accidental, but in both cases were more facilitated than impeded by that area's prevailing (i.e., easterly) winds. Some of the landings, and colonizations, took place on uninhabited islands, some others at places already peopled by non-Polynesians, whom the newcomers assimilated, both genetically and culturally, or by whom they were themselves assimilated. In addition, some of those settlements were subsequently augmented, and their cultures and gene pools to some degree transformed, by arrivals of other islanders, either Polynesians, Melanesians or Micronesians. These were, altogether, a very complex ethnic hodgepodge, but one that has been partially but skillfully disentangled by the anthropological linguist D.T. Bayard, in his 1976 monograph—that is, up to the point permitted by lack of data (except for such Outliers as Tikopia, Anuta, Rennell-Bellona and Kapingamaringi, which are well represented in ethnographic literature).[21]

The next question to be posed about the Polynesians' dispersal is When and by what stages did the successful colonizing voyages to the "pure" Polynesian, eastern islands take place?

Scholarly opinions concerning when the different Polynesian islands were first colonized have varied over time. Up to about 1950 some islands were viewed as having been colonized at times no earlier than about A.D. 400–500. Also, some of them were held to have been colonized by two or more ethnically distinct "waves." The most "authoritative" version of that "wave" theory was that of E. S. C. Handy, who postulated two of such: the first of a people bearing a socioreligious culture of Indic, specifically Vedic, origin, the second and later of a people bearing one of (ultimately) Chinese origin, and who spread only to the larger (central) islands, where they succeeded in dominating the first-wave people (E. S. C. Handy 1927, 312–28).[22]

Next, with the discoveries of the actuality and more remote antiquity of the ancestral homelands (i.e., Tonga, Samoa, etc.) within the borders of present-day Polynesia, it was, earlier, the majority scholarly view that there had been a centuries-long, even a millennium-long pause there, which had ended about A.D. 400, when canoeloads of colonizers set out from the ancestral homelands—some toward the east, others toward the north and northwest. According to this scenario the eastward-going migrants first reached and colonized the Marquesas (whence some of their descendants eventually colonized Hawai'i, Mangareva, Easter Island, the Tuamotus, the Cook Islands and Tahiti), while others were to colonize Tuvalu and the numerous Outliers (some of which had already been settled on by non-Polynesians directly from Vanuatu and the Solomons).

More recently there has surfaced a "minority" opinion (which had been earlier proposed by Irwin in 1979) to the effect that there had been no lengthy "pause" in the ancestral homelands—that canoes from there had continued exploring and colonizing in several directions fairly soon (how "soon" is not specified) after colonization of the ancestral homeland islands.[23] The time element in this minority opinion has not yet been widely accepted, but those subscribing to the majority opinion are now coming around to the view that while the Marquesas were indeed the staging area for Hawai'i, there had been numerous direct colonizations from various ancestral homeland

islands to various islands of east central Polynesia at about the same time (Green 1993; Irwin 1992; Pawley 1996; Rolett 1993). Moreover, as a result of the recent successful experiments in long-voyaging, there is now more of an inclination among Polynesianists (i.e., researchers into things "Polynesian") to accept the possibility, or even probability, of more postcolonization interisland contacts—except with Easter Island and New Zealand, which are believed by most researchers to have remained wholly isolated after first colonizations. Finney (1994b) provides a persuasive argument for some interisland voyaging, including a résumé of the wide geographic knowledge of a Tahitian sage, Tupaia, who accompanied Cook on some legs of the latter's first Pacific voyage. (See also Dening 1962.)

So much for "probabilities"; assigning credible dates to some initial colonizations is complicated by the possibility that archaeologists may not have discovered remains of an island's earliest settlement—either through oversight or through disappearance of an island's earlier shores. By "oversight" is not meant incompetence; in recent decades Polynesia has been favored with research by many talented and experienced archaeologists, but their work is very costly and therefore less than what they are capable of. As for "disappearance," in some cases early sites have been discovered, more or less accidentally, under thick layers of sediment—some of it run-off resulting from erosion caused by Polynesians' deforestation and gardening. In other cases, shoreline sites—the most likely locations of initial colonizations—have been submerged as a result of an island's tectonic subsidence.

Turning to the Outliers, the nineteen Polynesian-language islands and atolls west of those within the Triangle,[24] their cultural affiliations were more complex. The languages of all of their contact-era peoples were—still are—closely related to those of Samoa, Tuvalu, East Uvea and East Futuna, indicating that they were colonized from one or another of these in post-Lapita times. However, some of the Outliers contain archaeological evidence dating back to Lapita times, indicating the presence there of pre-Polynesian, perhaps Solomonese Lapita, peoples who had either vanished or been absorbed by the subsequent "true" Polynesians. However, just as Tongans and Samoans have continued to receive cultural, and

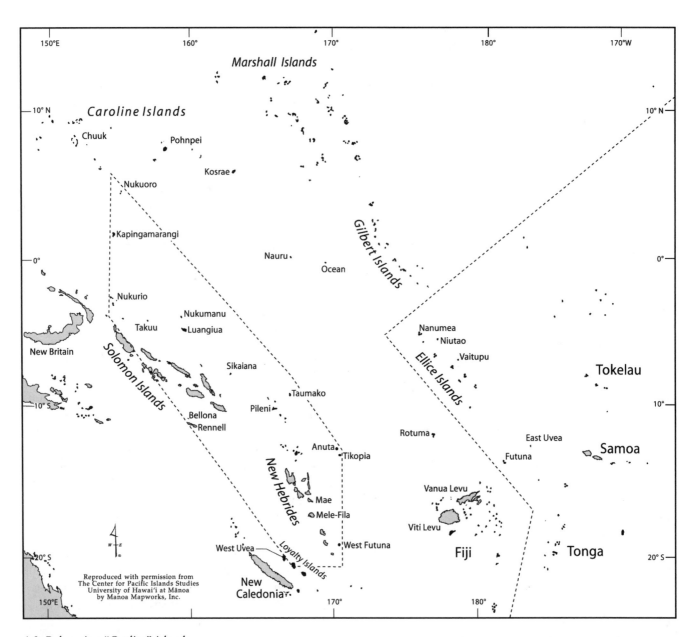

4.3. Polynesian "Outlier" islands

perhaps some genetic, influences from Fiji, so have some of the Outlier peoples received such influences from nearby Melanesians.

Figure 4.4 (Pawley 1996, 398), representing a chartering of relationships among all Triangle and most Outlier languages, provides the most recent and authoritative summary of linguistic findings. It confirms many of the findings of archaeology and ethnography, including, in most cases, the order in which language (and therefore cultural) branching took place. However, it tells nothing about the actual dates of that branching—i.e., about when particular colonizations took place (Biggs 1972).

Some estimates about such times have been obtained through glottochronology—the method based on counting the number of certain cognate[25] "core" word-meanings shared by two related "daughter" languages, in order to discover the duration of their separation from their common "mother" language. The two hundred (or four hundred) "core" word-meanings used in these exercises include such items as "one," "two," "I," "he," "blood," "foot," and "die"—i.e., those assumed to be present in all human languages. This method, which was first applied to languages of the Indo-European and Semitic families of languages, the histories of which are fairly well

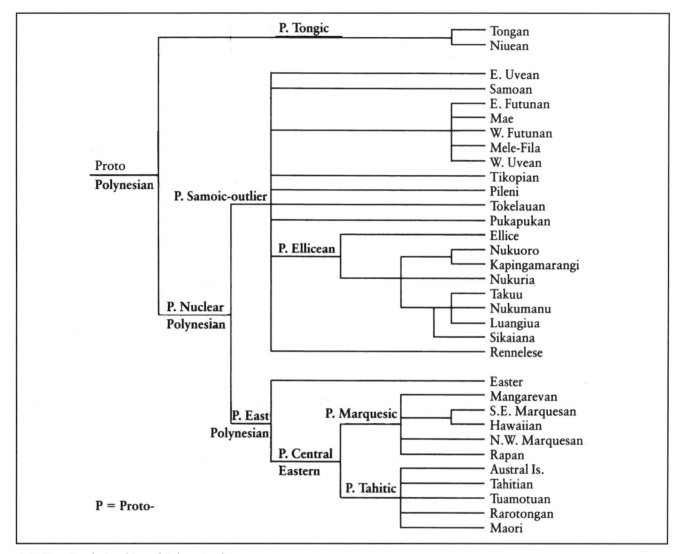

4.4. Genetic relationships of Polynesian languages

known, found that their two hundred (or four hundred) cognate "core" word-meanings had changed at a fairly constant rate over time—which was calculated to have been about 20 percent per thousand years—or, conversely, that they retain about 80 percent of their preseparation meanings.

Unfortunately, those "averages" cannot be applied literally in the case of many Polynesian languages, some of whose rates of change may have been slowed from that "universal" average by postcolonization interisland contacts (a possibility strengthened by the recent experiments in long-voyaging described earlier) or may have been accelerated by practices such as the Tahitian one of *pi'i* (name avoidance)—i.e., the prohibition of the use of the names of some tribal chiefs and of many words containing sound combinations more or less identical with such names. (For more on

this and other aspects of Polynesian languages see chapter 7.)

Finally, in the case of some fairly recent colonizations, rough estimates of their dates might possibly be reached by counting the generations orally transmitted in their chiefly genealogies and multiplying that number by twenty to twenty-six (i.e., the hypothesized duration of a "generation"). Until about 1950 this was the most widespread "scholarly" method available for dating a Polynesian people's past. Genealogies were the principle vehicles for legitimating positions of prestige and authority, and while parts of them may have been "doctored" for political purposes, that cannot have rendered them altogether useless for estimating the "generational" age of a descent line of persons.[26]

PART TWO

PREFACE TO PART TWO

Part Two describes the cultures of the peoples of tropical and subtropical Polynesia[27] just before they underwent major changes as a result of contact with non-Polynesians (in this case Westerners)—a time frame that anthropologists call the "ethnographic present." Admittedly, this exercise in reconstruction and comparison is complicated, in some cases thwarted, by several circumstances.

One such circumstance has to do with differences in judgment about what constituted a "major" change. In most cases the data on which this book's descriptions are based were recorded at times when a society was already undergoing some Westerner-induced changes—such as use of metal tools and the psychological and values-altering experience of confrontation with firearm-weaponed and culturally alien outsiders. Did such experiences as those constitute "major" changes? Or only preludes to "major" changes in allegedly "more important" domains such as, say, cosmology and subsistence technology? In the absence of agreement about this matter the decision rests with the writer—in this instance, me!

Another circumstance that complicates this exercise is the fact that the Western contacts that served eventually to transform every Polynesian society were somewhat different in kind and were widely separated over time. For example, while the Tahitians were "discovered" by Europeans in 1767, and much of their culture Westernized by 1825, the inhabitants of the small and off-track Tikopia Island remained largely "precontact" for another century and a half. If isolated "primitive" cultures had been essentially immutable, as some Westerners assume, no logical difficulty would be encountered in comparing the Tahitians of 1767 with the Tikopians of 1927 (when they were competently studied by the anthropologist Raymond Firth). However, archaeological studies in Polynesia and elsewhere have proved that assumption to be entirely false, thereby raising unanswerable questions about the validity of some of the concurrence implied in this and other books about precontact, so-called "ancient" Polynesians.

A third complication inherent in this exercise

derives from the unevenness of the reporting on which it is based. The sources of those reports range from observations by short-term visitors with no fluency in the local language, through long-term and language-fluent but sometimes closed-minded missionaries, to language-fluent anthropologists on one-or-two-year visits (few of whom, however, had carried out their field studies before their subjects had become largely Westernized).

Notwithstanding those and other caveats—along with the opinion of some present-day scholars that one cannot write knowingly about a culture other than one's own, and the view of some (usually Western-trained) Polynesians that Westerners should not presume to write about theirs—some anthropologists, including the present one, will persist in trying to do so.

Some Polynesianists will doubtless question this book's organization—i.e., its treatment of all tropical and subtropical peoples collectively, and separately from those of New Zealand. That separation (I reason) is based largely on environmental differences: granted that there were some far-reaching differences—in size, in topography, in climate, etc.—between the habitats of the former (say, between Hawai'i and Tongareva), only a few of those environmental differences were as wide as those between them and those of New Zealand—with correspondingly wide differences in several features of material culture. As for treating the tropical (including subtropical) peoples collectively and not in separate chapters for each people, as some books on Polynesia do, that is done for the sake of brevity and because of the many cultural features shared by those peoples.

Finally, the beliefs and practices written about in this book will be described in the past tense even though many of them (e.g., some foods and food-producing technologies, some intrafamilial relationships, some beliefs about magical processes, and many of the languages of everyday speech) still prevail—alongside imported canned foods, Christianity-sanctioned monogamy, Westernized schooling, and widespread literacy in English or French.

5

NATURAL ENVIRONMENTS

No knowledgeable anthropologist would now claim that a people's culture had been wholly shaped by its natural environment nor argue that any culture is wholly free of environmental influence—especially not in the case of Polynesian peoples, whose tools were relatively simple, however effectively they were employed. Thus, while the pre-Western cultures of tropical (and subtropical) Polynesia were alike in many respects—a heritage of their common origin—the circumstance that their subsequent natural settings were so varied, from small, dry, thin-soiled atolls to large and lush mountainous archipelagoes, resulted in many environmentally influenced cultural differences among them. In a book of this length it will not be feasible to describe separately each people's natural environment; instead, the major types of islands and the natural factors that served to differentiate them will be summarized.

First to consider are the geological fundaments of the islands.

The Earth's whole "surface," its lithosphere, consists of a layer of rigid rock sixty or more miles thick, which floats on a layer of molten magma. Further, that lithosphere is divided into a number of tectonic plates, of various sizes, which are themselves rigid but are constantly in motion: away from, toward or sideways with their neighboring plates. At boundaries where plates move apart, the underlying magma flows up through the gaps to build mountainous ridges, below or above sea level. Or, where two of them continually collide, one of them subducts the other and pushes it upward, thereby forming mountainous ridges and trenches—also below or above sea level. And when two plates move sideways to each other, that motion results in earthquakes and terrain-changing episodes (familiar especially to present-day Californians). As a consequence of all such movements the most unstable zones of Earth's surface are those along plate boundaries (Whitmore 1981).

Most of the islands inhabited by Polynesians are on the vast Pacific Plate and were formed not by the motions of neighboring plates but by the upward, volcanic flow of basaltic magma through so-called "hot spots"—i.e., relatively small holes in the underlying mantle. One exception to that location is Easter Island (Rapanui), which is part of the (largely underwater) ridge along the plate's southeast boundary. Other exceptions include New Zealand (where the Pacific Plate abuts and pushes under the Indian Plate), and the Tonga Archipelago (whose islands are volcanic extrusions along the western boundary of the Pacific Plate).

During the last fifty million or so years the Pacific Plate has been moving northwestward about 3.54 inches a year. Consequently, the "hot spots" permit the underlying magma to flow upward and enlarge or form new and originally volcanic islands. Thus, of the human-inhabited islands of the Hawaiian Archipelago, Kaua'i (the farthest one to the northwest) is the oldest and Hawai'i (the farthest to the southeast) is the youngest (and is still volcanically active).

Another fundamental process of island building in tropical seas, including most of tropical Polynesia, is coral, a rock-hard substance made up of the consolidated skeletons of certain marine animals and plants. The animals involved are polyps (coelenterates), which make their own shells by imbibing and secreting seawater; during their final life stages they attach themselves to rocks or to the shells of dead polyps and in this way build up solid calcareous structures of innumerable shapes and sizes. The plants involved in the process are microscopic algae, which first live within the cells of the live polyps—thereby stimulating their calcium metabolism—and eventually fill the dead shells of their hosts with their own calcareous corpses. Coral-forming polyps live and multiply only in warm, saline and clear sunlit

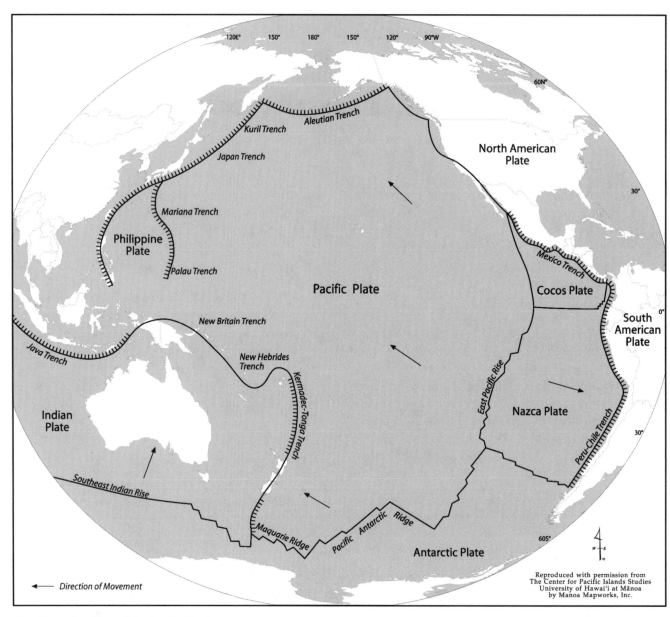

5.1. Tectonic plates of the Pacific Region

waters, which in the Pacific constitute a belt that extends from about 30 degrees north latitude to about 30 degrees south, and within depths of less than about 150 feet. Because of those limits, as a coraline-encrusted shoreline rises and falls relative to sea level so does its zone of coral formation. There having been many changes in shoreline level in the Pacific, including those resulting from tectonic movements (up, down, and sideways) as well as those accompanying the Pleistocene Ice Ages mentioned in chapter 2, dead coral reefs are attached to the slopes of some islands as much as four thousand feet above, or below, present sea level. Also, many former islands have sunk (tec-

tonically) or been sunk (by rising sea level) far below present sea level, or remain exposed only as shoals.

In a few places, such as in the Marquesas, most of the islands' lithic slopes are so steep that little or no coral has become permanently attached to them. However, on most other islands of tropical Polynesia, the spatial relationship between an island's lithic volcanic base and its coral crust differs from place to place—thereby resulting in widespread differences in human use. Thus, in some places the exposed or shallow crust of coral forms a direct extension of—a "fringe" to—the island's dry fundament of land, while in others it exists as an offshore—"barrier"—reef, forming a lagoon between it and dry land. In still other places, where the volcanic base of an island has sunk or been weathered down, with only its reefs or reef-fringed slithers of land remaining above sea level, those remnants are labeled "atolls." And in those places where all but the coral-capped summit of a mountain's volcanic rock base has sunk below sea level, the remaining island constitutes a landform known as a "pancake" island, or by the Polynesian term *makatea*. Most of tropical Polynesia's "high" islands are surrounded, wholly or completely, by both fringe and barrier reef formations, and some archipelagoes contain both "high" islands and atolls—plus, in some cases, *makatea*.

Once formed and elevated above sea level for long periods of time, the islands of tropical Polynesia have been transformed, in varying degrees, by surface winds, by rainfall, by earthquakes and tidal waves (tsunami), by continuing volcanism, by exogenous changes in sea level, by ocean currents, by animals and plants and—to extents seldom recognized—by humans themselves.

Beginning with winds: north of about latitude 25 degrees north and south of about latitude 27 degrees south strong westerlies (i.e., winds from the west) blow almost continuously year-round. In the wide band between them occur four major wind patterns: trade, monsoon westerly, doldrum and typhoon.[28] (See figure 5.2.)

Trade winds blow at times during every month of the year but do so more constantly, and strongly, from May to September—north of the equator from the northeast, south of it from the southeast.[29] Between them lie the doldrums, characterized by low wind velocities, high humidity and year-round even temperatures.

In tropical Polynesia, the westerly monsoon-pattern winds, which are generated by seasonal climatic changes in Asia and Australia, blow most regularly and protractedly in that westernmost part of the region in which the Polynesian Outlier islands are located, but also occur, for days or weeks at a time, farther east throughout the year

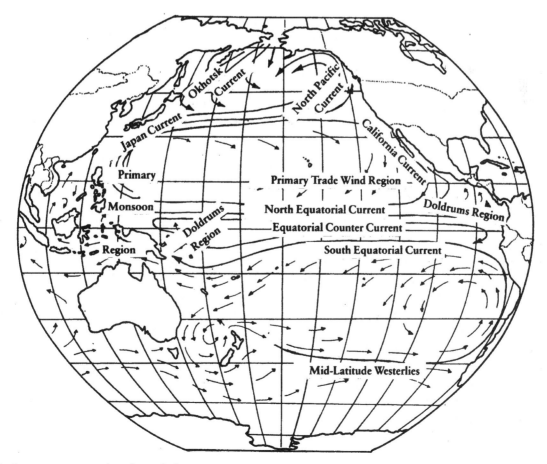

5.2. Pacific Ocean currents and surface winds

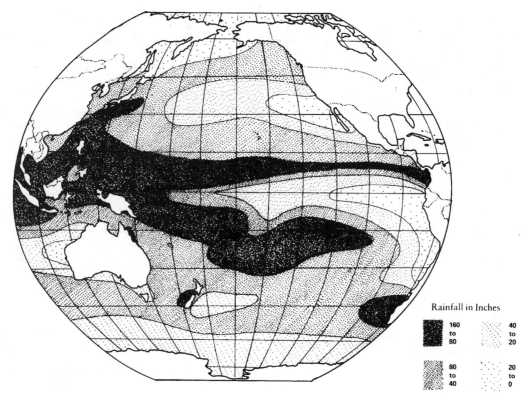

Rainfall in Inches

160 to 80	40 to 20
80 to 40	20 to 0

5.3. Rainfall patterns of the Pacific

but mostly during the Austral summer. As for typhoons (i.e., hurricanes), which occur throughout tropical Polynesia, and usually during the Austral summer, their high winds and torrential rains are devastating even in today's era of advance-warning communications; they are known to have wreaked havoc in the past upon many Polynesian peoples, directly and on their supplies of food.

Rainfall (see figure 5.3) in tropical Polynesia is marked by wide variability: between archipelagoes, between islands in the same archipelago and between different parts of single islands. In general, the nearer the equator the more the rainfall—except for some equatorial atolls, which receive virtually none, and except for some Marquesan high islands, which occasionally suffer severe drought. In the case of most other high islands, however, the amount of rainfall differs, in some places widely, by location—with more falling on windward than leeward sides, thereby producing important effects on land slope, vegetation and, of course, on human habitation and exploitation. Another type of variability is exemplified in the Hawaiian Archipelago, where the westernmost Kaua'i Island has an annual rainfall in some locations reaching over six hundred inches a year, in

contrast to Kaho'olawe Island, which lies in the rainfall "shadow" of Maui and has an average annual rainfall of only ten to twenty-five inches.

Earthquakes have occurred throughout tropical Polynesia ever since its islands originated, but it is not known whether any of them had been violent enough, since the times of human occupancy, to cause more than temporary damage to their occupants. The same may be said of the region's earthquake-engendered tidal waves (tsunami)—except in the case of some low islands, whose vegetation and inhabitants were doubtless destroyed by them, partly or wholly, from time to time. More certainty exists concerning the effects of volcanic eruptions, which are known to have occurred on a few populated (high) islands, with consequences that ranged from total destruction of an island's habitable areas—and decimation or evacuation of its populace—to restricted damage of only parts of it.[30]

Many Polynesian islands have also undergone sea-level oscillations after settlement, but none so wide as during earlier Pleistocene times. In fact the ocean had reached and maintained, more or less, its present shoreline levels millennia before any humans reached them.

Turning to ocean currents: two vast whorls, or

gyres, dominate water movements in the Pacific and in between them flows the Equatorial Countercurrent, which varies in width between five and ten degrees of latitude and shifts northward and southward in response to seasonal change. Polynesians were influenced by such currents in at least two ways. Indirectly the currents served to influence which species of ocean-borne plants and animals an island received from elsewhere. More directly, they served to facilitate, or to impede, canoe travel between islands, with all the cultural and social consequences of such interactions or isolations.

The flora and fauna established on the islands before arrival of the Polynesians had some physical impact upon the soils, etc., of the islands themselves, but rather than try to assess that impact it will be more relevant to list the kinds and distributions of those biota that the Polynesians met with on their first landfalls, before they had begun to alter them—which they inevitably did.

The factors—some of them interdependent—most influential in affecting the kinds and locations of terrestrial plants on tropical Polynesian islands prior to human habitation were distance from Asia (and, secondarily, from Australia and New Guinea), rainfall, soil (including groundwater level and salinity), altitude (translated into temperature) and insolation (i.e., amount of sunlight). Other factors being equal, the farther the island from Asia (and in some cases, Australia–New Guinea), the fewer genera of plants it had—a tendency greatly increased by the proportionately wider water gaps between archipelagoes from west to east. In other words, the only terrestrial plants that happened to migrate onto those islands before humans arrived were those whose reproductive parts could be carried by winds or birds or could survive long immersion in salt water. Thus, terrestrial plants "dropped out," numerically, in their passages from west to east, so that, for example, while hundreds of genera reached the (Outlier) Rennel Island (in the Solomons) only thirty reached and survived on Easter Island, about sixty-five hundred miles to the east. The "other factors" listed above served to modify somewhat this pattern. (Uninhabited) Canton Island, for example, is nearer to Asia and Australia than are the Marquesas Islands, but since Canton is a thin-soiled atoll and the latter are large high islands, Canton had fewer

genera. In general, however, the "distance from Asia-Australia" pattern prevailed. (See Kay 1980.)

A few terrestrial plants migrated successfully from the Americas to some Polynesian islands prior to their human occupation, but compared with those from the west the numbers were very small (Whitmore 1981).

New Guinea was the immediate source of most of the terrestrial vertebrates that reached islands farther east, and generally speaking, as in the case of plants, the farther the island from New Guinea the fewer its species of such vertebrates. For example, while opossums, tree rats, mice and bats (including "flying foxes") were present in parts of the Solomons before humans reached there, the only mammals found on most tropical Polynesian islands before humans were, perhaps, rodents—"perhaps" because even those may have been introduced by Polynesians deliberately or as stowaways in their canoes. The same kind of attenuation occurred with other land-based orders of fauna, including snakes and birds—except for the truly oceanic birds, such as gulls, terns, noddies, albatrosses and shearwaters (and except for some far-flying land birds such as the golden plover, which migrates annually between the Arctic and Hawai'i and beyond). And while freshwater fauna tended to be influenced by the same kind of distance rule that governed terrestrial fauna, the distribution of saltwater animals was determined by conditions of other kinds, including currents, water temperature, undersea topography and coral formations.[31]

When the forebears of the Polynesians reached Fiji they carried with them, perhaps unintentionally, some kinds of organisms, including rodents, that came to affect themselves and many of their descendants. Among those were disease-carrying mosquitoes—specifically, those that carried the elephantiasis-causing *fileria* parasite (but not, mercifully, the malaria-causing anopheles, which, however, did infest a few of the Outlier islands even before Polynesians arrived there).

Combinations of the above factors—geological, oceanic, meteorological, botanical, zoological, etc.—resulted in formation of numerous types of natural zones, which by scientific (including Western) criteria have been classified in ways that vary according to the criteria employed in classifying them. Thus, according to the criterion of physiographic profile (above sea level), the islands of tropical Polynesia are either "high," "pancake" (*makatea*), or "atoll" in shape, with several variants within each type. Or an island's coral growth is categorized as being either "fringing" or "barrier." Or in the case of some "high" islands, their phytogeographical (i.e., vegetation) zones are categorized into three major types: "coastal" (including "submangrove" and "littoral" subzones), "mesotropical," and "wet tropical" (including four subzones: "lower reaches of valleys," "plateaus and middle slopes of mountains," "rain forests," and "mountain summits"), each with its distinctive kinds of vegetations and, of course, soils, insolation, rainfall, temperatures and winds.[32]

The point of the above paragraph is that, contrary to the popular stereotype of Pacific islands, i.e., as consisting mainly of palm-clad beaches and towering volcanoes, they included in reality very wide varieties of natural habitats for possible use, and misuse, by their Polynesian colonizers.

The foregoing description of natural environmental conditions and biota refers only to the tropical (and subtropical) islands where Polynesians were to live. Entirely different were the natural environments of New Zealand, to which some Polynesians migrated (undoubtedly from eastern tropical Polynesia) and which will be described in Part Three.

The phenomena just described are—quite obviously!—conceptualized in Western, specifically Anglophonic, terms. It remains to consider if and how Polynesians perceived and explained them.

Consider, for example, movements of air. Most if not all adult Polynesians were, doubtless, capable of distinguishing by name winds from all compass points,[33] along with their usual and unusual velocities and their concurrence with other cyclical events. Moreover, each such wind was believed to be controlled by one or another god, who was therefore supplicated to assure its periodic occurrence or to curb its occasional excesses. (In this connection, in at least one society, Pukapuka, each such wind was said to "belong" to the community through which it blew upon reaching the island, and it was that community's god who controlled that wind.)

Or consider an island's contiguous sea. While science distinguishes such obvious parts of it as "lagoon," "tidepool," "surge channel," "outer bank," and "open sea," Polynesians made much finer and (to Westerners) less obvious distinc-

tions—including "holes" in the lagoon or seabed (where certain fish bred), and (to Westerners) barely perceptible submarine channels (where certain pelagic fish seasonally gathered), and concentrations of coral (wherein octopus lurked)—many of them associated with one or another god, either of the animal breed itself or of each particular place.

Similarly, nearly every Polynesian past childhood possessed detailed knowledge about the physical and phytogeography of his or her community's territory, including each area's utilities and inutilities, advantages and disadvantages—not in terms of the physical geography of science but of their applicability to their own lives.

With regard to the ways Polynesians explained the natural phenomena they perceptualized, in most of their cosmogonies nearly all such entities were believed to have been created by one or another godly activated method—sexual reproduction, vocal or mental command, fishing up islands from the seabed, etc. In addition, as later chapters will relate, some cosmogonies explained the origin of everything, including natural phenomena, in evolutionary terms—although not through the process conceived of by Darwin!

Finally, a few words concerning Polynesians' concepts regarding time. Despite their lack of mechanical clocks and written calendars, Polynesians in general were acutely aware of natural cyclical variations—in winds, tides, temperatures and rainfall, and in the courses of the sun and moon and of certain star constellations and individual stars. Moreover, they had names for such cycles and for points within them.

Within the diurnal cycle—which throughout tropical Polynesia is more evenly divided between daylight (*ao*) and night-darkness (*po*) than is the case in temperate latitudes—points of daylight "time" were identified most numerously and precisely by positions of the sun—in Tahiti, for example, by twenty-four such points, beginning with "bordering sun rays," through "the sun casts no shadows," to "the sun has sunk below the surface of the sea." And in the Marquesas nighttime points included "taboo chicken" (about midnight, when the first cock crowed), "tomorrow shade" (about 2:30 A.M., when the third cock crowed), "the light is near breaking" (about 3:30 A.M.) and "dawn" (Handy 1923, 347). (It should be noted however that such "points" were seldom utilized for scheduling events—sharp punctuality not having been regularly practiced in the conduct of their everyday, or even "official," lives.)

In addition, the daylight part of the cycle was everywhere divided into larger segments—of "morning," "midday," and "afternoon"—a reflection of the usual daily routines of productive labor, followed by preparation and consumption of the principal meal, followed by rest (including sleep) and diversions. Again however it should be noted that such periods were not sharply boundaried, and that their beginnings and endings varied in "time" (i.e., Western clock time) individually (or by household) and from day to day.

Most Polynesian peoples also reckoned "time" in cycles of named "moons" (i.e., lunar months) of twenty-nine or thirty "nights" each. The successive "nights" of each "moon" were correlated with moon phases and were characterized mainly in terms of the availability of this or that variety of (edible) marine animals. In some places there were twelve such "moons," in others thirteen, neither of which cycles can be synchronized with a 365-day solar cycle; therefore some methods of adjustment (of intercalation or subtraction) were required. Other cyclical methods of reckoning "time" included, here or there, the positions of certain stars or constellations—especially of the Pleiades; weather conditions at sea—especially of winds; and the ripening of major food plants. There was however wide intersocietal variation in all these "calendars" due to differences in temperature, wind, rainfall and food supply. Some of those differences will be described in later chapters, but the corresponding variations in local "calendars" were too numerous to attempt to describe in this compendious text. For fuller treatments of such "calendars" see the monographic works on particular societies, especially those published in the Bishop Museum series. Be it noted however that most if not all such "calendars" had to do with crucially important practical occurrences, such as fishing or plant ripening or canoe travel, and not with the passage of "time" in the abstract. For example, with one known exception (see chapter 17) such reckoning was not used to measure a person's "age," nor was it used for "dating" a past event—such as, for example, in stating that a war or a hurricane or the death of a particular chief occurred "six moons (or seven trade-wind periods, or eight breadfruit-ripening seasons) ago."

POPULATION

Estimates of the numbers of Polynesians alive at times of contact range from wild guesses to conscientious—albeit unconfirmable—reconstructions. In most cases credible censuses were taken only decades later, after Western-introduced diseases had taken heavy tolls. And except in the case of a few small populations, such as those on some atolls, the guesses of most Western contact-time visitors varied by magnitudes of five or ten.[34] (For example, for Tahiti Island the estimate of the Spanish navigator Boenechea in 1772 was 10,000, and Cook's in 1774 was 204,000—whereas a recent one based on several more realistic head counts and estimates arrived at a figure of 35–36,000 (Oliver 1974). Nor can archaeology—based on remains of houses and communities—provide better than informed conjecture. Nevertheless, it behooves me to summarize the most credible, or least incredible, figures that

scholars of various disciplines have reconstructed concerning those population numbers, along with estimates of their densities, where possible.

The first of such estimates (Table 6.1) represents contact-time numbers of whole high-island *archipelagoes* within the Polynesian Triangle, as summarized by the archaeologist Patrick Kirch from estimates of various other specialists (from Kirch 1984, 98, with his kilometers converted to statute miles).

On the same chart Kirch gives estimates for several *individual* high islands of the Triangle (Table 6.2).

Note however in all the above that "arability" was not of the same kind and quality everywhere. Thus, in terms of the production of food and other human-used resources, the quality of Samoa's 313 square miles of "arable" land was, mile for mile, far superior to that of Easter Island. And while

Table 6.1

Archipelago	Total population	Total land area (mi²)	Arable land	Population density per mi² of arable land
Hawaiian	200,000	6,420	642	312
Tongan	40,000	289	247	162
Society	45,000	592	178	253
Samoan	80,000	1,092	313	256
Marquesan	35,000	408	204	172

Table 6.2

Island	Total population	Total land area (mi²)	Arable land	Population density per mi² of arable land
Easter	7,000	62	41	171
Mangaia	3,000	27	15	200
E. Uvea	4,000	23	15	266
E. Futuna	2,000	24	15	133

both Easter Island and the Marquesas (as a whole) may have had the same density per square mile of "arable" land, the differences between the uses of those lands were very wide. Another limitation of the relevance of the above figures for comparing an island's natural human-supporting resources is their focus on dry land. That is, some of the islands were surrounded by food-rich lagoons or shallow and relatively calm ocean waters, while others by only turbulent or barren seas. (This difference was particularly sharp in comparisons of the natural resources of high islands with those of atolls, many or most of which were adjacent to food-rich lagoons.) Almost as critical, the figures do not take into account local differences in the frequency and destructiveness of natural cataclysms, such as hurricanes, tidal waves, volcanic eruptions and multiyear droughts. Nevertheless, the figures do serve to indicate that Polynesian peoples differed widely in the kinds and amounts of life-sustaining resources available to them—differences that were reflected not only in their numbers and densities but in their institutions as well.

At times of contact some peoples (such as the Hawaiians and the Tahitians) had not yet reached the full carrying capacities of their lands (i.e., in terms of their current methods of exploiting them),[35] while some others, such as the Tongans, had reached but not yet permanently exceeded theirs, and still others, such as the Easter Islanders, had exceeded a comfortable population-wide conformity to theirs—which resulted in more or less continuous land-contesting warfare. And the existence of the so-called "Mystery Islands" referred to in chapter 1—those once but no longer inhabited—indicates that not even the extraordinarily adaptive Polynesians were able, or willing, to live just anywhere.

However, warfare and exodus were not the only measures taken by Polynesians to adjust to the physical limits of their island homes. In

Tikopia, for example, where the risk of overpopulation was well recognized and authoritatively inveighed against,[36] concrete measures were taken to avoid it—including coitus interruptus, abortion, infanticide and celibacy (of younger brothers). Note, however, that there and elsewhere in Polynesia abortion and infanticide were also practiced for purposes other than overall population control, as will later be described.

Listed below are estimates of population for some other high islands within the Polynesian Triangle—most of them dated much later—after Western contact had, doubtless, reduced population sizes.

Table 6.3

Island	(Date) Total population	Total land area (mi²)
Aitutaki	(1906) 1,162	6.09
Mauke	(1906) 446	7.18
Mitiaro	(1906) 210	6.25
Rarotonga	(1906) 2,441	35.80
Niue	(1873) 5,000+	100+
Rapa	(?) 1,500+	16

For the atoll peoples of Triangle Polynesia, available (dated) population estimates are given in table 6.4.

To complete the list of Polynesian population figures—such as they are—I list below those of the Outlier high islands and atolls, identified by dates of earliest credible counts or estimates—which, as will be seen, were very recent, a circumstance that renders the figures somewhat less irrelevant to the early contact focus of this book, inasmuch as most of these populations had been much less affected by Western contacts than had been their Triangle counterparts. The list was compiled by Bayard (1976) and is in order of the islands' position, from north to south: Nukuoro (date of count, 1878) 124; Kapingamarangi (1971) 500+;

Table 6.4

Atolls	(Date) Total population	Total land area (mi²)	Population density per total land area
Pukapuka	(1866) 750	1.95	385
Tokelau	(1840) 1,000+	4.7	213+
Tongareva	(?) 2,000+	6.25	320+
Tuvalu	(1931) 4,025	?	?
Nukulaelae	(1860) 400+	?	?

Nuguria (1940) 80; Tau'u (i.e., Taku'u) (1940) 178; Nukumanu (1971) 100+; Luangiua (i.e., Ontong Java) (1939) 588; Sikiana (i.e., Sikaiana) (1935) 235; Pileni (1960) 489; Taumako (1966) 220; Tikopia (1929) 1,281; Anuta (1944) 133; Rennell (1951) 1,000+; Bellona (1930) 500+; Maeemae (1936) 150+; Mele (1934) 380; Fila (1934) 200; West Futuna (1936) 250; Aniwa (1936) 176; West Uvea (1917) 2,000–3,000 "métis" (mixed blood).

Eyewitness estimates of the gender composition of contact-era populations vary, from the careful personal numeration by Raymond Firth of Tikopians to the impressionistic opinions of the English missionaries about Tahitians (e.g., "three to four times as many males as females"). Likewise with estimates about age, which varied from "they live to a Good old age" to another (about the same population) that "we saw very few old people."

One might reasonably expect that precontact cemeteries would yield better data, at least on age. Unfortunately, only three large (and therefore less likely to be representative) cemeteries have so far been excavated and studied osteologically. The largest of these, in Hawai'i, contained 883 skeletons judged to be "adult" (i.e., over about twenty-one years of age). Of those, 473 (54 percent) had died before reaching thirty-one, and only 8 (0.01 percent) were over fifty (Pietrusewsky and Douglas 1994). (The causes of death could be determined in only a few cases, the deaths having occurred before the introduction of such skeleton-marking diseases as syphilis and leprosy.) Also, it should be noted that not all Hawaiians were buried in cemeteries, some having been buried singly or in small family burial grounds, some having drowned at sea, and some killed and their bodies left scattered on battlefields or ocean floor.

In this connection, the mortal diseases known to have existed in one or another Polynesian population included tuberculosis and filaria (which led to elephantiasis), but not malaria (except in some Outliers in the New Hebrides or the Solomons), and none of the diseases, such as gonorrhea, syphilis, influenza, leprosy and dysentery, that were unwittingly introduced by Westerners and Asians and which served to reduce some populations to near extinction.

Earlier in this book Polynesians were described as having had "lighter skins, straighter hair and less negroid facial features" than most present-day Melanesians, and their Lapitan forebears as having been "Mongoloid" in physical type. What more can be said concerning the physical characteristics of live, contact-era Polynesians that distinguished them from other Pacific Islanders? Answers to that question have been sought from three kinds of evidence: skeletal remains, the external physical features of living individuals, and genetic analysis.

Evidence from skeletal remains has been summarized most recently by Pietrusewsky (1996), and concerns post-Lapita crania. Using cranial measurements from many parts of Asia, (aboriginal) Australia, and Oceania, he concluded that his findings "confirm the distinctiveness and relative homogeneity of Polynesians and point to a homeland in Island Southeast Asia" (351). His term "relative homogeneity" refers to the slight differences found among the several geographically different cranial series—e.g., those between eastern and western Polynesia. Such differences derived not from natural selection, which, in evolutionary terms, is unlikely to have occurred during the short periods of the populations' separation one from another, but rather from operation of the "founder principle"—i.e., the result of colonizations having involved only small numbers of people, who, quite normally, would have differed somewhat from the "average" genetic compositions of the entire populations of their respective homelands.

A special feature of Polynesian crania worth mentioning is the "rocker jaw," a trait that occurs sparsely in a few other human populations but that was widely prevalent among Polynesians. It refers to the lower edge of the mandible, which unlike those of most other humans, is so convex in shape that it "rocks"—i.e., that it cannot sit firmly on a flat surface.

Turning to measurements and other observations on present-day living populations, the physical anthropologist William Howells summarized that "In general, Polynesians are (or were) large in size; relatively tall, large boned, and tending to corpulence. Polynesian women may not all approach the Majestic Queen Salote of Tonga or past royalty of other groups, but the females of Gauguin's paintings or living Maori—both pictorially familiar—would be representative. Skin color is variable, usually a light brown. Hair also varies, seldom being either frizzly or perfectly straight, but instead slightly to markedly wavy, and always dark. Faces are large, high and oblong, with noses that are neither prominent nor flat" (1979, 272).

Genetic studies of Polynesians, both living and dead, have been concerned both with their "original" origin and with their hybridization en route, and in neither case do the results of the studies totally agree. As reported in chapter 2, some evidence points to Taiwan as the original homeland, other evidence to mainland Southeast Asia. And regarding their hybridization en route, some studies suggest that the bloodlines of the particular, pre-Polynesian Lapitans migrated through Melanesia fairly speedily and with little or no mixture with Sundanoids en route, while other studies suggest that they tarried long enough to interact and hybridize with the earlier, Sundanoid inhabitants. For more on this matter see Hegelberg and Clegg 1993; Hill and Sargeanson 1989; Kelly 1996; and Stoneking and Wilson 1989.

7

LANGUAGES

At times of Western contact there were about thirty-five Polynesian languages—the exact number being uncertain, partly because of inadequacies of information. For example, in the case of Moriori, the vernacular of the former inhabitants of the Chatham Islands, there is uncertainty as to whether it was a fully separate language or a dialect of Maori, the language of the inhabitants of New Zealand, whence the Chatham Islands were colonized. (In this case the uncertainty is due mainly to the fact that the Chatham Islanders had become "re-Maoriized" sometime after Western contact and before their vernacular had been adequately studied. See chapter 25.)

Another kind of uncertainty derives from disagreements among linguists concerning the distinction between "language" and "dialect." One proposed qualitative distinction between any two vernaculars is that they constitute distinct languages if they are mutually incomprehensible and dialects if they are only partially incomprehensible variants of a single language—which raises the question of how to define "partially." Thus, in the case of Hawaiian and Tahitian, at times of contact the two vernaculars were in some respects "mutually comprehensible"—e.g., in both vernaculars the (unvoiced alveolar) t-sound and the (unvoiced alveolar) k-sound were variants of the same phoneme, as were the sounds "r" and "l" (e.g., in some early Western accounts Honolulu was spelled "Honoruru"). Later, however, missionaries moved in and after some debate decided upon "t" and "r" for Tahitian, and "k" and "l" for Hawaiian, and by embodying their decisions in printed translations of the Bible and other mission documents had perpetuated them, not only in printed spellings of words but eventually in everyday speech as well. In other words, the well-meaning lexicographers (doubtless unintentionally) actually decreased the mutual comprehensibility of the two vernaculars for all time (Walch 1967).

A more quantitative distinction proposed by some linguists between language and dialect is based on the number of words (i.e., "units of meaning") they share, (i.e., despite their phonetic difference): namely, if they share more than about 81 percent of them (out of a standardized list of two hundred "units of meaning") they are considered to be dialects of a single language; if less than 81 percent, they are considered to be distinct languages. This criterion might be useful to linguists for certain purposes, but to a nonlinguist (such as I) the cut-off percentage of 81—rather than, say, 75 or 85—seems somewhat arbitrary.

However, leaving aside such definitional nuances, there is no question that all Polynesian languages (including their constituent dialects) were "descended" from a common ancestral language. Moreover, the most prevalent method used for discovering their subsequent, contact-time interrelationships has been by counting, and evaluating, their nonaccidental shared innovations—in phonemes, morphemes, lexemes (i.e., words) and syntax.[37] It has been by this method that linguists constructed the "genealogy" of their relationships.

For all their differences, however, Polynesian languages were—still are—remarkably alike in comparison with, say, the comparable subgroupings of Germanic, which consist of German, Dutch and English, and were immeasurably different from, say, "standard" English, as the following examples will illustrate.

Beginning with phonemes (i.e., the smallest meaningful sounds of a spoken language), while one or another English dialect contains seven to nine vowels (vocalic phonemes), Polynesian languages contain only five (a, e, i, o and u)—although each of the latter consists of two meaningful (i.e., not merely rhetorical) forms, both "short" and "long," thereby raising the number of their vowels to ten. As for consonants (nonvocalic phonemes), the most noteworthy differences between English and Polynesian phonemes lie in their number; in most English dialects they number twenty-four, in Polynesian far fewer—and, as noted earlier, in the meaningful (i.e. phonemic) use of the glottal stop (represented in writing by the letter '), which occurs in all Polynesian languages but not in "standard" English. Also, unlike in English, all syllables in Polynesian words end in a vowel.

With respect to morphemes (i.e., the smallest meaningful expressive units of a spoken language) and to syntax (i.e., the many ways in which morphemes are combined into words and words into sentences), the differences between Polynesian and English are too numerous and complex to attempt to summarize here, but some (nonprofessional but intelligible) notion about the extent of those differences is indicated in the following examples, contained in a Hawaiian text about a legendary hero:

1. *I ka wa kahiko ua noho kekahi koa ma Kaua'i*
[In the era ancient (past) dwelt a-certain warrior at Kaua'i]
In ancient time a certain warrior lived in Kaua'i

2. *'O Palila kona inoa*
[(subject) Palila his name]
Palila (was) his name

3. *He kanaka ikaika loa i ke kaua*
[A (native man) strong very in the warfare]
A man very strong in warfare

4. *He la'au palaukana*
[A war club wooden stick his]
He had a war club/wooden stick

5. *Hiki iaia ke leleme keia la'au*
[to-be-able him the fly-leap-jump with this club]
He could fly-leap-jump with this club

6. *Ua lele mai kekahi mokupuni a hiki i kekahi mokupuni*
[(past) fly-leap-jump from one island be-able to one island]
He jumped from one island to/as far as another island

7. *Ua lele mai Kaua'i a hiki i O'ahu*
[(past) jumped from Kaua'i to/as far as O'ahu]

He jumped from Kaua'i to O'ahu
(Elbert 1970, 119; the lines giving literal translations, in brackets, are added.)

Another feature of Polynesian languages that differentiates them markedly from English is their more precise use of pronouns—namely, their use of separate ones for distinguishing two persons from more than two. Still another feature of all Polynesian languages that differentiates them from English—and that is indicative of Polynesians' concepts about "self"—was their distinction between two forms of possessives, namely, between the word *o* and the word *a*. The word *o* was applied mostly to entities deemed inherent, such as parts of one's own body or entities inherited (e.g., parents, siblings, land); the word *a* mostly to entities acquired (e.g., spouses, lovers, offspring).

Like all other peoples everywhere the Polynesians used their languages (verbally only) in several different ways, which in their case included conversation, narration (including the retelling of myths and legends and the reciting of genealogies), secular orations (salutations, harangues, laments, farewells), songs, prayers and magical spells.

Conversations were of course more informal than other kinds of speech, and in some societies varied somewhat according to the relative statuses of the conversers. In several of their societies, for example, when a person addressed someone of higher status he was required not only to adopt a conventionally "respectful" tone of voice, but to use certain more "respectful" words and phrasings as well. Also, while conversations were often rich in allusions of other kinds, they typically (and innocently) included such direct references to bodily functions and to sexual intercourse as to scandalize even Western seamen. Moreover, this feature was characteristic of more formal utterances as well—even to those addressed to gods, as exemplified in the common Tikopian prayer that prefaced many supplications with "I eat ten times your excrement."

Narrations varied widely in topic, from particularistic accounts of everyday events to society-wide, even Polynesia-wide, cosmogonic mythic themes. Most widespread of the latter were accounts of creation, including the creative exploits of the demigod trickster Maui (whose

Polynesia-wide adventures have been authoritatively and dramatically recounted in Katherine Luomala's classic *Maui of a Thousand Tricks*, which provides additional confirmation of the common heritage of all Polynesians).[38]

With respect to genealogies, many of the longer ones were delivered in the tone of chanting, which was characterized as follows by the nineteenth-century Christianized Hawaiian Samuel Kamakau: "The voice took a tone almost on one note and each word was enunciated distinctly. There was a vibration in the chanting together with a guttural sound in the throat and a gurgling in the voice box. The voice was to be brought out with strength and so held in control that every word would be clear" (as quoted in Beckwith 1951, 36). And, as Beckwith adds: "Evenness of voice was obligatory. A breath taken before the close of a phrase, a mistake, or even hesitation in pronouncing a word was a sign of ill-luck to the person or family thus honored" (Ibid., 35–36).

In some societies mnemonic devices, such as knotted cords, were used by reciters to keep count of names or phrases, but even then some of the recitations were so long as to require prodigious feats of memorization.

In several societies there were men who specialized in reciting, more or less publicly, lengthy formal utterances—in some cases mainly secular, in others religious, and in still others both. (I write "mainly" inasmuch as many if not most such "secular" utterances also included some religious content or intent.) Expertise in this profession required prolonged training and was rewarded, usually, with privileged social status. In most societies the training was done on an individual basis—say, by an elder relative (including cases in which the profession was an exclusive family prerogative)—whereas in a few more populous societies the training took place in organized "schools."

Unlike chants, which tended to be lengthy, and in which several syllables were intoned on a single note or on only slightly varying notes, the few examples of authentically pre-Western songs that have been musically recorded were (by Anglophonic definition) more melodic and rhythmical, and were quite short. Doubtless, most if not all Polynesian peoples composed and sang songs, but few if any of those songs have been studied, and published, as fully and insightfully as those of

Tikopia—thanks to the joint work of Raymond Firth and Mervyn McLean, whose publication *Tikopia Songs* (with an accompanying cassette) adds yet another chapter to the unparalleled corpus of descriptive and analytical studies on that people's culture. Helen Roberts' *Ancient Hawaiian Music*, published in 1926, remains the classic of the genre but was based on salvage research, whereas the Tikopia study derived from observations and recordings made in a robust and largely un-Westernized culture.

Most Tikopian songs were of one of two types: *mako*, those that were sung on occasions of pleasure and recreation, especially while dancing; and *fuatanga*, those sung on more serious occasions, such as mourning and formal eulogizing, plus some that accompanied rites that were specifically religious. The latter were composed by especially skilled persons and usually for specific occasions.

In Firth's words: "The oral text of a poem [i.e., song text] has two features which distinguish it from ordinary speech, and give it a poetic character. The first is its rhythmic pattern . . . combinations of stressed and unstressed syllables with some degree of regularity. The Tikopia have been completely uninterested in . . . parallel development of syllabic endings or phrase alignments . . . What does seem important [to them] is the stress pattern of syllables and words, and the phrasing of words, linking rhythm and meaning" (1990, 14–15). Regarding the latter, some songs were sung to the accompaniment of hand clapping or of percussive beats—made, e.g., by sticks struck on a wooden plank or by sections of bamboo bumped on the ground (Ibid., 18–19).

The words used in Tikopian songs sometimes differed from those of ordinary speech. And while vocalized poetry did make use of phrasal repetition—as it does in English—it did not employ consonantal alliteration. Here are a few examples of such poetry; first, about the fishing expertise of the composer's foster grandparent and his knowledge of the banks where fish were to be found:

Muna mai ke kou ono ki oi
He told me to gaze on it [a fishing bank]
Muna mai ke kou ono ki oi
He told me to gaze on it
Ki ona fakataunga i te moana
On his bearings from the ocean

Ki ona fakataunga ki uta
On his bearings to shore
. . . .
Fatio au ki oi
I bend over to it [a big fish]
Fatio au o veivei ki oi
I bend over to exclaim in astonishment at it
(Ibid., 41)

Next, the dismay of a canoe helmsman when confronted by change of wind and threat of storm:

Kau kitea te mate
I have looked upon death
Taufatea oko mai
Gale-borne it has reached me
Ra puroupurou e!
Oh sail curved over!
Ra riorioki e!
Oh sail flapping to and fro!
Se ne kau iroa
I did not know
Ko te vakaianga o te matangi
The circling of the wind
Ki te fokotiu
To the northwest
Tu a papa te tokerau
The north stands in storm clouds
Ka oko mai
Which will arrive here
(Ibid., 158)

Next, a song by a man in praise of his wife:

Utu ko te voi e toku soa
The water bottle is filled by my spouse
E neve saere
Walking with back burden
I o au katoongo
Amid your mass of affairs
Fakamau nofo ou ki
In security I dwell through
toku soa
my spouse
I taku kamu ma te paipi
With my betel and my pipe
Ka sori moi
Which you will give me

(Firth adds to this: "It may annoy a feminist in its calm assumption of the serving role of the woman

in a Tikopia household . . . [namely, in] . . . patiently filling the water bottles at the spring, then tying them in a basket on her back and making her way home . . . and contrasted with all the other things she has to do in and around the domestic dwelling—sweeping the house, tending to floor and bed mats, preparing food for the oven, caring for children" (Ibid., 171–72).

One of the Polynesians' lengthiest, most notable and most richly allusive narrational chants is the Hawaiian *Kumulipo* (*kumu*: beginning, source; [in] *li po*: deep darkness—i.e., "song of creation." Like others of this Polynesia-wide genre it was composed, and publicly recited, in order to validate and extol the high rank of a chief and of his family dynasty—in this case that of Kamehameha, the warrior-leader who succeeded in becoming, first, chief of Hawai'i Island and, later, with Westerner support, "king" of the whole archipelago. This particular kind of song-like chant (*mele*), known as a "lineage-pathway," consisted of over two thousand "lines" grouped into sixteen sections. The first seven sections dealt with the creation of the Universe, beginning with the following lines of the first section of the Kalākaua Text (Beckwith 1951) (there having been more than one text):

1. O ke au i kahuli wela ka honua
2. O ke au i kahuli lole ka lani
3. O ke au i kuka 'iaka ka la
4. E ho'omalamalama i ka malama
5. O ke au o Makali'i ka po
6. O ka walewale ho'okumu honua ia
7. O ke kumu o ka lipo, i lipo ai
8. O ke ku kumu o ka Po i po ai
9. O ka lipolipo, o ka lipolipo
10. O ka lipo o ka la, o ka lipo o ka po
11. Po wale ho-'i
12. Hanau ka po
13. Hanau Kumulipo i ka po, he hane
14. Hanau Po'ele i ka po, he wahine
15. Hanau ka 'Uku-ko'ako'a, hanau kana, he 'Ako'ako'a, puka
16. Hanau ke Ko'e-enuhe 'eli ho'opu'u honua

One of several different "literal" translations of the above reads:
1. At the time when the Earth became hot
2. At the time when the heavens turned about
3. At the time when the sun was darkened

4. To cause the moon to shine
5. The time of the rise of the Pleiades
6. The slime, this was the source of the earth
7. The source of the darkness that made darkness
8. The source of the night that made night
9. The intense darkness, the deep darkness
10. Darkness of the sun, darkness of the night,
11. Nothing but night.
12. The night gave birth
13. Born was Kumulipo in the night, a male
14. Born was Po'ele in the night, a female
15. Born was the coral polyp, born was the coral, came forth
16. Born was the grub that digs and heaps up the earth, came forth

The lines of the first section chronicled serially the birth (hanau) of sea cucumbers, mussels, and other shellfish, then of various kinds of seaweed. Then, in the next six sections, were chronicled seriatim the birth of various kinds of fish and eels, land vegetation, insects, birds, amphibians, food plants, pigs, rats and dogs—the whole having taken place in the era of Darkness (Po) and interspersed—poetically adorned—with mythic allusions of many kinds. After that, the final nine sections chronicled, in the era of Day (Ao), first the birth of gods (akua), then god-engendered demigods and humans, then those human-engendered—albeit godliness imbued—ancestral lines of humans that, according to this politically inspired version, coalesced to beget the Kamehameha dynasty.[39]

The above summary, exigently brief, provides little indication of the extraordinarily rich, colorful and often cryptic allusiveness of the chant as a whole. While its function was clear and obvious (i.e., to validate and glorify the status of the Kamehameha family dynasty), the many meanings of the early "Darkness" Era chronicle have led to different interpretations. In the words of Martha Beckwith (whose version I have summarized): "The general and orthodox view [of most interpreters] has been to look upon the Chant as an actual history of life on Earth from its beginning (kumu) progressively up to the coming of man, and thence through the family succession in unbroken line to the birth of the child [i.e., Kamehameha] to whom it was dedicated" (Ibid., 40). Another interpretation regards the first seven sections as symbolizing "stages in the development

of the divine taboo [kapu] chief from infancy to adolescence, when there begins in the second division the symbolic rehearsal of his taking a wife, house building, and the rearing of a family" (Ibid., 41). And still another sees the same sections of the first, Darkness, division as depicting "not stages in the growth of the child after birth, but those passed through while still dwelling in the spirit world as an embryo within the womb of his mother" (Ibid.). Or, as still another, present-day exegetist proposes, "Probably all [the above interpretations] are right" (Ibid.).

In any case, whatever the chant's "real" meaning, it is an excellent and in some respects typical specimen of Polynesian oral poetic art.[40]

Turning, briefly, to prayers, utterances addressed directly to gods, they too varied widely, from offhand, single sentences delivered in the course of everyday activities, to hours-long standardized, word-perfect chants—as will be mentioned in chapter 8.

The verbal utterances of most, probably all, Polynesian peoples also included spells, word formulas designed specifically to cause something to happen—in many cases something harmful—to another person. It might be argued that all such utterances were prayers for assistance addressed to one or another god, but there is a strong possibility that some of them were thought to depend entirely upon the direct magical power of certain words in the spell. (Also, it should be added that the requirement for verbal accuracy that accompanied delivery of some other formal utterances—such as genealogies and eulogies—suggests that word-magic operated in them as well.)

Another form of word-potency had to do with name avoidance, prohibition of the use of the names of some tribal chiefs and of many words containing sound combinations more or less identical with such names. The practice was most prevalent in the Society Islands, where it was known as pi'i, and, as mentioned earlier, where its best known example occurred during the regime of Pomare I, who was chief of the tribe, in northwest Tahiti, in whose waters the ships of Cook and other English visitors of that era anchored. Thus, in order to avoid common use of the syllables that make up "Pomare"—which meant "night" (po) and "cough" (mare), rui became the common name for "night" and hota for "cough." Violations of the avoidance were severely punished.

7.1. A *rongorongo* tablet of Easter Island and some of its pictographs

The substitutes prevailed at least during Pomare's chieftainship and at least among his subjects. What is not certain is whether they did so outside his tribe or after his death or replacement (White 1967, as noted in Oliver 1974, 1040–42).

Next, we come to the famous and controversial Easter Island *rongorongo*, small wooden boards on which were incised numerous pictographs set out in distinct horizontal lines and in reverse boustrophedon form—a form of writing in which the rows alternate in direction from left to right and then right to left (fig. 7.1). The individual pictures were either anthropomorphic or zoomorphic, and were about one hundred in number. They were used mainly, perhaps solely, as mnemonic props by chanters (also called *rongorongo*). They have been studied by numerous persons, some of whom have interpreted them as a form of ideographic script. (See, for example, Barthel 1971.) However, since the pictures evidently do not represent phonemes or syllables or whole sentences, other writers argue that they did not constitute a form of writing, and point out that they appeared on the scene in postcontact times, thereby suggesting that they were made in imitation of Western alphabetic writing (Métraux 1940; Emory 1972; Fischer 1997[41]). In any case, as long as the island's colossal stone statues serve to attract and intrigue the interest of outsiders, so will its unique pictographs excite and color their imaginations.

Finally—or as preface to subsequent descriptions in this book—it should be added that Polynesians, like all other peoples, used other, nonverbal, kinds of ways for expressing their real or culturally prescribed "thoughts," including body postures, manual gestures, dance movements, facial expressions, ways of proffering "gifts," etc. Such standardized behaviors were more elaborated in western than in eastern Polynesian societies and reached their height of refinement in Samoa, where "The ceremonial setting—the gesture, the word, the placement of person, the order of precedence, the sipping of the kava cup—the respect for the minutiae of decorum . . . is a statement of the very essence of social life," and where "protocol expertise and oratory, enjoyed as ends in themselves or as embellishments of the larger drama of honor, rank among the most esteemed of the Samoan skills" (Goldman 1970, 258).

8

COSMOLOGIES AND RELIGIONS

Unlike some other Pacific Islanders, Polynesians in general did speculate about, or accept speculation about, unseen aspects of their world.[42] What I wrote about eighteenth-century Tahitians in particular can be said of most other Polynesians: "There is evidence aplenty that some [Tahitians] were keen observers of their physical surroundings, and that at least some of them engaged more than casually in speculation and generalization about their universe. In fact, [such] sages occupied positions of honor and privilege" (Oliver 1974, 55).

I will begin this necessarily brief account of a very large subject by saying that I do not share the view of those scholars who argue that Polynesians in general regarded their respective[43] universes as consisting of an all-pervasive dynamism—a kind of belief that is labeled "animatism" (to distinguish it from "animism," the doctrine that among objects and natural phenomena that appear to be inanimate—including rocks, mountains, lakes, heavenly bodies, boats, tools, weapons, etc.— some were endowed with powers of moving, speaking, reasoning, etc., similar to those of live humans). The "classic" statement about the alleged Polynesia-wide belief in animatism is that of Edward Handy in his book *Polynesian Religion*, published in 1927: "The Polynesian cosmogony depicts a universe which is a psychic dynamism manifesting itself physically: behind and within all natural manifestation is life and psychic force. All objective phenomena of nature had their origin in the psychic dynamism; and all existed within its field or atmosphere. Concrete nature in all its parts was also in a sense regarded as a reservoir of dynamic power. Its different parts were the mediums of transmission of this force" (1927, 26). And in another passage of the same book: "The ancient esoteric teaching in [Polynesian] cosmology postulated the preexistence of a self-created World Soul which evolved the world and the universe out of itself, and called manifest existence out of nothingness by the power of the Word" (Ibid., 9).

Handy went on to say that the only direct evidence we have of such a belief is from New Zealand and the Society Islands, and that the reason other Polynesian creation accounts make no mention of this World Soul is that the informants either did not know or dared not reveal such esoteric knowledge.

In an exhaustive search through documents relating to pre-European Society Islanders (i.e., Tahitians) I failed to discover any credible basis for Handy's postulation of native belief in a "World Soul" or in an all-pervasive "psychic dynamism." And while granting—for the moment!—that such beliefs might have prevailed among the New Zealand Polynesians (i.e., the Maori), like Handy I can find no persuasive evidence of them among any other Polynesian peoples. Building blocks for such a concept can be inferred from some recorded beliefs and practices—although Polynesians' profuse use of metaphor can be deceptive in this respect—but it is my opinion that those "blocks" were not integrated into a unitary metaphysical edifice.

Instead, I am convinced that most or all Polynesian peoples viewed their respective universes as consisting of innumerable particular entities, some of which were essentially "active" (i.e., animate) and others essentially "inactive" but capable of being rendered "active." Regarding the latter, while most individual stones, trees, tools, weapons, etc., were essentially "inactive," some of them were made "active," temporarily or permanently, by gods for particular purposes. One kind of borderline exception to that included certain mythical entities, such as "Giant Stratum Stone," which though generically "inactive" did figure "actively" in some cosmogonic myths. Also, there were other entities, such as red feathers and the stem and branches of the *ti* (*Cordyline terminalis*), that were believed to have the power of attracting gods, and some others, such as fire, seawater, and certain words, which although usually "inactive" (in the sense now being considered) were on certain ritual occasions imbued with "active" qualities.

In the category of normally "active" entities, most if not all Polynesian cosmologies distinguished three major subtypes: gods, living humans and living nongodly-imbued animals (i.e., most birds, fish, insects, etc.). Here again, however, there were some borderline exceptions. For example, in most societies most humans were believed to have been conceived, and born, with some vestige of "godliness"—i.e., an impalpable but active constituent of that god who had engendered a human's primal human ancestor. Moreover, in some humans that constituent was so large (or powerful or whatever) that they were considered to *be* gods.[44]

I use the term "god"—reluctantly but deliberately—to label all types of supernatural[45] beings. While some Polynesian peoples distinguished, and distinctively labeled, two or more types of supernaturals, in terms of power or origin or function or domain, etc. (e.g., gods that had never been human, and humans-become-gods—i.e., ghosts), some others applied the same label (i.e., *atua*, or some cognate thereof) to most or all types. I shall do the same—partly for the sake of word economy and partly because it is often difficult or impossible to particularize. I shall, however, attempt to specify, when necessary and possible, a particular god's perceived function or power.

Regarding gods in general, in virtually every people's universe they were believed to be countless in number and immensely varied in function and power. Some were credited with having created all or some parts of the universe, including humans and other gods. Some others were believed to be in control of particular aspects of nature, such as particular winds, or parts of the ocean, or particular active volcanoes (although, as just noted, it is not always clear from recorded beliefs whether such and such a god controlled, say, the volcano, or actually was the volcano). Also, some other gods were believed to hold control over one or another domain of nature or of one or another activity of importance to humans, such as horticulture or fishing or warfare—or

8.1. Stone image from Raivavae, with Peter Buck

thievery! Throughout much of Polynesia the most important of such gods, whom several writers label "departmental," were (to name their Hawaiian versions) Kāne, Lono, Kū and Kanaloa—who, in the Hawaiian pantheon, exercised control over, respectively, fertility—of nature and man; rain and harvests; warfare; and healing. Cognates of those four (for Lono, e.g., Rongo or Ro'o) were worshiped in many societies, but not everywhere in association with the same "department." Thus, in Tahiti and some other societies Kanaloa—in Tahitian, Ta'aroa—was the creator of the universe, but in the Marquesas was god of the ocean. Moreover, some of the more powerful gods were considered to exercise control over more than one aspect of nature, or more than one human activity—including seemingly opposite ones, such as both war *and* peace.

In addition to the above widely worshiped, and usually very powerful, gods, there were in some societies one or more others who surpassed any or all of them in terms of this or that kind of supernatural power. One such was the Tahitian god 'Oro, god of both war and peace, whose devotees included members of the famed Arioi cult (see below) and whose patronage at time of contact was vied for by the society's most influential chiefs. And at the other end of the scale there were gods who played only minor and restricted roles—such as serving as the familiar of one particular magician, or controlling the use of one particular spring, or acting as tutelar to one particular family.

Altogether, whereas in some cosmologies some creator gods had become otiose (i.e., withdrawn), most others played active roles in the affairs of living humans. In the words of F. A. Hanson (whose résumé of Polynesian religion is comprehensive, economic and lucid):

> Although numerous variations may be found in different islands, Polynesians are [were] unanimous in [the following] beliefs: that [most of] the gods inhabit a realm distinct from the physical world populated by human beings; that they are frequent visitors to the physical world; that the gods are responsible for a great deal of what happens in the physical world, including events both beneficial and detrimental to human beings; that humans may exercise, through properly executed ritual, some control over the visits of the gods to the physical world and what they do here; and (what is one of the most distinctive features of Polynesian religion) that the gods may be ritually induced to withdraw from the physical world in circumstances where their influence is not, or is no longer, desirable. At bottom, Polynesian religion is a story of gods who are immensely active in this world and of people who attempt to control the activities of the gods by directing their influence into places where it is desired and expelling it from places where it is not. (Hanson 1987, 424)

In addition to the above (and as stated earlier), in some societies certain individuals were considered to be gods because of the large "amounts" of their godliness. Also, in some societies certain individuals, called *taura* (or *taula*, *kaula*, etc.), became "possessed" by one or another god in order to make known, through the voice of the *taura*, that god's thoughts: wishes, judgments, interpretations, prophecies, etc. Most such intermediaries underwent "possession" only occasionally, but

there were a few, here and there, who became permanently possessed and as such were respected as gods.

Before describing what Polynesians believed about godly influences in their (respective) worlds, and how they attempted to control those influences, it may be useful to summarize their cosmogonies, i.e., their views about the creation of those worlds—which, I must quickly add, is easier said than done, because there were several different versions of cosmogony, in some cases even among the same people. A large sample of those versions is provided in Handy's aforementioned *Polynesian Religion*—although skepticism is advised regarding the author's "World Soul" postulate. Only a few of the more widely prevalent themes of those many versions need be listed here.

In many cosmogonic myths the initial creator was a single, presumably self-created, god, named Tangaloa (Ta'aroa, Kanaloa, etc.), who created much of the universe, including a few other major gods, out of a void (a night-dark nothingness).[46] Thereafter, certain of those gods continued the process by creating other entities—by fabrication, or angling (from the ocean), or sexual reproduction, etc. (Incidentally, the most successful of the godly anglers was the culture-hero Maui, who in addition to fishing up many islands from under the sea, succeeded also in lengthening daylight by restraining the fast-moving sun.)[47]

Creation by sexual reproduction—either by a male and female pair of gods, or by a male god and a human female—occurs in many cosmogonic myths. In some of them such was the source of the first humans (thereby providing a mythic rationale for their inheritance of a quota of "godliness"). In many other myths the sexual embrace between the male god of the sky and the female goddess of the Earth was so close and enduring that their progeny and other entities existing between them were trapped in darkness, until one of the latter forced and propped them apart, thereby admitting daylight and permitting their progeny and other active entities to move about and grow.

In some other mythic accounts, Creation was represented as having been initiated not by intentional acts on the part of a self-made and more or less anthropomorphic Creator but through evolution of primordial abstractions such as Thought and Desire, etc. However, I am not convinced that the native texts containing such words were meant to represent doctrine, literally; instead, they may have been examples of Polynesians' undeniable talent for sonorous metaphor.

More concrete, and more credibly doctrinal, are those evolutionary cosmogonic themes that depict physical and earthly entities as having grown or spread by stages (as, for example in the *Kumulipo*, described in chapter 7). In the words of Edward Handy:

> The most common mode of transmitting or recount-ing the evolutionary cosmogonic records was by genealogical series. Creational genealogies are typi-cal of and peculiar to Polynesia. These picture the world as evolving by a process of generation or propagation. Evolution is pictured as being procre-ational, accomplished by successive impregnations of female by male entities resulting in the birth of new cosmic manifestations, elements, entities, and beings. It is scarcely accurate to speak of the results of these mythical unions as reproductions, for the offspring always differ entirely from both parents. It is more correct, and perhaps more suggestive, to speak of the process as one of continuous impreg-nation producing successive mutations. (E.S.C. Handy 1927, 22)

Another kind of scenario is represented by one of Samoa, which attributes the process not to pro-creation but to rivalrous conflict, as in the follow-ing:

> Fire and water married, and from them sprang the earth, rocks, trees, and everything. The cuttle-fish fought with the fire and was beaten. The fish fought with the rocks, and the rocks conquered. The large stones fought with the small ones; the small con-quered. The small stones fought with the grass, and the grass conquered. The grass fought with the trees; the grass was beaten and the trees conquered. The trees fought with the creepers; the trees were beaten and the creepers conquered. The creepers rotted, swarmed with maggots, and from maggots they grew to be men. (Turner 1884, 6)

In a book such as the present one there is not enough space to do justice to the wide variations among Polynesian cosmogonies—variations not only between one society's and another's but within each society as well. (For a résumé of some of those themes see Kaeppler 1989.) Instead I will

list some of the recurring themes that have rele-vance to other, nonmythical aspects of Polynesian cultures: (1) the mythmakers' detailed knowledge of and interest in natural phenomena, including some that seem to have had little or no relevance for their everyday lives; (2) the wide behavioral distinctions between gods and humans in terms of strength and versatility—notwithstanding the genealogical ties that, in many versions, linked them; (3) the distinction between the usual abodes of gods and of humans—the former in Po (night-time, darkness, etc.), the latter in Ao (daytime, light, etc.); (4) the wide intrinsic distinction between human males and human females, in terms of their relationships with gods.

Turning now to relations between gods and living humans, one fairly common way in which gods were believed to influence humans was through omens (phenomena or incidents regarded as prophetic signs). Some omens were there for everyone to see or hear—although not everyone had the knowledge to interpret what they por-tended. Examples of such were rainbows, bizarre cloud formations, a human's muscle twitches, unusual movements of birds and other animals, unexpected rainfall, etc. In other situations signs of future events and outcomes were actively sought, by expert diviners, by interpreting gods' messages in, say, the entrails or reflex movements of a chicken killed for that purpose. Such experts were also engaged to divine, say, the source of a person's illness or the causes of defeat in battle.

Messages from gods were also transmitted in dreams, which were believed to be the experiences undergone by a sleeper's wandering spirit. As with other omens, some of those experiences were so conventional as to be interpreted by nearly any-one, while others were arcane enough to require the services of an expert diviner.

As mentioned earlier, another and more direct way in which gods communicated with humans was to "possess"—to enter into—a human and use the latter's voice or other body movement to transmit messages about past or future events (including the god's advice and wishes). Most per-sons were susceptible to "possession," but some were regarded as being so characteristically so that they were engaged occasionally as mediums (*taura*, or cognate words). And, as mentioned earlier, in some societies there were individuals who became permanently possessed by one or another god.

On some occasions gods also took direct, unsolicited action vis-à-vis humans, not by merely communicating with them but by doing something to or for them. On average such actions were more harmful than beneficial—such as causing an individual to sicken or a whole community to be devastated by a storm. And while some of those actions were punitive (mostly in response to disrespect for that god), in other cases they were considered to be without justification: the gratuitous actions of some characteristically malevolent god or one who was "morally" neutral (which many if not most gods were thought to be).

Most of the above actions and interactions were haphazard; more orderly relations between humans and gods took place in patterned rites wherein gods were formally thanked for something done for them or were petitioned to do something for them—or not to do something against them. Such rites varied widely in form—from simple one-liners (such as perfunctory prayers before a household meal) to hours-long entreaties that continued off and on for several days (such as those dedicated to crop fertility or in celebration of a chief's inauguration or in preparation for war). One crucially important aspect of most formalized verbal addresses to gods was the requirement that their delivery be letter-perfect. In some cases any hesitation or error on the part of the speaker was believed to nullify the interaction and in some cases subject him and perhaps the whole congregation to godly displeasure and punishment[48]—an indication of the amount of training and practice needed for becoming and remaining a priest. To avert such errors, the priests in many societies made use of rosarylike mnemonic devices, such as bundles of small sticks or knots in a cord.

Another feature of formalized verbal addresses to gods was their mode of delivery—i.e., usually sing-song and repetitious and often in unnaturally high-pitched, even falsetto voice. Also, in some societies the effectiveness of a prayer required that lengthy sentences of it be voiced without a break for inhalation—a feat that served even further to distinguish the profession of priestcraft.

The usual sequence in most large-scale rites was (1) a request by humans to the relevant god (or gods) to leave his customary otherworld abode, the Po, and visit for a while in a place specially pre-

pared for him; (2) petitions to the visiting god for whatever purpose the ceremony was intended; and (3) a request to the god that he or she return to his or her customary otherworld abode.

Regarding (1), some gods—usually very "minor" ones, and either benevolent or malevolent or neutral—lurked much of the time, whether bidden or unbidden, in the mundane realm of humans, but the more powerful ones, especially those associated with whole groups of persons, or those identified with some culturally significant activity (such as horticulture, ocean travel, tattooing or warfare) had usually to be "invited." The kinds of places where such interaction took place varied widely, from clearings on a community's commons—including perhaps a small wooden god-house—to extensive stone-walled temples containing permanent altars, praying posts, edifices or images meant to serve as resting places for the visiting gods. (With respect to such places, the fabricated temples were more characteristic of eastern Polynesian societies; the simpler unwalled clearings, those of the west.) (Figs. 8.6, 8.7, 8.8, 8.9) In addition, some peoples had movable images, reserved for occasional occupancy by one or another particular god. (Figs.8.1, 8.2, 8.3, 8.4 8.5)

Regarding (2), although the petitions were ordinarily verbal (and characteristically highly stylized and obligatorily word-perfect), they were commonly accompanied by sacrifices, which ranged from token amounts of food to (in a few societies) live humans or those slain in warfare. In addition, in some societies the verbal invitations and petitions to the gods were enhanced by display of things believed specially attractive to them (e.g., red feathers, the *ti* plant, drum beats or dancing).

And regarding (3), it was considered essential (for the safety, i.e., normality, of the human participants) that the visiting gods end their visits and return to their otherworldly abode after the petitioning was completed, for their presence was believed to be inimical to everyday human actions. The most unequivocal example known to me of actions designed to accomplish that was one practiced by Tahitians:

Dismissal! Grand dismissal to make ordinary (*noa*)!—Let sacredness (*tapu*) remain here [in the temple] , that we [leave the temple and] become

8.2. Stone image from Marquesas

8.3. Wooden image from Rarotonga

8.4. Wooden image from Hawai'i

8.5. Wooden image from Hawai'i

8.6. *Marae* (temple) Mahaiatea in Tahiti

ordinary [*noa*]. Let holiness (*ra'a*) be thine, O god, let the priesthood (*tahu'a*) hold the sanctification (*mo'a*) of the sovereign (*ari'i*) and congregation. We are now retiring to use our hands and become vile (*ha'aha'a*); we shall do domestic work, wear flowers, paint ourselves yellow with *mati* (ficus Tinctorius), blow [kindle] fire, curse, give each other blows, practise [sorcery], caress [copulate], put on unconsecrated clothes, eat pork, cavalla fish, shark, bananas; and drink [kava]; look not upon us in anger for this, O god!—Remain thou here, in this holy place, turn thy face to Po, look not upon the deeds of [humans]. (Henry 1928, 172)

The motive expressed in the last line is particularly suggestive: i.e., "do not watch us behaving in ways that you might consider improper."[49] Or, as expressed in another Tahitian disengagement prayer: "Be not farsighted, be not farhearing to us.—Turn your faces to Po [darkness, the abode

of gods], and turn your back to the Ao [daylight, the mundane world of living humans]" (Ibid., 176–177).

Such prayers indicate that when the gods in question resumed their existences in their usual abode it was unlikely that they would know what humans did (much less thought?) during the latters' everyday, secular lives. Moreover, indications are that most interactions between humans and gods were initiated, or suspended, by humans. In fact, under some circumstances humans were able not just to suspend relations with gods *pro tem* but, in the case of some gods—i.e., family tutelars—to terminate relations with them permanently, as recorded in another passage about Tahitians: "When members of a family were stricken with long, protracted illness and with death and the prayers for their recovery to the gods (and goddesses) of their ancestral [temple] proved ineffectual, the family would hold counsel together and say, 'This god is no longer helping us; he is a man-devouring god. Let us cast him off and seek the favor of another deity!'" (Ibid., 178). Whereupon, the family's priest, who was usually its father or grandfather, went to the family's ancestral shrine and expelled its tutelar god in no uncertain words and selected another one in its place.

Speaking of "priest" (i.e., someone who mediates between humans and gods), Polynesian societies contained many kinds—due to the large numbers and varieties of their gods and to the latters' intervention in many of the things that people did. Correspondingly, mediation consisted of many different techniques—ranging from a perfunctory "thanks" accompanying, say, a family meal, to awesome days-long and tribe-wide ceremonies solemnizing, say, the inauguration of a chief, and including such practices as blessing, healing, divining, complaining, admonishing, etc.—and seeking assistance for, say, seducing or murdering someone. It is likely that most adults—or at least most male adults—knew and occasionally employed the techniques involved in some mediation practices, but many of the latter required specialized training or certain intrinsic personal characteristics.

Regarding these personal characteristics, some forms of mediation could only be accomplished by or through persons possessing large "amounts" (or whatever) of godliness—acquired by being firstborn of a long line of firstborns.[50] In some clans (i.e., common descent units) their senior member was both their top administrator and their practicing highest priest; in others, especially in the ascendant clans of large societies, their senior deputized his priestly duties to some specially trained priestly expert, but served on occa-

8.7. A human sacrifice on Tahiti

8.8. View on Easter Island showing two statues on stone platform

8.9. View of "Royal" temple on Hawai'i Island

sion to lend *ex cathedra* authenticity to the latter's ritual actions. And in other cases—especially where a clan senior was also a tribe's chief—that official relinquished, or was forced to relinquish, chieftainship over his tribe and served only as its highest priest.

At the level of families and extended-family households, it was usually their eldest male who represented the unit to its tutelar god(s)—a role that, usually, required little or no priestly expertise.

Focusing on such expertise, it is significant that nearly all Polynesian peoples applied the same generic label (i.e., *kahuna, tahu'a, tohunga*, etc.) to all types of experts deemed honorable in their society, e.g., expert carver, expert tattooer, expert in knowledge (sage), expert navigator, expert warrior, including "expert religious mediator"—i.e., "priest."

The latter—the "priest"—was, however, not the only type of mediator-with-gods. There were, for example, healers and sorcerers, whose techniques involved major assistance from one or another god, and in large temple congregations there were ritual assistants of many kinds (e.g., image keepers, sacrifice killers). In fact, most types of experts, including builders, warriors, etc., were on occasion mediators with their craft's or activity's tutelar gods. And in addition (as was noted above) every society contained one or more persons (*taura*, etc.) who had become "possessed" by some god and through whose voice or gestures the god transmitted messages to humans. In most cases the "possession" was temporary, and for some specific occasion, but in a few cases it was permanent, which—as noted earlier—led to that person's being treated as a god.[51]

Examples of gods' multifarious relations with humans, including the numerous kinds of settings in which that interaction took place, will be touched on later, but before ending this précis of Polynesians' views about arcane aspects of their conceptualized universe(s), I must attempt to explicate the meanings they ascribed to the almost Polynesia-wide words *mana, tapu* and *noa*. Note well the verb "attempt": scholars have been striving for decades to provide Polynesia-wide translations of these words.[52]

The fact that these words in all recorded Polynesian languages referred to sets of entities that were intangible—i.e., impossible to see, hear, touch, taste or smell—raises the possibility, indeed the likelihood, that they did not retain all of their proposed "proto"—i.e., "ancestral"—meanings throughout time and everywhere, especially between peoples as divergent—in numbers of years, in their environments, in size of population, in degree of isolation, etc.—as those of, say, Hawai'i and Tikopia.

Starting with *mana*, some scholars have translated that word as having referred, throughout Polynesia, to a psychic force that flowed, like electricity, into objects, including humans, thereby making them fecund or powerful or effective, etc. Others have translated it, also Polynesia-wide, as an adjective, one for characterizing the state of persons, places and objects made fecund or powerful, etc., by gods. And at least one translation (this one by an on-the-spot missionary lexicographer) defines the Tahitian version of the word as "power, might, influence; powerful, mighty, affluent; to be in power, possess influence" (Davies, 129)—all without specific reference to gods.

In view of the numerous scholarly disagreements regarding the "true" or Polynesia-wide meaning(s) of *mana* (and of the differences in cosmological concepts implied by them) I take sides only to the extent of rejecting the notion of *mana* as being the manifestation of "a universal, all-pervasive psychic dynamism." I do however accept at least three of the components of meaning that have been claimed for it here or there.

One nounlike component refers to what, earlier in this chapter, I labeled "godliness"—i.e., that component of a never-human god that was transmitted to his or her human descendants by the sexual act of procreation, and subsequently by them to theirs in the same way. A second component refers, adjectivally, to the god-imparted characteristics of some individuals, however transmitted, which conduced to their becoming outstandingly efficacious in some manifest way—e.g., in leadership, fighting, priestcraft, etc.[53] Third was the practice of some peoples in referring, also adjectivally, to those places or objects or humans or animals customarily visited by one or another god—i.e., temples, images, mediums, etc.—as being *mana* (or as herein translated, "sacred") at the time. And fourth was the outstanding efficacy, however acquired, attributed to certain individuals or objects (e.g., blood, red feathers, water) or processes (e.g., cooking) or words (singly or in context). According to some interpretations all such efficacies were directly or indirectly transmitted by gods; according to others some of them were intrinsically so. (Throughout the rest of this book "godliness," "efficacy" and "sacred" will be used instead of *mana*, in order to avoid ambiguity.)

The range of meanings that scholars have ascribed to the word *tapu* (*kapu*, etc.) is even wider than that ascribed to *mana*. At one extreme it has been defined as virtually synonymous with *mana*. At the other, it has been translated simply as "forbidden," for whatever cause. Or, for another wide variant, the Tahitian dictionary compiled by Protestant missionaries (after four decades of labor there) gives as one of its meanings "an oath or a certain solemn engagement to perform, or not to perform certain things" (Davies 1851, 253). In view of this wide range of ascribed meanings to *tapu*, within and between societies, it would be fallacious to assign a single, definite Polynesia-wide meaning to the word. However, many if not most of the recorded meanings do imply that it referred to an entity (including a person, an object, a place) or an event or a condition that was somehow inviolable to the extent that violations of it were in some way punishable. And in perhaps most cases the inviolability was sanctioned by and its violation punished by some god.

Turning now to *noa*, its meaning in most societies referred to states of being opposite to, and therefore adverse to, *mana* and *tapu*. One usage of *noa* referred to actions or activities: thus, whereas those activities involving gods (e.g., religious rites) were *mana* and *tapu*, those not involving gods (e.g., everyday activities) were *noa*—corollary to which was the practice in some societies whereby persons, usually males, had to become "de-*tapu*-ized" after participating in religious ceremonies before they could safely return to everyday (i.e., *noa*) life, as was exemplified in the prayer quoted earlier in this chapter Or, in many societies, females, who were characteristically engaged in and consequently identified solely with everyday, *noa*, activities, were not usually allowed to partic-

ipate in organized religious ceremonies, for fear of repelling the gods and thereby disorganizing the ceremonies—and perhaps causing harm to themselves as well.

Another usage of *noa* referred to objects considered to be characteristically *dis*-ordered, such as the putrefying flesh of a dead human, and in some societies menstrual (in contrast to ordinary) blood, contact with either of which, being "polluting," required ritual deletion. On the other hand, another scholarly view is that menstrual blood was not really nongodly but positively very "godly"—that in at least two societies: "menstruation is not understood as simply polluting, but as inherently dangerous because it represents a heightened time of female activity as the conduit between the worlds of gods and humans" (Shore 1989, 146, paraphrasing Hanson and Hanson 1983, 93), which not only serves to show that Western scholars differ in their interpretations of widespread Polynesian verbalized concepts, but also suggests that Polynesians themselves differed, from society to society, in the precise meanings attached to such words. It also suggests that not all members of any one Polynesian society entertained identical meanings of such words—and even that some individuals entertained different, and by Western standards, logically ambiguous meanings of such words—an inconsistency not unknown in our own literate society.

Specific localized usages of the above concepts, and localized examples of the "religious" practices listed earlier, will be mentioned in subsequent chapters of this book, as will particulars about other aspects of the Polynesians' religion(s). For now, however, we turn to other types of belief and practice—first, to the fabrication and use of their "primary" tools—for, while Polynesians attributed much of their well-being (and ill-being) to their gods, they evidently recognized that much of both also depended upon their own efforts to acquire food and other life-sustaining and status-maintaining (or status-enhancing) goods.

TOOLS AND CRAFTS

TOOLS

Although most Polynesians looked to gods to assist them in satisfying their wants for food, shelter and other tangible things, they relied also upon their own manual efforts to do so—with but a small number of kinds of tools and an even smaller number of kinds of machines (i.e., devices in which power is supplied at one point and does work at another). However, they compensated somewhat for those limitations by manual skillfulness in using those instruments—and by proficiency in using their own bodies as a kind of "tool."

While Polynesians everywhere evidently enjoyed "play," and spent many waking hours in "resting," there seems to have been no institutionalized devaluation of manual labor—nor any valuation of "work for work's sake." In the most highly stratified of their societies those at the top were usually relieved of the necessity of productive labor, but even in those many of the elite were not above lending a hand. Indeed, some of the latter were known to take pride in excelling in craftsmanship. And in the less stratified societies their leaders worked along with household mates in producing most if not all of their own food.

Another characteristic of the Polynesian variety of what Westerners call "work" concerns the sexual division of labor. Although many specific kinds of tasks were everywhere allocated by gender, that type of norm was observed far less strictly than in many other Pacific Island societies—a consequence, perhaps, of the "frontier" beginnings of many Polynesian societies. And although most adults were capable of performing a wide variety of manual tasks, they of course did not do so with equal skill—which led to the situation in all their societies of experts in certain crafts being admired, honored and in many cases remunerated.

With regard to the human body as a "tool," most Polynesians between late childhood and senile decrepitude have been characterized as

9.1. Tahitian carrying a load of bananas and breadfruit

tough-bodied, strong and dexterous. For example, except when walking on sharp-edged, flesh-piercing coral, they always went barefoot—which not only toughened the soles of their feet but left their toes free for grasping and picking up a variety of objects. Also, they used their generally strong teeth not only for chewing tough foods, but for tearing, cutting or softening other materials as well. As Captain Bligh wrote of Tahitians, "their teeth were always sufficient to clear a Cocoa Nutt of its Rind to give them food and drink" (Bligh 1789, II: 63).

Males usually carried heavy one-man objects, such as logs and large rocks, directly by hand or on their shoulders, but most other kinds of one-man loads, such as bunches of plantains or clusters of coconuts, were hung over the notched ends of a carrying pole balanced over a shoulder fore and aft (fig. 9.1). In contrast, females usually carried heavy objects—clusters of taro, baskets of shellfish, etc.—strapped to their backs. But neither males nor females carried objects on the head, which, as will be noted, was sacrosanct.

One observation concerning (some) Polynesians' abilities as walkers and hill climbers is recorded in Georg Forster's account of an excursion on Tahiti. (Forster was a member of Cook's second voyage, in 1772–75):

> From hence we proceeded up the valley, which having no rivulet in its middle, began to rise in proportion as we advanced. We resolved therefore to go upon the steep hill on our left, and with much difficulty accomplished our plan. Our Tahitian friend laughed at us, when he saw us faint with fatigue, and sitting down every moment to recover our breath. We heard him blow or breathe slowly but very hard, with open mouth, as he walked behind us; we therefore tried the same experiment, which nature had probably taught him, and found it answered much better than our short panting, which always deprived us of breath. (Forster 1777, I: 348–49)

Several other accounts bear witness to the capacities of some (many?) Polynesians to cover, nonstop, distances of great length and over exceedingly difficult terrain in astonishingly short times. Also, many early accounts by Westerners expressed wonderment at Polynesians'—male and female, young and old—capabilities and endurance in swimming. Children acquired those abilities at a very early age, and in some societies spent much of their days in the water.

Following chapters will describe other examples of the uses made by some or most Polynesians of their own bodies—in canoe paddling, tree climbing, adz using, weapon wielding, etc. For now however we turn to the ways in which some—or perhaps most—of them used "natural," unfabricated objects as tools.

One striking characteristic of Polynesians' technologies was their employment of a wide variety of unworked natural objects for a wide variety of purposes. The following list is not exhaustive for Polynesia as a whole, nor were all of the items in use everywhere nor everywhere used the same way, but the diverse nature of those objects will serve to indicate the Polynesians' ingenuity in making use of their insular resources—and, reciprocally, the formative influence of those resources on their ways of life. We can begin with plants, some of which grew on every island where Polynesians succeeded in establishing and maintaining residence.

Long-fiber leaves, mainly coconut and pandanus, were everywhere used for temporary tying, and large and broad ones for makeshift containers and rain capes and for lining and covering food stored in pits or baked in ground ovens. Leaves were also used for thatching, but usually after combining into thatch plates.

After some degree of working, wood served numerous purposes, as will be described, but even unworked wood was used for tools: splits of bamboo for knives, chips of wood for wedges, long, hard sticks for digging, shorter ones—sharpened and stuck into the ground—for husking coconuts, large unworked logs as canoe-hauling rollers and smaller ones as levers. Also, plant resins were used nearly everywhere as adhesives.

Unworked stones formed parts of several kinds of edifices; they also served as hammers, cutting tools and missiles, and wherever available were heated and used for baking food in earth ovens.

Other natural objects used for grinding and polishing stone and wooden artifacts included sand—with or without water—coral, sea urchins and the skin of stingrays. While bamboo slivers were used for cutting soft materials, mollusk shells and chips of volcanic rock served to cut harder things and to peel vegetables. In addition to its use in several types of fabricated tools, unworked but sharp-pointed bone was used as awls and needles. Uses were made even of the mounted teeth of sharks and rats—for awls, saws and weapons.

One purposive use of water, as a tool, was its channeling for irrigation. Other toollike uses of it included its employment in food preparation and, as a softener, in the fabrication of cordage and textiles.

As noted earlier, the availability of the above natural objects differed from place to place—the widest difference having occurred between large and lush high islands (such as O'ahu, Tahiti, Savai'i) and dry-zone atolls (such as some of the Tuamotus). In some places those differences were reduced by means of exchange with better-stocked neighbor islands, but in the case of several isolated atolls the poverty of usable natural objects was reflected throughout their inhabitants' cultures, as later chapters will describe.

Fire was used as a tool throughout Polynesia—for cooking, and in many (but not all) places for other purposes, such as roughing out canoe hulls and clearing sites for gardens. Moreover, it was always manmade—I know of no customary practices of making use of volcanic- or lightning-produced fire.

Some kinds of natural objects were made more efficient or easier to use by only a modicum of processing. For example, natural stones used for hammering were roughly shaped at one end for ease in holding, and shark skin used for smoothing was fastened around a piece of wood for harder rubbing. However, the most useful primary tools were more fully fabricated—the most ubiquitous and numerous among which were adzes. (An adz differs from an axe in being hafted so that its cutting edge is perpendicular to the line of its handle. Also, unlike blades made specifically for use as axes, the cutting edge of most blades used for adzing was shaped by beveling on only one face of the blade.)

Adz and axe blades were fabricated out of dense volcanic rock (basalt or obsidian) when available—or when not available (i.e., on many atolls) out of shell (most commonly that of the giant clam, *Tridacna*). (Basalt usually exhibits a columnar structure, obsidian a conchoidal structure. Both are susceptible to flaking, thus ideal for purposive shaping.) Adzes varied in size according to use, the larger ones having been used for felling trees and roughing out canoe hulls, the smallest for carving small wooden images. They also varied

in cross-section shape (from quadrangular to triangular), in presence or absence of a tang, in method of fabrication (chipping or flaking or grinding or pecking) and in finish (from very rough to finely polished). The oldest adzes thus far discovered (in earliest archaeological sites in Tonga and Samoa) were preponderantly quadrangular in cross-section. (In fact, adzes of that shape seem to have been introduced by the Polynesians' Lapita forebears into Melanesia, whose original residents made and used mostly lenticular-shaped adzes and axes.) Among the earliest Polynesian adzes were a few roughly triangular in cross-section, but triangularity became more definite and preponderant in eastern Polynesia with the passage of time. A parallel sequence applied to tangs—the thinning of a part of the butts of blades to provide firmer hafting. Tanging "evolved" from absent to incipient (in the earlier adzes, in western Polynesia) to common (in later, eastern Polynesian sites) (fig. 9.2).

With regard to methods of adz fabrication, those used for shell of course differed from those used for stone, the former made by chipping and grinding, the latter by flaking and pecking. Differences also obtained, not only between but also within societies, with respect to workmanship—some specimens having been meticulously shaped and smoothly finished, others left roughly shaped and pitted (not perhaps because of lack of skill but because of their intended use). In this connection it is relevant to note that the fabrication of adzes (and of chisels and gouges) required an expert's skill, and such experts were often identified with an occupational title and were usually remunerated for their products.

The most common methods of hafting adzes, both tangless and tanged, are shown in figure 9.3, which also illustrates the source of the haft. In nearly all known cases the cording employed for lashing was sennit (a large chapter would be needed to illustrate and account for the innumerable differences in lashing design—a task that will not be attempted here but one that would provide insight into an important aspect of Polynesian aesthetics.) A point worth noting about Polynesian adzes is their occasional use as axes, made possible by lashing them directly to the haft or by lashing them to an intermediate section of wood, which could then be fastened to the handle either adzwise or axewise. Another feature was their

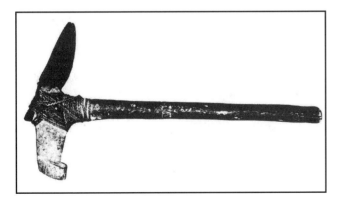

9.2. Stone adze on wooden handle

9.3. Detail of Figure 9.2

occasional use as weapons, and still another their widespread use in ceremonies, wherein those used were usually distinguished by extraordinarily fine finish and elaborate lashing.[54]

Two other primary tools used throughout Polynesia were chisels and gouges, which were made of either stone or shell, according to availability, but were generally smaller and thinner than adzes and were hafted in line with rather than perpendicular to their handles. Moreover, unlike some adzes, they seem to have been used solely for working purposes—i.e., not for fighting or ceremony. In addition, the indispensable tool of all or most households was the pounder, of various shapes and sizes and kinds of use.

Evidence bearing on the efficiency of Polynesians' primary tools can best be judged by their products, many of which will be depicted or described in pages to follow. When judging, however, two considerations should be borne in mind. On the positive side, what may strike a Westerner as crude (e.g., in the lineaments of many carved images) were due more to convention than to inefficient tools—or unskilled workmanship. And on the negative side, it should not be forgotten that the Polynesians themselves eagerly replaced their stone and shell blades for metal ones as soon as the latter became available. (To this should be added the fact that metal ores were nowhere present in tropical or subtropical Polynesia.)

CORDAGE

As noted earlier, Polynesians made use of untreated leaves and strips of bark for makeshift tying but fabricated more durable cordage out of coir (the fiber of coconut husk) and the bast of several kinds of trees (especially hibiscus and breadfruit) and the fibers of several grasses. In some places even human hair was twisted or braided into strings, mainly for necklaces. Bast was obtained by cutting off long strips of bark, scraping off the outer layer, washing the inner layer and allowing it to dry and then separating it into thin strands. Workable strands of coir were extracted from coconut husks by cutting the latter into longitudinal chunks, which were soaked and beaten to remove the unusable interfibrous material and then dried and separated into strands. Then, to obtain strands of the desired thickness, several fibers were rolled together either by hand or against the thigh (or occasionally against the "palm" of the foot), adding additional ones in the process. With enough strands in hand they were then braided by hand into cords (sennit) of desired length and strength, the most common braid having been three-ply.

The practical need for sennit was so large and constant that its fabrication was a continuing enterprise. Just as American and English women used to knit while they sat, so did Polynesians, especially elderly males, roll or braid coir threads into sennit as they sat (which was much of the time). Indeed, so essential was sennit for numerous practical purposes, and so valuable an article of exchange, that it behooved a household to have coils of it on hand.

Indeed, Buck's statement that sennit braid "is the most important single article in Samoan material culture" can be extended to most other Polynesian peoples as well. Moreover, sennit also figured, symbolically, in many Polynesian religions. Thus, in Hawai'i some incantations were "bound"—made durable—by having someone braid a length of sennit while they were being chanted. And elsewhere the power of a god was occasionally "bound" within an image made of sennit. In fact, the symbolic use of sennit to represent the "binding" of "sacredness" was, according to a leading expert on Polynesian religion, a Polynesia-wide practice (Shore 1989, 151–53).

CONTAINERS

Polynesians made a wide variety of containers. Unworked palm leaves were plaited into makeshift baskets in a matter of minutes—mainly for storing or carrying nonliquid materials—or such leaves were sun-cured, slit into fine strips, and fine-plaited into nearly leakproof baskets for more durable storage. Liquids were carried or held in lengths of bamboo or in gourds grown for that purpose or in coconut shells—some of the latter having been rubbed and polished almost paper thin. Out of wood were fabricated bowls, dishes, platters and boxes, some of them incised into designs. But no pottery had been made for many centuries prior to Western contact.

It will be recalled that "ancestral" Polynesians made and used pottery: hand- (not wheel-) made clay containers of numerous sizes and shapes, many of them finely decorated with incised designs. Also, as noted earlier, archaeology has revealed that—in western Polynesia, where it was centered—pottery making began to decline, in quality and quantity and amount of design, relatively shortly after pioneer settlement, and ceased altogether there about A.D. 0. The pioneer migrants from western Polynesia to the Marquesas evidently arrived there with a few pots, but appear not to have engaged in pottery making for very long after arrival. Nor has evidence of pottery making been found so far on any other eastern Polynesian island. (The emphasis, however, should be on "so far"; it was not until 1920 that any was found in western Polynesia.)[55]

Some earlier writers suggested that it was lack of suitable clay that "obliged" Polynesians to give up pottery making. That argument, however, could conceivably apply to only a few isolated and clayless atolls, since all of the high islands in question do contain suitable deposits of clay; also, the argument cannot apply to the discontinuance of pottery making in western Polynesia. Another argument, somewhat more credible, is that a shift of cooking method, from boiling to roasting and baking (the methods used throughout Polynesia when Westerners first arrived) removed the need for clay containers. That however may put the cart before the horse (or the baked pig before the earth oven!). Finally, there are those who argue that Polynesians found it easier to transform nuts and gourds into waterproof containers than to continue making pots: which raises the question,

Why did western Polynesians wait for centuries to do so?

PLAITWORK

In addition to making plaited containers, just noted, Polynesians used plaiting techniques to fabricate a wide variety of items, including clothing, sun eyeshades, sandals, fans, flooring, bedding, house walls and canoe sails.[56] Even wider was the variety of plants used in one place or another for plaiting, including grasses, sedges, hibiscus, seaweed and—most widely and frequently—leaves of the coconut and pandanus palms.

For most matwork products the leaves or strips of bark were prepared by only soaking or drying, but for finer-textured objects, such as clothing and mats used for ceremonial exchange, they were scraped clean and smooth as well. Speaking of texture: mats used as flooring and walls had wefts as broad as an inch or more, whereas those intended for clothing for high-status persons had in some societies wefts as narrow as one twenty-fifth of an inch (resulting in mats of remarkable softness and pliability).

In most societies plaiting for mats and clothing was done by females, although males were not unaccustomed to making rougher, makeshift articles.

In some societies the fine mats used for high-status persons or for ceremonial exchange were decorated with feather or plant-fiber fringes or with colored designs—the latter having been executed mainly by dyed-weft overlays. Speaking of the use of mats in ceremonial exchange, that practice reached its apogee in Samoa and Tonga, as will be described.

NETTING

In some places containers of netting were made and used for carrying or hanging things, but their primary use was for fishing. For all kinds of fishnets except those of very wide mesh the fabricating tools consisted of needles and gages; the former, consisting of a flat, rectangular piece of wood (or bamboo or bone or turtleshell),[57] served as the shuttle, the latter as a means of standardizing the size of the mesh.[58]

Several kinds of basts and fibers were used for net cordage, depending upon availability and the purpose of the net, the most common having been hibiscus and nettle bast and coconut coir. Net making was nearly everywhere done by males, and especially by expert fishermen.

FEATHERWORK

Polynesians' use of feathers merits special mention. The importance attached by most of their peoples to the color red in general and to red feathers in particular in matters of religion was noted in an earlier chapter. In addition, some peoples used red, along with yellow and black, feathers for decorating objects—although in many cases that "decoration" doubtless had religious as well as aesthetic purport.

In Tahiti, for example, both red and yellow feathers were used to decorate (or sanctify) several kinds of objects, including the girdles and helmets of incumbents of the society's highest-status officials, the images of its most important gods, and gorgets worn by official mourners for personages of high status. The framing of the girdles and gorgets consisted of network; that of helmets and images, of wickerwork.

It was in Hawai'i, however, that featherwork reached its acme. There, feathers were used to decorate cloaks and aprons (in network frames), on helmets and miniature temples (on wickerwork frames), and in *lei* (garlands, wreaths, necklaces). The demand for them was so large that some men occupied much of their time in catching the preferred upland forest birds, which were virtually exterminated to meet the demand. And no wonder: one feathered girdle seen by Westerners was twenty-one feet long and six inches wide, and contained "thousands" of feathers, and one Hawaiian cape contained the feathers of about eighty thousand birds. (The articles so decorated consisted of a network foundation to which single feathers, or bunches of them, were tied.) In writing about Hawaiian cloaks and helmets Captain Cook stated that "the surface might be compared to the thickest and richest velvet, which they resemble, both as to feel, and the glossy appearance" (quoted in Buck 1957, 215). In Hawai'i the preferred red-feathered birds were the 'i'iwi (*Vestiaria coccinea*) and the 'apapane (*Himatione sanguinea*), the yellow-feathered ones the 'ō'ō (*Moho nobilis*) and the mamo (*Drapanis pacifica*). Although red and yellow feathers only were used in the cloaks, etc., of high-status persons, some other befeathered articles contained other colors from less rare birds as well, including seabirds and domestic fowl.[59]

BARKCLOTH

We turn now to an item that, along with waving palms and enticing maidens, has come to symbolize Polynesia quintessentially to the Western world. That item is barkcloth (*tapa, kapa,* etc.). In fact, barkcloth is or was made by many peoples throughout the Tropics—Africa, South America, Southeast Asia, Melanesia, etc., but according to the highly knowledgeable Peter Buck: "From museum specimens, it is evident that Polynesian barkcloth is superior, on the whole, to that made in any other area." And he went on to say that among Polynesians the barkcloth (*kapa*) made by Hawaiians "displays the greatest variety of texture and ordered designs" (Buck 1957, 166).

In Polynesia barkcloth was made from the inner bark of Chinese mulberry (*Broussonetia papyrifera*), breadfruit (*Artocarpus* spp.), arrowroot (*Tacca leontapetaloides*), nettle (*Pipturus propinquus*), the aerial roots of banyan (*Thespesia populoea*), and certain thick climbing vines. Chinese mulberry and breadfruit were the most commonly utilized wherever they grew and were in some places cultivated for that purpose, the other plants having been gathered from the wild. (Note however that not all of the above plants grew everywhere; in fact on many atolls there grew no plants suitable for making barkcloth.)

The fabrication process was about the same everywhere and consisted of the following steps:

1. cutting the stem or limbs (or aerial roots of vine) of the plant into lengths several feet long, the desirable thickness of stem, limb or roots having been about two inches or less—anything thicker having had too thick and rough a bark;

2. removing the bark of the excised stem, limb or root by making a longitudinal split in it, and peeling it off by hand;

3. removing the outer from the inner bark of the strip—usually by soaking and scraping, and discarding the former;

4. widening—and thinning—the remaining inner bark by beating it with a wooden beater on an anvil. In most places this involved an initial "rough" beating on a stone or wooden anvil, and then a final beating on a wooden one. Before each beating the bark was usually soaked in fresh or salt water and then partly dried in the sun;

5. joining the finished strips to make them wider, either by felting or pasting or sewing them

together—or by doubling them (by felting) to make them thicker and stronger;

6. in some cases, coloring the whole finished cloth by soaking it in a liquid dye, or decorating it by painting designs on it or by applying to it dye-dipped wooden blocks of various designs.

Then, when finished and finally sun dried, the cloths were either fashioned into clothing or used as bedcovers—or were rolled into bundles and stored in house rafters for future use, which included, among numerous other functions, using them for exchange or for "taxes." We return now to the itemized stages to add a few details about the fabrication process, and do so purposely because of the central importance that barkcloth, and barkcloth fabrication, had in Polynesian life.

Several of the early Western visitors noted that their plantings of paper mulberry saplings, along with *Piper methysticum*, the plant used for kava, were the Polynesians' only "orderly," "well-tended"—i.e., European gardenlike—"plantations." In all cases recorded, it was the job of men to cultivate and harvest the domesticated barkcloth trees, or to obtain suitable alternatives from the wild, but it was usually the work of females to fabricate and decorate the barkcloth. (Although in some places men joined in the fabricating when large quantities were required on short notice—as, for example, in preparations for making donations to visiting celebrities.) In this connection it should be added that for no Polynesian society that I know of was barkcloth fabrication considered a menial occupation. On the contrary, in some places it was engaged in even by the highest-status women, and expertise in the craft was a focus of public esteem.

In step 4 of the fabrication process, the wood used as an anvil was usually a log flattened on top, on average a few feet long when used by one person, or much longer to accommodate several—for barkcloth beating was widely regarded as a socially enjoyable activity. Moreover, the drumlike sound of a beater striking the anvil was evidently pleasurable, and some anvils were raised on supports and their undersides hollowed in order to produce more sonorous sounds. Also, in some places anvil-drum patterns were devised to send messages, such as those announcing the approach of a visitor.

The mallets most used in the process were one of two kinds: round ones for a first, rough, beating, and ones with rectangular cross-section thereafter. Also, the faces of the latter were in many cases incised into shallow longitudinal grooves, which served to break up and flatten the bark fiber and to produce deliberately patterned watermarks (fig. 9.4).

The most widespread method for joining two strips of bark, or for combining two layers of them, was felting—i.e., matting them together by mallet blows. A second method, practiced mainly in Samoa, consisted of joining and combining strips by use of glutenous plant pastes. And a third one, practiced in some places either exclusively or along with felting and pasting, was sewing.

The art of decorating finished barkcloth reached its zenith in Hawai'i. In Buck's words: "[A] greater number of [vegetable] dyes and a consequently greater variety of colored patterns were produced in Hawai'i than in any other part of Polynesia. . . [having included] light green, light yellow, lavender (sea urchin), yellow-red, pale yellow, yellow, light green, brown, black, gray, light gray . . . " (Buck 1957, 186).

In addition to the widespread method of coloring barkcloth by immersing it in dye or painting freehand designs on it, the Hawaiians matted together white and colored sheets back to back and decorated them with block-printed designs—both methods having been uniquely Hawaiian. The blocks, or stamps, were made of bamboo or wood and were fabricated by men, who then "sold" them to the women barkcloth makers.

Designs differed widely from society to society; for one made in Samoa, see figure 9.5.[60]

It should be added that barkcloth, along with fine mats, constituted the nearest equivalent most tropical Polynesians had for "money," both items having been fairly durable and storable and exchangeable for a variety of other objects and services. Moreover, in some places their exchange values were fairly well standardized.[61] No wonder, then, that many households were at pains to accumulate them, and that they served in some places as a measure of affluence.

Finally, it should be noted that barkcloth fiber served in some societies to fabricate articles other than textiles, such as the Easter Island image shown in figure 9.6.

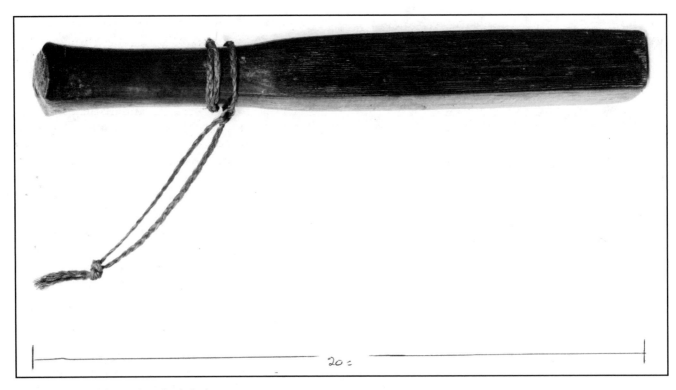

9.4. Mallet used for making barkcloth

9.5. Samoan barkcloth pattern

9.6. Easter Island figure covered with barkcloth

EMBELLISHMENT

Many of the kinds of objects listed in this and the previous chapter—tools, cordage, containers, mats, barkcloths and religious icons—were embellished, which in Western (dictionary) terms means "to beautify by adding ornamental features; to decorate"—i.e., to add to manmade objects features not directly related to their intended principal functions of, for example, making other objects, binding things together, containing liquids, covering nudity, and communicating with gods. In Polynesia such "additions" included the more than necessarily intricate ways of using sennit to bind an adz blade to its handle, the plaiting of colored strips into some baskets and mats, the attachment of feathers to sheets of barkcloth, the designs carved onto wooden bowls and gourds and the stylized patterns in which god images were carved. To most Westerners all such "embellishments" are just that; to Polynesians, however, some of them may have been essential to their principal purposes. Thus, for example, in the case of religious images, their particular shapes (which differed somewhat from society to society) may have been believed to be essential for inducing the local gods to inhabit and be communicated with. And a particular form of sennit binding may have had the purpose not only of securing a blade to its handle but also of assuring godly support for the tool's effectiveness. This is not to say that Polynesians were lacking in appreciation of what Westerners call "embellishment" (or "decoration" or "ornamentation") per se; rather, it is to suggest that some of their "embellishments" may have had other purposes as well.[62] That said, however, we can focus on the shapes, arrangements, colors, etc., of some of their embellishments of objects, including some already mentioned and some yet to be described. We begin with their carvings.

There were differences among Polynesian peoples, some of them wide, with respect to the materials used for carving, the kinds of objects carved, and their forms of design.

The materials used here or there in tropical Polynesia were wood, stone, coral, shell, bone and whale-tooth ivory. To only a few peoples were all such materials available—and even among those not all were utilized to the same degree. And in several cases the paucity or the inferiority or total lack of certain ones of them (e.g., the absence of stone on many atolls, the scarcity of wood on

Easter Island) obliged or inclined their residents to use others. Notwithstanding, availability was not the only factor that influenced use. For example, suitable wood was obtainable in both Samoa and Hawai'i, but for carvings Hawaiians focused on wood, whereas Samoans disregarded it almost entirely in their carvings.

The objects carved, here or there, were of four kinds: (1) those, mainly images, associated with religion; (2) decorative elements of various nonreligious objects; (3) articles of personal adornment; and (4) petroglyphs.

Carved religious objects consisted mostly of more or less anthropomorphic stone and wooden images of gods—including separate free-standing figures and free-standing and low-relief components of larger objects, such as "god sticks" (i.e., wooden staffs with upper ends carved into images of gods).

The very wide variety of nonreligious objects that were "embellished" with carving in one society or another included weapons; the handles of various kinds of tools (e.g., adzes, fans, combs, fly whisks, food pounders and carrying poles); house posts; stools and neck rests; bowls and food plates; the paddles, bailers, prows and sterns of canoes; and flutes, trumpets and drums.

Carved personal adornments (of ivory, shell or wood) included pendants, bracelets, rings, headbands, ear ornaments and gorgets (breastplates)—some of them minutely and exquisitely carved.

Petroglyphs—figures incised or chipped into immobile rocks or rocky surfaces—were very widely distributed, and have been aptly characterized as being "of simple narrative intent, perhaps to recount some event or tell of some practical need, or they may have been no more than the passing fancy of some dallying traveler" (Archey 1966, 462).

Turning to carving designs (and paraphrasing Archey), the most common Polynesia-wide form was a "naturalistic" rendition of the human form, which in some societies became stylized and then, in a few cases, abstract. Less common were renditions of plants and animals—which, like those of humans, were often stylized and many cases abstract. And in those and other forms of carvings their profiles were either in low or high relief or in the round, and their lines mostly consistently geometric or consistently curvilinear.[63]

Focusing on the so-called "basic naturalistic"

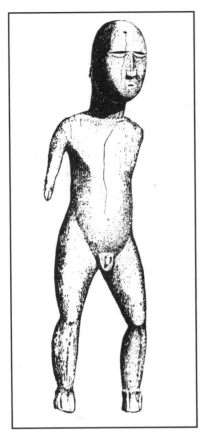

9.7. Wood carving from Mangareva

9.8. Wooden and shell figure from Rurutu

sculptures, a further "etic" distinction among them has to do with their material composition—i.e., between stone and wood. In most societies where both stone and wood were utilized for such sculpture, the available stone was too dense and columnar (as with basalt) or too coarse (i.e., vesicular) for the fine detailing possible with wood or with ivory and bone. On the other hand, stone figures themselves varied more widely than wood in size, from tiny to gigantic (the extreme examples of the latter having been those of Easter Island, where the largest was thirty-eight feet high and weighed ninety-four tons). As for wooden naturalistic figures in the round, while nearly all of them were anthropomorphic, they differed from society to society in characteristic features—as the samples illustrated in figures 9.7 and 9.8 reveal. Indeed, the same generalization may be extended to include the decorative patterns, anthropomorphic and abstract, applied to implements.

Turning finally to textiles, the embellishments of some of them consisted of pigments (applied to barkcloths), dye-colored strips plaited into mats, and feathers attached to mats and gorgets and onto network frames of cloaks and helmets. Some such additions were meant to signify the (high) statuses of persons wearing or otherwise using them, but it is reasonable to conclude that some of the shapes and colors of those additions were also thought to be aesthetically pleasing. Regarding their designs, some patterns occurred in only a few places (e.g., the naturalistic plant designs on Tahitian barkcloth), and some of them nearly everywhere. Among the latter were the conventionalized anthropomorphic ones (labeled *tiki*), along with conventionalized lizards, birds, fish, leaves and vines. Also widespread were linear patterns, both curvilinear and geometric.[64] As for colors other than black and brown, the most common were red and yellow, which in some societies bore the additional nonaesthetic meanings of high status or godliness.

10

CLOTHING, BODY ADORNMENT AND TATTOOS

10.1. Woman and boy of Tahiti in the dress of that island

10.2. A man of Tahiti in the dress of that island

With a few exceptions (e.g., on Easter Island in winter) tropical Polynesians had little need to protect their persons from daytime atmospheric cold. In many places they wore raincapes against downpours and cloaks against nighttime chill, and most of them had the good sense to remain out of the sun during torrid midday hours. Otherwise, most of their clothing was designed not for extremes of temperature but for one or another of the following nonclimatic purposes: for observing local conventions regarding differences in gender and age; for concealing from public view those

parts of the body considered too explicitly coital; for practical purposes of everyday activities; for personal adornment; for identification of status or occupation; for display of personal affluence; and for customary role-playing in ceremonies. Now for some details.

In most societies children of both sexes went naked up to a culturally defined stage of perceptible physical growth—that stage having varied from society to society, from about three to ten years of age (by Western reckoning). When that stage was reached all persons donned one or more garments designed, mainly, to conceal their genitalia: in most societies a loincloth for males, a short kilt for females. In some societies males or females or both concealed—more or less—their genitals by leaves hung from a belt; in others the loincloth or kilt was supplemented with a short cloak, or in some places a poncho.

Nowhere did the local concept of "modesty" include the necessity of concealing a female's breasts. And in most societies complete nakedness, in public, was considered appropriate or even required on certain occasions, such as, e.g., when working in the bush, when swimming or (as in Tahiti) parading before potential suitors. Also, in some societies, where males had even their groins tattooed, some of them dispensed with effective genital covering in order to display the distinctiveness of their tattoo designs (and implicitly, their fortitude in having endured the pain of so much tattooing).[65]

With respect to the differentiating factor of age (i.e., physical sexual development), it can be added that in some societies the conventional clothing of the aged also differed from that of younger adults. Thus, in one Cook Island society aged women wore longer kilts than younger ones, and in Mangareva, where younger males wore only girdles, longer loincloths were reserved for aged ones.

In many societies individuals wore special garments when engaged in nonusual activities—for example, full-length "robes" when conducting religious rites, cloaks when engaged in fighting, all-around bustles when performing ceremonial dances.

Clothing also served to identify a wearer's social class or exhibit his or her material affluence. In many societies members of the upper class wore garments that differed even in form from those of other classes—e.g., longer kilts or cloaks, garments of finer than ordinary tapa or matting, or garments decorated with rare feathers. And in some societies affluence was displayed, most strikingly, by the wearing of superfluous amounts of fine clothing—as exemplified in Tahiti, where "the rich seem to shew their greatest pride in wearing a large quantity of [bark] cloth . . . . The poorer sort have only a small allowance of cloth. . . . [I]t was no uncommon thing for the richest of the men to come to see us with a large quantity of cloth rolled round their loins, . . . sufficient to

have clothed a dozen people" (Joseph Banks, who accompanied Cook on the latter's first voyage: in Beaglehole 1962, I: 338). This practice reached such an extreme in a few societies that individuals were sometimes wrapped in such quantities of tapa or mats that they could barely move.

Mats or tapa worn only occasionally had long lives, but those worn for everyday use soon disintegrated. Thus, in Samoa the ordinary *ti* leaf kilt worn by men lasted only a day or two (Buck 1930, 253).

Turning to headwear, the range of types was very wide: from none in some societies, to several functionally different kinds in others (e.g., one kind for everyday, another for fighting, still another for religious ceremonies, etc.). Perhaps the most practically beneficial were the *tapa* turbans worn by Tahitians of all social classes, mainly for protection against the sun, and the stiff and pointed basketry military helmets worn by some Cook Islanders for protection against slingstones. In some societies (e.g., Hawai'i and Tahiti), form of headwear served also to show high social rank—

10.3. A *heiva* of Raiatea with helmet and gorget

which may have been useful in some situations but was clearly inexpedient in battles, where such helmets were typically worn and where they helped the enemy to identify and target their wearers.

In addition to their practicality—or in some cases their impracticality—some types of headwear also served, deliberately, as adornment, ranging from the feather or two added to an everyday turban to the huge and largely ornamental headdress of the Samoan "Sacred Maiden" (see below). In this connection, in most societies headwear in general, and different kinds of it in particular, were more characteristic of males than of females—a reflection of the circumstance that men's roles everywhere were more highly differentiated than females' (and also, perhaps, because men's activities kept them more in the sun).

From headwear we turn to coiffure. In most societies the head hair of both sexes was allowed to grow long, with males gathering theirs into a topknot when activity required. In some places, however, males wore their hair short and females theirs long, in other places the reverse. Nor did the variations end there. In Samoa, for example, men's long hair was "tied in a knot called a *fonga* and worn usually a little to the right side of the crown." However, Buck continues, "It could . . . be worn to the front, back or sides, as fashion directed . . . . [In fact] there were 12 different combinations each distinguished by a name denoting the position of the *fonga*" (Buck 1930, 631). In some places the varieties were even greater, especially among males. Thus, on the Marquesan island of Hiva Oa: "Some men never cut their hair, others did it up in two horns . . . still others arranged the crown in fantastic ways, as one half shaved the other long, or the front shaved and the back long, or in a series of shaved strips, with long hair between . . . [and] in time of war, finger bones or other trophies of slain enemies were attached to the hair" (Linton 1923, 419). Nor was hairstyling limited to males. In Samoa, for example, virginal females had their heads shaved in the middle from front to back, allowing the hair on both sides to grow long; and older women used lime in order to dye their cropped black hair to a favored brown (Buck 1930, 631).

(If the Western reader finds the above to be primitively bizarre let him recall parallels in his own society, such as periodic changes in women's hairstyles based on current fashion, and differences in men's (e.g., flowing locks, crew cuts, skinheads, Mohawk cuts, etc.) that are based not only on currency of fashion but serve to identify a person's occupation or social class or political views.)

To comment briefly on Polynesians' practices regarding other kinds of body hair, it should first be noted that, while the head hair of most of them was luxuriant, their body hair was, by Western averages, relatively sparse. And although in many places men allowed their beards to grow, fully or in goatee, some of their own compatriots, and in other places all adult males, were at pains to remove all facial hair—by shaving it off with sharp shells or pulling it out with shell tweezers. And in several societies both men and women pulled out all visible nose and ear hair as well. Summarizing: some of these and other "piliatory practices" (a worldwide survey of which would make an exotic, and not necessarily trivial, doctoral dissertation!) were based on standards of cleanliness or beautification and were associated with one or another conventional life-cycle stage.

Speaking of cleanliness and beautification, many pages could be written on Polynesians' ideals and practices regarding them—but that will not be done here. Instead, here are some of the most noteworthy ones. To begin with, there was consensus among Western observers that Polynesians valued body cleanliness very highly, and when possible bathed in fresh water at least once every day. In Tahiti, for example, even after spending hours in ocean or lagoon, fishermen would finish of with a freshwater bath.

In addition, most peoples valued sweet-smelling bodies and hair, and endeavored to attain them by pomading the hair and rubbing the body with flower-scented or, when available, sandalwood-scented coconut oil. Also, in many societies dyes were used to paint all or parts of the body, not only on ceremonious and festive occasions but often in everyday life as well. The most widely used cosmetic dye was a yellow one, derived from the root of the turmeric plant (*Curcuma longa/domestica*).

Also, "naturally" white skin was especially admired in many societies—a preference that led some peoples to respect, even venerate (for a short while!), the first Westerners to visit them. Among themselves skin whiteness was achieved in some places with dye, in others by prolonged protection from direct sunlight. In the Marquesas, for exam-

10.4. Various types of Society Islands hairstyles

10.5. Woman of Easter Island

10.6. Man of Easter Island

10.7. Man of Mangaia, Cook Islands

10.8. Man of Hawai'i in helmet-mask

ple, "the body, especially the face, was first painted with *ena* [turmeric] and coconut oil. Over this was smeared the juice from the crushed leaves of the *kokua* tree or *paya* vine. This gave the skin a green color. The person undergoing the operation [then] stayed in the house for seven or eight days, at the end of which time the skin was bleached" (Linton 1923, 161–62). And in Tahiti, where white skin was a cosmetic objective especially of upper-class women, that objective was attained mainly by staying in the shade.

All of which suggests (not proves) that the preference for lighter skin color may have derived (in some but not all Polynesian societies) from an aristocratic ideal that high-status individuals did not have to work in the kinds of activities that kept them in the sun—a suggestion that would appear to contradict an observation made earlier, that manual labor was generally not devalued. In fact, however, both attitudes may have prevailed; for Polynesians were quite capable of holding seemingly contradictory values—as do Americans, who value suntanned bodies (perhaps as a sign of leisured affluence) and devalue "red necks" (perhaps as a mark of rural lower-class laborers).

It should also be recorded that many Polynesian peoples valued corpulency, with or without white skin. In several societies (as will be reported), it was considered such a mark of beauty, male and female, that young persons of both sexes were fed excessively in order to make them more desirable marital choices. And in Tahiti, some upper-class women of older ages retired occasionally to a nearby islet for the purpose of fattening themselves by excessive eating and indolence.

Both corpulence and skin bleaching may have had other meanings—as was suggested above and as will be conjectured later on—but their cosmetic value, especially in terms of sexual attraction, seems undeniable.

Polynesians everywhere (like most other humans) made and adorned themselves with ornaments of many kinds and for one or more purposes, such as "purely" aesthetic enhancement, added sexual attractiveness, display of affluence, marks of high social status, etc.—even, in some places, to memorialize a dead relative (e.g., by wearing one of his or her bones). Flowers were perhaps the most common ornament—worn in the hair or over or in an ear, or as a head wreath or necklace.

Along with which, earlobe-piercing was widespread, to accommodate flowers or other ornaments.

Perhaps the greatest variety of body-adorning ornaments were made and used in Hawai'i, having included head ornaments (wreaths of leaves, flowers or feathers), necklaces and neck pendants (of flowers, feathers, human hair, dog teeth, marine and land shells, nuts, berries, whale ivory, etc.), bracelets (of boar tusk, turtle shell, bone, marine shell, whale ivory), etc. In contrast, the body-adorning ornaments of the atoll-dwelling Kapingamarangi consisted only of flowers, pandanus-leaf headbands, and necklaces and neck pendants of shell. Evidently (and correspondingly banal), a people's inventory of ornament was limited overall by availability of raw materials—but aside from that other factors also served to differentiate one society's inventory from another, such as the complexity of their institutions, the variety of their statuses and roles, the affluence of their economy, and last but not least, their aesthetic values, which, after centuries of separation, could hardly have remained identical.

Speaking of which, we come now to a mode of body marking for which Polynesians have become widely known, and which was performed by some with consummate skill. They were not the only peoples to practice this kind of marking, and the meanings it had for them were not only aesthetic. Reference here is to tattooing, which word is in fact derived from the Polynesian word *tatau*.

TATTOO

Tattoo, the practice and product of marking the skin with indelible pigment, has been a part of Polynesian cultures since, and before, their beginnings. It was doubtless a feature of their Lapita heritage and had roots in Island Southeast Asia. It was also practiced in Micronesia and in several areas of Melanesia, but nowhere with the elaborateness reached in several Polynesian societies. Among these latter the practice served four kinds of purpose: as a mark of physiological maturation, as a medal for individual fortitude, as a means of personal ornamentation, and as a badge of special social status. Regarding the first, the life stage at which an individual underwent his or her first (and only, or most extensive) tattooing varied somewhat from society to society but was in most of them coincident with the perceived onset of

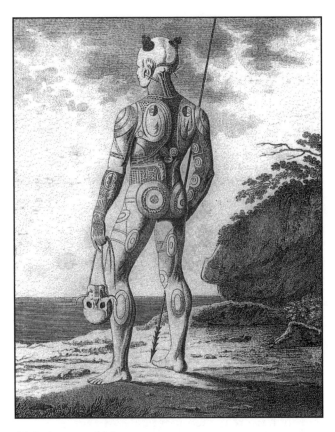

10.9. A tattooed Marquesan

10.10. A tattooed Hawaiian

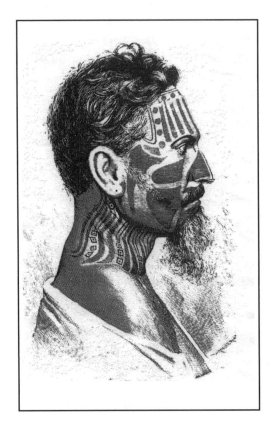

10.11. A tattooed Easter Islander

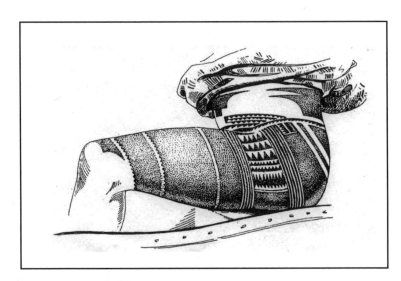

10.12. Tattoo of a Tongan

physiological puberty (and therefore generally earlier for females than for males). It must however be added that in some societies some individuals continued to be tattooed well beyond that life stage. Regarding the second purpose, tattooing was for the subject manifestly painful, even perilous—therefore an emblem of strength and endurance.[66] Third, when expertly and expansively performed it served—deliberately, I suggest—to "embellish" its possessor uniquely, conspicuously and permanently. And fourth, in some societies it served also to identify its possessors' membership in some particular organization or specialization in a particular activity, or to indicate his or her parents' material affluence—and usually, therefore, their social class.

Before exemplifying the above purposes of tattooing I need to say something about its distribution and techniques.[67]

Tattooing was practiced by all of the peoples within the Polynesian Triangle except those of certain sparsely populated "low" or relatively isolated islands, namely, Manihiki-Rakahanga, Pukapuka, Manuae, Niue, Raivavae and Rapa. In other words, it flourished mainly in the more populous and complex societies, including those having more fruitful natural resources. It seems to me likely that the existence of tattooing, as a technique for skin ornamentation, was known even to those peoples who did not practice it, but their lives were focused on activities more essential for their physical survival. Yet that correlation was evidently not complete. For, although it flourished very elaborately in resource-rich and socially complex Samoa, it was far less common in even richer and more socially complex Hawai'i. And in the Marquesas, whose people were exposed not infrequently to food-diminishing drought and to destructive intertribal warfare, tattooing flourished in popularity and in amount of body coverage. Clearly, factors of natural resources and social complexity had some effects on the elaboration of a people's tattooing practice, but were not the only or weightiest ones. As with several other institutionalized Polynesian practices—such as those concerned with featherwork, kava drinking, physical maturation, social stratification and cannibalism—the reasons for the efflorescence of tattooing in some Polynesian societies and not in others cannot now be discovered. However, as in the case of certain other beliefs and practices (such as

cannibalism and religious architecture), once begun their momentum evidently increased in some societies until their ultimate limits were reached, a development well exemplified in Easter Island with its stone images, and in Samoa with its kava ceremonial. (Although uncomfortable with the use of a mechanical metaphor for a historical process, I can come up with no other way of describing what I believe took place.) I turn now to the tools and techniques of the practice.

Polynesian-type tattooing involved tapping pigment into a subject's skin with a pigment-dipped tool. The tool consisted of one or more needlelike points attached to a triangular plate, which itself was attached adzlike to a wooden handle. Most commonly, the point used in single-point tappers was a tooth, either of fish or boar; those used most commonly in multiple-point tappers were pieces of bone or shell with serrated, comblike edges. Or, in order to make longer lines, additional points or combs were attached to a single plate. The tapper used in the procedure was usually a piece of wood, or where wood was scarce, the midrib of a palm frond. And the most common pigment consisted of soot (usually of burnt candlenut) suspended in a liquid (usually water).[68]

The tattooer began by sketching with charcoal a design on the supine subject, whose skin at that location was stretched taut by one or more apprentices. The tattooer then dipped the appropriate points—either a single one or a whole comb—into the ink (usually contained in a coconut-shell cup) and tapped it into the subject's skin, holding the blade handle in one hand and tapping it with the other.[69] The blood that usually trickled from the punctures was wiped away either by the tattooer or his apprentice, the latter having also served by restraining a pain-wracked subject from moving, for the operation was inevitably painful—a test of fortitude that tattooers sought to shorten by working as fast as possible. In fact, tattoos nearly always festered and often led to sickness—and in some cases death.

The following paragraph, from Sparks's unpublished manuscript, provides a concise description of the most common Polynesian technique:

When tattooing body pigment was implanted in skin the dye seeped into the surrounding area to some extent. Thus, a comb with closely spaced teeth actually printed a solid line approximately the width of the comb. Squares, rectangles, and stripes of this width were made by tattooing successive lines close together, until the desired pattern had been achieved. A comb with more widely spaced teeth made a row of dots. The singlepoint was used for single dots and for small details added to the edges of previously imprinted shapes . . . . Throughout Polynesia no color other than blackish blue was achieved . . . . There is no evidence that the artist deliberately varied the dilution of his pigment to produce different shades of the basic color. (Sparks n.d.,13-14)

The seepage of the dye enabled the tattooer to produce large or small patches of solid pigment by use of a comb blade with wide and closely spaced points, such patches having been components of several overall designs.

While all localized conventions differentiated between designs of male and female subjects in their placement and patterning, the designs differed from one another in other respects as well—in individual design elements, in overall design patterning, in the parts of the body tattooed, and in the sequence of tattooing. In Samoa, for example, the tattoos on males were continuous from just above the waist to just below the knees; the patterns were bilaterally symmetrical, one side of the body tattooed completely before the other side was begun; and the designs were mostly rectilinear. In Hawai'i, however, the most common sites for tattooing were face, chest and limbs; also, the patterns differed from one side of the body to the other, and the designs included triangles, circles and pictographs of humans and other objects. And in the Marquesas some males were tattooed from crown of head to feet, including eyelids, tongue and inside the nostrils—but not the genitals[70] (as was done, however, in Tonga).[71]

It is not unlikely that some individual designs implanted by tattooers were impromptu, but most of them were "traditional," and as such bore names related to, e.g., some natural or manmade object, a place or object in a legend, the part of the body on which it was conventionally implanted, etc. In other words, however adept a tattooer was in executing designs, he was constrained within fairly narrow, conventional limits in creating them. Moreover, according to some accounts, in some societies the subject himself (or herself) or the patron (i.e., financer) of his tattooing had a voice in selecting or approving the inclusion of individual designs or of their large-scale patterning.

In some societies the mark of a subject's social status was depicted in his or her tattoo design. Thus, in Hawai'i, members of the *kauwā*, the pariah underclass, were marked with designs that identified them as such. And in Tahiti, one's advance in rank in the exclusive Arioi cult was accompanied by the addition of specific tattoo marks, so that those at the top had their legs fully tattooed and were correspondingly named "Black Legs." More generally, however, the quality and extent of one's tattooing reflected the amount of material resources owned by, or otherwise available to, oneself or one's close kin. For high-quality tattooing required the services of experts, and in most societies the latter had to be recompensed—with pigs or fine mats or whatever kinds of objects that were locally used in extrahousehold exchange. Thus, in some societies it was only the firstborn son of a chief who received extensive and high-quality marking. (And in several such situations the youths of his age cohort received gratis and at that time a few lesser quality marks from the hands of the apprentices.)

Regarding the tattooers themselves, most communities contained at least one expert in the craft, with one or more other individuals—all of them males—serving as his apprentices. And, since the experts were not all of equal expertise, in some cases an affluent client employed one from another community to tattoo himself or his heir. However, such differences aside, all men recognized as specialists in this craft were so labeled, and enjoyed relatively high social status, equivalent in some cases to that of expert carpenters, canoe builders, navigators, etc.

POSTSCRIPT

Since writing the above there has come to my attention a larger, more recent, and much more sweeping work on Polynesian tattooing, namely, *Wrapping in Images*, by Alfred Gell, which does not invalidate any of the foregoing but places that tattooing in much wider cultural contexts—too wide, in fact, and too limitlessly speculative, to warrant summarizing here.

11

FOOD AND DRINK

Most books about Polynesians in general focus on their arts or their religions or their imposing stone edifices or their seamanship or their social and political institutions, etc. In reality, most Polynesians everywhere spent most of their waking hours obtaining, processing and consuming food. Moreover, quoting that peerless Polynesianist Raymond Firth: "[C]onsideration of what [Tikopians] eat leads to the examination of the economic reciprocity between husband and wife, methods of wider cooperation in work, systems of land tenure, ritual offerings to ancestors and gods for [crop] fertility. [And] from here one is led to family history, to political relations, especially those of chieftainship; to the obligations and privileges of adoption, as reflected in food; . . . " (Firth 1957b, 117). In writing this book it has not been my intention to focus on that "alimentary approach," but mention it here in order to assert how important food was, not only to the Tikopians but to all other Polynesians as well—and not just for sustaining them physically but in many other aspects of their lives. That said, however, it should be made clear at the outset that not all Polynesian peoples produced and ate the same kinds of foods.

According to linguistic evidence, the ancestors common to all Polynesians subsisted largely on an identical complex of foods, which consisted of certain species of marine animals, certain domesticated animals and certain cultivated and wild plants. Eventually, however, many descendants of those ancestral Polynesians left their western Polynesia home islands and colonized numerous others that differed from the home islands and from each other in many ways—including size, physiography, climate, native vegetation, native fauna, distance from other islands, etc. In order to survive, each of the branches of colonists was to adjust its food-getting efforts to a pristine natural environment that was in some respects distinctive.

In addition, during the following centuries every one of those branches effected some changes, wittingly or not, in its environment—including deforestation (and consequent redistribution of soils) and extinction of some fauna (e.g., birds and shellfish), and those changes led to further distinctive alterations in what they produced and ate.

Polarities in Polynesia's environmental differences are exemplified in the cases of Samoa and Tongareva.

Samoa, one of the Polynesians' original—formative—homelands, is a chain of high volcanic islands comprising about 1,092 square miles, a third of which consists of fertile, well-watered soil. Its contact-era population, of about eighty thousand, had access to a bountiful supply of food: pigs, dogs, chickens and wild fowl; tree crops (coconuts, breadfruit, bananas); cultivated food crops (taro, yams, sweet potatoes, arrowroot, turmeric) along with *ti* and sugarcane; seaweed; and a large variety and quantity of marine animals. From these were concocted scores of types of dishes, including (for example) six featuring taro roots, five featuring taro leaves or stalks, five featuring breadfruit, five featuring yams and nine featuring bananas.

Tongareva, in contrast, is an atoll consisting of a ring of islets enclosing a lagoon about twelve miles long and six wide. The islets, totaling about six and a quarter square miles, rise no more than fifteen feet above sea level and are composed of coral and sand. At time of first Western contact, in 1853, the population, of about two thousand— i.e., thirty-two persons per square mile—made full use of the lagoon's fish, shellfish, turtles, etc., but had no domesticated animals and no plant foods other than those provided by coconut and pandanus palms. (Pandanus palms also grew in Samoa, where their leaves were used for making mats and baskets, but their meager fruit was not needed nor used for food.) Nevertheless, the

Tongarevans concocted eight different cooked dishes out of coconut flesh and fluid and two out of the small edible pandanus "keys"—in addition to drinking the uncooked fluid of immature coconuts and eating parts of the pandanus keys uncooked. And with those and a plentiful supply of marine animals they appear to have been as healthy and long-lived as the Samoans—except when hurricanes starved them by stripping their palms.

Few Polynesian peoples resided in environments as fruitful as Samoa or as unfruitful as Tongareva, in terms of number and variety of land-based foods. On the other hand, a people's physical environment did not entirely determine which of their foods they produced and ate. On some atolls just as infertile, pristinely, as Tongareva, the residents succeeded in growing root crops by digging pits into the coral and sand fundament down to water lenses and filling them with imported soil or locally produced mulch. Again, the fact that Easter Islanders had no pigs or dogs was due not to the island's physical environment but, probably, to its isolation—i.e., few if any of those animals having survived the very long voyages required to reach that outpost, and none having survived for long once there. In addition, personal choices institutionalized into society-wide preferences resulted in peoples A and B concentrating their horticultural efforts on different staples even where their food-growing environments were alike. Examples of these and other intersocietal differences in foods and food getting will be given in due course. For the present, the focus will be on some generalized features of the foods themselves and the ways they were obtained, processed and consumed—meanwhile reminding readers once again that while such matters may not be as intriguing or awe-inspiring as some other aspects of Polynesian cultures, they were doubtless the very center of interest and action of most Polynesians themselves.

MAJOR FOOD PLANTS

Coconut palms (*Cocos nucifera*). These stately palms, the very symbols of tropical islands, almost certainly originated in the Indo-Pacific region—probably in Southeast Asia, whence they floated, or were carried, as far west as Madagascar and as far east as tropical America. European explorers found them growing throughout Polynesia, except in New Zealand, Easter Island and Rapa, where year-round temperatures, even at shore level, were not warm enough to permit their growth. (And even on the most tropical islands of Polynesia coconut palms did not grow at elevations above about twelve hundred feet.) How they reached their various Polynesian destinations has been a subject of lively debate—some specialists asserting that they floated to them with the help of current and wind, others holding that they were carried there by humans. The probable truth is that different islands were reached by one, or both, of these ways. Thus, expert consensus is that they were first introduced to the Hawaiian Islands by humans (i.e., Polynesians). Conversely, *Cocos* pollen, recently uncovered in the Cook Islands, has been found to be thousands of years older than the earliest possible arrival of humans there. In this connection, experiments with floating coconuts, combined with computer simulations of South Pacific winds and currents, have found that some sea-borne coconuts could have remained reproductively viable for periods long enough to have reached most Polynesian islands (Ward and Brookfield 1992)—but, this study adds, not long enough for them to have reached tropical America, thereby raising the question, presently unanswerable, concerning what humans carried them there in pre-European times.

As just implied, coconut palms are self-propagating, given the right conditions of soil, sunshine, moisture, and freedom from impairment by animals or weeds. However, most stands of palms on Polynesian beaches, and all of those inland, were almost certainly planted, and thereafter protected, by humans. Most palms begin to produce nuts about five years after germination and continue to yield them for forty to sixty years at a continuous (i.e., nonseasonal) rate, producing about fifty nuts a year. The immature nut contains a tangy liquid that in time transforms into a layer of hard, white flesh on the inner surface of the shell and, somewhat later, a spongy mass of embryo in the nut's cavity. The liquid of the immature nut was often drunk, and the spongy embryo of the mature nut often eaten, raw or cooked, but most nuts used for food were harvested after the meat had been deposited and before the embryo had begun to form. Because nuts usually fall after complete formation of the embryo, most of those wanted for drink or food had to be picked, which was done

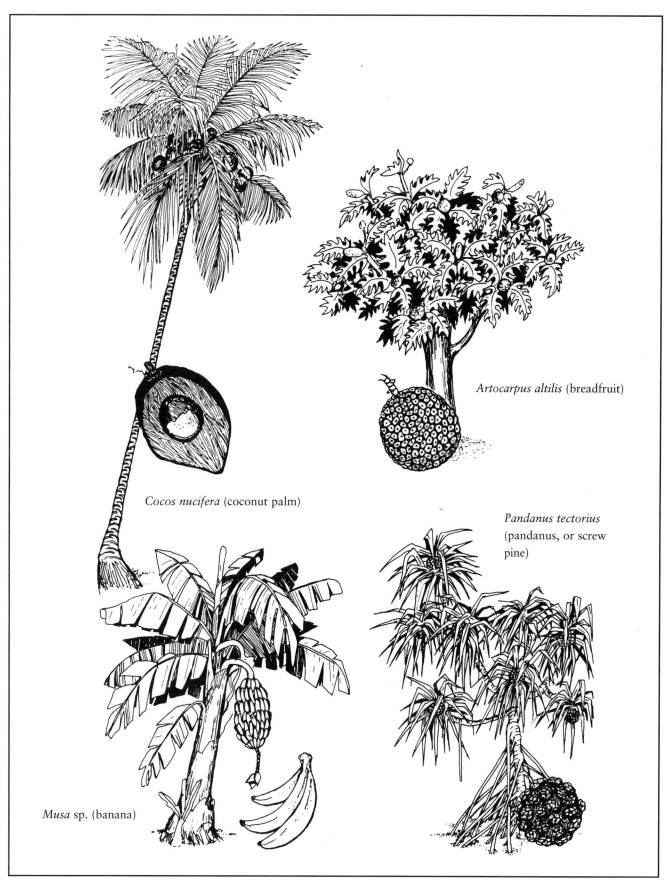

Artocarpus altilis (breadfruit)

Cocos nucifera (coconut palm)

Pandanus tectorius (pandanus, or screw pine)

Musa sp. (banana)

11.1. Principal food-bearing trees of tropical Polynesia

by climbing the palm and twisting or cutting them loose. (Climbing was done by means of a loop of cordage stretched between the feet to aid in gripping the trunk.) After the nut had been split, the most common method of extracting its hardened flesh was by scraping it out of the shell with a saw-toothed tool of wood, shell, or stone, usually lashed to a three-footed stand. The shredded meat was then eaten either raw or mixed with some starchy food and cooked, or had its oily cream extracted, by some form of squeezing, for cooking with other foods or for cosmetic or medical uses. (In some islands of Micronesia the sap of coconut blossoms was collected and drunk either fresh or fermented, or boiled and eaten as "candy"—practices not adopted by Polynesians, not even by those of Kapingamarangi, who were in contact with Micronesians.)

Those Polynesians fortunate enough to have coconut palms utilized their components not only for drink and food—in some places the most important, indeed life-supporting food—but also for building-frames, thatch, screens, caulking material, containers, matting, cordage, weapons, armor, cosmetics, medicine, etc. No wonder that the palms figured prominently in myth and legend. Among the most common of such myths were those having to do with their origin—as, for example, one concerning a family dying of famine-induced starvation. Upon the death of his wife—the story goes—the father went inland in search of wild plantains to feed his orphaned children. Having found some he returned home, to find his children also dead—except for their heads, which grew into coconut palms, the first in the land, and from which the whole island was eventually populated (Henry 1928, 422–23).

Pandanus palms (*Pandanus tectorius*). This palm, with its aboveground buttress roots, grew at low altitudes throughout most of tropical Polynesia, in some places both cultivated and wild—one of its advantages having been the capacity to survive in locations of little soil and low rainfall. On some atolls its fruit, which resembles a pineapple, was, along with coconuts, the only plant food; on others it shared its place as a food staple with root crops or breadfruit. And in some other places, mainly high islands, its sweet-tasting keys were eaten raw or were cooked and eaten during shortages of other foods.

The pandanus palm bears seasonally and pro-

duces up to fifty fruits a year, some of them weighing up to forty to fifty pounds each. Each fruit is made up of thirty to fifty "keys" (or "drupes") three to four inches long. It was the tapering, pithy inner part of the key (which contained significant quantities of carbohydrates and provitamin A) that was eaten. Cooking transformed the pulp of the key into paste or flour that remained edible for months, thereby making it a most valuable, even indispensable, food for those who engaged in long sea voyages and who resided in places subject to food shortages accompanying seasonal variations or to devastating hurricanes.

Breadfruit (*Artocarpus incisa*). The following was written by Joseph Banks in Tahiti in 1769, while with Captain Cook on the latter's first voyage to the Pacific.

> In [this] article of food these happy people may almost be said to be exempt from the curse of our forefathers; scarcely can it be said that they earn their bread with the sweat of their brow when their chiefest sustenance Bread fruit is procured with no more trouble than that of climbing a tree and pulling it down. Not that the trees grow here spontaneously but if a man should in the course of his life time plant 10 such trees, which if well done might take the labour of an hour or thereabouts, he would as compleatly fulfill his duty to his own as well as future generations as we natives of less temperate climates can do by toiling in the cold of winter to sow and in the heat of summer to reap the annual produce of our soil. (Beaglehole 1962, I: 341)

And so convinced was Banks about the potentiality of the breadfruit becoming a more economical means for feeding the slave laborers on British West Indian plantations that he promoted William Bligh's missions on the ill-fated *Bounty*, in 1787, and on Bligh's subsequent, and successful, *Providence* voyage in 1789, to collect planting stock for those plantations.

Nor were Banks's estimates about the trees' fruitfulness and the fruits' food values greatly exaggerated. One mature fruit—which is round to elliptical, up to ten inches in diameter, and up to ten pounds in weight—can supply an active adult with about one-half of his daily requirements in calories, one-fourth of calcium, iron and ascorbic acid, one-fifth of protein and fair amounts of several other nutritional needs. Moreover (in Tahiti, for example) the mature tree produces between 75 and 150 fruits a year (Wilder 1928)—one catch, however, being that the fruit ripens seasonally and has to be eaten (or preserved) within days of ripening, another that the trees are very vulnerable to drought and high wind and to destruction by enemies. Some of those disadvantages were, however, mitigated by preserving the fruit by fermentation, about which more will be said.

The most widespread Pacific species of breadfruit, *Artocarpus incisa* (which doubtless originated in Southeast Asia)[72] comprises a large number of varieties, seeded and seedless. The latter came to predominate in Polynesia, probably through human selection and also by purposive introduction—i.e., unlike the coconut, its sea-borne seeds do not remain viable for long and even its root shoots require careful tending to remain so. Once planted it requires year-round warm temperatures, much rainfall, and well-drained soil. Thus, although the pioneer settlers of such places as New Zealand, Easter Island and several dry or thin-soiled atolls may have attempted to grow the tree there, they evidently did not succeed. Where it does grow it fruits seasonally: more plentifully during the summer, less so in early winter, with two or more crops during the summer season.

The fruit was usually harvested just prior to its full ripening—the fully ripened fruit having been considered too soft and sweet. It could be easily harvested by one person but was usually done so more expediently by two—one to twist loose the fruit by hand or by a long-handled forked stick, the other to catch it or break its fall (i.e., to keep it from bursting).

The freshly picked fruit was prepared for eating in several ways. The simplest method, usually resorted to when away from home, was to roast it whole and then scrape off the charred rind. Usually, however, the fruit was baked in an earth oven, either whole and in its rind or in chunks (after removing rind and core). When fully baked it was eaten as is or mashed and mixed with coconut cream or other foods.

At the height of the plentiful breadfruit season it was customary in some places for neighbors, or for fellow subjects of a leader, to combine their surplus ripe fruit and bake it in an extra-large earth oven—baked fruit having remained edible longer than unbaked. Or surpluses were preserved

by storing uncooked fruit in leaf-lined pits; fruit fermented in this way remained edible for years, thereby providing some insurance against food scarcities—either brief interseasonal ones or longer ones caused by droughts or tree-destroying warfare. Season-long droughts occurred in several Polynesian islands, year-long ones in the Marquesas—where, in conjunction with frequent tree-destroying wars, whole tribes sometimes experienced near or total starvation. (And in the Marquesas, where breadfruit was the major food, precautions against those hazards were taken by digging and filling enormous fermentation pits in hidden locations, but even those were sometimes found and destroyed by raiding enemies.)

Among a people heavily dependent upon breadfruit, its temporal pattern of ripening served to chronologize their named seasons, and their season of greatest breadfruit abundance was, typically, a time of religious ceremony and secular feasting (that is, if any Polynesian feasting can be described as wholly secular).

In addition to its role as a source of food, the breadfruit tree provided a durable wood for construction of houses and canoes and for fabrication of bowls, carved images, fishing floats, etc. Also, its adhesive sap—mixed with shredded coconut husk—was used in several places for caulking and, mixed with other plant products, was smeared on tree limbs to catch birds and to trap small rats. And in addition to all those uses its inner bark was in many places made into high-quality barkcloth.

It is not surprising that many Polynesian peoples had myths regarding the origin of breadfruit. One version, fairly widespread, was that of a man who sacrificed himself to feed his starving family by transforming himself into a breadfruit tree, of which his head became its fruit. As would be expected, where breadfruit was a staple food its associated supernatural patron ranked high in the local pantheon, and religious rites regarding its planting and harvest were correspondingly momentous. In Tahiti, for example, upon the ripening of the year's largest crops (a few weeks after the summer solstice) members of each tribe assembled at their chief's residence and presented their first harvest to him and to the plant's patron god; then and only then were others permitted to eat the breadfruit.

Bananas (*Musa* spp.). Another important food-producing tree that grew on many islands was the banana, of which there were two species, *Musa paradisiaca* and *Musa troglodytarum*, both comprising many varieties (the starchier of which are in English called plantains). The former species doubtless originated in southern and southeast Asia, the latter possibly in Melanesia—both having been carried by humans, and not by ocean currents, into Polynesia, where most varieties of the former were cultivated, in groves or individually, near dwellings, and most of the latter grew wild and untended in mountainous areas. (Those growing wild were usually collected only when cultivated foods became scarce or when adventurous men wanted a change of diet—"adventurous" on account of the arduous nature of carrying the heavy bunches down mountain slopes.) Both species are fast-growing and highly productive, and propagation was (is) by suckers or by shoots that grow from the root stock. Bananas thrive only in rich soil, thus cannot grow on most atolls. Some varieties of *M. paradisiacum* are naturally sweet and were eaten raw; others, along with all *M. troglodytarum*, were cooked and were a highly favored food.

We turn next to Polynesians' so-called "root" crops (fig. 11.2), represented mainly by aroids, yams and sweet potatoes, secondly by arrowroots and *ti*, and far less widely and usefully by kudzu and turmeric.

Four species of aroids (i.e., members of the *Araceae* family) were cultivated by Polynesians: "true" taro (*Colocasia esculenta*), "giant" taro (*Alocasia macrorrhiza*), "swamp" taro (*Cyrtosperma chamissonia*), and *teve* (*Amorphophallus paeoniifolius*). All four species grew year-round—although only in year-round warm climates. In all four species the edible portion was its corm, the bulblike enlargement of the underground part of its stem. (In the case of "true" taro the tender ones of its leaves were also eaten.) Also, they were all propagated vegetatively—by replanting the stem shortly after cutting off most of its corm. Moreover, the corms of all four species required cooking—but they differed from one another in other respects.

"True" taro was everywhere the most highly favored aroid in terms of flavor and texture, but it required wetter soil than the others—ranging, according to variety, from rain-watered slopes to natural or manmade freshwater pondfields. And, although it was ready for harvesting seven to nine

months after planting, its corm rotted soon after reaching maturity and remained palatable for only a few days after harvesting or cooking. In the course of the species' (human-borne) diffusion throughout Polynesia it became differentiated into numerous varieties—Hawai'i alone contained about 250—largely as a result of purposeful selection and propagation to suit distinctive natural settings or specific requirements of flavor or texture. By times of Western contact "true" taro was also found growing on many islands in the wild—not autochthonously but as an escapee from cultivation.

As just stated, all varieties of "true" taro required some (freshwater) moisture in the soil, but they differed with respect to how much—and, consequently, so did their methods of cultivation—the drier varieties having been grown by shifting cultivation, the wetter ones by human-engineered water control.

Shifting cultivation consisted of planting crops in the same site until its fertility diminished (as indicated by the deterioration of the harvest) and then moving onto another site, or series of sites, thereby allowing each site to remain fallow long enough for its fertility to become restored (i.e., as indicated by size of the site's natural secondary regrowth). In some especially fertile settings a plot was replanted two or three times and then allowed to remain fallow for only a year or two; in less fertile settings a single planting had to be followed by several years of fallow, such cycling having been established through observation and experimentation. (It is likely that the pioneer settlers of most islands had to do a great deal of experimentation, in various settings, before achieving satisfactory solutions.)

As summarized by Patrick Kirch (1984), three methods of horticultural water control were practiced here or there by tropical Polynesians. One was practiced mainly on atolls; it involved planting the taro in pits dug through the coral rubble and sand deep enough to tap a lens of fresh water (i.e., rainwater that had sunk through the porous ground). Also, because the soil of such locations lacks organic nutrients it had to be enriched by mulches of decaying leaves and humus, the latter sometimes brought by canoe from other islands. In this connection it should be noted that nowhere in Polynesia was use made of animal fertilizer (Douglas Yen, pers. com.).

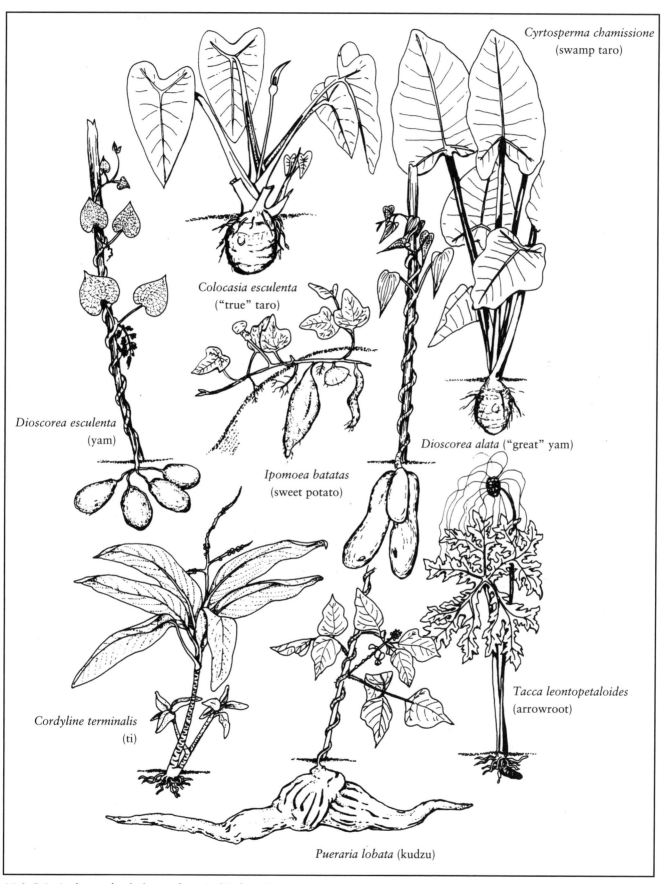

Cyrtosperma chamissione (swamp taro)

Colocasia esculenta ("true" taro)

Dioscorea esculenta (yam)

Ipomoea batatas (sweet potato)

Dioscorea alata ("great" yam)

Tacca leontopetaloides (arrowroot)

Cordyline terminalis (ti)

Pueraria lobata (kudzu)

11.2. Principal root–food plants of tropical Polynesia

The second kind of water-control method was the so-called "raised bed" (or "garden island") system, which was applied on land having too much permanent surface water (i.e., freshwater marshes). It consisted of a network of ditches dug throughout the marsh, the taro having been planted abovewater on the mounds formed by the excavated soil.

The third method, "pondfield irrigation," involved the transfer of water from a more or less continuous source (e.g., a stream or spring) to a site that was not watered enough by rain for cultivation of hydrophytic varieties of the taro. The engineering of the transfer ranged from simple measures—such as damming a stream in order to divert water to a streamside plot—to construction of lengthy irrigation ditches that tapped large streams and discharged their water into descending series of manmade terraces. The terraces were usually bordered by earthen or stone-faced dikes, which were periodically breached to permit water to flow into their lower abutting fields. Pondfield irrigation was practiced in several high islands, its apogee having been reached in Kaua'i and by that island's famous Menehune Ditch, which was 1.8 miles long and had banks of clay and stone that in some sections were 24 feet high (Bennett 1931, 22–23).

Mention was made earlier of the use of plant materials for mulching and fertilizing pit-cultivated taro. Similar functions were performed by ashes produced by the land-clearing burning that accompanied shifting cultivation and by the vegetation uprooted in the process of renewing the ditches in raised-bed gardens and in the process of weeding pondfields and repairing their dikes. On the other hand, the only known example in Polynesia of the purposeful practice of soil enriching by crop rotation occurred on the small Outlier island of Anuta, where taro and yams were alternated on the same plots with little or no fallowing between them (Yen 1973b, 125).

"Swamp" taro (*Cyrtosperma chamissonis*) was grown in coastal freshwater marshes and in manmade pits. It grew mainly in the Ellice Islands (now Tuvalu), Tokelau and the northern Cook Islands, and was probably introduced into those atolls from Micronesia. Its edible tuber is generally larger than that of "true" taro and takes three to five times longer to mature. It is also more fibrous, and consequently less favored for food

than "true" taro, but has the advantage of remaining edible in the ground for years—a capacity for "storage" that "true" taro lacked.

The tuber of "giant taro" (*Alocasia macrorrhiza*) is also larger than that of "true" taro, and the growing plant requires less moisture. On the other hand, its edible part and its aboveground starchy stem contain mouth-burning oxylate crystals, which have to be washed out before eating, and even after that its taste was less favored than that of "true" taro.

Turning now to yams (genus *Dioscorea*), several species grew in Polynesia, but only two, *D. alata* ("great" yam) and *D. esculenta* ("lesser" yam) were cultivated regularly, and those mainly in western Polynesia, where they were about as important as taro in quantity of production, and because of their longer after-harvest edibility were more important than taro as an object of accumulation and exchange. And, although they needed less moisture for growing, they had the disadvantage of ripening only seasonally and required more labor to cultivate.

The sweet potato (*Ipomoea batatas*), which originated in South America, was introduced into the Pacific along three different routes and at different times. The earliest introduction, circa A.D. 400–700, was into eastern Polynesia, whence it spread, eventually, as far as Tonga, New Zealand and Hawai'i—all of its local vernacular names having been cognates of its Peruvian name, *kumara* (e.g., *kumala*, *'umala*, *'umara*, *'uala*, etc.). Its second introduction was by the Portuguese into Indonesia, thence to New Guinea; and the third was by the Spanish, from Mexico into the Marianas and Philippines (Yen 1973).

How the sweet potato reached Polynesia prior to Western contact remains a problem: whether by Peruvians or by round-trip voyaging Polynesians is still being debated by scholars and maritime adventurers. Thor Heyerdahl in his *Kon Tiki* raft demonstrated the possibility of the former, but the experimental voyages of the Hawaiian canoe *Hōkūle'a* suggest the greater likelihood of the latter.[73]

The wide diffusion of sweet potato cultivation throughout Polynesia is easy to comprehend. In most places it was considered somewhat inferior in taste and texture to "true" taro but proved to be easier to grow, to have higher yields, and to prosper not only in drier and cooler locations—as, for example, in the Hawaiian uplands, and even in the temperate climate of New Zealand's North Island, where taro and yams could be grown only in the island's far north and where sweet potatoes could be grown more widely (but only seasonally).

"WET" VERSUS "DRY"

As noted in the foregoing, the growing of most varieties of "true" taro required more—in fact, much more—moisture than did the growing of yams and sweet potatoes—the distinction between the two agronomic regimes having been aptly labeled the "wet" and the "dry."[74] Moreover, that distinction entailed not only methods of cultivation but also kinds and quantities of land and labor required to feed a tribe's residents, and consequently a tribe's intertribal relations as well.

With regard to yield: in view of its more or less continuous cultivation—in pondfields or on raised beds— taro required less land than was needed for the shifting cultivation characteristic of yams and sweet potatoes. On the other hand, taro growing was largely limited to areas that were typically "wet"—i.e., those on the rainier, usually windward, sides of most high islands. And with respect to labor, while a large amount of it was required initially to construct the pondfields and raised beds for taro, the subsequent planting and replanting of them was considerably less labor-demanding, per capita, than the continuous land clearing associated with the shifting cultivation of yams and sweet potatoes—which included, on some islands, the labor of females as well as males (work which in most "wet" gardening was allotted mostly to males). As for the political aspect of "wet" versus "dry": in tribes undergoing population increase (which was the case with most of them at some stages of their histories), many of those dependent on shifting cultivation for most of their food experienced, and became conscious of, shortages of available land, which induced their leaders to engage, or abetted them in engaging in, territorial conquest, especially if the neighboring tribal territories were "wet."

SUPPLEMENTAL FOOD PLANTS

Four other edible starchy roots of more localized distribution, or of lesser use, were arrowroot (*Tacca leontopetaloides*), *ti* (*Cordyline fruticosa*), kudzu (*Pueraria lobata*), and turmeric (*Curcuma longa*).

Arrowroot thrives naturally in sandy corraline soil but in a few places was also cultivated. Its edible root was usually made into a flour that was combined into cakes with coconut or other ingredients—and as such was, because of its preservability, used on long voyages and between the seasonal ripenings of, say, breadfruit. However, the starch extracted from its root contained a bitter and mildly poisonous element, which therefore had to be washed out before eating.

Throughout much of Polynesia the slender, long-stemmed, leaf-crowned *ti* plant was valued mainly for its colorful leaves, which were used as ornaments, food wrappers and ceremonial props. In a few places, however, its starchy root was eaten, and favored on account of its high sugar content and its keeping qualities. (Because of its sugar, in postcontact times Polynesians learned from Westerners to use it for making an alcoholic beverage, in the process of becoming "civilized.")

The starchy root of the kudzu vine was an important food staple in parts of Melanesia, but in Tonga and Samoa, its easternmost extension into Polynesia, it grew mainly in the wild and served only as a standby "famine food."

Turmeric, a member of the ginger family, was cultivated widely in Polynesia, mainly for the yellow-red dye extracted from its root. In some places, however, the starchy root itself was occasionally cooked and eaten.

Other supplemental food plants cultivated here or there included sugarcane (*Saccharum officinarum*)—whose stalk was chewed to extract its sweetness, "Tahitian apple" (*Spondias dulcis*) and "Malay apple" (*Syzygium malaccense*)—the two latter having been among the few edible fruits.

In addition to the above, their forebears introduced and some Polynesians continued to cultivate a number of plants whose fruits or nuts were eaten infrequently or in times of famine. Among these were an almond (*Terminalia catappe*), a melon (*Cucumis melo*), a fig (*Ficus tinctoria*), two fruits of the *Solanum* genus (*repandum* and *viride*) and the "lesser yam" (*Dioscorea esculenta*). For the nonspecialist reader the importance of the above listings of supplementary and occasional or famine-food plants is not their specific identities, but what they reveal about the horticultural skills and the colonizing foresightedness of the pre-, ancestral and subsequent Polynesians.

It is not surprising that the planting and harvesting of a people's major food crops were accompanied by religious rites, including supplication to the relevant god(s) for assistance in their flourishing and thanks to them for providing that assistance—plus, in many cases, the rendition of a portion of the harvest to the producers' clan senior or tribe chief. In some societies and for some crops the rites were performed simply and perfunctorily by the individual producer at times of his own choosing and without wider reference. At the other extreme, however, such rites for major food crops were carried out by tribal officials for their entire clan or tribe in series of episodes that, in the case of harvests, included universal interdiction against eating any of the harvest until completion of the rites; "first-fruit" offerings to the crop's patron god(s), typically only token amounts of the crop itself; "first-fruit" tribute to the clan's senior or the tribe's chief, typically a more substantial portion of the crop (i.e., a tax); and in many societies feasting or dancing or sports events.

Hawai'i's Makahiki and comparable large-scale horticultural ceremonies such as Tahiti's Parara'a Matahiti ("Ripening of the Year," Oliver 1974, 259–62) and Mangareva's Marae Uaikai (Buck 1938a, 433–43) have, justifiably, attracted much scholarly attention, but knowledge about their actual performances is based mainly on sketchy accounts by on-the-spot Westerners or by the decades-old memories of Westernized native informants. The only eyewitness account by a professionally trained anthropologist of extant pagan Polynesian horticultural rites is that of Raymond Firth about Tikopia (1967A, 1967B). And although Firth's account does not contravene any of the major generalizations about such rites offered in this book, it adds rich details about them and their relevance to other aspects of Tikopian society.

Cultivated food plants constituted the largest component, by far, of the things eaten by tropical Polynesians. Next in order of quantity were fish and other marine animals, then domesticated animals, and, least of all, wild birds.

DOMESTICATED ANIMALS

Before the arrival of humans in what was to become (tropical) Polynesia the only land-based mammals living there were fruit bats, and even those were present only in some islands of Tonga and Samoa. And while numerous species of birds nested in those and other Polynesian islands—although of genera that diminished in number from west to east—none were subsequently domesticated except as pets. In other words, at times of first Western contact and except for a few avian pets, the only domesticated animals found, here or there, among the tropical Polynesians were pigs, dogs and chickens (fig. 11.3). Moreover, all three had been introduced into the region by the Polynesians' forebears—but not all three had eventually reached, or survived, on all the islands subsequently colonized.

At times of Western contact pigs existed, either domesticated or feral, in none of Polynesia's atolls (where the supplies of plant foods were insufficient to support them), but were present in all but a few of the region's high islands—the notable exceptions having been Easter Island and Tikopia. Their absence in the former may have been due to their having expired, or been killed for food, during the long colonizing voyages to that isolated outpost. As for Tikopia, pigs were once kept there but were subsequently killed off (and presumably eaten) in an intentional effort to end their heavy drain upon scarce plant foods (Kirsch and Yen 1982). (At the time of Western contact pigs were also absent in New Zealand, for reasons that will be opined in Part Three.)

The pigs of Polynesia—and of elsewhere in the Pacific—were of the species *Sus scrofa*, descendants of the wild boars that were native to large parts of Eurasia extending south and east as far as Sulawesi, and perhaps even Buru—but not across the ocean gap into Sahul land (Darlington 1957). By about six to five thousand years ago, however, domesticated pigs had been carried by humans across that gap to New Guinea. Also, it is fairly safe to assume that they had already been introduced into the New Hebrides by the time the Lapitans began colonizing there, and as just noted were carried by them thence to Fiji, Tonga and Samoa. In fact, pig-raising was an inherent element of ancestral Polynesian culture, as indicated by presence of a word for "pig," *puraka*, in the reconstructed proto-Polynesian lexicon (Pawley and Green 1971). It is also likely that subsequent colonizing expeditions eastward would have carried pigs (along with planting materials)—although, as noted above, not all such expeditions

11.3. Domesticated animals of tropical Polynesia

succeeded in establishing pig-raising in their new colonies.

Such pigs were described as being smaller than European breeds, and as having longer legs and snouts. The domesticated ones were also noted as being more docile than their European cousins.[75]

Some peoples (e.g., Samoans) kept their pigs in enclosures, but in most pig-raising communities the animals were unfettered and left free to roam and forage for most of their food. To sustain their domestication, however, they were usually fed daily at or near their owners' residences. Most or all of that food was vegetal, consisting of the same kinds of staples, cooked and raw, eaten by their owners (the same "kinds" but not necessarily of the same quality—such foods sometimes having included a household's meal leavings or substandard pieces of tuber or breadfruit). Indeed, in some places domestication reached a level at which some or all of a household's pigs were treated as pampered pets—even to the extent of feeding very young ones by hand, or as witnessed by scandalized Westerners—by breast. Nevertheless, the invariable fate of most of them was to serve as food—in most societies as the most desirable of all foods—"most desirable" perhaps but seldom eaten, except by some affluent upper-class pork-eating persons in a few resource-rich, highly class-structured societies. For most other pork-eating persons in pig-raising societies it was a very infrequent treat, eaten only on rare ceremonial occa-

sions. (I specify "pork-eating persons" inasmuch as some persons in many societies—e.g., all females and children—were denied pork altogether.)

The most widespread way of killing pigs was by strangling—stabbing having been ruled out in order to avoid losing any of their blood, which was a highly regarded delicacy. Pigs were usually cooked whole in earth ovens and then butchered in conventional patterns, with specific cuts reserved for specific categories of individuals (e.g., chiefs, chiefs' servants, adult commoner males). Thus, in Samoa (where women were allowed pork on occasion) the cuts and allocations were as shown in the following diagram (from Buck 1930, 121):

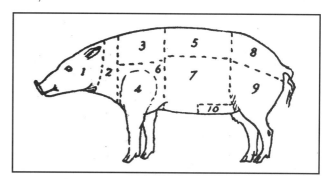

11.4. Traditional distribution of pork cuts of pigs at Samoan feasts

Figure 11.4. Pig, ceremonial divisions: 1. *ulu* (head) to the *au manga* (young men who cook); 2. *ivi muli ulu* (neck) to the *tulafale* (talking chief); 3.

o'o (back) to the *ali'i* (chiefs) of second grade; 4. *alanga lima* (shoulder) to the *tulafale* (talking chief); 5. *tuala* (loins) to the *ali'i* of the first grade; 6. *itu mea tele* (big side) to the *ali'i* of the second grade; 7. *itu pale asu* to the family of the chief; 8. *muli* to the women; 9. *alanga vae* (leg) to the *matai* (chief of lesser tank); 10. *alo* (abdominal wall) to the *taupou* (i.e., village "sacred" maid).

In several societies pigs were also an important item of exchange—including prescribed "gifts" between the principal parties of a marriage, payments for specialized services, taxation (i.e., exactions from subjects to their chief), and offerings to gods. However, they invariably ended up as food—i.e., mainly for mortals, since most of those offered to gods were eventually eaten by the human worshipers—only the "essence" of the animal having gone to gods.

In terms of numbers, pig-raising reached its zenith in Hawai'i, where pigs constituted a part of the land rent regularly paid to chiefs,[76] and where, according to Western accounts, "hundreds" of them were levied by chiefs for ceremonies and feasts.

Like pigs, dogs were among the baggage of the Lapitans who colonized what was to become Polynesia. The naturalist Georg Forster, who accompanied James Cook on the latter's second Pacific voyage, described the dogs of Tahiti this way: "[They are] short, and their sizes vary from that of a lap-dog to the largest spaniel. Their head is broad, the snout pointed, the eyes very small, the ears upright, and their hair rather long, hard, and of different colors, but most commonly white and brown. They seldom if ever barked, but howled sometimes, and were shy of strangers to a degree of aversion" (G. Forster 1777, I: 378).

Other Western visitors to Tahiti during that era characterized them as, for example, "the ugliest and most stupid of all the Canine tribe," and "by no means ferocious, and excepting their shape and habits, [having] few characteristics of the English dog"—which, according to one of those visitors, came about as a result of their food (i.e., plant foods rather than meat). Early reports about dogs in other parts of Polynesia suggest that they resembled those of Tahiti—in shape and in temperament.[77]

Except in New Zealand, where there was sufficient quarry, precontact Polynesians did not use dogs for hunting. However, in one or another tropical Polynesian society dogs' teeth were used for ornament, their bones for tools—including fishhooks—their hair for decorative cordage, etc., but their main practical use was as food, which was considered as delectable as pork, and as such served also as munificent offerings to gods.

Also, in some societies dogs were treated as pets (which, however, did not prevent their owners from killing and eating them on occasion). Quoting again the naturalist Georg Forster (who reports having seen a Tahitian woman suckle a puppy),[78] "[T]he dogs in spite of their stupidity, were in high favour with all the women, who could not have nursed them with a more ridiculous affection, if they had really been ladies of fashion in Europe" (Ibid.). In the same vein an English missionary to Tahiti wrote: "We are at present surrounded with a great multitude of useless mischievous dogs, which the natives kiss and hug as much as they do their children, and call them good property and food" (quoted in Oliver 1974, 276).

It was in Hawai'i that dog domestication reached its Polynesian acme. There, an English missionary recorded that they were kept in yards and provided with small houses to sleep in, and that a part of the land rent of every tenant was paid in dogs "for his landlord's table" (Ellis 1969). In Hawai'i dog flesh was deemed superior even to pork, and was the principal meat at feasts, the same missionary having counted "nearly 200" of them cooked on one such occasion.[79]

Like other domesticated animals—indeed, like most other animals known to Polynesians, dogs figured in myths, and in some cosmologies even in their pantheons. (For descriptions of which, see, for example, Buck 1938b/1959; Titcomb 1969; Henry 1928; and Stimson 1934.)

The chickens present on many Polynesian islands at times of contact were descendants of the Southeast Asian jungle fowl, *Gallus gallus*, and bore the vernacular name *moa* nearly everywhere. They were raised mainly for food, and in some cases for their feathers as well; in a few societies they may have been used also for cockfighting—but perhaps only after contact. And, like other valuables, they sometimes served as offerings to gods. On the other hand, their eggs were seldom eaten, even when available—which was uncommon, since cooping up chickens occurred only sporadically.

The domestication of chickens reached its Polynesian peak on Easter Island, where they were the only domestic animals at times of contact—i.e., probably the only kind that had survived the pioneer voyage to and settlement of that isolated island. According to that island's principal ethnographer, Alfred Métraux: "When the ancient culture was functioning, chickens were the usual gifts to people who must be honored; they were raised for feasts and appear as a favorite motif in art. The feathers were used in making circlets, eyeshades, and hats. The economic value that chickens once had for the natives is manifest in the care they took of them. Near the sites of most ancient villages or settlements, hen houses are found. Often they are the only testimony of the former existence of a village. One [early visitor reported] that 'the islanders breed fowls in little runs scraped out in the ground and thatched over'" (1940, 19).

The native rat (*Rattus exulans*), a small brown animal, was introduced into Polynesia by Lapitan colonizers, and their descendants were eventually carried to nearly every colony. Whether they were transported intentionally or as stowaways cannot now be discovered, but probably the latter, because among contact-era Polynesians they were considered pests in most societies and eaten in only a few (as, for example, on Easter Island, where there were neither pigs nor dogs). However, not even when serving as food were rats intentionally domesticated. Nevertheless, the little creatures succeeded in domesticating themselves, as evidenced by the swarms of them that infested household buildings in many islands. In some places baffles were constructed to protect stored edibles from them, and people sought to reduce their numbers by killing them—in some places by bow and arrow. In other places, however, no efforts were made to kill them, in the belief that they were avatars for certain gods. Thus, in Tahiti: "The rat . . . was a shadow [*ata*] of ghosts. When it visited people at night and uttered strange sounds with its tongue or scratched the thatch inside the roof of the house until daybreak, it was communicating mysteries and reminiscences of war and times of peace from dead warriors to living men. But when it approached a sick bed articulating strange sounds, it was the shadow of a devouring ghost announcing the near approach of death to the patient" (Henry 1928, 385).

(Regarding those night visits, so heavily did some Polynesians sleep that the visiting rats—more likely the houses' "domesticated" ones—were known to have gnawed off patches of callus from their feet—and often without waking the sleeper!)[80]

HUNTING

Here or there tropical Polynesians hunted—i.e., shot with bow and arrow or trapped or netted, etc.—land-based game (e.g., feral [wild] pigs and chickens, rats, birds, land crabs, etc.) for food or recreation—and in the case of birds, for feathers. (As will be described in chapter 23, hunting was a much more important activity for the Polynesians of New Zealand than for their tropical counterparts.)

Two categories of (land-based) animals were hunted: those species that were indigenous (lived there prior to humans) and those that the Polynesians' forebears had brought to the area and that had subsequently gone wild. With respect to the indigenous fauna generally it will be recalled that most species of them had originated in Southeast Asia or in Australia–New Guinea, and that those had decreased in number (of species) from west to east—a cline that was however complicated somewhat by an island's geography (e.g., given the same distance from Southeast Asia and Australia–New Guinea, atolls supported fewer than high islands). Thus, while fruit bats were indigenous in islands as far east as Samoa, islands farther east of there supported no land-based mammals at all (i.e., before humans introduced pigs, dogs—and rats).

Birds able to fly (as distinct from the flightless birds of New Zealand) are of course not as land-bound as most mammals, but even so, Samoa had only 32 land-bound species of them (Watling 1982), and Easter Island only 6 (Stedman 1995), compared with New Guinea's 570 (Ryan 1972, 68). In contrast with species, however, the isolation and geographic diversity of some Polynesian islands resulted in much local *sub*speciation—i.e., "adaptive radiation." Thus, in Hawai'i, one ancestral species of honeycreepers (family *Drepanididae*) had evolved into 22 up to the time of Western contact.

Of the three human-introduced domesticated species, some pigs and dogs went wild, probably because of insufficient domestic feeding, and then proliferated. That may also have been the case

with some chickens—but even uncooped domesticated chickens appear to have spent as much time
in the "wild" (where they laid most of their eggs)
as they did close to their owners' residences. (On
those few atolls with animal domesticates they
could not "escape" into the wild, there being little
or no "wild" to support them.)

Except in the case of those birds valued mainly for their feathers, the objective of most hunting
was food—along with the recreation often associated with it. In fact in some places recreation
seems to have been a more important motive for
hunting than was food, as, for example, in Samoa,
where fowling was a competitive sport.

The methods used for hunting, in one society
or another, were numerous. At one extreme were
the practices of catching the quarry by hand (e.g.,
in the case of land crabs) or throwing rocks at it
(e.g., certain species of birds). At the other
extreme was the use of complex spring traps with
decoy baits. Concern with hunting ranged from
that of the people of Kapingamarangi Atoll
(where none were engaged in it, since there were
no wild mammals and since wild fowl were not
valued as food) to Samoa (where the quarry were
varied and relatively plentiful, and where the
methods of obtaining them were correspondingly
numerous and diverse). The following description
of those methods is taken from Buck 1930,
524–41:

- baited spring traps: for catching rats and pigs,
  which in trying to obtain the bait, released a
  trigger that freed a running noose;
- self-acting fowl traps: for catching chickens
  gone wild;
- manipulated fowl traps: for catching chickens
  gone wild—sometimes used with bait or a roost-
  er decoy;
- dove trap: used with a decoy bird;
- bow and arrow: for shooting pigeons, rails, fruit
  bats, and wild chickens—done from concealment in a small house (note that in some
  Polynesian societies the bow and arrow was
  used also for shooting fish, but not as a weapon
  against humans—except, possibly, in
  Mangareva);
- fruit bat hook: a hook attached to a long handle;
- pigeon net: a bag net with a long handle, yielded by hand—sometimes in association with a
  (tame) decoy bird used to bring the quarry within reach;

- netting platform: earthwork platform constructed on hilltop ridges, on which a fowler, assisted
  by decoys and concealed inside a small house,
  awaited his prey with nets; platforms were also
  constructed in trees for similar purposes;
- tern netting: used for catching that bird, which
  frequented seaside cliffs. "The fowler sat nakid
  . . . in a clear space near the cliff edge with his
  net on the ground before him. The decoy had a
  string about two fathoms long tied to its leg and
  it flew about to attract the tern. As the tern came
  up over the cliff edge the fowler caught it with
  his net."

Another bird-catching technique, not practiced in Samoa but quite widely elsewhere, was the
use of an adhesive plant sap (e.g., of breadfruit).
In some places it was spread onto tree limbs
known to be resting places for birds; in others
(e.g., the Marquesas) the gum was smeared onto a
long pole, which was thrust among the branches
and aerial roots of banyans where birds regularly
nested (E.S.C. Handy 1923, 180).

In some societies some methods of hunting
were engaged in mainly by men of upper-class status, or certain kinds of quarry were reserved for
them. Thus, in Tonga: "All pigeons (lupe) caught
were taken to chiefs, and eaten only by them. If
commoners ate pigeons [and were detected] they
were punished by whipping or even death. Pigeon-
snaring was perhaps the most popular of chiefly
sports. A host of words refer to it. Many of them
are used metaphorically of women, successful
lovemaking being likened to successful pigeon-
snaring" (Gifford 1929, 117). As in Samoa,
Tongan pigeon snaring was done with nets from
manmade mounds, and the areas surrounding
such mounds were in some cases taboo to commoners.

GATHERING

While producing most of their plant food by
cultivation, most Polynesian peoples obtained
some of it by gathering it from the "wild"—i.e.,
from sources other than their gardens and groves.
The kinds and amounts of wild foods gathered
varied from place to place, not only in consequence of each area's available supply but also of
each people's conception of edibility—and, not
least, the sufficiency of other kinds of food.

At one extreme in this respect was Hawai'i.
Under normal weather conditions its people culti-

vated plentiful supplies of a number of food plants—taro, sweet potatoes, yams, arrowroot, bananas, breadfruit, coconuts, etc. Or in case of need they were able to *gather* some of those staples that had been or had gone wild. In addition, however, among Hawai'i's rich and diverse indigenous wild flora, its people considered at least twenty-six dry-land species to possess edible components—either leaves, pith, berries, nuts or corms—any of which could be resorted to when their cultivated staples were in short supply (E. S. C. Handy 1927, 234–36).

At the other extreme was Tongareva Atoll, where, as described earlier, only two food plants, coconuts and pandanus, were cultivated, and where there grew no wild plants that its residents believed to be edible (a belief that was doubtless factual, in view of Polynesians' penchant for dietary experimentation). This shortage of edible plants left them very vulnerable to food scarcity in face of the nut- and fruit-damaging hurricanes that sometimes occurred—scarcity that could be relieved only partially by the atoll's rich marine food resources.

Between the extremes represented by Hawai'i and Tongareva with respect to the gathering of wild food plants, the other peoples of tropical Polynesia exemplified a wide range of mix. Some, such as those of Pukapuka (atoll), cultivated only one or two staples but had access to a plentiful supply of uncultivated plants (in Pukapuka, mainly pandanus). Others, such as those of the Marquesas, were heavily dependent on one or two cultivated staples but so deficient in wild plants (i.e., those considered to be edible) that when supply of the staples was reduced, by drought or destructive warfare—as was sometimes the case—the accompanying famines resulted in starvation or, in some cases, emigration in search of a more life-sustaining land. (Indeed, that kind of motivation might well have been the one responsible for several Polynesians' voyages of discovery and colonization.)

Here and there in tropical Polynesia people collected and ate one or more kinds of *limu* (*rimu*, etc.), a word applied mainly to "edible" algae, principally seaweed (but which in Hawai'i at least also included freshwater algae, mosses, liverworts, lichens and some soft corals (Abbott 1992, 45). In most if not all Polynesian societies *limu* served as a condiment—a welcome supplement to peoples'

usual bland meals. In Hawai'i, where the subject has been best investigated (thanks to the efforts of Isabella Abbott), some twenty-nine species were eaten—more, perhaps, than elsewhere in Polynesia. There also—and probably elsewhere in Polynesia—the collection was done, and probably originated, by women, a custom that Professor Abbott attributes, persuasively, to the circumstance of women having been conventionally forbidden most other savory foods. (See also Abbott 1991.)

FISHING

We turn next to fishing, which Polynesians engaged in mainly for food. The topic is vast, complex—and fundamental for understanding those peoples' ways of life. In fact, one of the principal authorities on Polynesian origins argued that their forebears were "oceanic strandloopers"— i.e., a wholly maritime, fishing people who had migrated fairly swiftly down the Melanesian chain of islands, dwelling only along the shores and obtaining what plant foods they needed from the preceding, mainly horticultural, residents in exchange for fish (Groube 1971). As has been amply demonstrated through archaeology and linguistics, those forebears were indeed fishermen— but seasoned horticulturists and animal domesticators as well. Nevertheless, the vocation of fishing was, or became, considerably more multiform and technical than horticulture in terms of tools and methods, and much more heterogeneous in end product. In fact, so diverse were the end products of fishing and so particularized the techniques for obtaining them that the ensuing description will follow suit, beginning with a schema of where those creatures lived and were obtained.

First to be noted is the sharp difference between their freshwater and saltwater habitats. Unlike many of the larger islands of Melanesia, few of Polynesia's high islands and none of its atolls or *makatea* ("pancake islands") contained freshwater streams large enough to shelter potentially edible marine animals. Moreover, the freshwater streams of tropical Polynesia harbored many fewer species of fish than did the islands of Melanesia: thus, Tahiti's streams contained only about 15, compared with the 111 or so that bred and lived in New Guinea's. With saltwater fauna the differences were not so wide—the waters around Tahiti having contained about 625 species as compared with New Guinea's 2,000 or so.[81] However, within tropical Polynesia there were— still are—some large differences among the islands with respect to their marine environments, and therefore to the edible fauna present and fished for—it being true, with few exceptions, that if such fauna were present the local Polynesians did fish for them. (One such exception prevailed at Easter Island, where the absence of large trees limited the construction of seaworthy canoes and hence potentially fuller exploitation of nearby deep-sea faunal resources.)

The most ubiquitous type of coastal-zone topography of tropical Polynesia is that schematized in figure 11.5. Generally speaking, the larger fish inhabit the seaward side of the bench (i.e., barrier) reef, while the smaller free-swimming fishes, along with mollusks, crustaceans, octopuses, squids and the like, live in the lagoons and tidepools. Truly pelagic species, such as tuna and bonito, usually roam about in the open sea but come occasionally to the face of the outer reef or enter the lagoon itself. Complicating that pattern is the presence of channels through the outer reef—which, typically, lie opposite the mouths of freshwater streams. The nutrients carried by the streams into the lagoons attract small fishes, which in turn are fed on by larger fishes, etc., so that such places are usually quite densely populated with fish, especially after shoreside rains. Another typical complication is the presence in lagoons of numerous heads of coral of various sizes and shapes, which provide bases for stationary creatures (e.g., mollusks and crustaceans) and

havens for movable ones (e.g., octopus, eels, and numerous varieties of small fish).

In many cases all or part of an island's shoreline is unprotected by barrier reefs—the result either of continually strong wave action, which occurs along the windward coasts of many islands, and of steeply plunging coastlines. Moreover, in many places with or without barrier reefs the shoreline itself is coated with fringing coral, either narrow and discontinuous or continuous and broad. Still another variant occurs in those groups of atoll islets that constitute the surviving rim of a single submersed volcano crater. While the inner shores of such islets face the relatively shallow and quiet waters of a lagoon, their outer flanks are usually precipitous and wave whipped.

Needless to say, a people's fishing activities (i.e., the creatures they fished for and their techniques for securing them) were in large part determined by their coastal geographies—in large part, but not entirely, since cultural conventions also circumscribed who fished for what, where and when. Thus, while Tahitians in general had access to a full range of fishing locales—lagoon, fringe and barrier reef, open sea, etc.—Marquesans, with their largely precipitous shorelines, were limited mainly to fishing in open seas. An island's natural resources also limited the kinds of fishing tools, and therefore in some respects, the kinds and amounts of catch. One example was Easter Island's lack of large trees, which curtailed the building of canoes suitable to the island's turbulent seas; another example was Tongareva's lack

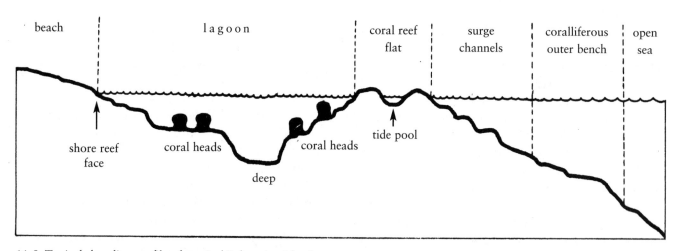

11.5. Typical shoreline profile of tropical Polynesian islands

of hibiscus, whose bast elsewhere was deemed superior to sennit in the fabrication of certain kinds of nets.

Notwithstanding those and other interisland differences in fishing, the following account will treat (tropical) Polynesians' manual and mechanical methods overall, touching on those of a particular people only if they differed markedly from the rest. In one or more places the following methods were utilized: catching by hand—and sometimes by foot, by poison, by netting, by noosing, by trapping, by spearing and by angling. In many places torches were also used at night in order to attract the prey to within reach.

Groping. Catching by hand was common practice in shallow waters, fresh or salt, in fishing for mollusks, crayfish and other non- or slow-moving creatures, the prey having been located by sight or by groping with hands, feet or sticks. Peter Buck describes the method as it was practiced in Samoa: "Both men and women are expert at groping . . . in the crevices between rocks for the rock-frequenting fish which rest there. The men often use the short spears but women use the bare hands . . . . [T]he narrow clefts from which there is no escape are naturally productive of the best results. The constant search that commences in childhood naturally leads to the villagers coming to know every suitable cleft and crevice in the lagoon that adjoins the village. They submerge and with open eyes swim around the rocks peering and feeling in the crevices. When a fish is caught, it is brought up, the head bitten to kill it and the catch deposited in a basket . . . tied around the waist or slung over the back" (Buck 1930, 418).

In some places rocks and coral were piled up in the lagoon to furnish extra resting places to attract fish.

Another common practice was "treading"—walking about in shallow lagoons and using one's feet to detect creatures burrowed into the sand—taking care to avoid stepping on those with needlelike and in some cases poisonous spines, such as sea urchins and scorpion fish (which however were also captured and eaten). As reported about Tahitians by one of the *Bounty* mutineers:

> They . . . are excellent hands at diving after [rock] fish and I have seen a Diver in Clear Water and Calm weather pursue a Fish from one hole in the

rocks to another without coming up to breathe; . . . the most curious part of this fishery is that of taking the Hedge hog fish and Sea Cat—the one being so full of prickles that they can take hold no where but by the Eyes, which is the Method by which they get them as very few are caught any other way—and the others adhere so close to the rocks, that it is as much as two men can do at times to haul them off and I have seen them in 3 or 4 fathom forced to quit them and come up several times before they could accomplish their end; if a Stone lies handy below they kill the fish there, & then they get it off easy. This may seem an odd Method of Fishing but I have seen it attended with good Success and the Divers return in a few hours with large Strings of fine Fish. (Morrison 1935, 155)

To a Westerner the most hazardous type of groping was that used in some places for catching octopus (which were utilized both for food and for bait). Those frequenting lagoons tended to be smaller, and were driven out of their rock shelters by sticks and then caught by hand. The larger ones, usually used for bait, kept to deeper waters and had to be dived for. Here is a description of the method as practiced in Mangaia:

> The successful fisherman must have good sight and a sound wind. Each man carried three sharpened sticks . . . to assist in driving the octopuses out of holes. They had no fear of the tentacles fastening upon their arms once the octopus was within reach. For a firm grasp upon the [octopus's] body caused the tentacles to relax. However, when an arm was thrust into an occupied hole, the octopus seized the arm with its tentacles and pulled [it] toward its body. If the [fisherman's] arm was pulled back, the octopus pulled the harder and the fisherman was likely to be kept prisoner until he drowned. The native fisherman, however, did not pull back, as he was anxious to get his hand on the body of the octopus. He accordingly pushed his hand farther, and Mangaians say that when the octopus found the arm was drawn in without opposition, it let go. (Buck 1944, 214)

Whereupon, the account continues, the fisherman would seize the octopus by its body, surface with it to his canoe, and kill it by biting or stabbing it between its eyes.[82]

Poisoning. Catching fish with poison was

widespread. The most common agent, almost everywhere, was the grated kernel of the fruit of *Barringtonia*, a shrub of the myrtle family. Next most common were the bruised stems, roots and leaves of a shrub, *Tephrosia piscatoria*. The intent was usually to narcotize the fish so as to collect them by net or by hand, but the practice sometimes resulted in killing some of them, especially the smaller ones. (I have come across no report of the eating of poisoned fish having sickened the eater.) The most common technique was to scatter the poison into tidal pools or to place it in coral crevices, which stunned or killed nearby fish and brought them to the surface. On a much larger scale, whole communities would cooperate in closing off sections of a lagoon at low tide and poisoning its waters. Such actions were festive in atmosphere and often caught more fish than the participants could eat, but were undertaken infrequently because of their recognized wastefulness and the slowness of the waters to repopulate.

Netting. Nets of many types were used, from small fine-meshed, one-person scoops to huge large-meshed seines up to about two hundred yards long and twenty yards deep. In Samoa alone Buck counted (and meticulously described) fifteen types—of various uses, sizes, net materials and mesh size: four types of dip nets, scoop nets, arched hand nets, arched nets with line, mullet hand nets, shrimp nets, casting nets, three types of seines (the largest about one hundred yards long) with wooden floats and rock sinkers, shark nets (made of thick, three-ply cord) and turtle nets—plus one of cobwebs collected on a forked stick and used to capture small garfish. A description of these, and of the numerous other types of fishnets used by Polynesians elsewhere, would require more pages than are justified here. Suffice it to say that the Polynesians had expanded net making to adjust to the catching of scores of different sizes and behaviors of prey and in numerous kinds of marine environments.

Sweeps. In shallow waters sweeps were used to drive fish into fixed nets or onto the shore. They were made by attaching leaves, most commonly coconut fronds, to cords or vine stems and were in some cases hundreds of yards long. Members of a whole community—male and female, old and young—would drag the sweep through the shallows in the desired direction, under the supervision of a recognized (and suit-

ably titled) expert. As with large-scale poisoning, such sweeps were festive events and were carried out only occasionally because of their acknowledged wastefulness and their recognized depleting consequences.

Weirs. In the lagoons of many islands weirs of leaves or rocks were constructed in shallow tidal channels in order to capture fish as they returned seaward with falling tides. Most of them were V-shaped, with their openings facing shoreward. In some cases the fish were caught in a net placed at its seaward end; in others fishermen were on hand to spear or scoop them up as they congregated at the closed end.

Fishponds. Ponds were constructed on several high islands, and reached their acme in Hawai'i, where the larger ones, constructed along the shore with stone and mud walls, were hundreds of yards long. Typically, fish entered the ponds at high tide through sluices, which were then closed to impound them. In Hawai'i the trapped creatures (including mullet [*Mugilidae*], "sea pig" [*Kuhlia sandvicensis*], eels, shrimp, guppies and occasionally larger species) were sometimes fed with plant food and were reported to have grown in captivity, and even to reproduce—in other words, a case of fish farming. In Hawai'i and a few other places smaller fresh- and brackish-water ponds were also constructed and stocked with fingerlings—the same purpose having been served in some places by wetland patches of taro.

Less widespread but much more bizarre was the practice of "domesticating" eels; the most unusual example of it I have encountered was one observed by the English missionary, Wm. Ellis: "Eels are great favourites, and are tamed, and fed till they attain an enormous size. . . . These pets were kept in large holes, two or three feet deep, partially filled with water. On the sides of these pits, the eels formed or found an aperture in a horizontal direction, in which they generally remained, excepting when called by the person who fed them. I have been several times with the young chief, when he has sat down by the side of the hole, and by giving a shrill sort of whistle has brought out an enormous eel, which has moved about the surface of the water, and eaten with confidence out of his master's hand" (Ellis 1829, 285–86, quoted in Oliver 1974, 286).

Nooses were used in many places and to catch a variety of prey, especially eels. In Hawai'i even sharks were sometimes noosed, after having been stupefied with kava (Buck 1957, 288–89).

Traps. The mechanical devices used by Polynesians for catching and holding marine fauna were nearly as varied as their types of fishnets. In Samoa alone Peter Buck saw six types of them, one of them manipulated by the fishermen, the others self-acting and constructed on the principle of an American lobster pot (i.e., with a funnel-shaped entrance), some of them baited, others unbaited, their shapes and sizes having varied according to intended prey (which included crayfish, crabs, sea eels, small and large fish). In addition, Polynesian fishermen nearly everywhere used traplike containers for holding, and later for "preserving," live marine fauna caught by other means.

Spears. Two basic types of fish spears were in use: a short, usually one-piece one for jabbing (while swimming or walking in shallows) and a long one for throwing (consisting either of one piece or with one or more separate points; Buck saw one with thirty-two attached points, used for throwing into shoals of fish). Spears were thrown either from the shore or from canoes—reportedly with remarkable accuracy by some men, who were usually rewarded with praise (and, presumably, with many fish!) for their skill. One particularly difficult but occasionally very rewarding method was for a spearman to stand on the outer edge of a barrier reef and aim for the large fish brought in by breaking waves. As there was no cord attachment, spearmen had to retrieve their spears by swimming after them.

Evidently, many Polynesians took great delight in long-spear fishing and spent much time practicing to improve their skills—not only for the food obtained but for the pleasure, and verbal rewards, achieved in surpassing one another.

Spearing also took place on moonless nights with the aid of torches (of dried leaves), which served not only to illuminate the fishermen's way but to attract fish to within reach. In some places torch fishing was on occasion a communal, and festive, affair, involving spearing as well as other fishing techniques.

In Samoa bows and arrows were used not only for shooting pigeons (as will be described) but also for shooting fish swimming near the surface. (I have no evidence of such use elsewhere in Polynesia.)

Angling. Fishing with hook and line was engaged in by Polynesians everywhere: by day and night; with or without rods; from shore or canoe; alone or in groups; specialized for one kind of catch or generalized for several; common to both sexes or restricted—by common usage or strict rule—to males. It often entailed long and grueling labor but was usually undertaken with evident enjoyment. And it attested, par excellence, to the Polynesians' success in applying their relatively simple primary tools in exploiting their complex natural environments. Let us begin with an inventory of their hooks.

Simplest of these was the gorge, a short, straight piece of wood or bone sharpened at both ends and attached to the line at the middle. The gorge and line end were held together and parallel, and a bait impaled over both. When the bait was swallowed, the fisherman pulled in the line, thereby releasing the gorge crossways, like a trap, in the fish's gullet. As for true hooks, they were made in a very wide variety of sizes and shapes, and from several materials: wood, bone (including human), shell (both mollusk and turtle) and echidna spine. Some were of a single material—e.g., large wooden hooks for sharks, smaller ones of shell for lagoon fishing. Some consisted of two or more different materials—e.g., wooden shank and bone or shell point, pearlshell shank and turtleshell point. Some were barbed, some barbless. Some were used plain, some with lures or hackles. And as for lines, some were held by hand, others attached to rods. Two examples will indicate the degree of specialization associated with particular types of angling (but scores would be required to describe the full range of Polynesian techniques). The first example is from Hawai'i and involves an individual fishing alone; the second is from Tahiti and involves canoeloads of men. (Although Hawaiians also did other types of fishing in groups, and Tahitians also did other types of fishing individually.)

Beginning with Hawai'i: beyond a reef and down to twenty fathoms an experienced fisherman could explore and fish the bottom visually after spitting onto the surface mouthfuls of chewed, water-clearing kukui nuts. But beyond twenty fathoms, and to depths of four hundred fathoms (twenty-four hundred feet!), he used several baited hooks on the same line, and lowered by stone sinkers). Having found a profitable spot and fixed it mentally by taking cross bearings with prominent landmarks, he would return to it again and again, taking pains to guard its location from other fishermen—except from members of his own family (thereby creating a family heirloom). The secrecy was guarded by leaving for the prized area before morning light. Then, after discerning that all his hooks had been taken, he towed his line to a distant spot before hauling it, in order to deceive possible onlookers.

The second example, from Tahiti, concerns deep-sea dolphin fishing. During the known season for such fishing, canoeloads of men set out early and, upon sighting a hovering flock of fish-eating birds, made for the spot, knowing that their own prey would be nearby. Upon reaching the school they paddled or sailed alongside it as long as they could, meanwhile trolling their lines and making a catch almost as soon as the hooks, consisting of light-sparkling pearlshell shanks, were returned to the water. For such fishing the hooks were barbless, thereby saving the extra time it would have taken to remove the barb from the fish. Some men were skillful enough with rod and line to flick a fish into the canoe from midair and return the hook onto the water without pause. Sometimes a canoe became so overloaded with fish that its crew had to swim alongside in order to return it safely through the waves breaking on reef and shore.[83]

The barbless hooks used in this and some other types of fishing have been characterized as follows: "In one respect the use of all these in-curved or angular native hooks differs from that of ours. When the fisherman using a European hook 'gets a bite,' he strikes to set the point and barb in the fish's mouth. With the native hook, on the other hand, one must never strike; a steady gentle tension is kept on the line and the fish allowed to hook itself. The pull of the line, leading from the inner head of the shank and causing the hook to revolve, sets the point deeper and deeper in the fish's jaw" (Nordhoff 1930a, 156).

The fabrication of some types of fishhooks was an exacting and highly specialized craft. Each type of fishing—even, in some cases, each kind of prey—came to have a distinctive kind of hook: in size, shape and raw material. And although effectiveness in catching prey was in some measure believed to be dependent upon supernatural considerations—e.g., offerings to a protective god—

fine craftsmanship was also recognized as having an influence upon the hook's success. Consequentially, expert craftsmen were usually recompensed for their services, and finely crafted and historically effective hooks kept as valuable family heirlooms.[84]

In addition to the widespread methods and tools of fishing generalized about above, there were some others worth mentioning that were peculiar to one or two places. Easter Islanders made some fishhooks out of (basalt) stone, the only people, except possibly Pitcairn Islanders, who did so. And the Marquesans are reported to have trolled for fish by swimming with a hook and line in tow. And on a larger scale were the Tahitian *tira* method of fishing for albacore and the Samoan practice of catching *palolo*.

Tira-type fishing was unique to Tahiti, where it was used to catch albacore (i.e., "tuna"—large-sized members of the *Scombridae* family of teleost fishes). One of the characteristics of albacore, which were a much favored prey, was to congregate in certain areas called "holes," not depressions in the seabed but places where fry also congregated and provided food for larger fish. There were about a dozen such holes in the waters around Tahiti Island, and they were regularly fished by various methods of angling, including the *tira*, which was designed to catch the larger albacore, i.e., those weighing up to a hundred pounds and more. This method consisted of long and heavy angling rods fixed to canoes at about 45-degree angles; when the intended prey took the hooks the rods were raised to vertical positions by means of pull-ropes, the device having acted as a crane (Oliver 1974, 297–98).

Palolo are the reproductive segments of a sea worm (*nercis*) found in the waters of many Melanesian islands but only of the western ones of Polynesia. At certain invariable times of the year (i.e., during the nights of certain moon phases in the Western-labeled months of October and November) their *palolo* are freed from the adult worm (whose head remains at the bottom of the reef) and wiggle to the surface in vast quantities, where they were scooped up in nets by throngs of people, who cooked them with coconut cream into a highly esteemed savory that could be reserved for months by repeated recooking.

Up to this point the description of Polynesian fishing has been presented in Western—specifically

Anglophonic—terms. The question that now aris-es is, How did the Polynesians themselves "think about" the marine animals they fished for, and the ways they caught them? Published dictionaries (written by Westerners) indicate that they classi-fied—"thought about"—their physical marine environments in categories quite similar to those of English speakers—e.g., as consisting of beach-es, lagoons, fringing reefs, barrier reefs, reef chan-nels, open ocean, etc., while recognizing and label-ing certain other features, such as the albacore "holes" just mentioned, not usually categorized in English. On the other hand, their taxonomy of marine fauna was a far remove from science's Linnaean one. For example, present-day, and per-haps pre-Western, natives of Niutoputapua distin-guish between *ika* ("free-swimming creatures with scales, a head and eyes") and *fingota* ("creeping and crawling creatures without head or eyes"). Since their broad category *ika* contained not only fish (and eels) but also turtles, cetaceans and cephalopods, and *fingota* all the rest, the classifi-cation at this level was clearly un-Linnaean, and incorporated, unlike the Linnaean system, behav-ioral, as distinct from morphological, criteria. But of course, the Niutoputapuans were more con-cerned with catching the creatures than with tax-onomizing them (Kirch and Dye 1979).

The study just excerpted also recorded the amount of catch from each of Niutoputapua's fishing domains—and inferentially the amount of effort applied to each. It concluded that most by far of their fishing took place on the island's fring-ing reef. Moreover, using archaeological data, the authors of this study also concluded that the Niutoputapuans had favored such "inshore" strategies ever since their settlement there during the first millennium B.C., a finding that adds to the evidence, from several other islands, that some of the differences among Polynesian peoples in their fishing activities can be assigned to their differ-ences in marine environments—some, but of course not all.

Throughout Polynesia the availability of marine prey was subject not only to location but in many cases to regular cycles of time as well—to season of year, to phases of moon, to night versus day, even to time of day (and, of course, to more irregular occurrences such as hurricanes). Moreover, knowledge of those regular cycles was everywhere known, and incorporated in the scheduling of each people's fishing. The depth and comprehensiveness of such knowledge is not sur-prising in view of its importance for survival and in view of the many centuries during which suc-cessive generations of the same people had lived in the same narrow areas and had experienced the same cyclic changes.[85] For example, Polynesians everywhere "knew" about the effects that diurnal changes in tide and sunlight had upon the behav-ior of reef- and lagoon-based animals, and sched-uled their fishing accordingly. And those dwelling on high islands also knew to expect that during the rainy season fish would congregate at the mouths of streams, to feed on the animal and plant nutrients flushed seaward by those rains.

Moreover, as noted earlier, the finer cyclic scheduling of fishing was (verbally) recorded and perpetuated in many a society's locally adapted and more or less "official" lunar calendar—a named sequence of nights, from the rising of the new moon until its setting. Here are a few charac-terizations of such "nights" perpetuated by Tahitians (as was recorded in Frank Stimson 1928):

Night One (Tireo). The radiations of the moon have become visible, it (is) a new moon, and the moon rests upon the horizon; the fish have risen, all species of fish; the *iihi* have commenced to run on this night; the method of fishing is with a net, but the opening of the trap-pocket should face the shal-lows; this (is) a night of very many fish.

Night Two (Hiro-hiti). The moon has risen, she has revealed her form; the fish have also come in from the sea, and all species have risen and are mov-ing about; the *manini* run on this night; the method of fishing is with hook and line. This is the night when Hiro [God of thieves] was born.

Night Three (Hoatu). The moon has appeared, thereafter she is visible, and she has shed her light; creatures of the sea propelled by their tails, those having hard shells, and also those that crawl, move about on this night; the method of fishing is with hook and line, and also by torchlight on the deep sea for the *paoe*, the *orare*, the *maunauna*, the *vau*, and the *omuri*. . . .

Night Seventeen (Turu). Beautiful children are conceived on this night; all the sea-creatures having hard shells, the sea-crabs, the spiny sea-shells, the one-sided sea-shells, the *maoa*, and the land-crabs as well, have come together in the act of fecundation;

not on any circumstances go fishing on this night lest you meet disaster from fatigue. . . .

Night Twenty (Ara'au-muri). This (is) a fishless night, nevertheless *iihi* run in great numbers on this night when the months have come when they deposit their spawn; a net (is) the fishing method of this night, the opening of the trap-pocket should still face the shadows.

Social as well as environmental, temporal, and technical factors influenced Polynesian fishing—especially as to who did what kinds.

Most basic of such considerations was gender: in every Polynesian society thus known about there prevailed not just a conventional practice but a rigid rule that prohibited females from engaging in deep-sea fishing. In some places the rule was explicit and direct, in others indirect, and inferable from the prohibition against females' riding in canoes used in deep-sea fishing. Again, in many places females were forbidden by rule, or disinclined for reasons of strength or skill, to engage in certain nonpelagic practices such as octopus catching.

Another socially differentiating aspect of fishing was expertise. Outstanding achievement in any type of fishing—spearing, angling, shark snaring, etc.—was rewarded with praise and over time with enhanced prestige. And expertise in group-sized enterprises—such as communal net sweeps or bonito expeditions—led to an individual's becoming titled as such (e.g., *tau-tai*, expert-sea) and to his consensual selection as leader of such enterprises. Indeed, in some societies his leadership was absolute, superseding the authority of all other participants, including that of the community's headman or a tribe's chief. In Samoa, for example, the saying was "The authority (*au*) of the land does not apply to the sea" (Buck 1930, 518). Moreover, as also pertained to several other kinds of expertise, the attribute, and its title, tended to become hereditary—not necessarily by birthright but because of the likelihood that an expert would have transmitted knowledge and skills to a son or other relative.

In addition to expertise in fishing per se, skills in crafting certain fishing implements—mainly nets and hooks—were rewarded not only with payment for services but with public praise.

In some societies every man, and most women, engaged in some kinds of fishing, but in most of

them some men did so more frequently or productively than the rest—a circumstance that was institutionalized in a few societies in the existence of distinct fishermen guilds. In Tahiti, for example, men of the same tribe or subtribe who specialized in fishing (*feia taia*, persons-who-fished) had their own guildhouse *cum* temple, where they congregated and, among other actions, tendered offerings, of supplication and thanks, to their occupational god.[86] But it was as individuals, not guild members, that some of them engaged in contracts with men specializing in gardening to exchange fish for garden produce.

The sharpest institutionalized delineation of expert fishermen seems to have occurred in the Marquesas. There, such men, called *ava ika*, dwelt in separate, males-only houses, where they slept, cooked and ate, and kept their canoes and fishing gear, and where there were shrines containing images of the members' occupational deities. One account of them states that "Such professionals did not go to war," and adds, "hence they were little honored" (E. S. C. Handy 1923, 164)—a somewhat dubious non sequitur, inasmuch as most fishing in the Marquesas was in unsheltered deep-sea water, and involved not only considerable skill but strength and courage as well.

Another social aspect of fishing had to do with the differential ownership of fishing locations. In some societies all marine locuses—reefs, lagoons, channels, "holes," weirs, open seas, etc.—were open to everyone (at least, to all residents of the adjacent tribal territory). At the other extreme were societies where parts of reef, lagoon, and even open ocean were "owned" by residents of the adjacent dry land, who had to be solicited by outsiders (including tribe mates) for permission to fish there, and paid with part of the latters' catch.

With fishing gear, however, the situation was different. With few exceptions most of the larger pieces of equipment (e.g., multiman open-sea trolling canoes and long seine nets) were owned by some but not every individual or kin unit, and nonowners (including neighbors) paid for their participation in using them by service or parts of catch. In Samoa, e.g., kin units (in this case, "families") held exclusive rights not only over use of certain types of hooks and nets but over the catching of certain varieties of marine fauna as well (Buck 1930, 522).

More complex were the arrangements concerning fishing and tribal chiefs. Throughout most of Polynesia a tribe's chief (or subtribe's subchief) received, by sanctioned tradition, some portion of a subject's catch whatever its kind, and especially if it was larger than that needed by the fisherman's own family. In some societies such transactions constituted chiefly entitlements, i.e., "taxes," in others "gifts," being given more or less voluntarily in order to curry favor or to retain a chief's goodwill. There was, however, still another kind of "ownership" that was also very widespread. It was based on the convention that certain kinds of marine fauna belonged only or mainly to chiefs whoever caught them. In fact, in some societies it was believed to be not only politically risky but supernaturally dangerous for a nonchief to eat the forbidden animal. In most societies in which such conventions prevailed the forbidden animal was the turtle, and in some others, sharks.

Turning to allocations of other kinds of fishing catch, it was in most societies divided, ideally, in three ways: one (usually small) part going to the fisherman's chief, one (usually very small) part going to the fisherman's tutelar household or fishing god, and the rest to the fisherman himself (and his household)—or, in the case of group fishing, to all members of the crew—with the largest share going to the owner of the boat or net. (Note inclusion of the word "ideally"; needless to say all parties to the allocation were not always satisfied with their portions.) In addition to the above, and as noted earlier, in some cases a habitual fisherman gave some of his catch to a habitual gardener in exchange for vegetables—either occasionally or regularly and subject to verbal contract. And finally, quite apart from the widespread rule that certain kinds of marine animals were reserved for chiefs, it was a commonplace in several societies that certain other kinds of them were reserved for males in general.

The aesthetic side of fishing is less easily identified. Some specimens of some types of fishhooks may appear to Westerners to be "beautifully" made, and to some Westerners the synchronous motions of fishing-canoe paddlers may be judged the same—but whether Polynesians perceived them in such terms I cannot discover. No such uncertainty, however, exists about the religious side of fishing.

Fishing, like gardening, was for Polynesians what Handy calls a "consecrated industry" (1927,

282). A human skilled in the activity could of course do what was humanly possible to ensure a successful outcome, but in a universe containing and in part governed by gods, human action alone, however skillful, was never enough. As in producing plant food, Polynesians took several measures to secure beneficial supernatural intervention in fishing; these will be described in the following numbered paragraphs. (Some but not all of the following derives from Handy 1927, 282–96.)

1. Prior supplication of patron gods. Before many if not most fishing events fishermen undertook to secure the favor, or avoid the disfavor, of one or more of the gods associated with the event—e.g., the god of the ocean (who in some places was Tangaroa, in others Ku'ula, etc.); the god of fishing in general (in some places Rata); the patron god of the particular kind of fauna to be fished for; etc. Such supplications ranged from an individual fisherman's adding a prayer-laden rock onto a rock-pile shrine of the relevant god, to an elaborate ceremony (including prayers and offerings) at the sacred precincts of a fishermen's guild preceding a large-sized expedition. Besides supplications for success, persons contemplating a large-sized or especially unpredictable expedition would sometimes be attentive to, or would actively consult, omens concerning the outcome and be guided by their "readings."

In this connection, in some societies (e.g., Tahiti, Marquesas, Hawai'i) some gods associated with fishing in general, or with particular marine fauna, were characteristically embodied in, or could be induced to enter into, certain sacred stones, and as such exercise control over the fishing. Thus, in Tahiti, such a stone could be pointed inland in order to draw the fish shoreward, or, if the stone's human agent desired to frustrate the fishing, pointed seaward to drive the fish out of reach.

2. Prophylactic measures. Special restrictions were often imposed or rites performed to insulate a fishing venture from god-engendered difficulties—e.g., to protect the fishermen, to avoid canoe mishaps, to preserve the catch. Thus, in connection with hazardous, large-sized deep-sea expeditions, it was widespread practice to remove from the fishermen the antisacred profaneness (i.e., *noa*) associated in some societies with females in general and with coitus in particular. In Hawai'i,

e.g., fishermen, with all their gear, spent the night engaging in absolution rites at a fishermen's temple before embarking on such an expedition. And in the Marquesas "[the] tribe as a whole was placed under a consecrational *tapu* requiring silence and cessation of all [sic?] activity, when their fleet of fishing canoes was out, similar to that in wartime and during the great communal rites. Especial *tapu* was imposed upon the wives of the fishers while their men were at sea. They had to fast, to remain within the sleeping house, and to refrain from any casual sexual intercourse" (Handy 1927, 285).

3. Gear preparation. In addition to consecrating and specially empowering the intending fishermen, it was widely believed to be necessary to do the same with their canoes and fishing gear. In many societies that was done at the time when such items were first fabricated, particularly in the case of canoes and large nets, but in some societies it was done with other gear as well.

4. In-progress rites. In some societies supplications were made during fishing expeditions in order, for example, to attract certain kinds of fish, to calm heavy seas, or to summon desirable winds. In most such situations the requests were specifically to those particular gods having jurisdiction over the creatures or weather phenomena under consideration, rather than to gods in general.

5. Terminal rites. After many fishing operations, including most large-sized ones, rites were performed either to discover or remove the causes of failure or to celebrate and offer thanks for success. The usual means of discovering failures was by divination, followed by removal of cause by supplication to the offended god or discontinuation of the divinated cause (e.g., an error in ritual, an omission of offering, some kind of sacrilege—and even, in some cases, elimination of the individual who had committed it). As for celebration of success, that usually included a ceremony of thanks to the responsible god(s), including at least a token share of the catch.

COOKING AND EATING

All Polynesians ate some plant foods raw—including, in one place or another, sweet bananas, the flesh and the spongy embryo of coconuts, the fleshy keys of pandanus, Tahitian chestnuts, native mango, Malay apples, the nuts or berries of several wild plants, certain species of seaweed,

etc.; also, raw sugarcane was chewed for its juice. In addition, here or there several kinds of marine animals (e.g., octopus, crayfish, crabs, shrimp, mussels and several species of fish) were eaten raw, or marinated lightly by dipping in salt water. Indeed, according to Handy, in the Marquesas all fish was eaten uncooked—in (partial) support of which he quotes a passage from Herman Melville that I cannot refrain from adding: "I grieve to state so distressing a fact, but the inhabitants of Typee [a region of Nuku Hiva] were in the habit of devouring fish much in the same way that a civilized being would eat a radish, and without any more previous preparation. They eat it raw; scales, bones, gills, and all the inside. The fish is held by the tail, and the head being introduced into the mouth, the animal disappears with rapidity that would at first nearly lead one to imagine it had been launched bodily down the throat" (quoted in E. S. C. Handy 1923, 197). (Melville seems to have forgotten that "civilized" individuals of his own homeland and era delighted in eating raw oysters, mussels and clams.)

On the other hand, most of the other foods eaten by Polynesians was first cooked; indeed the "origin" of cooking was heralded mythically as having been a major step in the beginnings of humanity's career (Buck 1930, 98–99). Three methods of cooking prevailed. Roasting over an open fire or in hot ashes was resorted to when circumstances demanded—e.g., when traveling or working away from home, when reheating cooked food for a secondary meal or snack. Second, liquid foods were in some places boiled by placing hot stones in wooden-bowl containers (or, very likely, in clay-pot containers before pottery making was discontinued). However, the most common method by far was baking, in earth ovens.

The typical oven, for an average-sized household, was a simple but effective device; it consisted of a rounded pit about one to two feet deep and four to eight feet across. In most cases a household's one or two ovens were permanent installations and were located under thatch-roofed shelters near its sleeping houses. (In some societies most households had two ovens, to accommodate the circumstance that the food of adult males required separate cooking from that of females.) To prepare an oven for baking, layers of firewood and fist-sized rocks were placed in the pit and the wood burned to ash, which usually left the stones "red" hot. (Where available, rocks of basalt were preferred.) In some cases the food to be baked was placed directly onto the heated rocks; more commonly it was protected from scorching by placing it on leaves spread over the rocks. In all cases, however, layers of leaves—sometimes including discarded mats or those plaited especially for ovens—were placed over the food and the whole left to bake. (Variations on this procedure included placing hot rocks over the food as well, and covering the leaf overlay with earth.) In some places a little water was poured onto the covering leaves in order to soften the baking food in steam; elsewhere the food was baked dry and softened only by its own moisture. European observers reported that most food items were sufficiently baked in about two hours' time. Without clocks, of course, precontact Polynesians had no equivalent way of measuring "hours," but seem to have judged correct baking time by comparing it with other food-processing activities that usually accompanied the baking—such as preparing the coconut cream intended to eat with the baked food. In this connection, some foods, mainly meat, were on occasion deliberately undercooked; that occurred when visitors, or participants at a feast, were given portions intended to be taken away and cooked additionally at home. (It was this practice that led some European guests to complain of underdone meat.)

Some foods were partly or completely processed—e.g., cleaned, peeled, scraped, grated, cut up, mashed, blended, etc.—before cooking, others after. The usual implements for such processing included knives of bamboo strips, peelers of wood or shell or bamboo, scrapers of mollusk or coconut shell, graters (usually mounted on seat supports), pounders of stone or wood, strainers and wringers of shredded plant fiber, wooden adzes for splitting breadfruit, stirrers of coconut-leaf midribs, bowls of wood or stone, etc. Some implements were austerely functional, others shaped or decorated in locally pleasing ways (fig. 11.6).

We turn next to the topic of culinary plant-food recipes, which, however, can be only touched on here because of their extraordinary number and variety.

Leaving aside the plant-food recipes of the Hawaiians or Tahitians or Samoans (whose large and topographically complex islands produced a very wide variety of edible plants, from which their natives concocted a correspondingly large number of food recipes), consider, for example, those of the Tikopians, whose one island, though "high" (i.e., mountainous) was only about four-and-one-half square miles in area. Nevertheless, the thirteen hundred or so Tikopians (in 1929, the date of Firth's study there) were able to concoct—and eat—some thirty-three different recipes out of plant foods alone (i.e., in addition to several combining plant foods with fish or bird flesh—but not pork).[87]

Compared even with Tikopia's, however, the atoll environment of Tongareva provided a very limited range of edible plant foods, namely, coconuts and pandanus. Nevertheless, consider how the Tongarevans had adapted to that limitation in terms of their culinary practices.

Beginning with the coconut palm, they distinguished and named eleven stages in its (uninterrupted) growth, from its fertilized flower to its putting forth of roots and leaves—i.e., its readiness for replanting. They also distinguished thirteen stages in the growth of the nut itself, its later stages having been identified by shaking the nut and listening to the sound of its fluid, if any. The fluid of the nut was drunk at stages 3 through 7; because of the paucity of fresh water on the atoll, coconut fluid was the people's principal beverage. The nut's flesh was eaten raw at stages 4 through 11, or used in eight different cooked dishes from stage 6 through 11. In addition, the developing husk (stages 3 through 5) was chewed for its sweet liquid, or was mixed with the nut's flesh in a cooked recipe. Even the nut's dry spongy embryo (uto) was eaten raw or mixed and cooked with grated nut flesh or flesh cream or liquid. According to Buck: "No term is used to indicate the fruit [i.e., the nut] in general. The different stages [of its growth] have become so distinct that a general term is not only vague but useless. If a European should ask for a "coconut" the word would convey no meaning to the Tongarevan, for the Tongarevan associates directly the name for the kind of nut and its uses" (1932, 111).

One of the most important of the Tongarevans' culinary items was roro, the oily liquid expressed from the grated flesh of the nut at its mature, sakari, stage and used either as a raw drink or purgative or in combination with other cooked foods. In Tongareva—whose residents knew

11.6. Hawaiian food implements and utensils

about kava but were unable to grow it—*roro* took its place. An indication of its cultural import is indicated by the following song, supposedly sung by a male appealing for some female to extract *roro* for him: "Oh *roro* for me / that I may drink / and so be satisfied./ I grow fatigued / but my strength will return through the *roro*."

The edible part of the pineapple-shaped pandanus fruit—i.e., its separable drupes, or "keys"—was treated with almost as much attention, in terminology and in diet, as the coconut (details of which will, however, not be summarized here). Indeed, for most readers the details per se of the foregoing description about Tongarevans' uses of coconuts are superfluous. What is, however, worth knowing is that these atoll dwellers had developed a viable, complex, and evidently satisfying existence while adjusting to a physical environment that was extremely deficient in edible plants. Nor is there evidence that the Tongarevans lived shorter or sicklier or more toilsome lives than, say, the resource-rich Samoans or Tahitians or Hawaiians—except when hurricanes denutted their palms. Moreover, while their numbers were fewer, their social institutions less complex, their buildings less diverse and elaborate, etc., than those of many other Polynesian peoples, they succeeded in maintaining a core of distinctively "Polynesian" beliefs and practices and were, seemingly, as "happy" as those elsewhere. Now to leave off evaluating and return to "facts."

Throughout most of tropical Polynesia main meals, in contrast to secondary meals and "snacks," consisted of a base food—a starchy plant staple or plant-staple pudding—along with a savory supplement (e.g., fish, morsel of meat, taro leaves, seaweed). Most "puddings" were composed of a grated or mashed starchy plant food along with coconut cream or oil—sometimes combined before and sometimes after cooking. However, that summary statement does not begin to describe the numerous varieties of their meals—in terms of menus and recipes. In fact, one could fill pages with such descriptions; hopefully, however, enough has been stated to indicate that the ingenuity of the Polynesians was not limited to, say, seamanship and fishing—which leads into consideration of how, and how much, they ate.

With very few exceptions persons past infancy ate with their fingers—exceptions occurring when they used a pointed stick to handle a painfully hot morsel, or when by custom they were restricted from feeding themselves (e.g., when in some societies persons of very high rank were in official mourning). In some societies all members of a household ate out of a common receptacle or from a common heap placed on a "tablecloth" of broad leaves; in others the food was parceled out into individual baskets or plates of leaves; and in others males and females ate entirely separately and from separate ovens and containers.

The most graphic accounts I know of concerning how as well as how much some Polynesians ate were recorded by members of Captain Cook's expedition during their visit to Tahiti in 1769, the first by Joseph Banks, an upper-class Englishman who was himself a gourmet. (The following excerpt is lengthy but deservedly so, because of the importance of the topic in any comprehensive and balanced description of how Polynesians lived.)

> I will describe the manner in which one of their principal people is servd; they commonly eat alone unless some stranger makes a second in their mess. He setts commonly under the shade of the next tree or on the shady side of the house; a large quantity of leaves either of Bread fruit or Banana are neatly spread before him which serves instead of a table cloth, a basket is then set by him which contains his provisions and two cocoa nut shells, one full of fresh water the other of salt [water]. He begins by washing his hands and mouth thoroughly with the fresh water which he repeats almost continually throughout the whole meal. He then takes part of his provision from the basket. Supose (as it often did) it consisted of 2 or 3 bread fruits 1 or 2 small fish about as big as a perch in England, 14 or 15 ripe bananas or half as many apples [probably the native mango, *Spondias dulcis*]; he takes half a breadfruit, peels of[f] the rind and takes out the core with his nails; he then cramms his mouth as full with it as it can possibly hold, and while he chews that unlapps [i.e., unwrapps] the fish from the leaves in which they remain tied up since they were dressd [cooked] and breaks one of them into the salt water; the rest as well as the remains of the bread fruit lay before him upon the leaves. He generaly gives a fish or part of one to some one of his dependents, many of whom set round him, and then takes up a very small peice of that that he has broke into

the salt water in the ends of all the fingers of one hand and sucks it into his mouth to get with it as much salt water as possible, every now and then taking a small sup of it either out of the palm of his hand or the cocoa nut shell. In the mean time one of the standers by has prepard a young cocoa nut by peeling of[f] the outer rind with his teeth . . . which when he chuses to drink he takes from him and boring a hole through the shell with his finger or breaking the nut with a stone drinks or sucks out the water. When he has eat his bread fruit and fish he begins with his plantains, one of which makes no more than a mouthful if they are as big as black puddings; if he has apples a shell is necessary to peel them, one is pickd of[f] the ground where they are always plenty and tossd to him, with this he scrapes or cutts off the skin rather awkwardly as he wastes almost half the apple in doing it. If he has any tough kind of meat instead of fish he must have a knife, for which purpose a peice of Bamboo is tossd him of which he in a moment makes one by splitting it transversely with his nail, with which he can cut tough meat or tendons as least as readily as we can with a common knife. All this time one of his people has been employd with a stone pestle and a block of wood beating breadfruit by much beating and sprinkling with water he Reduces to the consistence of soft paste; he then takes a vessel made like a butchers tray and in it he lays his paste mixing it with either bananas sour paste or making it up alone according to the taste of his master; to this he adds water pouring it on by degrees and squeezing it often through his hand till it comes to the consistence of thick custard; a large cocoa nut shell full of this he then sets before his master who supps it down as we would do a custard if we had not a spoon to eat it with; and his dinner is then finishd by washing his hands and mouth, cleaning the cocoa nut shells and putting any thing that may be left into the basket again.

It may be thought that I have given rather too large a quantity of provision to my eater when I say he has eat 3 bread fruits each bigger than two fists, 2 or 3 fish and 14 or 15 plantains or Bananas, each if they are large 6 or 7 inches long and 4 or 5 round, and conclude his dinner with about a quart of a food as substantial as the thickest unbaked custard; but this I do affirm that it is but few of the many of them I was acquainted with that eat less and many a great deal more. (in Beaglehole 1962, I: 346–47, as quoted in Oliver 1974)

The spectacle just depicted was exceptional enough to have caught the attention of European observers; it is unlikely that all Tahitians, or even all upper-class Tahitians, regularly ate as voraciously as that. Nevertheless, Tahitians were inclined to put away large quantities of food when it was available—as, for example, during the height of the year's most plentiful breadfruit season (an adjustment, perhaps, to seasons of breadfruit scarcity). In any case, rotundity was looked upon with approval, and—as will be described—fattening was undertaken deliberately to beautify young females and males. This is all very well for Tahiti, with its usually plentiful food resources. Similar appetites and practices seem to have prevailed in some other Polynesian societies—or at least among the upper classes of those having access to plentiful supplies of food. But what about those peoples less well-provided?

It might be supposed that an atoll, such for example as Pukapuka, with fewer kinds and quantities of plant foods than most high islands, and with no domesticated animals, would not provide enough comestibles to encourage gourmandizing. In fact, however, the Pukapukans seem to have admired rotundity as much as did the Tahitians and, like the latter, engaged in practices designed to make young females and males "fat and fair"—and thus more desirable as spouses (Beaglehole and Beaglehole 1938, 282). Such attitudes, there and elsewhere in Polynesia, could be interpreted in part as fortification against the hunger that many of them experienced from time to time—due to shortages caused by weather or warfare, or to fasting prescribed by religious regulation or chiefly fiat—but only in part. For the Polynesians, as for many other peoples elsewhere, eating was evidently one of life's greatest pleasures, and was unconstrained by rules regarding a nutritionally "balanced diet."

In this connection, I sample again the ethnographic sagacity of Raymond Firth, whose statement about Tikopian eating habits can be applied to Polynesia as a whole: "In a civilized environment one is apt to look upon a meal as an interval in the real business of life: a pleasant social relaxation, a gastronomic indulgence or a conventional interruption for bodily refuelling. In . . . Tikopia [on the other hand] it is the main daily business in itself. To this the work of the fore part of the day leads up, and after it is over, the time of recreation has come. People in this island community do not arrive home to snatch a meal and return to work; the attainment of the meal itself is the fulfillment of their work" (1957b, 53).

In addition to several kinds of temporary abstentions—e.g., fasting during some religious rites, the banning of coconut eating in preparation for a feast, the prohibition of eating certain seasonal harvests until the relevant chief or god had eaten (i.e., "First Fruits")—some foods were permanently denied to, or reserved for, persons according to gender or social rank. The prohibitions varied somewhat from one society to another but included, very widely, the reservation of turtle flesh for chiefs and the denial of pork to females.

In some societies certain forms of kinship also played a part in limiting what one could eat—specifically, which pairs or sets of kinfolk could not eat food baked in the same oven, or eat in one another's presence. And with respect to the latter, the conventions concerning who ate with whom were numerous.

As later chapters will indicate, food played an important part in many other social-relational contexts as well: e.g., in initiating or cementing relationships, in celebrating life-cycle events, in paying for services and in acknowledging servitude. Moreover, gods were worshiped not only with verbal praise but with offerings of food—or at least small tokens or essences thereof. Several of the staple food plants were hallowed in myths, were symbolically regenerated in elaborate ceremonies, and were in some societies associated with specific social units. Moreover, the gods who were credited with creating or were otherwise associated with one or another food or food-producing activity (such as fishing or taro growing) were among a people's most revered and actively worshiped.

Finally, it would be worthwhile to know what effects Polynesians' eating habits had upon their health and energies—worthwhile but no longer possible to reconstruct. In the first place, the contents of diets differed too widely from society to society to permit areawide generalizations on the matter. And second, too little is or can be learned about the actual relationships between any particular people's average diet and their state of health. With the use of hindsight it can now be stated that certain peoples' attachment to corpulence, and the excessive consumption of certain foods, were "unhealthful"—but at this late date I suspect that it would be impossible to establish, for example, what certain known eating habits contributed, specifically, to the (fairly well proven) short life spans of most tropical Polynesians.

KAVA AND BETELNUT

Kava (or its cognates *kawa, 'ava, 'awa*) is the Polynesian name for a shrubby species of pepper plant, *Piper methysticum,* and for the beverage made of an infusion of its root with water. The plant also grew—still grows—in several other Pacific islands; in Polynesia it grew everywhere except on a few thin-soiled atolls and on those high islands lacking year-round tropical temperatures (i.e., Easter Island, Rapa, New Zealand and Chatham Islands). On some Polynesian islands it grew wild, but those plants used for the beverage were usually cultivated—in some places very carefully cultivated. Thus, in Tahiti one of Cook's associates described it, along with the barkcloth plant, Chinese mulberry, as "almost the only [cultivated plants] to which they seem to pay attention; and these they keep very clean" (Anderson, in Cook 1784, 145, quoted in Oliver 1974, 256). And the captain of the missionary ship *Duff* wrote: "Here [near a dwelling] I thought I got a sight of an European garden; the plats of ava-ground were laid out in such nice order: each bed formed regular parallelograms, trenched two feet deep, and disposed with a great deal of taste; the whole enclosed with a fence of bamboo" (Wilson 1799, 193).

The beverage was made by pulverizing the plant's root and soaking it in water. The resulting somewhat cloudy liquid tasted (as one present-day Westerner put it) "like the smell of a cedar lead pencil when it is sharpened." The drug contained in the root produces soporific and euphoric effects and seems to be more potent in fresh green roots than in older dried ones—i.e., in many cases roots were kept, sometimes for weeks, after harvesting, to be used on subsequent occasions, or to serve as gifts or taxes. The potency may also have been increased by the saliva added by chewing. Melville provides a graphic picture of kava preparation in the Marquesas: "Some half-dozen young boys seated themselves in a circle around an empty wooden vessel, each of them being supplied with a certain quantity of the roots of the 'arva' ['ava]

11.7. Poulaho, King of the Friendly Islands (Tonga) and his subjects drinking kava

11.8. Kava plant

11.9. Tongan kava bowl

broken into small bits and laid by his side. A cocoa-nut goblet of water was passed around the juvenile company, who, rinsing their mouths with its content, proceeded to the business before them. This merely consisted in thoroughly masticating the 'arva,' and throwing it mouthful by mouthful into the receptacle provided. When a sufficient quantity had been obtained water was poured upon the mass . . ." (194–95). (Elsewhere in Polynesia the masticating was done not by "young boys" but by young females or older males. The process was evidently jaw-straining and cannot have been pleasurable.)[88]

After the root had been pulverized it was, as Melville stated, soaked in a bowl of water, into which were dissolved its narcotic elements, the remaining root fibers having been removed by straining.

The Polynesian form of the concoction is only mildly narcotic. Nevertheless, "large" amounts of it—how "large" is not reliably reported—are said to reduce food appetite and to induce sleep and some paresis of the lower limbs. Early Western visitors recorded seeing individuals suffering from undernourishment and scaly skin as a result of "overdose"—a condition that appears to have been readily cured by a few weeks of abstention and return to customary diets.

With a few exceptions the uses of kava differed significantly between western islands (e.g., Tonga, Samoa, East Uvea, East Futuna) and those in the east (e.g., Hawai'i, Marquesas, Tahiti, Rarotonga, Mangaia, Aitutaki). In the former its preparation and imbibing were usually done communally and ceremoniously, and mostly for social or ceremonial purposes. In eastern societies, however, the concoction was often made and imbibed individually, with little or no ceremony, and for a variety of purposes, including alleviating ordinary thirst and fatigue, medicating, inducing trance (by a psychic) and satisfying personal addiction. And in both east and west the concoction was used for greeting guests, for formalizing agreements and as libations to gods. Also, in some places dried roots of the plant served as gifts or taxes. And finally, it must be added that its imbibing was everywhere limited in one way or another—e.g., in some societies to persons of high social status (mostly where the supply was limited), and to males nearly everywhere.

The custom of betel nut chewing was—still

is—very widespread, throughout much of South and Southeast Asia and on into Melanesia and western Micronesia. In Polynesia it was practiced only in a few of the western Outliers—i.e., those subject to influence from Melanesia. The nut is that of the palm *Areca catechu*, which when ripe is about the size of a large cherry, is hot and acrid in taste, aromatic and astringent (Burton-Bradley 1972, 66). Among Polynesian users the nut, along with some lime (obtained by burning coral) was wrapped in a leaf of the betel vine (*Piper betle*, a member, like the kava plant, of the pepper family), and chewed. Or, in the case of individuals with fewer teeth, the ingredients were first ground together in a wooden mortar. Working together the three ingredients irritated the mouth's mucous membrane, thereby producing a local sensation that experienced users (including some visiting anthropologists!) found pleasurable—the nicotine-like properties of the nut having been responsible for the euphoria, which one writer characterized as "a feeling of well-being good humour, and an increased capacity for work." In Tikopia, especially, betel-chewing was a sociable activity—quite literally, inasmuch as wads of it were sometimes shared—for both men and women, having been engaged in when meeting together unceremoniously or after completing some cooperative action.

Finally, the pleasures and hazards of tobacco use—an American Indian gift to civilization—were unknown to Polynesians until introduced by Westerners, but, like alcohol, tobacco use was received with gratification and was widely and swiftly adopted.

CANNIBALISM

Accounts of cannibalism among tropical Polynesians range from eyewitness reports by credible Western observers to sporadic references in myths and legends—or, even less verifiable, to one people's disparaging characterization of another—for contact-era Polynesians quickly learned, and parroted, Westerners' disgust for the practice. Sifting through the numerous bits of "evidence" leads me to classify (some) Polynesians peoples' cannibalistic practices into four kinds of function: commemorative, assimilative, punitive and alimentary.[89] Commemorative cannibalism consisted of eating some token part of a corpse, usually that of a close relative. Assimilative consisted of eating, or pretending to eat, part of a corpse (e.g., an eyeball) in order to acquire one or another of his (very seldom, her) characteristics, such as strength or specialized knowledge. Punitive consisted of inflicting revenge upon the corpse of an enemy or his kinfolk or tribal mates by means of what was regarded as a quintessential expression of contempt, and expressed, in some cases, a personal act of bravado. And alimentary cannibalism consisted of eating for eating's sake—i.e., because one likes the taste of human flesh, or is hungry enough to eat anything edible. There was also an element of sacrifice in some forms of cannibalism—i.e., of sharing the subject with some god.

It should be noted at the outset that for some Polynesian peoples (e.g., of Tongareva, Kapingamarangi, Pukapuka, Tikopia) there is no record of any precontact cannibalism. Assuming such to have been true, one proposed explanation for its absence is that there were in such places plentiful enough supplies of comparable foods—which, however, was certainly not the case in Tongareva and Pukapuka—nor in Tikopia (even after its residents' purposeful extinction of their pigs). Another possible reason for the absences is that such peoples were so harmoniously peaceful that eating, or even killing, one another could not have occurred—a situation that certainly did not prevail on Tikopia, and probably not on Pukapuka. Moreover, even where grounds for eating humans because of hunger or revenge did not exist there remained the possibility of doing so for magical reasons of "assimilation." In any case, I gladly leave such speculating to those scholars who have nothing better to do.

Turning to positive reports of cannibalism, the best-documented instances of its assimilative variety occurred in Tahiti and Hawai'i, where in fact that seems to have been the only variety practiced. Both of these peoples were accustomed to killing one another—in warfare, in private feuds, and in executing infringers of religious codes and political wills. Also, many of those killed were used as offerings to gods—as well as were some that were killed solely or mainly for that purpose. However, the only part of any such victims that was actually—or in some instances, symbolically—swallowed was an eyeball. Moreover, the customary reason for doing that seems to have been assimilative—although in some cases other purposes may also have been involved (such as, for example,

religious offering or symbolic revenge). In this connection, in both Hawai'i and Tahiti the rest of the corpses of most enemies slain in warfare were left to decompose, either where they fell or at some temple site.

In some other societies, such as East Uvea, whole bodies were eaten, and were killed specifically and exclusively for alimentary purposes, but (as recorded in legends) only a few chiefly individuals engaged in the practice.

In still other societies, such as the Marquesas, where cannibalism seems to have occurred frequently and was well institutionalized, it was practiced in warfare both for revenge and as a means of enjoying a highly favored food—many instances of the former also serving as token offerings to cooperative patron gods.

Another high point of cannibalism was reached in Mangareva, where it occurred frequently and was mainly alimentary in purpose—the result, according to Buck, of commoners' hunger resulting from the island's meager supply of plant food and the chiefs' tyrannical control over it. And, Buck goes on to state, "Fugitives and refugees from a defeated group were fair game . . . and even corpses [of fellow tribesmen?] were sometimes stolen for food" (1938, 196). There were, however, limits to the practice even there: human flesh was forbidden to females; some people "showed repugnance to eating their own relatives"; and "it was considered a disgrace to be eaten" (Ibid.).

Whole-body cannibalism was also practiced in some of the Cook Islands, but "usually after battles when the victors utilized their slain enemies" (Buck 1944, 16). Also in the Cook Islands there were individuals addicted to human flesh. Such human ogres, according to Buck, lived apart and preyed on women and children, and were popularly detested and eventually killed by relatives of their victims.[90]

In Samoa (again according to Buck) cannibalism was practiced in an "earlier period," as evidenced in their "traditional narratives," but was subsequently discontinued—there having been "no lack of different kinds of flesh foods to give them variety in their diet" (1930, 127). One turning point was reached—at least legendarily—when a powerful chief unwittingly ate one of his own sons! Buck also reports that during that "earlier period" it was customary for a lesser chief to offer himself as an edible offering to his superior as an apology for some act of *lèse majesté* (Ibid.).

Turning finally to Tonga, it was stated by a seaman, Wm. Mariner, who was marooned there from 1806 to 1810: "There can be no doubt as to the existence of cannibalism in these islands in former days. It never became so prevalent as it once was in New Zealand, nor so truly atrocious in its character, as it now is, or has been in very recent years, in the islands of Fiji. It was customary, however, in times of war" (Mariner 1817). Tongan legends also refer to instances of cannibalism practiced for alimentary reasons alone—the perpetrators (who were the consumers) having been powerful chiefs (Gifford 1929, 227–29).

Regarding Polynesia as a whole, the eminent ethnologist E. S. C. Handy conjectured that "The original motives at the basis of [cannibalism] were first revenge; and second, . . . ceremonial practices" (1927, 267–68). In the present climate of anthropological scholarship this kind of speculation is very unfashionable, but in my opinion there is some plausibility in Handy's conjecture—along with the possibility that starving crewmen on drifting canoe voyages or desperate pioneer settlers on barren shores might well have eaten one of their number in order to remain alive, thereby proving to themselves (and perhaps to their descendants, if any) that human flesh was indeed edible. This is not to say that cannibalism was reinvented by Polynesians—the routes taken by their Lapita forebears, through Melanesia, were peopled here and there by communities in which man-eating was customary and probably very old. (For further information on Melanesian cannibalism see Oliver 1989b, 315–20.)

12

BUILDINGS

The kinds of buildings constructed by tropical Polynesians ranged from chicken pens to pyramids, from makeshift shelters to generation-bridging dwellings, and included specialized ones for working, for governing, for recreation and for worshiping. This chapter will concern the architectural aspects of those buildings, leaving for later chapters discussion of their use. I begin with "domestic" buildings—i.e., those associated with households.

DOMESTIC BUILDINGS

As will be amplified in chapter 18, the basic residential social unit of all Polynesian peoples was the household, a type of group that ranged in composition from one married couple and their own or adopted offspring to a large three-generation extended family plus one or more other relatives—and in a few cases, nonkin servants. (Exceptionally, some households were composed of only one married couple or one widowed individual, but in most places such persons were accommodated in larger households.) Unlike in some other Pacific Island societies, where all the older males of an entire community ate, lounged and occasionally slept together in a separate and usually male-only building, it was customary in most Polynesian societies for all males to eat, sleep and spend much of their waking hours within the areal borders of their household compounds. (In Hawai'i each cluster of closely interrelated households contained a male-only building where males past childhood lounged and ate, but even they usually spent their nights in the sleeping-house of their own household.)

Again, unlike in some other Pacific Island societies, where all of a household's activities took place in a single building, those of tropical Polynesia took place in two or more, always including one for sleeping and a separate one for cooking, and sometimes one or more additional ones designed for working or for storing goods or worshiping the household's tutelar god(s). There were, however, differences both between and within Polynesian societies in this respect. Even in those typified by a two-building pattern (i.e., one for sleeping and one for cooking) it was usual for the households of influential or affluent families to have one or more additional buildings (including, in some places, one for receiving guests).

Beginning this survey with the ubiquitous sleeping-house, it was in some societies literally only that, but in some others it served other purposes as well—e.g., eating (but almost never cooking), craft-type working (e.g., making mats) and storage, there having been several differences between societies in this respect. At one architectural extreme were the sleeping-houses of Easter Island, described as having been ten to fifteen yards long and one-and-one-half to two yards wide, with standing room only in the center and a small crawl-sized doorway (which was its only source of daylight). Georg Forster, a naturalist on Cook's second voyage, wrote of them: "We crept in [through the doorway] on all fours and found the inside of the hut perfectly nakid and empty, there being not so much as a wisp of straw to lie down upon. We could not stand upright in any part except in the middle, and the whole place appeared dark and dismal. The natives told us they passed the night in these huts, and we easily conceived their situation to be uncomfortable, especially as we saw so very few [sleeping huts] that they must be crammed full, unless the generality of the people lie in open air, and leave these wretched dwellings to chiefs, or make use of them only in bad weather" (quoted in Métraux 1971, 199). (In extenuation it should be added that Easter Island is seasonally colder than most other tropical Polynesian islands, and that there was very little vegetation there suitable for house frames.)

Tahiti

Tuamotu

Hawai‘i

Tonga

Samoa

12.1. Dwelling house types of tropical Polynesia

At the other end of this range was the average sleeping house of Samoa—where, it should be added, the climate was tropically warm year-round and where there were large quantities and varieties of excellent house-building vegetation. Most Samoan houses were erected on mounds and floored with rubble and mats. They were also much larger, broader and higher ceilinged than those of Easter Island—spacious enough to contain separate sections (but not separate rooms) for sleeping and for sitting. Moreover, they were completely open-sided—thereby admitting light and cooling breezes—but closable with movable shutters to provide occasional privacy and protection from driving rain. Also, in contrast with the simplicity, even crudeness, of construction of the average Easter Island sleeping-house their Samoan counterparts were architecturally complex and, in many cases, of superbly delicate craftsmanship—especially in the use of sennit for binding joints and for attaching thatch.

In some other societies people sometimes slept in rock shelters or caves (including lava tubes)—e.g., when traveling, or fishing far from home, or escaping from enemies—but the typical sleeping-house was everywhere made mostly of parts of plants and in architectural patterns now to be summarized.

The most widespread, and perhaps the oldest, type of sleeping-house was rectangular in floor pattern and had a longitudinally ridged straight-sided roof—or in a few cases a slightly curved roof, so shaped by adding a row of secondary, more pliable, rafters onto purlins or chocks attached to the main rafters or onto rafters bowed outward by collar beams and attached to what in English is called the "king" post above a tie beam. Within this general pattern there were several subtypes. In some cases the roof reached to the ground, thereby forming sloping sides; in all other cases the rafters ended aboveground and rested on a wall plate supported by wall posts, or in a few cases, by a stone wall. In some houses the walls were left open or were closable with movable shutters; in others with this type of roof the wall space under the eaves was closed off with either thatch or wooden stakes. Treatment of the ends of rectangular sleeping-houses also differed from society to society. In some, both ends were left completely open, in some others completely closed—usually with thatch, and in still others thatched from the top only partway.

Each of these features had both advantages and disadvantages. A roof that sloped all the way to the ground was advantageous in locations subject to high winds and, when associated with fully closed house ends, helped to keep out chilly night air. On the other hand, such interiors, as on Easter Island, were gloomy in the day and doubtless stuffy at night (especially when full of people). Also, in houses with a ground-ending roof, little or no use could be made of the low-roofed floor space bordering the sides. In contrast, the open-sided houses, such as those of Samoa, were well suited to that area's year-round tropical temperatures, but had to be manually shuttered against driving rains—or to provide the privacy that was sometimes wanted. (I have not had the experience of residing in a Samoan village, but imagine that a house shuttered during a bright rainless day might have provoked unwanted salacious or suspicious comment from neighbors. It certainly would have done so with the Tahitians among whom I lived!)

Generalizing from the above: It seems fairly certain that many of those architectural variables had come about as a result of a people's deliberate adjustment to current local circumstances—a conscious weighing of advantages versus disadvantages of particular features. However, it is just as likely that age-old traditions, including ones no longer advantageous, also figured in architectural plans of sleeping-houses.

Continuing consideration of the most widely prevalent, rectangular, house: two different methods were employed to support its upper ridgepole. One was by use of a post reaching from ground to ridgepole; the other was by use of a forementioned "king" post supported by a transverse tie beam that was itself supported on posts. The advantage of the latter consisted of its having freed a house's ends, when open, of obstructive middle posts.

Still another kind of variation in the plan of rectangular houses—and indeed of all other houselike buildings—lay in their methods of roofing. All of them were covered with thatch—of which, however, there were two kinds. One consisted of branches of long-fiber grass or grasslike materials, the other of plates made by combining broader leaves (e.g. of coconut or pandanus). In some places the choice between the two was evidently based on availability, in others on current practicability—i.e., in terms of durability or rainproofing; although here again "tradition," includ-

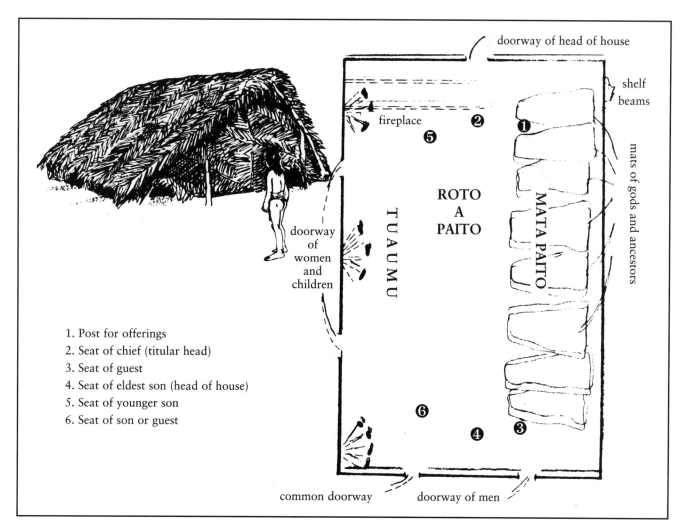

1. Post for offerings
2. Seat of chief (titular head)
3. Seat of guest
4. Seat of eldest son (head of house)
5. Seat of younger son
6. Seat of son or guest

12.2. Tikopian dwelling house, outside and inside

ing features no longer practicable, doubtless played a part.

Another variation in roofing technique had to do with ways of attaching the thatch. The simple way was by attaching it directly to the main rafters; the more complex, and possibly more durable, way was by attaching it to secondary, outer, rafters, which were fastened onto purlins affixed over the main rafters.

Nearly as widespread as the rectangular-floored type of sleeping-house were those with one or both ends rounded. In some of those the rafters stretched, either straight or curved, from house ridge to ground; in others they rested upon a curved wall plate, usually coincident with those of the side walls. Unlike some straight-line house ends, the curve-end rafters were always closed in, with thatch or latticework, at least partway to the ground.

Speaking of which, in most places all sleeping-houses were built directly on the ground, either unaltered or purposely raised. Anyone familiar with house architecture in Melanesia might be struck with the uncommonness in Polynesia of houses built on poles aboveground. The reasons for that were doubtless varied; the only reported one known to me pertains to the Marquesas, where such types of sleeping-houses were specifically disfavored on account of the taboo against a person being directly over another person's head.

Continuing with Polynesia's predominant (ground-level) sleeping-houses, in some places, where available or desirable land was sloping or otherwise uneven, level foundations were constructed with earth or stones or combinations of the two. And in still other places—especially, e.g., in Samoa—many houses were built on artificial mounds even where the underlying land was flat,

12.3. A view of Hawai'i, showing a priest's house

12.4. Round-ended dwelling house of Tongatabu

one or both of two purposes having been thereby served: to avoid flooding by rainwater or abnormally high tides, and to symbolize the importance of the occupants, or their forebears, by this highly visible and permanent evidence of their ability to mobilize mound-building labor. Also, in addition to such practical or political reasons for building houses on mounds, there were in some places social-architectural reasons as well. Such was the case in Mangareva and the Marquesas, where a house occupied only about one half of its mound, the other half having served as a broad porch, where the occupants often sat and where guests were received.

A wholly different sleeping-house pattern prevailed in a few places, mainly in those lacking trees large or abundant enough for building the types described above. The frame of such a house has been characterized as looking like an upturned boat with upward-pointing keel. On Easter Island, where they were most prevalent, the frame of one of them was described by an eighteenth-century visitor as follows:

> The rafters were slender poles fixed at their lower ends in the holes of the stone curbs. They were bent over and crossed at their upper ends with the opposite rafters, being lashed to the ridgepole structure. . . . The Middlemost rafters were the highest. . . . The other rafters gradually diminished in length, those at the ends of the house being hardly 2 feet high . . . . The [lengths of wood composing] the ridgepole were supported by ridge posts fixed in the ground [or into curbstones] at intervals of [several] feet. The need for ridgeposts is explainable only if we remember that, owing to the scarcity of wood, the rafters must have been of poor quality. . . . The rafters were connected by purlins reaching along the whole length [of the frame]. They gave strength to the whole structure and supported the thatching. (quoted and paraphrased in Métraux 1971, 196–97)

Concerning that thatch, another early visitor to Easter Island wrote: "The interstices [between rafters and purlins], which are all of oblong shape, are closed up and covered over with a sort of rush or long grass, which they put on very thickly, layer upon layer, and fasten on the inner side with lashing [?] . . . so that they are always as well shut in against wind and rain as those who live beneath thatched roofs in Holland" (Jacob Roggeveen, as

quoted in Metraux 1971, 197). And as noted earlier, the doors of such houses were only large enough to permit entry by crawling (which might be viewed not only as a means of reducing cold outer air but also as a protection against unwanted visitors). And finally, the frames of such houses were evidently rigid enough to permit the whole structure to be moved—for example, in case of war.

Turning next to the interiors of sleeping-houses, most of their floors—whether of dirt or rock or coral rubble—were carpeted with either dried leaves or mats, or both. In some of the larger ones the central areas were reserved for sleeping and were raised from the floor level by earthen platforms or piles of mats, or both. Artificial lighting was provided in most of them by small fires or by lamps of coconut oil or candlenut. Otherwise, sleeping-house furniture was scarce, having usually consisted only of sleeping mats, a few seats (of wood or stone) (fig. 12.5), and neck-rests of wood or bamboo (fig. 12.6). Most houses did, however, provide storage for food (usually protected from rats by baffles) and for tools and other implements and weapons. In some places sleeping-houses also contained small shrines for family god(s), and in

12.5. Rarotongan stool

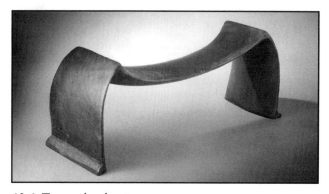

12.6. Tongan head rest

some of them small fireplaces for cooking modest meals—most cooking having been done in separate buildings—to which we now turn.

Virtually every household establishment contained one or more separate buildings—kitchens—for cooking its members' food. (Those with two or more kitchens were found in societies, or segments of societies, that discouraged, or in some cases proscribed, men and women eating jointly cooked food.) The architecture of cooking houses varied widely, both between and within societies. At one extreme were crude lean-to sheds, at the other partially walled houses that resembled their associated sleeping-houses in nearly everything but size. However, they were all alike in having an earth oven either inside or just outside the house. And most of them contained arrangements for storing both cooked and uncooked food.

Another kind of household-associated structure found in several societies was sheds, where the owners' canoes were housed and where household members (usually only older males) lounged and worked (i.e., fabricating things by hand). Most work sheds were open-sided and when used to house canoes were located as near as possible to the shore. In a few societies—notably Hawai'i—some of the same functions (except canoe making) were served by a house (in Hawai'i called *mua*, "in-front-of"), reserved for the household's males past early childhood, where they not only lounged and worked but often ate as well.

Still another kind of building found in some societies, and associated there with the more affluent households, has been labeled "guest houses"—places where (usually male) visitors from other households were received. In some societies, notably Samoa, such houses were typically better constructed even than their owners' sleeping-houses, and in some cases were entirely round-shaped in floor plan.

An unusual variant of the domestic guest house was that found in some of the southern Cook Islands, where, writes Peter Buck: "Large houses termed *'are karioi* (houses of younger persons) were sometimes built by chiefs for their favorite daughters. Here the young people of both sexes gathered at night to sing and dance, and here visitors were entertained" (1944, 43).

Unlike many other Pacific Islanders, Polynesians in general did not consider menstrua-

tion to be so polluting, magically, as to require females to reside in a separate building during their monthly periods, but in some Polynesian societies a separate domestic building was provided for women during childbirth and, in some cases, for a few weeks thereafter. For quite different reasons, a few Polynesian peoples consigned their aged and helpless invalids to makeshift domestic shelters, where their deaths were hastened by neglect, or in some cases by deliberate liquidation. (See chapter 17.)

Many Polynesian peoples built simple, temporary lean-to shelters at their gardens for protection against downpours, for respite from midday sun, and for occasional overnight stays—mainly while in gardens relatively far from home. Also, here and there were built shelters against hurricanes (usually with low roofs and with rafters from ridgepole to ground). And although pigs were seldom if ever kept in pens, in at least one society (i.e., Easter Island) it was customary to keep chickens—their only domestic animal—in well-built pens.

Finally, in some societies many households had a chapel devoted mainly, or exclusively, to communicating, by prayer and offerings, with their own household guardian god(s). In some of those societies the chapel was located inside a household's sleeping-house, in others in a separate and often miniature houselike building, and in still others in a separate roofless structure similar in some ways to that people's public temple—which brings us to a consideration of those and other buildings constructed for "public" purposes—i.e., those used by groups and gatherings of persons larger than single households.

PUBLIC BUILDINGS

Application of the label "public" to the structures now about to be itemized is somewhat inaccurate in at least three ways. To begin with, most of them were usually accessible only to members of one or another of a society's tribal units. Second, even within a single tribe some of its "public" buildings were reserved exclusively for particular categories of individuals (e.g., expert fishermen, older males). And third, in the tribes of many societies some of its "public" buildings were in fact personal possessions of one or another chief, who permitted, or in some cases required, his subjects to use them on certain tribe-wide occasions. Indeed, in many if not most societies a chief owned some proprietary rights in all of his tribe's "public" buildings—and through rights or powers of expropriation in all his subjects' "domestic" buildings as well. With these reservations in mind, the Polynesians' "public" buildings will now be categorized—not according to ownership but to use.

As indicated earlier, in several societies the otherwise privately owned guest house of a community's headman or of a tribe's chief served also as the "official" guest house or meeting place of the whole community or tribe. In some places this structure consisted of a roofless stone-paved area (for example, a large porch in front of the headman's or chief's sleeping-house), in others a separate—and usually open-sided—building, similar in size and roofing to the locale's better-built sleeping-houses. And in some other societies such houses were larger, in some places much larger, than ordinary guest houses, and used for a wider variety of purposes, including dancing and theatrical entertainments.

Fortresses of one kind or another existed in some Polynesian societies. They ranged in size and shape—and use—from stone-walled houses (which in some war-ridden places were occupied permanently) to structures that were resorted to only in time of war or threat of war. Some of the latter consisted of natural caves (some of them reinforced with stone portals), others of manmade forts, some of which were located on inland high points or insulated by ditches). More details about their architecture and defenses will be presented in chapter 16.

In some societies there were structures built and used exclusively by local groups of one or another type of specialist (e.g., fishermen, warriors and builders—of buildings or canoes). Little or nothing has been recorded about the architecture of such structures except mention that some of them—perhaps most of them—contained altars dedicated to communications with the group's own patron god.

In a few places highly distinctive structures were built and used for one or another type of competitive sport—principally archery, dart throwing and pigeon catching. Those and other aspects of "diversion," many of which activities, and their associated structures, included religious components as well, will be described in chapter 15.

Speaking of which, there were in every Polynesian society manmade structures used exclusively for religious purposes. Such structures ranged from small wayside shrines—composed of rocks added to by passersby one at a time, to huge multistepped pyramids located in acre-sized temple compounds containing shrines, altars, images, pulpits and areas for lay worshipers, along with special places for priests. Architectural details of such distinctively religious structures varied widely from society to society and would require scores of pages to describe. Instead, the reader is referred to the accompanying illustrations of a wide range of types—and for additional information, including numerous illustrations, to Peter Bellwood's excellent survey mentioned earlier.[91] Meanwhile it may be helpful to point out here the existence of a major region-wide difference between western and eastern Polynesia with respect to the size, quantity and complexity of religious structures, they having been smaller, fewer and simpler in the west than in the east. This does not necessarily mean that easterners were more "religious" than westerners—a generalization that would be difficult to substantiate—but it may be pertinent to note that the word *marae* (*malae, meae,* etc.), which meant "place of worship" in most eastern societies, was applied in the west to a community's nonexclusive and partly secular meeting plaza.

Last, it can be added that there were some wide differences between societies, and within some of them, in the kinds of places used for housing the physical remains of their dead—that is, the remains of those they wished to house (it having been widespread practice, for example, to leave enemies killed in warfare where they fell, and to sink thieves and some other malefactors into the sea). With respect to the remains of other persons, their treatment differed widely, both between and within single societies, as will be mentioned in chapter 17.

EXPERT BUILDERS

Many Western visitors recorded, either explicitly or implicitly, that among the various Polynesian peoples known to them, nearly every adult male had the ability—the knowledge, strength, and skill—to build an "ordinary" house (i.e., one of small or average size and of average architectural complexity). In addition, several accounts refer specifically to the existence, in one or another society, of a category of "carpenters" (expert [of] houses), who specialized particularly in the construction of better-than-average buildings—or in some societies, of better-than-average buildings and canoes. Most accounts of expertise in buildings focus on that concerned with wooden ones, but presumably it included those made of stone as well. In at least one society the experts in decorative sennit binding—the craft of lashing house and canoe elements together in sennit patterns deemed aesthetically pleasing—constituted a separate status, but in most societies most expert carpenters included that proficiency also among their skills.

Another question about the role(s) of carpenters has to do with their actual functions: in addition to making plans for an edifice, did they only supervise its construction or also assist physically in the actual work? An impression gained from most writings on the subject is that carpenters' roles varied somewhat from society to society and according to the size and nature of the edifice.

Still another query about skillfulness in carpentry—and indeed about most other kinds of expertise—is how it was acquired. The answer is, of course, demonstrated ability gained through learning and practice. However, in most Polynesian societies access to such learning was available only to a close relative of an established expert himself—and usually to the latter's eldest son, or if that son proved incapable or unwilling to assume the mantle, to a younger son or some other close relative.

In some societies one or more carpenters were attached to the staff of a chief; in others all or most of them operated independently and on commission. Also, in a few societies those carpenters residing in the same community were associated in a guild. For example, in Samoa—where carpentry reached a high point in terms of skill and artistry—such guilds traced their professional status back to the high-god Tangaloa, who was credited with having built the very first house. And in Samoa, notwithstanding the colleagueship among a guild's members (which was expressed in part by the distinctiveness of their patterns of thatchwork and sennit lashing), they evidently vied with one another for lucrative commissions.

Accounts about Samoa also contain the fullest descriptions of the social aspects of house building. In one of these—by who else but the prolific

and minutely detailing Peter Buck?—relations between owners and builders differed according to type of contract. In one type the two parties behaved like members of the same family, with mutual respect and friendly indulgence—the owners having to rely upon the builders' sense of honor in fulfilling their agreement. In the other, more "businesslike" type of contract, each party could insist on the other's correct performance: if the owner was dissatisfied with the work, he could demand, and receive, rectification. Or, if the owner was unwilling or unable to provide the agreed-upon payment (i.e., in food, mats, etc.), the builder and his assistants left the job—an explanation, adds Buck, for the existence of numerous unfinished houses.[92]

Needless to say, any (Polynesian) activity as important, both socially and economically, as the construction of a large and well-made building involved religious actions as well: prayers and offerings to relevant spirits, omens foretelling the outcome of the enterprise, restrictions upon other behaviors of the builders, etc.—and of course religiously colored celebrations and dedications upon completion. Moreover, in some cases, god-backed protective devices were built physically into the building's structure—including, in some places, the humans sacrificed for the occasion.

One eloquent and richly allusive invocation attending the construction of a building—in this case a house—was a Marquesan chant intoned by a ceremonial priest at the beginning and end of construction. In the words of E. S. C. Handy:

> The pu'e [invocation] begins with an account of the origin of the land. It ends by summoning various children of [the Creator God] Atea, personifications of the different materials utilized in building [both] platforms and houses, each being called upon to come and contribute his or her share to the erection of the house of Atanua, wife of Atea, and traditional ancestors of all Marquesans. Soil (epo), personified, is summoned to come and fill and level the platform of the mythical house of the goddess Atanua; next, red stone (ke'etu), personified, is summoned to come and make the curbing along the front edge of the house . . . just as the man who was going to build a new platform and house sent messengers (ke'e'e) to his various relatives and friends, summoning them to help and requiring them to bring the various articles such as stones, used in the

constructions—so the *pu'e* chant relates how messengers are sent to the personifications of the various elements used, summoning them to come and bring their contributions. (1923, 151–52)

In the above example, the religious act (i.e., invocation) was performed by a specifically religious expert, a "priest"; in some other societies the religious acts attending building (or canoe making, or large-scale fishing expeditions, etc.) were performed by the technical experts of those particular occupations—the rationale having been that the expertise of those specialists owed something to the interception of the patron gods of those occupations and therefore had some influence with them.

13

WATERCRAFT

13.1. Single-hull Tahitian sailing canoe

Since humans did not evolve there they could not have reached Australia or any Pacific island without some kind of watercraft. And without an advanced form of watercraft—one capable of carrying several persons and a fairly large cargo—no humans could have reached and populated any Pacific islands east of the Santa Cruz and New Hebrides islands. That some of them did have such watercraft is attested by the fact that some of them did succeed in colonizing Fiji and islands far beyond. Moreover, this patently obvious conclu-

sion is confirmed, linguistically, by the circumstance that their reconstructed "ancestral" language, so-called proto-Polynesian, included words for seaworthy equipment such as outrigger beam (*kiato*) and sail (*laa*). Words for such equipment were included even in proto-Austronesian, from which proto-Polynesian derived, suggesting that the cultural forerunners of those colonizers had had similar watercraft many centuries prior to the colonizing of Fiji.

With one exception there is no direct *material*

(i.e., archaeological) evidence regarding the sizes and shapes of watercraft used by Polynesians, from the time of their "ancestral" beginnings—in Fiji, Tonga and Samoa—up to a few decades prior to the various times of their discovery by Europeans—periods of at least three thousand years. That one exception consists of parts of one canoe—i.e., two long boards and a large steering paddle—that were preserved in a waterlogged site on Huahine, one of the Society Islands, and dated by their discoverer, the Bishop Museum archaeologist Yoshi Sinoto, to A.D. 850–1200. From such remains the length of the boat's hull is calculated to have been about eighty feet, therefore capable of carrying twenty to thirty persons along with some cargo. Other evidence bearing on the sizes and designs of watercraft during those three thousand years is indirect, but suggests that all branches of the Polynesians had both (single) outrigger and double-hulled canoes. Moreover, it is reasonable to conclude that there had been periods in their histories when their canoes had been larger and better designed for long voyage than those seen by Europeans, who—it turns out to be—had arrived among them after their longest intentional voyages had ceased. With that in mind we proceed now to summarize the designs and uses made of

Polynesian watercraft as they were at times of European contact and before they underwent changes prompted by that contact. The focus will be on canoes—"canoe" being an English word taken from a Haitian Indian language and defined commonly as "a narrow boat with pointed ends, and propelled by paddles." Except in New Zealand (as will be noted in Part Three), at times of contact all Polynesian canoes were "narrow" and were kept upright either by joining together two hulls or by attaching a balancing float, an outrigger, to a single hull by means of transverse beams.[93] (After contact some Polynesian peoples constructed canoes broad enough to require no outside balancing, based on the design of Western whaleboats.)

I begin this survey—logically—with canoe hulls, of which there were two major types: dugout and composite. The simplest variety of dugout was shaped entirely out of a single log, or by two or more logs joined end to end. Such canoes were commonly used for fishing in quiet waters, and usually by no more than two or three persons. In a common variant of this type, one or more strakes were attached to the dugout's (upper) edges in order to increase freeboard, thereby adapting the canoe to rougher waters. And in many such cases

13.2. Two men in a canoe off Mangaia

separately fashioned (wooden) elements were added to raise bow and stern. In some models the strakes were attached to the underbody, and successively to each other, edge to edge; in others they were fitted together by double scarfs, thereby constituting partial overlapping (and producing more waterproof seams).

Composite hulls were made either by attaching successive rows of planks, edge to edge, to a shallow dugout underbody or, where plank-sized trees were scarce or lacking, by putting together pieces of various shapes and sizes.

The joining of hull components, to underbody or to each other, was done with sennit passed through holes pierced into or through adjoining pieces. In most places the holes as well as the adjoining edges were caulked with plant fibers and resinous gums, and in some places the junctions were given additional waterproofing by covering them with narrow strips of wood or bamboo. Despite all that, most hulls, especially composite ones, leaked so much that bailing was necessary—in some cases continually.

Many larger hulls were strengthened or otherwise equipped with struts or spreaders, bulkheads, breakwaters and partial decking. In addition, hull shapes differed somewhat from society to society, and within each society as well, in accord with their local uses—and evidently with local aesthetic considerations as well.

Only one float was used to stabilize a single-hulled canoe (in contrast to most canoes in, say, Island Southeast Asia, where floats were attached on both sides of the hull). Also, floats were invariably smaller, in most cases much smaller, than their companion hulls, and were always placed on the hull's port side. The wooden poles—beams—that connected float to hull varied in number from two to eight—depending partly on length of hull and partly on local tradition, and were attached transversely to the hull's gunwales. In some places all of a canoe's beams were straight, inboard and outboard the hull, and attached to the float indirectly, by stanchions. In other places the outboard part of this boom curved downward naturally and was attached directly to the float. And in at least one place (i.e., the Society Islands) the front one of a canoe's two beams was attached to its float by stanchions, the rear one directly—an arrangement that provided more rigidity forward and more play aft.

In some societies having canoes equipped with sail, one or more of its booms (usually the forward one) projected outward from the hull's starboard side (i.e., the windward side, opposite the float) far enough to provide standing or sitting room for one or more persons, whose weight was intended to keep the float in balance when sailing in stronger-than-average winds. And in a few places such projections were planked over in order to accommodate a heavier balancing weight of people and cargo when required.

Although most smaller canoes were propelled by paddling, the larger ones, and especially those built for heavier seas, were also equipped for sail—a topic to be treated after some discussion of double-hulled canoes.

Polynesian double-hulled canoes—two hulls joined by transverse beams—had an advantage over single-hulled outrigger canoes in being more stable and in accommodating more passengers and cargo. On the other hand, they were heavier to paddle and less maneuverable under sail. Regarding their larger carrying capacities, some of those measured by early Western visitors exceeded one hundred feet in length and could carry from one hundred to three hundred persons—thereby making them suitable for transporting large numbers of warriors on military campaigns or enough persons and supplies to survive and establish colonies on islands hundreds of miles overseas. In fact, the largest double-hulled canoe seen and reported by a Westerner, one of Fijian design but built in Samoa, was capable of carrying five hundred to six hundred persons. (In comparison, the largest of the Viking ships, which were making their longest voyages at about the time that the Polynesians were making theirs, could carry no more than about two hundred.)

In contrast to those of some other Pacific Islanders, the hulls of Polynesian double-hulled canoes were nearly identical in size and shape. Moreover, the beams connecting them were in many instances planked over to form platforms for accommodating both passengers and cargo. Also, the oversized paddles by which they were steered were in most cases located on the after boom midway between the two hulls—as was, or were, the one or two masts that supported the sail(s).

Speaking of sails, those of tropical Polynesian canoes were of matting, mostly pandanus; they were more or less triangular in shape but were rigged in two fundamentally different ways.

Type One rigging consisted of a triangular sail tied apex downward. In the Hawaiian variety of this type, one side of the sail was attached to the (fixed) mast, the opposite side to a spar, whose lower end was attached to the foot of the mast.[94] The upper end of the spar was drawn in by a rope toward the mast, thereby causing the slender spar to curve inward—and to shape the free upper margin of the sail into a crescentic curve. The fixed and forward repositioning of the mast precluded the vessel from sailing any way but in the direction of its bow(s). Moreover, being attached to mast and spar prevented the sail from being lowered without taking mast and spar down as well.

Type One form of rigging prevailed throughout eastern Polynesia, except in Mangareva, where canoes had become supplanted by rafts. There were, however, some other kinds of localized differences among them. In some places, for example, double-hulled canoes carried only one mast, in others two. Or, in the Society Islands, sails were "triangular" in a peculiar way. Or, in some Tuamotuan canoes, it was possible to move—i.e., shunt—the mast forward or aft, thereby reversing direction of movement.

Type One riggings—including sail(s)—had also been prevalent in western Polynesia until the late eighteenth century, when they were largely supplanted by the lateen form of rigging (i.e., Type Two), in which the triangular sail's mastlike yard became a "true" yard and was supported in the crutch of a "true" mast—a change that had diffused from Fiji to Tonga and Samoa.[95]

The (single) mast of an outrigger canoe—when sailed, which was mainly for longer than usual voyages—was stepped inboard over its forward boom, whereas the single or forward mast of a double canoe was usually stepped forward of midships on a boom or platform between the two hulls.

Steering methods varied with size of canoe. In small outriggers it was done by the single or the rear paddler himself with his usual paddle. In larger canoes it was done with larger and specially shaped steering paddles, and either by one steersman at the rear of each hull or by a single steersman located at the rear end of the between-hulls platform. (In some other Pacific islands—mainly

13.3. Single-hull Samoan sailing canoe

13.4. Single-hull sailing canoe of Marquesas

13.5. Mangarevan raft under sail

in those of Micronesia—steering by paddle was supplemented by manipulation of sail—a method unavailable to Polynesians because of the fixity of their canoes' sails.)

Mention was made earlier of the large sizes of some canoes; observations have also been recorded concerning their numbers. For example, when James Cook's vessels first anchored in Kealakekua Bay at Hawai'i Island in 1778, his officers reported

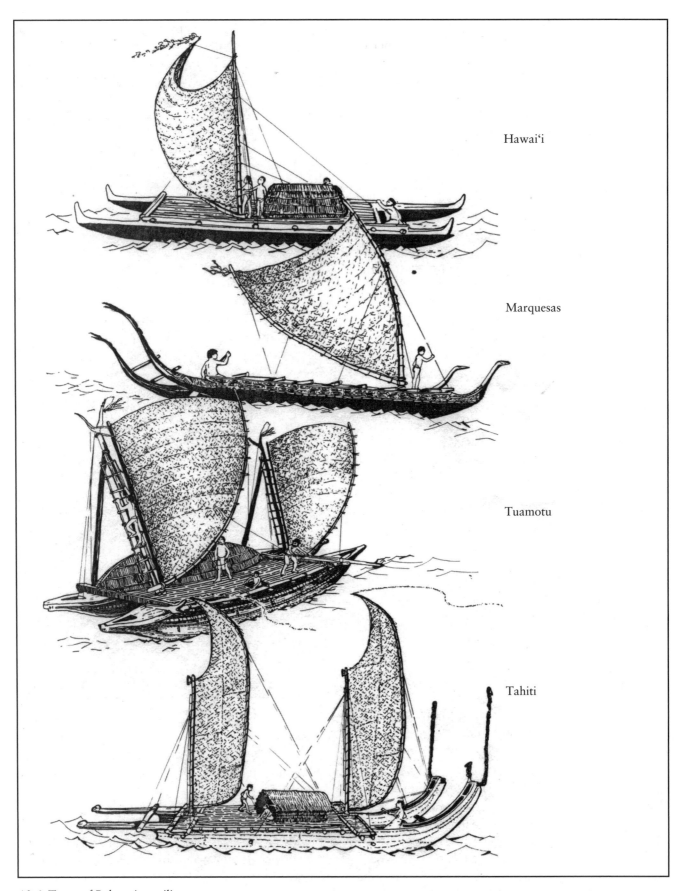

Hawai'i

Marquesas

Tuamotu

Tahiti

13.6. Types of Polynesian sailing canoes

that the number of canoes that came out to greet them "exceed[ed] 3,000," and that the number of their passengers was at least 15,000—besides those "who were swimming and sustaining themselves on floats" (Ledyard, quoted in Hornell 1936, 20). And on Tahiti Island, in 1774, when Cook witnessed the assembly of a fleet of canoes preparing for a military expedition against nearby Mo'orea Island, he estimated that it consisted of 160 large double canoes, carrying an average of 40 men each, and 170 smaller supply craft carrying about 8 men each—i.e., about 7,760 out of a total population (of Tahiti Island) of only about 35,000 (Oliver 1974, 401).

It is not surprising (i.e., for peoples given to decorating some of their tools), that many of them added ornamentation to some of their canoes—although they differed widely in this regard. At one extreme were the Hawaiians, who left their canoes almost totally plain (except for the patterning of the sennit used to fasten, say, outrigger boom to hull). At the other extreme were the Marquesans. Moreover, in those societies in which canoe ornamentation prevailed, not all types of canoes were equally well ornamented—e.g., those designed for fighting having been more extensively ornamented than those used for fishing. But here a caveat is in order. Some of that "ornamentation" may have been purposefully "decorative," some strictly "religious" (e.g., magical or supplicatory), and some a blending of the two. (As with many other cases of what Westerners would label "art," Polynesians doubtless also had other purposes in mind.)

Many more pages could be written about other features of the Polynesians' canoes: their breakwaters, weather screens, cleats for belaying ropes, decking, thwarts for paddles, and so on. However, rather than devote more space to such matters in this introductory text, the reader is referred to the encyclopedic work of Hornell (see Bibliography) and is asked instead to focus on the performance and building of those canoes and on the persons who built them.

Regarding the performance of canoes under sail, that of course varied from place to place, influenced weightily by differences in design. The best known tests of it were made by anthropologist Ben Finney with the reconstructed Hawaiian canoe mentioned in chapter 4. Finney concluded that "under ideal conditions of moderate-to-

strong trade winds (approximately 22 to 46 km per hour), expert trimming and steering, and a smooth sea, [the canoe] could make good course of up to approximately 75 degrees off the true wind. [Our measurements] also indicated, however, that when winds were light, when the canoe was not properly sailed, or when rough seas were encountered, windward performance fell off significantly. [Moreover,] windward performance falls off even further when seas become rougher and higher, and . . . when the canoe is heavily loaded . . . she is even more sensitive to sea conditions. High seas, particularly breaking seas coming at close intervals, appear to reduce windward performance both by slowing the craft and increasing her leeway" (1977, 1281).

This is not an impressive performance when compared with that of some modern racing craft. And yet such canoes were evidently capable of transporting enough people and cargo over distances of up to nineteen hundred miles to establish viable colonies in previously uninhabited places. Also, over long distances, movement under sail was markedly superior to paddling.

Polynesian paddles varied widely in shape. As for canoe performance by paddling, I turn again to tests designed and monitored by Finney with the modern facsimile of the Hawaiian double-hulled canoe mentioned earlier. Using experienced Hawaiian paddlers and subjecting them to various physiological tests, the experiment yielded the following results:

The paddlers showed that they could move the test canoe through calm water at slightly over 3 knots when paddling at a relaxed rate for eight consecutive hours (maximum speed at a racing pace was over 6 knots), and felt that they could if given sufficient rest, food, and water, keep this up for at least several consecutive days. The apparent food and water requirements would appear to be high. Although data on caloric expenditure are not yet available, preliminary figures on water loss indicate about 5 pounds per day per man. Paddling against wind and current, though possible, proved to be extremely difficult and slow (even though, as would be done on a voyage, mast and sail were lowered to reduce wind resistance). The speed of the canoe was slowed to about 1 knot when paddling against a slight current and a 20-knot headwind. The paddlers estimated that if there had also been a strong

13.7. Six men in a double-hull of Manuae

13.8. A double-hull sailing canoe of Hawai'i, the paddlers masked

headsea (the paddling was done in the lee of Oahu), little or no forward progress would have been possible. Paddling would, therefore, appear to have been useful to voyagers in calms or light wind and sea conditions, but not in the face of contrary wind, current, and seas—at least for any long distances. (Finney 1977, 150)

Larger canoes with alternate paddlers would have been able to travel farther, but not necessarily faster, on account of the increased weight of the boat and of its human passengers and essential cargo. Hence, while paddling was a useful method of propulsion for many purposes, it could only have been supplementary to sailing on long voyages.

Turning now to the building of canoes, it is reasonable to assume that any adult (male) capable of using an adze could have constructed a small dugout hull and its outrigger. However, the adding of washstrakes to a dugout hull would have required better-than-average carpentry skill—and the construction of composite canoes called for skills possessed by relatively few, who were in fact labeled experts (*kahuna*, *ta'ua*, etc.) and were commissioned, and usually remunerated, for performing such work for others—as well they should be, inasmuch as the construction of a medium- or large-sized canoe, especially composite ones, represented the acme of Polynesian carpentry skills. Leaving aside the craftsmanship revealed in the shaping and ornamentation, the skill involved in that carpentry is well shown, for example, in the joining of planks to hull and planks to planks, in such a way that the sennit used for doing so was invisible from outside the canoe (thereby rendering the join almost watertight). A second example consisted of the fashioning and installation of a wooden spreader inside the hull—done in order to strengthen its attachment to a boom. (The skillfulness embodied in these procedures can be better appreciated when one realizes that they were accomplished with tools of stone and shell.)

Speaking of those tools, during the building of a large canoe, and especially in shaping the hull underbody and adding planks, several adzes of different sizes were used, and the actual shipwrights were usually assisted by other men whose job it was to sharpen the adzes—most of which became quickly blunted by use. As reported by

Peter Buck (of Hawaiian practices): "One group [of assistants] undid the lashings of the blunted adzes and sharpened the edges, the second group took the sharpened adzes and lashed them to the handles. Thus a primitive production speeded up the work by enabling the master craftsman to devote full time to the more difficult part of production" (1957, 256).

As mentioned earlier, the generic term *kahuna* (*tafunga*, *ta'ua*, etc.) was applied to individuals who were expert in certain occupations, each of which was usually specified (e.g., *kahuna pule*: "expert [in] supplicating," i.e., priest; *kahuna kalai*: "expert [in] carving," i.e., sculptor). Not all peoples applied the same term to the same type of expertise, but the expert carpenter was so designated everywhere. In some places house building and canoe building were differentiated both in occupation and designation, but in others the expert canoe builder was expert in house building as well. Moreover, in most societies the expertise (and the corresponding title) in carpentry in general, or of boat building in particular, was heritable, usually passing from father to son, but "heritable" not necessarily as a familial privilege but because an expert father usually trained a son to continue in his occupation—usually his eldest son, but if the latter proved incapable, another son or close relative (including adoptees) instead.

In some highly stratified societies some chiefs had one or two expert builders on their staff, but in those and other societies there were other boatbuilders who sold their services to anyone affluent enough to acquire a large canoe. In Samoa, for example, anyone desiring a canoe of first quality had to mobilize his kinfolk and resources beforehand. Continuing the account by Peter Buck: "Everything being ready, he approached the desired builder with a fine mat and over a ceremonial bowl of kava made his request and proffered his mat. The builder replied and if he accepted the mat, the contract was sealed. If he refused, the chief sought another expert with the rejected mat . . . etc." (1957, 415–16).

Something about the size of the labor force utilized in building a large canoe is recorded in this report on the Marquesan island of Hiva Oa: "Four hundred men were employed in the building of a certain canoe at Pua Ma'u, working under the direction of four *tuhuna* (experts). The work was done where the tree was felled and where a

13.9. A view of the island of Raiatea, with a double canoe and boathouse

13.10. Double-hull sailing canoe of Tonga

decorated house was erected for the workmen. Workmen and *tuhuna* were fed by the chief, twenty men being employed in this work. The place was *tapu* (forbidden) to women and to strangers. Any intruder from another valley would be killed and eaten. When the canoe was finished a great feast was held at the place of manufacture, the workmen's house being decorated with ferns and wild vines" (E. S. C. Handy 1923, 155).

In some societies neighbor building experts combined into an exclusive guildlike association, with patron gods of their own to aid them in their work. And in those and other societies such experts had priestly roles in the several religious acts that accompanied building of a large canoe. Such acts included supplications and offerings to the gods of the trees from which the hull was made; empowering and protecting, from evil influences, the men and tools employed in the work; prognostications concerning the outcome of the enterprise; consecration of the launching of the finished canoe; and attempts to insure its successful performance—upon which in the lives of Polynesians so very much depended (including their own lives) and which was subjected to so many natural, and to Polynesians, supernatural hazards.

Finally, something needs to be added about the other kinds of watercraft that were in use at the time of first Western contact, namely, rafts and bodyboards.

Rafts were in active use in Tonga, the Societies, the Marquesas and Mangareva, and they were "remembered" as having been made and used in Samoa. In Mangareva they were the only kind of watercraft and were sometimes propelled by sail. There and elsewhere they were propelled by paddling, or by poling or pushing (evidently by persons standing in shallow water). And in Tahiti they were sometimes propelled by kites—i.e., when transporting blocks of coral in protected waters. Being made of logs or bamboo, they varied in size from a few feet long and broad to Mangareva's huge composite ones, made by joining together, on occasion, several individual rafts and capable of carrying up to one hundred persons (Hornell 1936, 2–94).

One-man (or one-woman) bodyboards, or floats, were doubtless used by several Polynesian peoples for support while swimming, and in at least two places, Tahiti and Hawai'i, they were used for recreation as well—as will be described in chapter 15.

14

SEXUAL ACTIVITY

Western ideas about Polynesians' sexual behavior were formed, first and most enduringly, by contact-era, eyewitness reports about Tahitians: "The great plenty of good and nourishing food, together with the fine climate, the beauty and unreserved behavior of their females, invite them powerfully to the enjoyments and pleasures of love. They begin very early to abandon themselves to the most libidinous scenes" (J. Forster 1778, 231, quoted in Oliver 1974). And "For deception, lasciviousness, fawning eulogy, shameless familiarity with men, and artful concealment of adulterers, I suppose no country can surpass Tahiti. She is the filthy Sodom of the South Seas. On her shores chastity, and virtue find no place. The predominant theme of conversation from youth to old age is the filthy coition of the sexes. From the King and Queen to the lowest grade, all are alike guilty, and if secrecy can be obtained, a very small reward will seduce any female" (John Orsmond, quoted in Oliver 1974). (Forster was a naturalist on Cook's second expedition, Orsmond a missionary of the London Mission Society.)

Few other Polynesian peoples were characterized at that time as having been as sexually unbridled as those of Tahiti, but it is doubtless true that most if not all of them were described as having regarded copulation as natural and pleasurable, and as being free of the kind of attitude—characteristic, for example, of some Christian sects—that enshrines chastity as a moral ideal.

That being said, while chastity itself may not have been to Polynesians a "moral ideal," the premarital virginity of a daughter or sister was in some societies valued as being one of her family's most prized (and well guarded) social assets. Thus, in Samoa: "[F]emale virgins [were] both highly valued and eagerly sought after. Moreover, as those values are [and were] especially characteristic of the higher levels of the rank structure, they also permeate to its lower levels, so that vir-

tually every family cherishes the virginity of its daughters" (Freeman 1983, 236). A culmination of that attitude occurred in the west Polynesian "Sacred Maiden" institution, wherein young and virginal females were selected to be ceremonial aides, or "ornaments," of important men and as such were expected to remain chaste until marriage—or, in at least one society, until death. To which it should be added that some acclaim was bestowed upon the man who preempted a rival family's prize virgin by deflowering her—that, plus the éclat attached to sexual prowess per se (as exemplified in the legend of a man who boastfully deflowered eleven *taupo* (i.e., a family's "official virgin").

Those and other practices aside, all or most Polynesian peoples shared several other beliefs and practices concerning sexual activity in general, as will now be summarized.

To begin with, all or most peoples believed that conception of a human fetus required copulation between a female and one or more males (either human or god), and in the case of a human male, not once but several times. In other words, although copulation incurred the chance of conception—a weighty consideration for many—belief was that females avoided the burden of pregnancy, and males the responsibility of fatherhood, by "sleeping around."

Further to the widely held belief that human females were sometimes impregnated by one or another god, sometimes by some figurative action such as hovering over a sleeping female, the method of impregnation between humans was thought to be by direct copulation.

Another widespread facet of Polynesian sexual behavior, corollary to the generally positive ways in which it was viewed, was the social openness it enjoyed—including unconstraint regarding representations of genitalia, as for example in some of the images pictured in this book. While Polynesian languages contained numerous synonyms for various aspects of copulation, few if any of them were prudishly euphemistic, and discussions of sexual matters were not limited by factors of situation or age or gender. In fact, knowledge about copulation was learned at an early age—partly by direct observation (which was facilitated by the absence of partitions in sleeping-houses), and partly by adult conversations, which did not seek to "protect" children from typically realistic gossip concerning neighbors' sexual affairs. Indeed, in some societies children's play at copulating was not only tolerated by older persons but greeted with huge amusement. And in some societies—mainly those of eastern Polynesia—deliberate measures were undertaken to instruct and initiate adolescents in the techniques of copulation: boys by adult women and girls by adult men.

Areawide generalizations about those techniques are unattainable, because of the paucity of credible reports. There is no shortage of accounts about sexual intercourse between Polynesian females and Western males, but few wholly believable descriptions of corresponding indigenous techniques. One such however is that by Ernest and Pearl Beaglehole, trained and experienced anthropologists, about the inhabitants of Pukapuka, whom they studied in 1935: "[Initially] the couple sit facing each other, the man with his legs folded under him, the woman with her legs resting on his thighs. In intercourse [however] the man lies on top of the woman. Chanting before or after copulation, as part of the fore- or after-play is a well established phase of the sex experience . . . . Both lovers chant together an old love song, or the man chants one of his own composition to his mistress" (1938, 288).

Turning again to Tahitians—who have been characterized in countless reports as having been even more sexually active and uninhibited than all peoples of the legendarily paradisical "South Seas"—there is actually very little credible information in print about their own copulation techniques—except for a few broad intimations. One was that it differed in body position from the usual Western mode—which was characterized by Tahitians and some other Polynesians as "missionary style." Another is that foreplay caressing did not include the female's breasts—those having had, in fact, little or no erotic significance. Still another is that some females became so frenzied during coitus that they inflicted deep scratches on their partners' bodies.[96] That practice aside, several reports about Tahitians, and about Polynesians elsewhere, state that males were expected to be, and actually were, more forward than females in initiating sexual encounters and more vigorous in carrying them out—which, however, does not signify that females were required to be reluctant or passive in those respects. Nevertheless, reports about some peoples indicate that while the male philanderer received plaudits for his successful conquests—except from jealous husbands—conspicuously promiscuous females were publicly denigrated—especially by jealous wives!

Information concerning when copulation took place among non-Westernized Polynesians is fuller than information concerning how it took place. Focusing first on the stage(s) of a person's life when copulation began, several reports directly state, or at least imply, that in many societies most boys and girls began attempting to copulate even before reaching physiological puberty, and that, as noted earlier, in some societies imitating copulation was a childhood game. (As was also noted earlier, in some societies deliberate efforts were made by adults to instruct, even initiate, adolescents in coital techniques.) Concerning the climax of a person's sexual life, that doubtless coincided with his or her physiologically empowered, and culturally defined, stage of "youth"—i.e., between physiological puberty and durable "marriage." This is not to say that being married diminished the overall frequency of a person's sexual acts, but it did undoubtedly limit somewhat the number of his or her sex partners, even in those societies where unrestricted copulation by unmarried young persons was not only permitted but encouraged and institutionalized.[97]

The best known of such institutions was the Tahitian Arioi cult, an exclusive society-wide set of tribally based sects dedicated to the worship of the peace-keeping personification of the god 'Oro, and whose members, both males and females, spent part of each year traveling intertribally giving dramatic and dance performances in return for (extorted) hospitality, meanwhile engaging sexually, and unrestrainedly so, not only among themselves but with residents of their host communities. Moreover, admission to a sect was limited to the unwed, and active membership in it was forfeited upon marriage. And while most of the members were young, some remained active, and therefore unmarried, for life. (For more on this cult see chapter 21.)

In several other societies a community's youths, male and female, banded together—in some societies actually resided together—and devoted themselves mainly to self-indulgent activities, including copulation. And while such groups—some of which bore labels cognate with Tahitian *arioi* (e.g., *kaioi, karioi*)—lacked the religious dedication and formal social structure of Tahiti's Arioi, their membership was usually limited to unmarried, and therefore sexually unconstrained, youths and maidens.

In some other societies, where extramarital sex was less formally institutionalized, young males and females customarily assembled on some uninhabited beach or in some secluded woodland spot to sing and dance—and eventually pair off and copulate. (Such gatherings were in some societies labeled "nesting parties," due to the circumstance that the trysts often took place in prepared "nests" of leaves and fronds.)

As to when in a person's life sexual activity typically ceased, it is of course evidential that orgastic frequency diminishes along with other measures of physiological juvenescence, but with most Polynesian peoples—who generally recognized that circumstance—it was not accompanied by norms that dignified senescent asexuality. On the contrary, in some of their societies admiration, colored with amusement and perhaps envy, was expressed for the aged philanderer—less so however for the aged philanderess.

Focusing on whole societies, there were times in the careers of several of them when some or most of their sexually capable members—married and unmarried, young and old—engaged in normatively sanctioned—i.e., "licensed"—sexual revels. On Pukapuka, for example:

The occurrence of periods of [sexual] license after the chanting and dancing over the village sporting triumph is well authenticated. . . . Married men and women and unmarried young people were all mixed together on these dance occasions. No tapus [taboos] seem to have been observed save those for related kin. Intercourse on these occasions seems usually, but not always, to have been under the friendly cover of darkness, on any space near or on the dance ground. On certain other occasions, as at

the end of the day when the canoes returned from a fishing competition, the women went to the beach to meet the men, and a period of wild lovemaking followed, all the more enjoyable because the men and women had been chaste for five or six days before and during the contest. It was customary during this license for women of one paternal lineage in the village to select lovers from among men of the other lineages in the same village. (Beaglehole and Beaglehole 1938, 289)

Another example of licensed group-sized sexual activity was the Hawaiian game of *'umi*, to be described in chapter 15. On a larger scale, in Hawai'i and some other large and multistratified societies, episodes of general tribe-wide sexual license also took place after a universally fateful happening—such as victory or defeat in warfare, or the death of a powerful chief. Such liminal episodes (from Latin *limin*, threshold) included not only feigned (or real?) madness and wholesale destruction of goods, but often general unrestricted sexual pairings as well.

However, it must be added that those and the other kinds of institutionalized promiscuous sexual activities just mentioned were somewhat exceptional. Much more common were those premeditated and fairly durable matings, which correspond to Western concepts of "marriage," and which were based, in most cases, on socially approved criteria of more or less mutual choice—including, in many cases, of *parental* choice. But before I enumerate those criteria, three cautions about Polynesian sexual activities need to be added.

First is the circumstance that in most if not all Polynesian societies there were families that acted, sometimes murderously, to safeguard the virginity of some or all of their young unmarried females—not, as was mentioned earlier, for reasons of abstract notions of "morality," but in order to secure what those parents considered to be suitable marriages for them—"suitable" in the sense of social equality or social advance, and hence "eugenically" acceptable progeny. (There are many, more or less disapproving, Western accounts of Polynesians having proffered their daughters or sisters, or even wives, to Westerners in return for valued items such as axes and firearms. Most such transactions were described as having been proposed by native "commoners," but even some members of native aristocracies took part in the trade, despite their usual eugenic concerns—or, in several credibly reported instances, because of those concerns—i.e., the desire to advance not only their own local affluence and influence but the social status of any resulting progeny as well.)

A second kind of restriction upon Polynesians' vaunted sexual freedoms was the fact that in all of their societies there were certain categories of persons, including some of a person's relatives, between whom sexual relations were permanently proscribed—a matter that will be amplified in later chapters.

A third kind of restriction on sexual activity to be noted is that in all of their societies there were specified occasions when copulation was interdicted—even, or especially—between spouses. Such occasions included, here or there, preparations for and during warfare, deep-sea fishing and large-scale religious ceremonies.

Leaving all such institutionalized restrictions aside, we turn now to listing the personal criteria applied by individuals who were free to choose sexual partners for more than casual, impromptu affairs. (By "personal" is meant choices made without respect to politics: it having been the practice in some of the more highly class-stratified societies for high-ranking persons to choose spouses for political purposes and without regard to the personal characteristics of the one chosen.)

Starting with a person's body, throughout much of Polynesia the major physical desiderata in choosing a sexual partner were overall plumpness and lightness of skin. (Some peoples judged thinness to be a sign of sickness—which indeed it often was.) Presumably, other features such as body size and symmetry also counted, but as most pre-elderly Polynesians possessed largish and well-proportioned physiques, such attributes may have been taken for granted.

I will postpone for the moment the question of why so many Polynesians peoples favored plumpness and paleness and address their methods of achieving it. Their high-calorie diets would doubtless have contributed to population-wide plumpness but for the active outdoor physical lives led by most of them, which also served to darken their skins. To remedy unwanted leanness and darkness, some older persons indulged individually in housebound food-gorging binges, but more orga-

nized multiperson measures were undertaken to fatten and bleach unmarried young males and females—for whom plumpness and paleness were especially requisite for attracting sexual partners and spouses. Institutionalized measures of this kind existed in several societies,[98] those of Tahiti having been the most fully reported. First, however, a description of the later-life fattening-bleaching which took place on Tetiaroa, an atoll owned by the chiefly dynasty of northwest Tahiti Island. William Ellis described it as "a kind of watering-place for the [Pomare chiefly dynasty], and a frequent resort for what might be called the fashionable and gay [fun-loving, not necessarily homosexual] of Tahiti. Hither the *areos* [members of the Arioi cult], dancers, and singers, were accustomed to repair, together with those whose lives were professedly devoted to indolent pleasures. It was also frequented by the females of the higher [social] class, for the purposes of *ha'apori* [fattening], increasing the corpulency of their persons, and removing, by luxurious ease under the embowering shade of the cocoa-nut groves, the dark tinge which the vertical sun of Tahiti might have burnt upon the complexions" (1829, I: 173).

The vacationing on Tetiaroa served purposes in addition to *ha'apori*, including recuperation from kava-drinking binges. Not so the more widespread and organized procedure for fattening and bleaching only young males and females. The male version of it is described in accounts by members of the Spanish expeditions to Tahiti in 1772–75: "This custom is that at certain times, or Moons, the youths of each district meet together and repair to one of the large sheds they have for keeping their big canoes under. . . . On being ensconced therein, and provided with their eatables, they lay themselves in the dry grass spread for the purpose, and a wrap that each one brings serves him for pillow and covering. . . . They do not get up except for their bodily necessities; they eat and sleep as much as they can. An old man serves them with meals; they go on in this way for the space and time of one moon in order to grow fat and lusty and high-spirited" (Corney 1915, 329–30, quoted in Oliver 1974).

Upon completion of their isolation the youths were paraded before their chief amid a large gathering of people, who expressed admiration for their plumpness and lightness of skin.

Accounts of female *ha'apori* are more specific

about their procedures and purpose: "According to an old custom in these isles, plumpness was considered a mark of aristocratic beauty. To accomplish this [young] women were fed *popoi*: fruits, bananas, and mashed breadfruit mixed with water and made into a semiliquid. During this time, all exercise was interdicted; they were allowed only to walk to bathe themselves in the river. Before appearing again in public it was customary for them to undress and be inspected by men; after which they became the object of admiration by young men, and were sought after more than ever" (Moerenhout 1837, 286–87, quoted in Oliver 1974).

Similar group-sized practices took place in several societies, as typified by Pukapukans:

> Some time after a group of boys and girls had attained adulthood [i.e., puberty?] a paternal lineage (*po*) might decide to hold a *kaitau wakayawi*, an institutionalized seclusion period intended to fatten their bodies, whiten their skins, and so make good marriages for the children of the *po*. . . . The [houses chosen for the purpose, one for boys and one for girls, were] made quite dark by covering the walls . . . with several layers of overlapping wall sheets and mats. The floor was first covered with mats, then with . . . fern leaves over which coconut oil was liberally spread. The secluded children were made to lie on the leaves, their bodies and heads completely covered with mats. They might eat, lie or sleep in any position provided they kept well covered. They were given especially fattening foods in large quantities. . . . When the house was opened up, the children, fat and fair, were taken to the beach to bathe. After being inspected by the members of the paternal lineage, each girl was dressed in two kilts, each boy in a new *malo* [breechclout]. Decorated with pearl-shell and flower ornaments, they were paraded through the village for all to admire. All the people came to see their beauty, expressing admiration in such terms as, "How beautiful, how fat, how fair," and wondering what men or women would be lucky enough to get such husbands and wives. Only a man who was a good fisherman and rich in [coconuts and taro] could hope to get a fat, fair wife, and only a fat woman would be able to get a [seclusion-fattened] husband. (Beaglehole and Beaglehole 1938, 282)

Elsewhere, however, fattening—usually coupled with skin bleaching—was undergone by, or

required of, only certain of a family's offspring, either its firstborn or its pampered "cherished-child." (See chapter 18.) Thus, on Mangareva:

> A well-nourished body and fair complexion were considered the physical attributes of chiefly rank. To add to the prestige of families, the parents secluded their first-born sons from the rest. They were fed on the best available food . . . . [A]t short intervals they had to eat great bowls of fermented breadfruit; the food was placed in their mouths and if they vomited, they had to eat again what they had rejected. Often a cudgel was used to make them eat more. They had to eat and drink reclining and physical exercise was forbidden. In spite of the hardships of getting fat, they all wanted to be submitted to such a regime because, during the rest of their lives, they felt the benefit of the period of fattening. They were always stronger and stouter than the others and hence came the idea that to be a good looking man and a great chief it was necessary to have a large stomach and big limbs. . . . The first-born sons and daughters who were kept in seclusion were called . . . "cherished children," while others who were not of such rank but were fattened were . . . "fattened children," having undergone the fattening process. Such children were kept in confinement until or near puberty, when they made their first public appearance at some special festival. (Buck 1938a, 117)

The practice of fattening or skin bleaching provides a fertile field for conjecture, and one that has been well sown. In addition to the possible reasons, mentioned earlier, for their everyday practice of what lean-loving Westerners would label "overeating," one credible explanation for their intentional institutionalized fattening is that it was an attempt to fulfill, or simulate, the idealized features of a society's upper-class individuals—who, because of their privileged statuses, ate more and better foods. It is also possible, but no longer provable, that the practice originated, or was encouraged, at times when survival from long and short-ration voyages depended upon body reserves of fat. Another partial—and delightful!—explanation is offered by Goldman, who wrote that in Manahiki-Rakahanga: "the symbol of food abundance was not the full storehouse as [it was] in New Zealand, but the well-fed and pubescent daughter of families of rank" (Goldman 1970, 60). And finally, there is the possibility that some cases of institutionalized fattening—i.e., those involving "Sacred Maidens" (who were also required to remain chaste), were magically empowering similes for the undisturbed fecundity, and therefore plenitude, of nature.

One aspect of fattening that invites particular attention was the immobility associated with it. Thus, individuals being fattened were required to remain inactive, and the well-fattened Samoan "Sacred Maiden" (taupo) was addressed as "sitting maiden."[99] (Moreover, in some societies the role of chief was also characterized by immobility, his physically active functions having been performed by one or more deputies.)

Concerning the goal of paleness, it may have derived from idealization of those upper-class individuals who in some societies spent less time than commoners in being in the sun—although that reasoning cannot be extended to those of Hawai'i, many of whom, male and female, were ardent surfers. (But then, I can find no evidence in the literature that light skin was in fact an aesthetic-cum-eugenic goal in Hawaiian society.)

Other physical features considered pleasing, and hence sexually attractive, in some societies were tapering fingers and a wide flat nose in females, and a peaked cranium in males—features which in those societies relatives sought to mold in infants in their care. Long, glossy tresses in females were also considered physically, therefore sexually, attractive in some societies, but in others all the head hair of unmarried females was cropped. In fact, preferred hairstyles differed so widely from society to society that no Polynesia-wide pattern is discernible in this regard.

Unlike many Westerners, Polynesians did not romanticize the size or shape of a woman's breasts. Nor are there enough published accounts available to permit any Polynesia-wide characterization about preferences for shape and size of genitalia. Some peoples considered a large clitoris an aid to heightened coital pleasure, and hence a desirable trait in a mistress or spouse, and in some societies attempts were made to enlarge that organ by manipulation during childhood. (Marshall 1962, 249). And as for males, in Tahiti William Bligh witnessed, and graphically described, a public spectacle that included several men who gave "the most uncommon and detestable demonstrations of their extraordinary capabilities in distorting the penis" (1789, II: 35, quoted in Oliver

1974)—but whether this indicated a sexually relative preference for an "acrobatic" penis I do not know—nor have I found evidence of similar practices, or of suggestions of such a preference, elsewhere.

On the other hand, cleanliness and redolence in a sexual partner were considered desirable virtually everywhere. The former required no exceptional measures—most Polynesians having usually bathed once or twice a day; the latter was effected by application of perfumes (made of aromatic plants mixed with coconut oil) and by the wearing of fragrant blossoms.

In many societies an individual's tattooing was a sign of a youth's fortitude, and therefore readiness for postchild behaviors, including actual—rather than playlike—copulation. In a few societies the same applied to girls—although their tattooing was seldom if ever as extensive as males'. It may be that the diffuseness and artistry of a male's tattoos also contributed to his sexual attractiveness, but about that I have no evidence.

Turning now to the kinds of behaviors that enhanced a Polynesian's sexual appeal, the first question to face concerns a person's capabilities in the sex act itself, and the first point to note about that is the Polynesia-wide difference in the models for males and females, especially young females. In every tropical Polynesian society that I know about, males were expected to be more experienced[100] than females; the widest of such differences seem to have prevailed in western Polynesia, especially Samoa, where a male's sexual repute usually increased with the number of his known "conquests," whereas, as noted earlier, virginity was highly prized in a young unmarried female. There is evidence also that strong sexual potency—i.e., ability to achieve frequent orgasms—also served to increase a male's desirability to females, but I cannot discover whether the same applied to females (who, in any case, might have been difficult to score in this respect).

It is also likely—but not demonstrable—that a male's prowess in warfare and his triumphs as an athlete enhanced his desirability as a sexual partner. Less likely was the case with the craft expertise of either males or females. On the other hand, in several societies skilled dancers, male and female, won praise during their performances and sexual rewards thereafter—often immediately thereafter. (In this connection: in many societies some forms of dance movements were explicitly erotic and some others indirectly so.)

Finally, as for the sexual advantages of superior social rank, that doubtless obtained in many societies, especially in the case of high-status males vis-à-vis lower-status females. However, social rank was a much weightier factor in spouse selection than in casual sex encounters. (The same can be said of the factor of kinship ties, as will be described in chapter 18.)

Turning now to abnormal sexual practices—the topic can be vividly introduced by that hardy Western seaman William Bligh: "It is strange that in so prolific a country as this [i.e., Tahiti], men should be led into such beastly acts of [sexual] gratification, but no place in the World are they so common or so extraordinary as in this Island"(1789, II: 16–17, quoted in Oliver 1974).

The "beastly acts" Bligh referred to were mainly homosexual practices, but in this section will be described those and other sex-related ones that differed from actual or simulated heterosexual copulation. (In this context "simulated" is meant to include the imitative sex play of children.) I label the following practices "abnormal," but abnormal in the sense of being different from heterosexual copulation, not of being indigenously "unlawful" or morally "wrong"—although some Polynesians did indeed consider some of them to be "abnormal" in the latter sense.

Perhaps because of the reluctance of early Western visitors to report them, facts about masturbation are scarce. Where it did occur, reportedly, it was indulged in by boys individually or mutually, sometimes alone and sometimes in groups. Girls also engaged in it, individually or mutually but not (reportedly) in groups.

Sexual acts between adult men or between man and boy have been reported in a few societies, mainly the more populous and class-stratified ones. In Tahiti, where such practices were prevalent, and extensively reported, they included "reverse" masturbation, sodomy, fellatio, and copulation between the subject's thighs. (There is some uncertainty about whether sodomy also was an indigenous practice or one acquired from early Western visitors.) In most cases the interactions between the participants were disparate: the one who played the male copulatory role having usually been bisexual, married and usually of chiefly status; the one who played the female and fella-

tio-active role usually unmarried, a commoner and consistently homosexual. Moreover, most of such pairings were stable, nonclandestine—and evidently publicly countenanced (including, it would seem, by the wife or wives of the "male" male). Also, the "female"-acting one of the pair usually belonged to a category of males labeled *mahu*, which may be broadly defined as a "male behaving as a female"—a characterization offered by James Morrison, the boatswains mate of the *Bounty*, who lived among Tahitians for about eight months in 1789–90: "Besides the different Classes & Societys already described they have a Set of Men Calld Mahoo. These men are in some respects like the Eunuchs in India but are Not Castrated. They Never Cohabit with weomen but live as they [i.e., women] do: they pick their Beards out & dress as weomen, dance and sing with them & are as effeminate in their Voice; they are generally excellent hands at Making and painting of Cloth [barkcloth], Making Matts and evry other Womans employment. They are esteemed Valuable friends in that way and it is said, tho I never saw an instance of it, that they Converse with Men as familiar as weomen do—this however I do not aver as a fact as I never found any who did not detest the thought" (1935, 238, quoted in Oliver 1974).

Some other early Western visitors to Tahiti were broader in their use of the word *mahu*, having included homosexuality as only one of its invariable features. Thus, according to Bligh, who was given the following "Account of the Mahoos" by "a dozen people": "These people . . . are particularly selected for the caresses of the men. . . . The women treat [one particular "Mahoo"] as one of their own sex, and he observed evry restriction that they do, and is equally respected and esteemed" (1789, II: 16–17, quoted in Oliver 1974). And by James Wilson, Captain of the missionary ship *Duff*, writing in 1799:

> These mawhoos chuse this vile way of life when young; putting on the dress of a woman, they follow the same employments, are under the same prohibitions with respect to food, &c. and seek the courtship of men the same as women do, nay, are more jealous of them who cohabit with them, and always refuse to sleep with women. We are obliged here to draw a veil over other practices too horrible to mention. These mawhoos, being only six or eight

in number [i.e., in Pomare's tribal district of north-west Tahiti, is probably meant], are kept by the principal chiefs. So depraved are these poor heathens, that even their women do not despise those fellows, but form friendships with them. This one was tayo [*taio*, bond-friend] to Iddeah [principal wife of the local chief]. (1799, 198, quoted in Oliver 1974)

It is my view, based on Morrison's statement and on early reports from other Polynesian societies, that one has to do here with two separate phenomena that were in some societies, sometimes but not invariably, related: male homosexuality (in contrast to male heterosexuality) and behavioral effeminacy (in bodily mannerisms, dress, occupations, etc., and in social relations—but not necessarily in sexual orientation). Regarding behavioral effeminacy, I repeat a suggestion made in an earlier publication, that "certain behavioral distinctions [made by Tahitians] between male and female roles—that is, males unable or unwilling to play the physically demanding and often hazardous roles expected of [Tahitian] men in climbing, canoeing, fighting, and so forth, were permitted and, perhaps, even encouraged or required to play female roles" (Oliver 1974, 1112)—as, for example, serve as cooks for upper-class females (who were forbidden to eat food cooked by "true" males). And as for male homosexuality, it may have been an underlying factor in a male's femininity—but perhaps not always so. As reported by George Hamilton (surgeon of the vessel sent to capture the *Bounty* mutineers), some of the upper-class men of northwest Tahiti, who were themselves married and presumably heterosexual, had some boys physically prepared—i.e., fattened and skin-bleached—to use them for their (avocational?) "abominable purposes" (Edwards and Hamilton 1915, 113, quoted in Oliver 1974). There is therefore the possibility that some

instances of Tahitian homosexuality in particular, and effeminacy in general, were due to purposeful selection and implantation. And, finally, it is a reasonable conjecture that the role of the male sex partner of an upper-class Tahitian man carried with it many advantages, both tangible and intangible. In fact, it was one of the most rewarding of achievable careers in that society of largely ascribed statuses.

Males labeled *mahu* (or cognates of the word) were to be found in a few other societies of eastern Polynesia, notably in Hawai'i, but accounts of them are much less informative than those about Tahitians.

In western Polynesia, "only three scant references to [male effeminacy] are found in the early records of Tonga, and for neighboring Samoa there are none at all. The earliest reference to Tonga—the first decade of the last century—denies that effeminacy and homosexual practices exist there" (James 1994).[101] This is not to say that male effeminacy and homosexuality did not exist in western Polynesia—only that those phenomena were not overt enough nor institutionalized enough to catch the attention of the Western visitors of that era—including the missionaries, who would have known about Tahitian *mahu* and would have been eagle-eyed in their notice, and vehement in their condemnation, of local parallels.

Turning now to female homosexuality (i.e., lesbianism), there is little to say. As among present-day Polynesians—and among many other peoples as well—there were doubtless many intimate "crushes" between young females, but the only reported case of lesbianism that I know about was from postcontact Easter Island (Métraux 1940, 108; note however that Métraux's report refers to the time of his fieldwork there in 1934–5).

15

OTHER DIVERSIONS

For anyone attempting to provide the sharers of his own culture a comprehensive description of markedly different ones, one of the most elusive problems of composition is how to combine the data into larger topically distinct categories. It may seem intelligible (to Anglophones) to compose or read articles or chapters on, say, "Gardening" or "Warfare," when writing about ancient Polynesians (or about Aztecs or Zulus, etc.), but the practices to be described in this chapter cannot be so logically combined. (Although, for that matter, even in the United States, growing radishes in a backyard plot is a very far cry from growing wheat on a Kansas megafarm; and with respect to "Warfare" we are told that it is but an "extension" of politics.)[102] And while many Polynesian languages contain cognates of the Tahitian word āre'are'a (pleasurable divertissement), it is not clear just what practices other Polynesians included in that term. Certainly, sexual activity was considered by most Polynesians to be so. Moreover, it is well attested that many Polynesians experienced pleasurelike feelings in some of the non-āre'are'a activities they engaged in—such as fishing, the collection of mountain plantains, even lethal warfare. And as with members of U.S. professional sports teams, it is almost certain that many of them engaged in certain competitive āre'are'a with anything but lighthearted feelings. In other words, the practices described in this chapter have been combined more to fit Anglophonic classification than for any underlying conviction about how Polynesians might have classified them.

Toys, Games and Sports

I begin with what most Anglophones would label "children's diversions"—although in Polynesia such practices were not necessarily "diversionary," but constituted the principal activities of most children's lives.

Like children everywhere (I suppose) those of ancient Polynesia played with toys, the most widespread forms of toy-playing having been top spinning, kite flying, leaf spinning, ball throwing and catching (with balls of rolled-up leaves), rope jumping, stiltwalking, jackstone tossing, and the sailing of leaves shaped into miniature canoes. In a few societies children also enjoyed the excitement, and hazard, of swinging and of sliding or sledding down hillside slopes. Also widespread were "social" games such as blindman's buff, hide-and-seek, and sham battling. In some societies children also engaged in imitation copulation. And in most seaside places children spent much time in the water—swimming, diving and playing tag—which culminated in their superlative aquatic skills. In some societies they engaged even in verbal and mind-developing games, such as the Marquesan contest of reciting the greatest number of words while holding one's breath, and the more educational one of Mangareva, which "consisted in enumerating all the names of men, women, and children of the archipelago; of plants, corals, shells, and even stars" (Buck 1938a, 183). Except, possibly, for sham-battling, all of the above seem to have been engaged in by both girls and boys—in some instances separately, in others together.

Turning to "adult" diversions—i.e., those played by persons past what Polynesians labeled "childhood"—some were mainly mental, others mainly physical. Prominent among the former were checkers and guessing games (e.g., finger matching, riddles and shell games). In addition, the making of string figures (i.e., cat's cradles) was very widespread (and engaged in by children as well), having been played in some instances to accompany and illustrate storytelling, in others to demonstrate dexterity and either memory or imagination.

Most adult physical diversions were in the nature of contests, involving physical strength or some form of physical skill. Moreover, some of those contests were between groups and some between individuals—although in the case of the latter, while individual winners were recognized, and lauded, they were usually regarded also as representatives of their respective groups—community, clan or tribe—in terms of overall score-keeping.

Most widespread of the physical contests between individuals was wrestling, and the most vivid eyewitness descriptions of it I can find took place in Tahiti. William Bligh, who watched several matches, wrote of them: "A fair fall like as it is in England is to be thrown on the back, but if they [Tahitian wrestlers] fall to the ground any way the trial for that time is over. They grapple by the Hair, Legs or any part they can lay hold of, however they have the art of Cross buttock as in Cornwall, but the Man who takes that method is generally thrown or Obliged to quit it, if the opponent is stronger than himself" (1792, I: 412, quoted in Oliver 1974). And in one match witnessed in Tahiti by the missionary William Ellis: "Mape, a stout, and rather active, though not a large man . . . was a famous wrestler. He was seen in the ring once, with a remarkably tall heavy man, who was his antagonist; they had grappled and separated, when Mape walked carelessly toward his rival, and on approaching him, instead of stretching out his arms as was expected, he ran the crown of his head with all his might against the temple of his antagonist, and laid him flat on the earth" (1829, I: 289–90, quoted in Oliver 1974).

There in Tahiti wrestling matches were held during nearly every large gathering, which included in some instances thousands of persons. And while the onlookers were usually silently attentive during the matches the scene changed instantly when one contestant was thrown, upon which "a shout of exultation burst from the victor's friends. Their drums struck up, the women rose, and danced in triumph over the fallen wrestler, and sung in defiance to the opposite party. These were neither silent nor unmoved spectators, but immediately commenced a most deafening noise, partly in honour of their own clan or tribe, but principally to mar and neutralize the triumph of the victors" (Ibid.).

Most of the Tahitian matches witnessed and reported by Westerners were characterized as "good-natured." However a later observer wrote,

"If it should happen that one side is beaten in match after match it usually ends up in real warfare" (Moerenhout 1837, II: 141–42).

Champion wrestlers were applauded and highly esteemed, but it is not reported whether they received any material rewards. Some of them were persons of upper-class status, but the sport was open to all—including women, some of whom wrestled publicly not only among themselves but also with men. Indeed, according to Bligh, women's wrestling was if anything more savage than men's and included such tactics as eye-gouging. But after a fall, reported one observer: "the affair was terminated, and the parties, after adjusting their hair, would tenderly embrace, and be as fond friends as ever" (Turnbull 1813, 286).

Despite the emphasis on individual skill, however, the religious element was ever present: "In this, as in most of their public proceedings, the gods presided. Before wrestling commenced, each party repaired to the marae [temple] of the idols of which they were devotees. Here they presented a young plantain tree, which was frequently a substitute for a more valuable offering, and having invoked aid of the tutelar deity of the game, they repaired to the spot where the multitude had assembled" (Ellis 1829, I: 288).

Wrestling was a favorite sport also on the small atoll of Pukapuka, where one form of it served as jural process in establishing the contested boundary between two parcels of land. Reference here is to a variant similar to Japanese sumo. As reported by the Beagleholes: "The technique . . . is a form of stick wrestling. A [wooden] weapon about 4 to 6 feet long is held by two men facing each other, each trying to push his opponent backward. The boundary advances or retreats according to the position of the weapon" (Beaglehole and Beaglehole 1938, 33).

Other variants of wrestling included free-for-all (boxing and wrestling) in Mangareva, tripping (in East Uvea), and arm wrestling (in the Marquesas).

Boxing (fig. 15.1) was less widespread than wrestling, but in some places, such as Tahiti, considerably more damaging, as the following by William Ellis records: "[W]hen the combatants engaged the combat was much sooner ended [than in wrestling], and no time was spent in sparring or parrying the blows. These were generally straight

15.1. A boxing match in Tonga

forward, severe, and heavy; usually aimed at the head. They fought with the naked fist, and the whole skin of the forehead has been at times torn or driven off at a blow. No one interfered with the combatants while engaged; but as soon as either of them fell, or stooped, or shunned his antagonist, he was considered vanquished, the battle closed, and was instantly succeeded by the shouts and dances of triumph" (1829, I: 292). To which Ellis adds that boxing champions "were proud to boast of the number of men they had maimed or killed," and that while it was practiced mainly by "the lower classes" was not confined to them, and that "chiefs and priests were often among the most famous boxers and wrestlers" (Ibid.).

Even more damaging was a kind of club dueling (fig. 15.2), practiced mainly in western Polynesia. In Samoa, for example, combatants used the midrib of a coconut frond and, standing face to face, struck at each other with bruising blows until one of them was disabled or lowered his hands in token defeat (Buck 1930, 573).

Most of the above competitive diversions were, and were perceived to be, useful training for actual warfare; and in a few places such training was made even more realistic by engagement of numerous persons in lethally realistic sham battles. I have come across no reports of sham battles having been fought by adults for diversion alone, but for children in some societies it served as a popular game. Thus, on Easter Island: "The sham battle was one of the favorite entertainments of children. Divided into sides, they threw at each other spears tipped by pieces of gourd shell in the shape of obsidian points. Legend states that children frequently discovered and substituted obsidian points for their [normally] harmless spear points" (Métraux 1940, 353). (In one such legend there occurred a "playful" battle that cost nineteen lives!)

A more specialized form of "playful" combat was fighting on stilts. Stilt walking was practiced in several societies, by both children and adults, and in some places (e.g., the Cook Islands) stilt-walkers engaged in a game with the object of knocking one another down. It was in the Marquesas, however, that stilt walking became a major and highly institutionalized diversion—and stilt making a fine art. There, the use of stilts was forbidden to women, and contests between tribal champions were the central feature of certain memorial feasts for the dead. The goal of such contests was to knock one's opponent off his stilt—which being done earned the loser the scornful laughter of the onlookers (E. S. C. Handy 1923, 297).

Another kind of combative diversion that may have been engaged in by some precontact Polynesians was cockfighting. I write "may have been" inasmuch as descriptions of it appear in accounts written decades after first Western contact, suggesting that the practice might have been introduced by Westerners. (For details concerning this activity in the Society Islands the reader is referred to accounts by Ellis and Moerenhout, reproduced in Oliver 1974, 322.)

Turning to noncombative contests, they varied widely: from mental games of guessing to foot and canoe racing, from exhibitions of dexterity (in juggling and jackstones) to combinations of strength and skill. Limitations of space permit description of only the most distinctive or widespread of them: namely, archery, pigeon catching, the pitching of discs, the throwing of darts, downhill sledding, and surfing.

Bows and arrows were used throughout most of Polynesia, but, with one questionable excep-

15.2. A dueling match in Tonga staged for Captain Cook

tion, only for sport and, in some societies, for practical purposes of shooting fish, birds and rats. (The exception was Mangareva, where reports of its use in fighting are however open to doubt.) As a sport, archery was most highly developed in Tahiti, where according to one authority it "was the most refined of the native athletic sports, and was a favorite amusement of the upper classes" (Henry 1928, 276). Bows were about one-and-one-half meters long and arrows (of bamboo tipped with hardwood points) about one meter long. In shooting, the archer knelt on one knee and let go the bow as the arrow was fired. Distance rather than marksmanship was the objective and ranged up to three hundred yards. The shooting was done from stone platforms (fig. 15.3). Arrow spotters, posted in the area aimed at, signaled back to the contestants whether a shot had gone farther or fallen short of the preceding best shot. Such contests also constituted religious events: the archers prayed to the tutelar deity of the sport, wore consecrated garments, and during participation were in a state of *ra‘a* (sanctity); like participants in temple services they underwent

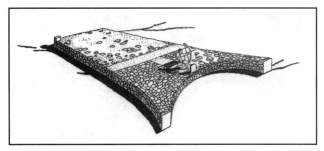

15.3. A Tahitian archery platform

rites before and after the contests in order to acquire and then rid themselves of the aura of sanctity deemed necessary for communicating with deities.

In some societies pigeons were either netted or were shot with bow and arrow—partly for food (for upper-class consumption) and partly for sport (by upper-class men). In both Samoa and Tonga the netting was largely a competitive pastime, to see who could catch the most birds, and was done with long-handled nets and the assistance of captured and trained pigeon decoys. In Tonga, where pigeons could be eaten only by upper-class persons, their snaring has been described as "perhaps the most popular of chiefly sports" (Gifford 1929, 117)—a judgment that is strengthened by the existence there of numerous large stone and earthen mounds, including some star-shaped ones, on which the players stood.

Disk pitching, somewhat like shuffleboard, was a popular competitive game in several societies. The disks, typically of basalt or of coconut shell, were thrown from one end of a long narrow strip of matting toward the other end, the object having been to position them as near to the far end as possible while keeping them on the mat. Disk throwing, in contrast, was done with a larger and much heavier disk of coral or stone, and for either distance alone or for distance and direction.

In a few societies contests took place to see who could throw common fighting spears the farthest, but the throwing of (nonmartial) darts was more widespread and more elaborately institutionalized. Indeed, dart throwing was one of Polynesia's most popular and widespread competitive games.

The darts used in the game were about sixteen to forty inches long and one inch thick and consisted, in some places, of a single shaft of wood (or cane or bamboo), in others of a heavier wooden head attached to a shaft. The object was to throw, by ricocheting the dart, as far as possible along a long and narrow strip of cleared and hardened ground. In some societies the strip was banked on both sides so as to form an alley, and was slightly mounded at both ends to serve as a base for the ricochet. The dart was held between thumb and middle finger, with the forefinger at the thinner back end. The throw was done after a short run and against the top of the beginning mound, in order to make it ricochet but to do so with as little angle as possible so that the dart did not dig into the ground short of its intended goal. Thus, winning required both strength and skill; and in some recorded instances the darts reached distances of as much as about three hundred yards.

In most dart-pitching societies the matches were between teams of throwers, and while individual winners were acclaimed, and consistent ones of them widely honored, the emphasis was on the teams and the community or tribe they represented. Moreover, when matches were between traditionally rival communities or tribes, they attracted large throngs of onlookers, and, like most populous Polynesian events, were conducted

with religious actions, including ritualistic movements and petitions to each team's patron spirit.[103]

Downhill sledding was a favorite diversion, especially for children, in several Polynesian societies, the most common children's sled having been a bunch of leaves. In Hawai'i, however, the pastime was also engaged in by adults, who, according to Buck, "developed it into an aristocratic game . . . which called for a highly specialized sled and carefully constructed runways" (1957, 379). Eyewitness accounts describe the wooden sleds as having runners up to five yards long, while remains of downhill runways reveal them to have been up to two hundred yards long and built on foundations of stones covered with packed earth which, when in use, were covered with grass. To begin a slide, a person, grasping his sled, ran to the top of the runway and threw himself forward onto it with all his strength—and, if expert, could slide "with velocity and apparent ease for 150 or 200 yards" (Ibid., 283–84). In competitions the sled that went farthest won; and as far as I can discover, only males engaged in the adult form of the sport.

Surfing (fig. 15.4), with or without a board, was engaged in in many places in Polynesia where wave action permitted—and indeed in some places where more cautious swimmers would judge it to be too hazardous to try. The practice was not limited to Polynesia, and certainly was not invented by Polynesians, but just as certainly attained its acme there.[104]

In Polynesia the boards used for surfing ranged in size from one to one-and-a-half yards

15.4. Hawaiian surfing

long and a few inches wide (enough only to help support the trunk of a swimmer) to some exceptionally large ones, six yards long and two feet wide (used in Hawai'i—where, however, those of average size were about half that length). Also, the riding position of surfers on the board ranged from prone to kneeling to sitting to standing, depending upon size of board and expertise—both of which factors varied from society to society. A third intersocietal variation had to do with age and gender: in some places surfing was a diversion mainly of children, in others of children and adult males, in still others (as in Hawai'i and Tahiti) of both males and females, old and young.

Surfing was, of course, practiced only in places where waves were of ridable form—i.e., mostly (but not exclusively) around the high volcanic islands of eastern Polynesia. In Tahiti, for example, where wave conditions were suitable, some boards were large enough to permit experts to ride, at least momentarily, on them, but it was in Hawai'i that surfing reached not only its Polynesian but its worldwide peak. Throughout the Hawaiian archipelago over one hundred coastal areas were used regularly for the sport, ranging from those with "safe" smooth bottoms and gentle waist-high rollers to some with dangerous rocky coastlines and eighteen- to thirty-foot waves (such as O'ahu's Waimea Bay). As for participants: "[The Hawaiians'] variety of skills, on long boards, together with the widespread participation of all classes was unequaled in any other Pacific island group" (Finney and Houston, 33). Not surprisingly, contests took place, and champions—i.e., those riding faster or on the biggest waves, both male and female, were widely acclaimed. Also not surprisingly, Hawaiian surfing was enmeshed in religious beliefs and practices, from the fabrication of a board to the winning of a contest, and including prayers and offerings for favorable waves.[105]

Finally, and to add spice to the above descriptions, mention should be made of the Hawaiian diversions of 'umi and kilu—counterparts of which, though unreported, might have taken place in other Polynesian societies as well. Here are Peter Buck's accounts of those games:

The game of 'umi derived its name from the term 'umi, to draw or attract. It was played by the commoners and by chiefs of lower degrees in [a] house (hale 'umi) set apart for the purpose. . . . The people seated themselves in a circle. . . . A man called the mau came forward and chanted a gay song, at intervals waving a long wand . . . trimmed with bird feathers. . . . [T]he mau passed around the circle and touched a man and a woman with his wand. The pair so designated went outside and enjoyed themselves. [One source] states that the selection of couples was not left to the mau, rather that the man indicated his choice by putting something of value in the hand of the mau to give to the woman to attract her toward him. Evidently the couple had to go outside, though the woman possessed the power of veto. If she exercised this power, they returned to the house. (1957, 367–68)

The aristocratic counterpart of 'umi was kilu, which only members of the upper, ali'i, class played. Unlike 'umi, however, it consisted of a quoitslike contest between male and female, and the prize of the winner, whether male or female, was to "kiss" (i.e., rub noses with) the loser—clearly a more dignified form of embrace than "going outside" (Ibid., 368–69).

Now to cap this sample list of Polynesian diversions, a few generalizations about them can be made:

• Most adult diversions were in the form of contests rather than of chance—thereby revealing an element of achievement in societies that were ascriptive in many other respects. (Ascription did however prevail in some diversions—e.g., in Tonga and Samoa only upper-class Tongans and Samoans engaged in pigeon netting.)
• Likewise, several of the diversions included both males and females—a somewhat unexpected situation in societies where males and females had separate roles in so many other activities.
• Although many kinds of contests involved groups of players or players representing whole communities or tribes, most of the actual contesting was between individuals and not teams, and while the group containing the winning individual shared in his victory, the latter was also individually acclaimed.
• Speaking of winning, in most kinds of contests the only prize was fame—material rewards having been bestowed in very few.
• Although the outcomes of contests were

attributed to the players' own strengths or skills, it was generally believed that gods were also involved—to what extent, however, I am unable to discover.

- Some diversions served practical purposes—such as learning to survive in the sea or to defeat an enemy in warfare. However, except in the case of explicit fighter training, I can find no evidence that Polynesians themselves purposefully engaged in such diversions with such practical objectives mainly in mind.

- In fact, most of the activities herein labeled "diversions" seem to have been considered only such—or, in some cases, to have been thought of as including features that served as models for other situations in life. Thus, just as Americans use "strike out" and "miss the mark" for other kinds of failure, so some Polynesians (in this case Samoans) likened clear thinking to a straight-flying dart; or being successful in general to a spear landing in the target's bulls-eye; or the need to hide one's feeling after any kind of disappointment to the forced cheerfulness required of the loser of a disk-pitching match (Buck 1930, 564–71).

Dancing

Turning again to the writings of the Dean of Polynesian ethnographers:

All Tikopia are extremely enthusiastic about dancing. A favorite expression meaning "I want to dance" implies not so much voluntary action as that the person has been taken over by his involuntary drives— literally, the "dancing impulse" has entered into him. When a dance has been "set up" and the beat of the sounding board begins, even old people are often stimulated to join in. A dance may take place at any time of the year, but traditionally the most formal festival dances tended to occur in the monsoon season, which had many fine weather periods and when food supplies tended to be readily available. When dancing was at its height, on a large scale, no work was done apart from the collection of food for the occasion. People went to their orchards, brought back provisions, cooked them and carried them off to the dance. In reference to this almost obsessional behavior [one of their chiefs] said to me: "The one work of Tikopia is the dance."

. . . When the community was caught up in dancing many people did not sleep at night. Only children and old people retired to rest before the early hours of morning. . . . Traditionally, since dancing was such an important interest of the Tikopia in this world, it was believed to be also a primary occupation of gods and spirits in the afterworld. Consequently, it was thought that dance songs could be composed by spirits. Indeed, some songs used in dances were attributed to spirit composers, having been chanted by human mediums in trance. (Firth 1990, 66)

And here is another quote, this one about early nineteenth century Tahitians: "Any little melody played on their nose flutes, or even the muted sounds from their drums, was enough to set [Tahitians] in movement; and as soon as one of their favorite tunes was heard to the accompaniment of these instruments, their faces and bodies became animated, moving in rhythm and showing the pleasure given them" (Moerenhaot 1837, II: 127, reproduced in Oliver 1974).

These kinds of observations, which are duplicated in accounts of several other Polynesian peoples, reveal something about their fondness of and readiness for dancing. However, dancing was for them not simply a matter of yielding spontaneously to impulsive high spirits. In addition, most of it was done on set occasions in prescribed costumes and with precisely choreographed movements tailored to each particular kind of gathering.

The occasions for dancing differed somewhat from society to society, but most of them included the "rites of passage"—especially funerals—of important persons; before or after battles and public sport contests, and in mainly religious ceremonies of many kinds. (I write "mainly" in view of the fact that most formal secular events also included some religious elements.) And, as indicated above, in many societies there were "recreational" gatherings specifically devoted to dancing itself—plus, in many cases, the lovemaking that such dancing stimulated as well as initiated. (Speaking of which, in some societies dancing with what Westerners characterized as "erotic" or "indecent" or "obscene" movements was also performed during religious ceremonies devoted to "fertility," both of nature and humans—possibly with magical intent.)

Dance costumes (which were intended to con-

15.5. Tahitian dancing

form to occasion) ranged from ordinary everyday wear to extreme elaborateness, from complete nudity to nearly immobilizing bulkiness, and from plainness or purposeful dishevelment to rich adornment—with flowers, leaves, feathers and skin painting (the dye of the turmeric plant having been especially favored nearly everywhere).

The wide variety of dance movements is exemplified by those of East Uvea, where, according to Burrows (1937), there were at least twelve named types that took place at feasts on community meeting places and that combined large numbers of dancers. Some of them were danced by males only, one by females only, one by females or by males and females, and one by either males or females or both. In most of them the hands of the dancers were empty, in others their hands held either plain sticks or broad paddles or coconut-leaf clubs, etc. Some involved standing only, others sitting only, and some both. Each type was characterized by what the observer described as a distinctive "emotional tone"—either "formal" or

"lively-jovial" or "erotic" or "plain martial" or "martially boastful." And each was either unaccompanied, prescriptively, or was accompanied by singing or hand clapping, or drumming. And in addition to those "formal" types of dancing there were in East Uvea other named types that were impromptu, took place in houses or in public, and involved fewer persons. (Unlike several other Polynesian peoples, however, the Uveans did not engage in dances by individuals. And except for some of the body movements in imitation of fighting or copulating, they did not practice the kinds of symbolic body movements included in the dancing of several other Polynesian peoples, especially in Hawai'i, Tonga, and Samoa.)

For most Americans Polynesian dancing is exemplified in the Hawaiian hula. In fact, the hula that tourists now watch (and relentlessly photograph) are a far cry from the ancient forms, of which there were two genres: *ha'a*, ritual movements performed during religious rites at temples, and *hula,* performed mainly for enjoyment.

15.6. Night dance by Tongan women

The most intensively studied of present-day, nontouristy forms of Polynesian dance are those of Tonga, by the anthropologist Adrienne Kaeppler, who in addition to describing them in technical choreographic terms has sought to show how present-day Tongans themselves conceptualize them, and how their dancing relates to other forms of "structured" movements—such as those that attend the ceremonial making and presentation of kava. Also, and on the basis of present-day descriptions by Bradd Shore, Kaeppler has proposed that the same kind of distinction exists in Samoa—i.e., between "structured" and "improvised" types of body movement, including dance (Kaeppler 1989, 226–27; Shore 1982, 258).

In an article on "Art and Aesthetics" Kaeppler (1989) proposed that all forms of a Polynesian people's "arts"—visual, verbal, musical, performing, etc.—along with their social institutions "partake of an underlying structure," and that "the various artistic and social domains are surface manifestations of underlying structures of the society, . . . which may be some of the unconscious, or at least unstated, principles by which individuals help to order their lives" (220–21). Perhaps so; a bold and stimulating thesis, but one which I shall not pursue here in this introductory text, partly because of limits of space but mainly because of the lack of germane data about pre- or early contact Polynesians. In her article Kaeppler is critical of what she calls the "Art Historian's" approach, saying that the study of Polynesian art and aesthetics "cannot simply focus on objects or artistic products per se; rather, such studies must be part of competent ethnography . . . . [They must show how] visual and verbal modes of expression are embedded in social structure and cultural philosophy, as well as how ritual and belief systems are integrally related to artistic and aesthetic systems" (220). All very true: as she has demonstrated in her studies of present-day Tongan dance—a study, however, that took place two centuries after the Tongans began to become Westernized in many ways, including cosmology, religious practice, economics, etc., and which may—just may!—have included aesthetics as well. In the case of the Tikopians studied so comprehensively and competently seventy years ago, their ethnographer's conclusions about relations between their aesthetics and other cultural domains are doubtless relevant for reconstructions about ancient Tikopians, but can the same be said about present-day studies of Tongans—or Samoans, or Hawaiians, etc.? Judging by my field work in 1954–55 and 1959–60 among Tahitians (who characterized their pre-Westernized past not just as *tau tahito*, "era-ancient," but as *tau tatani*, "era-Satanic), the answer is, most certainly not. [106]

SOUND–MAKING INSTRUMENTS

Polynesians had sound-making instruments of many kinds and for several purposes: for signaling, for announcing notable events, for deepening the solemnity of religious ceremonies, for increasing the terrors of battle, for accompanying or accenting dancing and chanting, for making what Westerners call "music"—and for reasons none other than the pleasure experienced in producing unusual sounds (as, for example, in the case of children's bull roarers). Also, in several societies women working together making barkcloth rendered the task more pleasurable by beating out the bast in resonant unison. In this section, however, the only instruments to be described are fabricated ones made specifically for sound making, and begin with those that Westerners classify as percussive (more technically, "ideophonic").

Instruments unequivocally classifiable as percussive were wooden drums, wooden slit-gongs, drums composed of matting, gourd drums, coconut knee-drums, bamboo tubing, dance sticks, stone castanets, xylophones, and foot boards of wood or of gourd or stone.

The most sonorous of the above were drums and slit-gongs. They were also the most widespread, but with partially separate distributions: slit-gongs only in western Polynesia, drums only in most of eastern Polynesia—both having occurred in only a few places (e.g., some Cook Islands, which also contained other traits found mainly in either western or eastern Polynesia). There were however a few places (e.g., Tuvalu and Tongareva) where there were neither drums nor slit-gongs.[107]

Drums consisted of a cylindrical section of tree trunk hollowed out partway from the top to form a resonance chamber, over which was attached a head, most commonly of sharkskin, attached by sennit cords (fig. 15.7). The wooden body usually rested on the ground and was in many cases ornamentally carved. Drums ranged widely in size, from a few inches in height and diameter to heights great enough to require a drummer to stand on a platform to beat them. The smaller ones were used mainly to accompany dancing, the larger ones mainly in religious ceremonies. Some were beaten by sticks, others by hand.

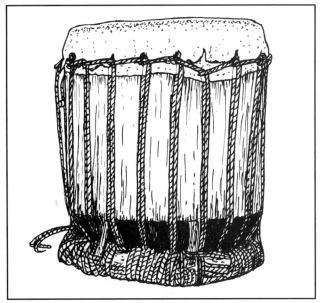

15.7. Common form of Polynesian drum, this one from Tahiti

Gongs consisted of a section of tree trunk or branch hollowed out short of its ends through a narrow longitudinal slit. They ranged in size from small hand-held ones to some (in Samoa) that were several feet long and three and more feet in diameter. The smaller ones were used to accompany dancing and were beaten by one or two sticks; the larger ones served to announce important events and were beaten with the end of a stick close to its slit.

In some places impromptu percussive instruments were made by use of canoe hulls, or by rolling up a mat, with or without a length of bamboo inside. And here and there a length of bamboo by itself served as such. Equally unspecialized were "dance sticks" and stone castanets, struck together while dancing. More specialized forms included those made of gourds, of half coconut shells (tied to the knee), pieces of discarded board (the remains, say, of a derelict canoe), and lengths of large banana tree trunks, struck end-down onto the ground.

What Westerners would classify as "wind instruments" included conch shells, flutes and pipes of bamboo, trumpets of wood, and whistles of bamboo, gourd and leaves.

Cone-shaped marine shells were widely distributed and were used mainly for announcing or signaling. Some of them were blown directly through a hole made near the shell's apex, others through a hollow bamboo tube cemented into the hole. According to one witness, "The sound is extremely loud, but the most monotonous and dismal that it is possible to imagine" (Ellis 1829, I: 283–84).

Almost as widely distributed was the bamboo flute (fig. 15.8), which in most places was blown only by the nose, in a few only by the mouth, and in a few by either nose or mouth. In blowing by nose the most common method was for the player to hold the flute's nose hole against his right nostril and play the notes with his right hand while using his left thumb to close his left nostril—flute holes having varied from one to six. The flute was characterized by one listener as producing "a soft, sensitive, and plaintive sound" (Henry 1928, 276). On some occasions it was played "privately": for courting, according to some witnesses, as a form of reverie, according to others. Or, on other occasions, it was played to accompany dancing or singing.

Pan pipes were present only in the western islands. They too were made of bamboo—i.e., of five pieces of varying lengths, and like flutes their sounds were described as "plaintive."

Wooden trumpets were distributed only sporadically. Those of Samoa were fashioned from the trunk of a wild palm and, being larger, produced louder sounds than flutes or pan pipes. According to one eyewitness quoted by Peter Buck, "It was formerly used by parties of warriors on their march, or at their general musterings and reviews" (1930, 579). Those of the Marquesas consisted of a hollowed piece of wood narrowing to a small hole to which was attached a mouthpiece of bamboo.

Solid whistles, of bamboo or gourd, were present in only a few places, and even there might have been copies of European ones. Impromptu whistles, on the other hand, were indigenous and more widespread. They were usually made of leaves and were used mainly by children.

The only stringed instruments known to have existed were so-called "musical bows." In the Marquesas the instrument consisted of a thin, slatlike piece of wood about three-and-one-half feet long and one inch wide (in the middle). Its single string, made of coconut fibers, was attached at each end of the bow and raised from its surface by small bridges of wood. Surviving specimens of the Hawaiian bow are shorter and composed of two to three strings. In both places the bow was played

15.8. A Tahitian boy playing a nose flute

15.9. A Hawaiian dancer holding a gourd rattle

by putting one end in the mouth and striking or plucking the string(s), letting the mouth serve as resonance chamber. Simpler forms of musical bows were found in several other places, where they were used mainly as toys.

Finally, some peoples used rattles of one kind or another, either to accompany dancing by others, or, by wearing them, to intensify their own dance movements (a purpose served in some places also by use of "dancing sticks"). The most notable kinds of rattles were those of Hawai'i, which consisted of gourds that contained seeds and which were elaborately decorated and fitted with handles (fig. 15.9).

One especially noteworthy aspect about Polynesians' sound-making instruments was their uneven distribution. Thus, while the Hawaiians had a dozen or more kinds, and the Samoans about ten, the Pukapukans had only three and the Easter Islanders only two (i.e., shell trumpets and wooden percussion plates sunk into the ground and stamped on for sound). Some of those disparities might be attributed to the environment (e.g., Easter Island's shortage of suitable trees and of bamboo), others to population size (and hence degree of cultural complexity). But some dissimilarities in kinds of instruments are attributable to situations more specifically "historical." Thus, the presence of large wooden gongs in western Polynesia—and not in most of eastern Polynesia—was likely due to the west's proximity to Fiji, where gongs, rather than drums, were the principal instruments for announcing and signaling. And the presence of large musical bows only in the Marquesas and Hawai'i is further proof of the close historical connections between the two (i.e., the original settlement of Hawai'i by Marquesans and its subsequent isolation, relatively if not totally, from the rest of Polynesia).

SINGING

Many of the stylized chantlike utterances discussed earlier—prayers, genealogies, eulogies, harangues, laments, love lyrics, etc., approached what Anglophones would call "singing" in their delivery; in addition there were others that Western visitors unequivocally called "ditties" or "songs." Some singing was done by individuals, some by pairs or choruses, and either antiphonally or in unison. Also, some singing was accompanied by instruments or dancing (including pan-

tomimic gestures)—or, conversely, served as accompaniment to other activities—such as beating barkcloth, paddling a canoe or forming string figures, or as part of the ritualized foreplay to coitus.

Some songs were composed for specific occasions—such as particular battle victories or larger than usual catches of fish; others were "traditional"—i.e., long-established types composed for generalized occasions, such as births, deaths and the winning of specific contests—the latter often having consisted of unbridled taunts. (Contrary to Western notions of "good sportsmanship," Polynesians evidently did not consider it necessary to comfort losers.)

Being unfamiliar with the technicalities of "music," I shall not attempt to generalize about its Polynesian forms, nor attempt to classify, by Anglophonic or Polynesians' criteria, the numerous kinds of topics represented in Polynesian songs.[108] However, before ending this regretfully superficial mention of Polynesian singing, I quote with partial agreement one scholar's sage remarks concerning Polynesian chanting, which likely may refer to some types of singing as well. The remarks, made by Adrienne Kaeppler, refer to a statement written by the anthropologist Ralph Linton about Marquesan chanting: "Although Linton (1941, 38) wrote that 'the maker of images accompanied his work by chants,' it is equally likely that in the Marquesan view a chanter accompanied his chant by making images. Linton thus gives primacy to making the image while I would give primacy to the chant, even though the perceived necessity for making the image may have occasioned the chant. The fabrication of a stone image while chanting a curing prayer and then placing the image into a me'ae 'temple' gives permanence to the prayer and substance to the chant. An integral association of visual and verbal modes of expression was found in many parts of Polynesia and is, I believe, a fundamental characteristic of Polynesian art and aesthetics" (Howard and Borofsky 1989, 217).

DRAMA

While some of the dances of many Polynesian peoples included pantomimic storytelling, in a few societies the dramatic element of some public performances was central. Such performances were particularly popular in Tahiti, where they took place either along with other entertainments or as separate events. There, moreover, in addition to a community's own occasional players—i.e., amateurs—there were a number of "professional" troupes, of males only or of males and females, which went on tour and were compensated not only by praise but with more tangible goods as well. In some places the performances took place in impromptu settings, in others in more or less permanent (outside) "theaters."

The themes of Tahitian dramas were more "historical" than "mythical," most of them having dealt with the deeds, and misdeeds, of their fellows, including farces about the characters and misdeeds of their own superiors—actions which in most other Tahitian contexts would have been severely punished, and which in some other societies, such as Tonga, would not have been permitted even "on stage." [109]

Touring and Visiting

Finally, much evidence establishes that in times of peace one of the Polynesians' most popular diversions was visiting distant communities either individually or in small or large groups. It was customary in many societies for youths or adult males to travel widely, including interisland, out of curiosity and desire for novelty and (hope-fully safe) adventure (including sexual conquest). But it was also the practice in several societies for numbers of persons, males and females, to travel together beyond their tribal borders, overland or interisland—sometimes to attend festivals but also for what can only be characterized as a desire for novelty. [110] The best-documented and most-institutionalized of such large-scale visiting was the Samoan *malanga*.

For many Samoans a *malanga* was their society's most stirring event, having taken place for each community about once a year. In it, a large proportion of the members of one whole community—in Samoa a nucleated village—traveled to another one, far distant or nearby, for one or another stated purpose—in addition to the unstated pleasure of visiting. Upon arrival, at a mutually agreed time, they received lavish hospitality, in food and entertainment, to the accompaniment of the elaborate and strictly performed ceremony that marked all formal Samoan gatherings. But unlike at many other formal gatherings (such as the weddings of important personages, when the parties engaged in strictly reciprocal exchanges) the guests at a *malanga* were not required or expected to reciprocate—until, that is, their current hosts eventually returned the visit at some unspecified, but implicitly expected, time.

16

WARFARE

Like many other peoples, Polynesians practiced numerous ways, physical and magical, of killing or otherwise harming human enemies both within and outside their own social units. This chapter, however, will concern only those practices undertaken by all or most members of a social unit intended to inflict deadly injury of a palpable bodily kind and by mainly physical means upon any and all members of a different social unit. In most cases the units referred to were whole tribes,[110] but sometimes were subtribes, clans, or subclans—but not individuals per se (which in present usage would have been not "warfare" but "homicide"). In many if not most cases of unit-to-unit killing, magical measures were also employed, but the kinds of practices now being considered consisted largely of physical actions.

As is customary in comprehensive writings about "warfare," something needs saying about its causes—but here at the outset only a few. For, as is well known, such causes may be exceedingly complex and usually included numerous kinds of situations: environmental, demographic, "traditional," idiosyncratic—and often long chains of them. Thus, where warfare had become continuous and especially ferocious, a case can be made for underlying environmental, (i.e., "population pressure") causes; in other places just as warlike even the underlying causes can be attributed to the ongoing personal ambitions of individuals and, even more basic, to encouraging and enabling features of a people's social structure. Several of these and other causal situations will be described later on, but for now I list only the most discernible *proximate* causes that led members of one social unit to kill or try to kill members of another unit looked upon as enemies en masse.[112] However, before doing so it must be emphasized that warfare was pervasive in most Polynesian societies—as much a part of life as, say, periodic religious

festivals. There were only a few societies—including that of Manihiki-Rakahanga, that did not experience frequent intertribal wars. For example, even on Tongareva, an atoll with a population of only about two thousand, its people experienced almost continual states of war. And in the Hawaiian Islands—now sloganized as the "Aloha State" (*aloha*: "love, affection, compassion, mercy, pity, kindness, charity, etc.")—warfare was frequent, large-scale and merciless.

The most impelling and widespread proximate reason that led (tropical) Polynesians to engage in warfare (as herein defined) was revenge—i.e., to avenge real or imagined wrongs, however defined, committed against themselves or other members of their tribe (or subtribe or clan, etc.). Such wrongs included not only abductions and bodily injuries, real or imagined, but also insults and indignities, especially those suffered by the unit's leaders.

A second and almost as common a cause—often supplementary to the desire for revenge—was social enhancement for a unit's leader(s)—and, consequently, for their supporters. Also, besides leaders, some other men sometimes encouraged and engaged in warfare in order to enhance their own individual statuses—as, for example, when the leader of a junior branch of a clan sought to win control over its senior branch.

In some cases the most compelling reason for warring was economic, i.e., for possession of an enemy's material goods and productive resources, including land (as expressed in the Tahitian saying that "warfare is growth")—although in many other instances the winners were content to destroy those goods and resources (e.g., by burning houses and destroying crops and trees) rather than by appropriating them.

Next, in many cases the most immediate reason for warring was religious. Religious beliefs were included in the rationales of other motives for warring but in some they were paramount, as, e.g., in the requirement for obtaining human victims for ceremonial sacrifice.

And finally, it seems fairly certain that some Polynesians encouraged and engaged in warfare not only for the rewards of winning but also for the pleasurable excitement of engaging in combat—a pleasure which in some societies was wittingly or unwittingly indoctrinated by processes of socialization, including the playing of certain games. And now, leaving the "whys" of Polynesian warfare we turn to its "hows."

WEAPONS

The most widely used weapons were spears, clubs and slingstones. (Many peoples had bows and arrows but used them for fishing and in a few cases for sport. There is no evidence, except, possibly, on Mangareva, that they were being used for fighting at times of contact.) In some places rocks were thrown by hand, and one or two peoples also used one or more of the following: swords, rasps, daggers, stone adzes and axes of stone and shell, throwing sticks, knuckle dusters, strangling cords and bolalike tripping weapons. The variety of a particular people's weapons ranged from virtually none (as, for example, on Kapingamarangi, where warfare occurred only rarely, and only when raiders from nearby Micronesian islands attacked) to Hawai'i, where there were ten types of clubs, ten of daggers, three of clubs, and four of tripping weapons—along with slingstones and strangling cords.

Societies also differed with respect to the ornamentation of weapons, which ranged from none at all, in a few places, to the elaborate fine-grained carving that characterized, for example, Marquesan and Rarotongan clubs, including those used wholly for fighting (i.e., and not those used ceremonially).

Now for some details on the ways weapons were used.

Spears varied in use, therefore in length, from short thrusting ones to throwing ones up to about six yards long. Some of them were one piece, others had separate points (of wood or bone or stone). The heads of some had single points or blades; those of others were barbed or multi-pronged. In addition, some points were made so as to break off upon entering their targets, thereby hindering their removal. Statistics concerning spear-throwing accuracy are lacking, but some

observers recorded the skill of some warriors in warding them off; thus wrote Vancouver about a sham battle witnessed by him in Hawai'i: "[Unlike most others, who retreated after throwing their spears, the experts] marched up toward the front of the adverse party, and in a vaunting manner bid defiance to the whole of their adversaries. In their left hand they held their spears, with which in a contemptuous manner they parried some of those of their opponents, whilst with their right they caught others in the act of flying immediately at them, and instantly returned them with great dexterity. . . . [One expert] defended himself against six spears that were hurled at him nearly at the same instant; three he caught as they were flying, with one hand, two he broke by parrying them with his spear in the other, and the sixth, by a trifling inclination of his body, passed harmless" (Lamb 1984, 833).

According to some witnesses the throwing of stones, by slings or by hand, was more accurate than the throwing of spears. On Easter Island, for example: "Stones were the weapons most commonly used in the beginning of a fight. To grasp a stone was an instinctive gesture. . . . as soon as an argument started. In all skirmishes with European seamen the natives attacked by pelting them with stones, which they threw with remarkable dexterity" (Métraux 1940, 165). Hand-throwing prevailed in a few other societies as well, but in some others martial stone throwing was done with slings. In Tahiti, for example, during the more organized of battles slingsmen kept together and confronted the enemy in a group: "The most expert slingers were celebrated through the islands, as well as the most renowned among the warriors; and when one of these presented himself, a cry ran through the opposite ranks. Beware, or be vigilant, *e ofai mau o mea*—an adhering stone is such a one; or *e ofai tano e ofai buai*—a sure or a powerful stone is such an one. . . . The slingers were powerful and expert marksmen" (Ellis 1829, II: 490–91, quoted in Oliver 1974).

One Western ship's captain who fought against Marquesans reported: "The stones are thrown with such a degree of velocity and accuracy as to render them almost equal to musketry" (quoted in Linton 1923, 391). Linton goes on to write, "Evidence of the force of slung stones is offered by a missile of the sort in the valley of Omoa, Fatu Hiva. The stone [had] been driven

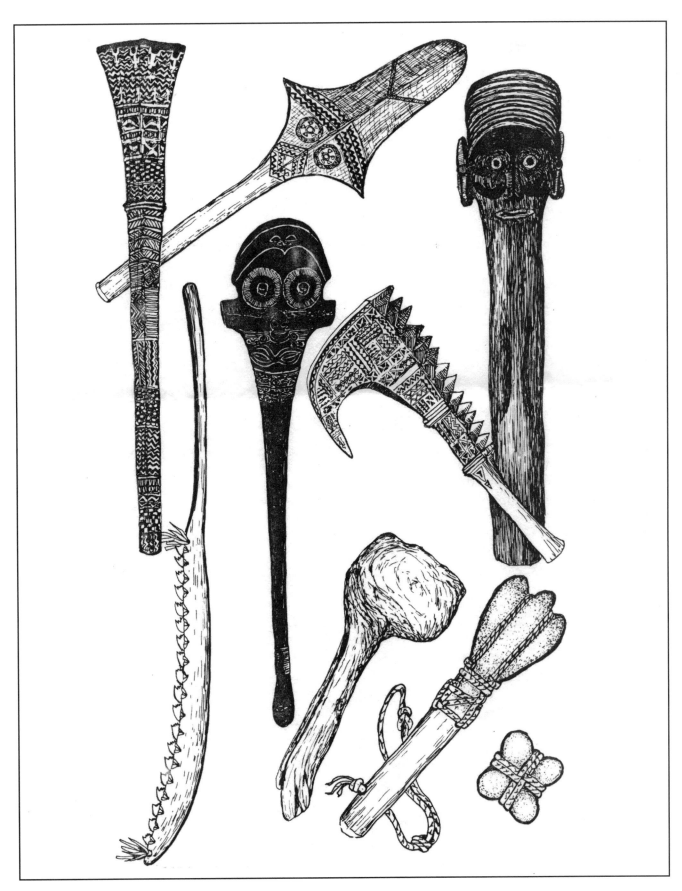

16.1. Weapons of various Polynesian peoples

into a crack between two rocks so solidly that the repeated efforts of curio hunters have failed to dislodge it" (Ibid.).

In most societies the slings were made of plaited sennit; in some the stones were unworked pebbles; in others purposefully shaped ones.

Some clubs were designed and used for throwing, with what effectiveness is not reported, but most of them were designed and used for close-in bashing and as such were reportedly the most widely employed and destructive weapons of all. They were made in many shapes and sizes: long and short, one piece or with a separate head of wood or stone, totally plain or elaborately embellished. Other close-in fighting weapons, used for stabbing or cutting, included daggers, serrated backbones of the stingray fish, swords or clublike rasps edged with sharks' teeth, and pearl shells mounted on wooden handles.

Another kind of offensive "weapon" employed was body painting or tattoo. Tattoo was used in several places—most vividly, perhaps, in the Marquesas, where "one of the main reasons for the men's tattooing was to inspire fear in the minds of enemies (Handy 1928, 127) (fig.16.2). Here or there successful warriors also armed themselves with the bones of battle victims—partly for magical purposes and partly to intimidate enemies (i.e., with such evidence of their ferocity). In some cases the bone consisted of a whole skull, and while such a token was doubtless intimidating it must also have been physically impedimental.

Speaking of which, another custom that cannot but have had unintended consequences was the practice of leaders to identify themselves, conspicuously, and thereby target themselves, by wearing highly visible garments—such as headgear or cloaks or demigorgets and the like. Some of those items may also have been protective—but hardly enough to offset the vulnerability they exposed.

Turning now to defensive devices, it is noteworthy that Polynesians, unlike some other Pacific Islanders, employed no shields per se in warfare. One reason for that, perhaps, is that most of their warriors, except specialist slingsmen, were armed with two or more kinds of weapons—say, clubs and spears—therefore had no hand free to hold a shield. Another possible reason is that most of them used clubs or spears to parry blows or missiles—i.e., thereby rendering shields unnecessary.

As for garments, the most widespread practice was to protect the head and trunk with thick wrappings of barkcloth.

Other defensive measures practiced in a few societies were traps, fortified residences, and forts per se. The traps consisted of camouflaged pits lined with sharpened stakes, in some cases poisoned. In a few places experiencing continuous warfare, whole communities were surrounded by walls of logs or stone and soil. More widespread, however, was the practice of constructing forts per se as refuges for noncombatants (i.e., children and aged persons) and fleeing warriors, in times of "total warfare." In some places fortified caverns were used for that purpose; more commonly some remote height was fortified, and its access narrowed, with additional barriers of wood or stone. Also, in several of the latter, huge rocks were positioned so as to be rolled down upon attackers.

In addition to the above defenses, some peoples used certain of their normal peacetime locales, such as temples and chiefly burial grounds, as sanctified places of refuge, not only for individuals fleeing particular acts of retribution but for whole groups of persons escaping from wartime enemies. Most notable of those were Hawai'i's "cities of refuge" (pu'uhonua), some of which were under the protection of certain gods and were manned by priests, who were armed and ready to "defend the fugitives and safeguard the temple to see that its sanctity was not violated by bloodshed" (Anell 1956, 190). Three types of persons obtained refuge in them: war fugitives (who were obliged to return to their own communities after cessation of hostilities), criminals (who were obliged to remain there until the gods "purged" them of their guilt), and the wives, children and elderly relatives of men actively engaged in warfare.

Polynesian warriors were also "armed" with intangible defensive weapons, such as god-assisted dodging, but this and other religious aspects of warfare will be listed later on.

TYPES OF WARFARE

For present purposes Polynesian warfare will be classified as brawls, raids or open battles.[113]

Brawls were a fairly common, and usually unintended, climax of interunit gatherings—occasions on which members of separate and more or less autonomous subtribes or of whole tribes

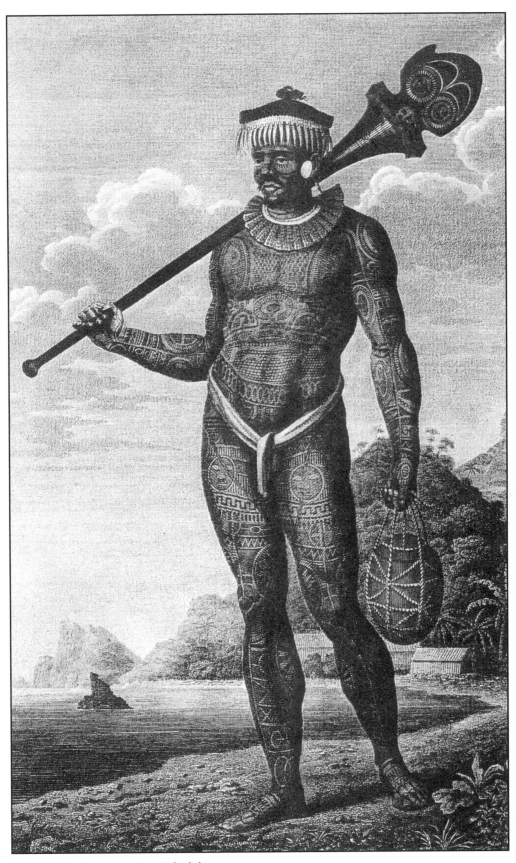

16.2. A Marquesan warrior with club

assembled for some shared event—such as religious ceremonies, sporting contests, and formal visits of their respective leaders. For many such occasions fighting was normatively interdicted by both parties, but that did not always succeed in preventing small quarrels' sometimes becoming widened into interunit brawls. For some kinds of "peaceful" gatherings even weapon-carrying was also normatively prohibited, but that also was a rule difficult to enforce—and many otherwise peacefully inclined participants doubtless carried secreted weapons, "just in case."

The most common type of military conflict was raiding—an attack, more or less stealthy, usually by a small number of men, into enemy territory. The most frequent reason for raiding was revenge for some real or imagined wrong committed by some member of the targeted unit against some compatriot of the raiders—preferably but not necessarily by close relatives of the wronged person, and in most cases against any member(s) of the "guilty" unit: man, woman or child. The "wrongs" that provoked, or in some cases provided a pretext for, raids ranged all the way from the actual killing or abduction of a compatriot to a real or imagined slight (e.g., an insult to one's leader or an unreciprocated "gift").

One of the most common tactics used in small-scale raiding was ambush—whereby the raiders hid near garden sites or groves and killed or captured persons (including women and children) arriving there to work, or whereby they lay in wait for persons arriving at a beach or stream to bathe.

The second most frequent purpose of raiding was to secure one or more victims for some religious purpose—e.g., to provide a human sacrifice for a ceremony, as in the following account by the ethnohistorian Greg Dening:

E ika ta was a Marquesan phrase meaning "to go fishing." Marquesans fished for more than shark and bonito. They "fished" for heana, the [human] victims that were sacrificed and sometimes eaten. At times of major social crisis, such as the death of a haka'iki (chief) or tau'a (priest), or at the failure of a breadfruit crop, or at a celebratory and tapu moment in the life of the haka'iki's firstborn, raiding parties would go out to snatch enemies from their fishing canoes, or capture them as they wandered alone along the shore or deep in the valleys. If the raiding parties went by canoe, as they mostly

did, they followed all the ritual preparations and sang all the chants that belonged to fishing for the most tapu of catches, the turtle. Heana, when caught, were brought back, a large hook in their mouth, baskets of bait tied to their limbs, their bodies painted red in token of the tapu fish of which they were part. They were carried to the me'ae [temple] with fishing chants and either hung as sacrifices from the trees or ceremonially eaten by tau'a [priest] and haka'iki [chief] and toa (warrior). (Dening 1980, 134)

Dening estimated that during the periods 1798–1805 and 1832–37 about eighty to one hundred men, women and children were captured this way each year in the Marquesas, whose population at those times had been reduced to about twenty thousand.

In contrast to some other Pacific Islanders, tropical Polynesians seldom raided nearby enemy communities for the purpose of obtaining slaves or concubines. Most of those captured and not killed after warfare and subsequently treated as slaves were a by-product and not a main reason for fighting. And the kind of quasiviolent wife-capture raids that took place on the Polynesian island of Tikopia were more simulated and game-like than purposely lethal. (See chapter 17.)

Entirely different from the above were the overseas raids carried out by Tongans, who voyaged to Fiji, Samoa, East Uvea and East Futuna to trade, and now and then, to raid. In addition, they sometimes made raiding voyages, for loot and captives, to places as far away as Sikaiana, Tikopia, Anuta, the Ellice Islands (now Tuvalu) and (the Micronesian) Gilbert Islands.[114] (Firth 1954, Lewis 1972)

Samoans also made long overseas voyages, but evidently with less predatory intent. Also different, in intent and scale, were the shorter expeditions of, say, some Tahitians and Hawaiians, who mounted military expeditions to nearby (intra-archipelago) islands for territorial conquest[115]—although such operations were usually conspicuous enough to allow their forewarned opponents to mobilize and meet them in open battles, to which type of military conflict we now turn.

Open battles occurred less frequently than raids and took place mostly in societies divided into large and hierarchically structured tribes. They involved more or less balanced and forewarned armies engaging in fierce clashes whose objectives were the extermination or rout of the enemy. They differed from the military games that took place on some occasions—i.e., encounters between currently "friendly" rivals that were circumscribed with rules of fair play and that produced few casualties. Be it noted, however, that such games sometimes turned into warfare.

Although the immediate aim of most open battles was enemy extermination, in many places they were nevertheless conducted, at their beginning, in mutually honored patterned ways. And although such "rules of battle" differed somewhat from society to society in details, most of them included preliminary duels between champion warriors of the two sides, along with much reciprocal boasting and menacing. At the beginning the mass fighting that occurred was more or less "organized"—i.e., all spearmen or slingsmen of each side acting together. Then, however, the fighting usually degenerated into more or less chaotic man-to-man combat. And it very often ended not in organized last-ditch efforts but in the flight of those who believed themselves to be losing—including, in many cases, those whose fight-leaders had been felled. (And speaking of the felled—in open battle they were more usually finished off at the spot than taken capture.)

Turning from generalities to particular peoples, here is one pronouncement about Tahitian battle tactics: "The chief modes of attack were: the *fa'atea*, in which two armies advanced for action face to face; the *tu'umata*, in which all aimed one way; the *marua*, in which picked men united and forced their way into the fiercest of the enemy's ranks, to throw them into confusion and rout them; the *aro nee*, in which only a small portion of the army was open to view and the greater part stooped low or crept along in the bushes; the *moohono* (jointless backbone), in which the different ranks held fast together; the *aro-ro* (ant fight), in which a line behind relieved the one before as it was getting worsted by the enemy; the *pu-toa*, in which the army stood in a body as a rock to resist the foe; the *rapa-tahi*, in which they aimed singly at the chiefs . . . etc." (Henry 1928, 305–6).

Needless to say, credible accounts of actual battles do not confirm an impression of precise military tactics and disciplined command control that one might infer from such pronouncements.[116]

Most of the foregoing applies specifically to battles on land; it should be added that Polynesians in some places also fought battles on the sea. I have come across no first-hand reports of such battles; there are, however, some published reconstructions based on second- and third-hand accounts. One such is that of the missionary William Ellis, again about Tahiti:

When the engagement took place within the reefs, the canoes were often lashed together in a line, the stem of one being fastened to the stern of the other before it. This they called *api*, and adopted it to prevent the breaking of their line, or retreat from the combat. The opposing fleet was, perhaps, lashed or fastened in the same way; and thus the two fleets, presenting one continual line of canoes, with the *revas* or streamers flying, were paddled out to sea, the warriors occupying the platform raised for their defence, and enabling them to command each part of the canoe. At a distance, stones were slung; on a nearer approach, light spears or javelins were hurled, until they came close alongside of each other, when, under the influence of rage, infatuation, ambition, or despair, they fought with the most obstinate and desperate fury. It is not easy to imagine a conflict more sanguinary and horrid than theirs must have been. Although the victors, when *faatini*'d or supplicated, sometimes spared the fallen, it was rarely they gave any quarter. Retreat there was none—knowing that death or conquest must end the fray, they fought under the power of desperation. At times, both fleets retired, but when victory was evidently in favour of one, the warriors in that fleet sometimes swept through the other, slaughtering all who did not leap into the sea, and swim toward the canoe of some friend in the opposing fleet. I have been informed by some of the chiefs of Huahine, who have been in their battles, that they have seen a fleet towed to the shore by the victors, filled with the wounded and the dead—the few that survived being inadequate to its management.—When the canoes of a fleet were not fastened together, as soon as the combatants perceived they were overpowered, they sought safety in flight, and, if pursued, abandoned their canoes on reaching the shore, and hastened to their fortress in the mountains. (Ellis 1829, II: 509–10, quoted in Oliver 1974)

More credible—at least concerning the size of naval forces—is Cook's account of a fleet of

16.3. Tahitian war canoe

canoes that assembled off northwest Tahiti for an attack on nearby Mo'orea Island. According to that scrupulous observer's count, the fleet—as was noted earlier—included 160 large double canoes carrying an average of 40 men each, and 170 smaller "supply" craft carrying about 8 men each—a total of 330 craft and 7,760 men.

Finally, mention should be made of sieges, which took place when tribemates sought refuge in a fortified place to escape slaughter or capture (usually slaughter) by enemy raiders or battle victors. As mentioned earlier, fortifications included caves, walled residential settlements, and deliberately constructed nonresidential forts. In some places accustomed to endemic warfare (e.g., the Marquesas) fortifications contained stocks of potable water and durable food (such as fermented breadfruit) along with ammunition (e.g., spears, throwing and slingstones), and in many cases did indeed survive siege—i.e., in such cases, it seems, besiegers lacked the patience or the supplies to conduct lengthy ones.

PEACEMAKING

In several societies peacemaking did not take place—the losing party of a military conflict was usually exterminated or forced off to sea or assimilated or, if not totally vanquished, able to recoup and fight again (an outcome which in some societies resulted in perennial feuding). Nevertheless, formal peacemaking action did sometimes take place—mostly when fighting became inconclusive or when leaders of one side, nearly but not yet totally defeated, initiated a truce. (Not unusually, however, the initiating peace envoys were not only unsuccessful but were slain on the spot.) The ceremonies accompanying, or rather constituting, peacemaking varied from society to society but usually included numerous—and lengthy!—oral declarations of reconciliation, imprecations against peace-breakers, and exchanges of tokens of peace—all of course religiously ratified by prayers and sacrifices to the principals' patron gods.

SOCIAL ASPECTS OF WARFARE

Which of a tribe's members engaged in warfare seems to have varied with type of conflict. In conflicts, whether raids or open battles, that concerned a chief personally, and in those otherwise sponsored by him, nearly every able-bodied male, and in some societies, some of its female members, took part. On the other hand, some raiding involved only a section of a tribe's membership— say, the close clanmates of a wronged individual, or the subjects of a subtribal leader (as if, for example, the citizens of Maine were to unite to raid Nova Scotia). As for which males were deemed "able-bodied," that doubtless depended upon physical strength and vigor; in some societies even pubescent boys served, say, as carriers of reserve weapons, and even men of "old" age went into battle if able to fight—and run.

Training for warfare occurred in several different forms. Not least were the everyday activities of most men—i.e., the generally body-strengthening nature of subsistence work coupled with specific proficiencies acquired by oft-repeated actions such as pounding, hacking and throwing. (Unlike, say, most Westerners, most Polynesian males did not have to undergo "basic training" in order to become physically fit for warfare.) Second were the skills learned in some competitive games, such as spear throwing and dodging, pigeon shooting, boxing and wrestling. And third were the sham battles that took place in several societies—some of which resulted in serious casualties or in bloody brawls.

Focusing now on military leadership in open battles and large-scale raids, it was almost always a tribe's chief (or a clan's senior, etc.) who decided if and when to wage them and who mobilized its forces, but in most cases it was one or more of its champion warriors, or warrior leaders—its *toa* (or *koa*, etc.)—who decided on strategy and tactics and who personally commanded its forces in fighting (at least, during the initial, less chaotic, phases of a battle).[117] In the tribes of some societies there was only one "official" *toa*, in others a whole band of them.

In some societies—notably those with large and hierarchically complex tribes such as Hawai'i and Tahiti—each tribe's *toa* resided and were subsisted at or near their chief's residence, to fight for him in war and serve him in other ways in times of peace. In some places they were members of their chief's own household, in others they dwelt in their own family households, and in a few places they slept, ate, and lounged in a separate and more or less sacrosanct place of their own—a kind of "standing army" whose principal, or in

some places sole occupation was to serve their chief. Given the privileged position enjoyed by many such *toa*, plus their fighting skills and doubtless pugnacious temperaments, they acted in many reported cases as bullies and extortioners among their patron's commoner subjects when, as often occurred, he and his entourage traveled about his realm—"like a plague," as someone complained.

On the other hand, in some societies a *toa* who was also a battle leader was enabled by his status to achieve practical political leadership as well, despite what may have been his lower hereditary rank—a matter that will be addressed in chapter 21.

The roles of females in warfare varied widely from society to society. In many they were dissociated from all phases of fighting—though not, alas, from its consequences. In some societies women were not only excluded from fighting areas (and in some places sent to places of refuge along with children and elderly men), but required to forgo certain behaviors of everyday life, such as eating or lighting a fire.[118] And in those and several other societies men were required to live apart from their wives during preparations for warfare. On the other hand, in a few societies women accompanied their spouses into battle, including (in some places) not only encouraging and helping them to fight, and tending to their wounds, but also taking active parts in the fighting as well.

Speaking of "active parts," the following practice, included in Tongarevan warfare, may well be anomalous, but is too bizarre to ignore: After the opposing parties had met and decided to fight out their differences,

hostilities commenced with a shower of stones and spears thrown at a distance of about 100 feet. These were thrown by the men, while the women of either side went out in front and with their light *tamutu* clubs beat down the flying spears that were projected toward [their] men. No spears were thrown at the women by either side, nor was any physical violence offered to them by the men, as it was strictly against custom to do so. After . . . stones and spears had been expended, the forces came into closer contact, and the men fought with their clubs or with truncheons . . . . After the women had lost their protective function of guarding against the spears, they engaged women of the opposite side in hand to hand fighting. Their light clubs seem usually to have been discarded, and they fell back on the primitive instincts of seizing each other by the hair. It was the object to get the best of a personal encounter rather than to kill. If the woman managed to get a handful of hair from her opponent's head, the hair was afterward boastfully displayed as a trophy of prowess in the field. (Buck 1932, 55)

"Primitive instinct" indeed!

Next, a word about live battle captives, of which, very likely, there were relatively few—most members of the defeated force unable to flee having been finished off on the spot. Of those captured alive, their usual fate in many societies was to be killed later, and as sacrifices to the victors' gods—or, in some societies, to be eaten by their captors. It was mainly in the more populous and highly stratified societies that some captives were allowed to live—but usually as slaves.

However, not all open battles ended with the slaughter or capture of the losing combatants. In some cases large enough numbers of the defeated warriors escaped to foil or otherwise discourage the victors from capturing and occupying significantly large portions of their lands. Or, as sometimes happened, it was not the intent of the victors' leaders to do so. In such situations what typically followed was either an uneasy truce, lengthy enough for the losers to recoup enough strength to fight again, or the chief of the defeated tribe's declaring subjection, and thereafter rendering material tribute, to the winning chief—without however reducing all his noncaptive subjects to slavishness.

RELIGIOUS ASPECTS OF WARFARE

Religious beliefs permeated and religious acts accompanied every phase of Polynesian warfare—indeed, so pervasively that it resembled a religious event.

To begin with, many if not most of the weapons—tools made and used specifically for fighting—were empowered by acts of magic and god-dedication during their fabrication, and again before each fight. Moreover, in some societies they were believed to become progressively more empowered with each casualty they inflicted—to the ultimate (and counterproductive!) extent of becoming "retired" from fighting service and kept solely as sacred objects.

When warfare was impending, either a raid or an open battle, resort was typically had to divination in order to learn the outcome, both in general and with respect to individual warriors. (It is not credibly reported, however, whether leaders intent on warfare actually heeded negative messages.) Concurrently, persons intending or expecting warfare became sensitive to omens foretelling its outcome, of which there were many kinds. (And again, there is little or no evidence as to whether hawkish leaders actually complied with unfavorable portents.)

It goes without saying that supplications, sometimes including sacrifices, were addressed to relevant gods before going to war. In some cases that was a group's particular tutelar; in other cases the group's society-wide god of war (who in much of Polynesia was Tu (or Ku, etc.), and in still other cases both tutelar of a particular tribe and society-wide god of war. (Like several Western peoples, Polynesians evidently perceived no contradiction in an enemy's supplication to the same god.)

In several Polynesian societies godly assistance was sought also during fighting, either at one's own tribal temple or on the field of battle or both. Typically, the specialist assigned to that role was a priest, who in some societies was charged also with tending the wounded and preparing enemy captives for sacrifice, in others the official exhorter. (In Tahiti, for example, the job of exhorter (*rauti*), himself a man of "commanding person" and "military prowess," was to "animate the troops by recounting the deeds of their forefathers, the fame of their tribe or island, and the interests involved in the contest" (Ellis 1829, II: 487–89).

As noted earlier, in most societies women did not engage in actual fighting, having remained on the sidelines to cheer their men or, more typically, in places of refuge or at home. Wherever they were and whatever else they did during the fighting, in several societies they contributed religiously to the success of their side's warriors by reinforcing the latters' ritually induced, and sanctified, austerity by, for example, abstaining from eating and from all sexually related behavior (including not letting down their hair).

Turning now to the kinds of religious actions that followed decisive battles, they differed according to a side's victory or defeat. For the victors the principal acts consisted of thankful offerings (often including the bodies of captives) to their patron gods. In several societies such offerings were accompanied by magical acts aimed at denigrating enemy captives or securing control over their ghosts—acts that included eating part of them, or keeping and vilifying one of their bones by wearing it or using it, for example, for fishhooks.

In the event of defeat or near defeat, one or more of the following religious actions took place. One was to petition one's god to forgive whatever human impiety (as indicated by divination) had led the god to cause or permit the defeat. A second, and antithetical, course was to blame that god for causing or permitting the defeat, and to transfer allegiance to another god—accomplished partly in some cases by expelling (e.g., burying, sinking, etc.) an icon of the former. Somewhat similar—but more animatistic than theistic—was the practice of scapegoating. This measure was based on conceptualization of the defeat as a form of epidemic illness, which was cured by concentrating it upon a scapegoat, animal or human, which was then expelled (e.g., by sinking it into a deep ocean grave). Still another measure, taken either alone or in addition to those just listed, consisted of rites aimed at purifying and reconsecrating a place, including restoration of its fruitfulness, after it had been invaded and its groves and buildings destroyed.

EPILOGUE

The foregoing paragraphs will have provided only an outline, and that a sketchy one, of the subject of (tropical) Polynesian warfare. A very large volume would be required to describe fully the wide varieties of ways that tropical Polynesians fought one another—for fighting was for many of them a consuming preoccupation and its outcomes, literally, matters of life or death, not only of individuals but of whole communities. Moreover, while expertise in, say, food getting or priestcraft or navigation was respected and acclaimed, successful warriors were not only highly respected—and feared—but, as will be reported in chapter 21, rewarded sometimes with positions of authority as high as or higher than those ascribed by aristocratic descent.

17

INDIVIDUALS: FROM CONCEPTION TO DEATH—AND BEYOND

All Polynesian peoples distinguished between living humans (*kanaka, tangata, ta'ata*, etc.) and all other animate humanlike beings (i.e., gods and demigods). Also, except for the mythic primal humans—who were generated in one way or another by gods—all subsequent humans were believed to have come into being through impregnation of a human female by a human male—or, in a few cases, by a male god. Concepts about human procreation will be described in the next section; before that something needs to be said about their beliefs concerning the composition—"physical" and "psychic," "palpable" and "impalpable"—of a human: an exercise easier said than done. Indeed, the adjectival oppositions just mentioned are Anglophonic and do not necessarily correspond to any Polynesian ones.

Differences between, say, Tongan and Marquesan artifacts (e.g., fishhooks, canoe paddles, etc.), or dance routines, or music making, etc., are apparent enough to verbalize in English (or German or French, etc.). Not so with several of the concepts now under consideration. In the first place, many of the original glosses of those concepts in English were clearly too simplistic to reveal differences between, say, Tongan and Marquesan (or Tahitian and Uvean, etc.) concepts in this respect. And differences there were—and indeed must have been. As argued earlier, by the times of their "discovery" and portrayal by Westerners most of those peoples had been separated from one another, totally or partially, for many centuries. And just consider the changes that have taken place among (literate) Anglophonic peoples over time concerning, say, a human's "temperament"—which as recently as three or four centuries ago was characterized by savants as consisting of four "humors," based on the proportions among one's "cardinal body fluids": blood (sanguine), black bile (melancholic), yellow bile (choleric), and phlegm (phlegmatic). In

other words, it would be unreasonable to suppose that such correlates regarding "temperament" had retained the same meanings among the various peoples of Polynesia, some of whom had had little or no contact with one another for many more centuries, and no systems of writing to preserve word meanings even within each society.

Nevertheless, all Polynesian peoples do appear to have retained through the centuries a conceptual distinction between, and in many cases cognate labels for, what Anglophonic lexicographers label "body" (*kino, tino*, etc.) and "spirit" (*wairua, vairua; kuhane, 'uhane*, etc.). Moreover, according to Western observers, Polynesians held similar views about those entities, namely, that the "body" invariably disintegrated after (physical) death, but that the "spirit" usually survived and unless deliberately or accidentally extirpated (i.e., by gods) could continue existing indefinitely. Also widespread, and universal, was the belief that during a human's waking state his or her spirit remained inside the body (exactly where is not universally agreed upon), but that during sleep or some other sleeplike state (e.g., trance, some forms of sickness) it sometimes left the body and experienced "dreaming." Other widely held, and labeled, concepts (which Westerners would describe as nonpalpable) were "thinking" and "emoting" (both located in the stomach or intestines), "healthfully alive," "breath and consciousness" and a person's "individuality" or "essence."[119]

As for widespread concepts regarding the more palpable components of human bodies, bones were considered (reasonably) to be more lastingly important than their flesh and other soft parts. After death the latter were allowed to rot away, or were deliberately removed and discarded, while the bones, or at least some of them, were usually preserved, and either buried, hidden away (from enemies), or kept as cherished mementos.

The most sacrosanct palpable part of a living

person was his head (and of a corpse its cranium)—why, however, is not entirely clear. (Some writers argue that the sacrosanct nature of the head derived from the location there of a person's *mana*, an opinion I am unable to support or reject because of the many uncertainties regarding the nature of *mana* itself.) To be sure, the head contained—obviously!—the organs of hearing, smelling, seeing, speaking—and of eating—but was not believed to be the site of "thinking" or of "emoting," which, as noted above, was believed to be located in the stomach and intestines. Throughout Polynesia there were proscriptions against touching, stepping over, passing items over, etc., a live person's head. Also, the preserved skull of a person was believed to be the most likely avatar for his or her (visiting) spirit—i.e., ghost.

In addition, for most, perhaps all, Polynesian peoples a male's genitals constituted an important, in some societies the second most important, part of his body—mainly if not wholly so because of their recognized generative function in procreation. Also, in men possessed of large "amounts" of "godliness," their genitals bore the capacity to empower other humans by contiguity or direct contact—for example, if the person crawled between their standing outspread legs. It is not clear what that "power" consisted of. Some writers attribute it to *mana*, that work-horse concept to which many scholars attribute all Polynesian "psychic" phenomena not otherwise accounted for. In any case, not only did the genitals of high-ranking men (i.e., those possessing very large "amounts" of godliness) figure prominently in legends and in fertility rites, but phallic representations were numerous and often exaggerated in sculpture.

Less significance was attributed to the human eye, although in some societies an eye of a sacrificial victim was symbolically eaten, as substitute for "eating"—i.e., vanquishing—his whole (enemy) tribe.

As for blood, a sharp distinction was made between ordinary and menstrual. The former figured prominently in standardized metaphor and in ritual, but it is uncertain what it was thought to be or to represent. As in English, some Polynesians used the word to distinguish consanguines from affines and relatives by adoption, but whether metaphorically or literally I am not sure. In any case, some peoples used ordinary blood ritually:

for example, by smearing some of a victim's blood over his body when sacrificing him to a god, by mingling a few drops from bride and groom at their wedding, and by lacerating one's head till blood flowed to express, or feign, strong grief or joy. (However, since redness per se was an oft-used symbol of sanctity, a victim's blood might have been offered mainly because of its color. Or the laceration might have been designed to express painful abnegation or deep feeling in general rather than blood-giving in particular.) In contrast, menstrual blood was in most or all societies the subject of negative reactions (by men at least), ranging from mild disgust (in some societies) to religion-founded dread (in some others).

Any of the above, and other physical parts of a person (e.g., hair, nail parings, saliva, food leavings—even footprints) and things touched by a person, could be used by magicians (specifically, sorcerers) to attract, entrap, and then injure a person's spirit, and thereby his whole body. Such a practice induced many persons (mostly those who thought themselves to be likely targets) to guard such exuviae (labeled "bait" by some writers) by, e.g., hiding or destroying their hair cuttings, keeping their spittle in a gourd and effacing their footprints.

Finally comes the psychic-*cum*-physical entity of "error" (or "mistake"), which in several societies was labeled *hara* (or *hala*, etc.). "Error," in contrast to "godliness," was acquired after birth. By Anglophonic classification it referred to two kinds of behavior (which, however, Polynesians themselves might not have differentiated): namely, errors vis-à-vis gods (e.g., mistakes in performing religious rites or eating an animal destined for sacrifice), and those toward certain other humans (e.g., disobedience to one's chief, unfriendliness to a bond friend—but not, it would seem, unfaithfulness to one's spouse). In at least one society it was believed that a person's "errors" accumulated substantially within his (or her) body, and were harmful to his well-being inasmuch as they attracted malevolent gods. In most cases, however, specific "untie-error" rites could be performed to atone for such errors and thereby diminish one's accumulation of them—although some of that substance remained and had to be drained away, along with a corpse's body fluids, after death. In some societies the nonpalpable aspect of the entity became attached to whole communities, as a result of its members' communal "errors" (e.g., vis-à-vis powerful gods or defeat in warfare—which in some cases was believed to have resulted from a god's displeasure). And, as noted earlier, "untie-error" rites also existed to atone for and remove such "errors," thereby rendering a community's territory habitable again.

CONCEPTION AND PREGNANCY

As noted earlier, most or perhaps all Polynesian peoples believed that conception of a child required copulation between a female and a male (either human or god). Most peoples also believed that some components of each parent, including some of their godliness, went into the composition, physical or psychic, of a child.[120] However, a problem arises—in my mind, and perhaps did so in the minds of some Polynesians—when two or more males were believed to have had intercourse with a woman just before or during her pregnancy. In at least one society—that of Hawai'i—children believed to have been sired, and "accepted," by two males were labeled "two-headed" (po'olua), and, according to one authoritative source, "this acceptance increased the number of relatives of the child who gave their loyalty to him as kinsman" (Pukui and Elbert 1957, 315). (Yet, it is not recorded which of such a child's inherited entities, physical or psychic, came from which "father.") A similar kind of question is raised by the Tahitian variant of "telegony"—a belief that in centuries past led some European breeders to mate cows with two or more bulls of superior qualities in the hope of transmitting those qualities collectively. In the case of the European breeders the favored qualities were likely thought to be physical. Tahitians likewise believed in the possibility of a child's inheriting some physical features from two or more of its mother's sexual partners, but I cannot discover their dogma with respect to the transmission of psychic traits, including godliness, to a child believed to have been multisired. Perhaps that question was settled when a man publicly "recognized" his wife's child.

Before I proceed, the variations just mentioned call for some sociological asides. Broadly speaking, they conform fairly closely with each society's distinctive methods of reckoning socially significant descent—i.e., each one's ways of assigning an individual to its consanguinity-based social units.

As will be argued in later chapters: in most Polynesian societies, wherein a child's supposedly inherited components were believed to come from both its mother and its (publicly recognized) "father," the child became a member in both of their descent units (i.e., clans)—if they differed (which was not always the case). If, on the other hand, it was believed that a child's inherited components derived only or mainly from its "father" (as was the case in Tikopia), the child was assigned to the latter's clan—the only type of clan in Tikopia having been patrilineal.

Reverting to the entities believed to have been transmitted from parent to child, we can begin by eliminating a child's spirit. Credibly accepted stories were told in several societies about the ghost—the spirit-become-ghost—of a dead person having entered into (having "possessed") some human temporarily, for one purpose or another. But I know of no belief, either general or specific, that all or part of a parent's spirit was transmitted to his or her child.

Too much uncertainty surrounds such recondite but in some societies labeled nonpalpable components (as, for example, "healthfully alive," "breath and consciousness," and a person's "individuality" or "essence") to permit characterizing them as either inherited or acquired. Not so, however, for the entity herein labeled "godliness." In those societies most concerned with this entity—mainly the more highly class-stratified ones, it was believed to be indisputably "genetic," having been inherited directly from both parents (or, in Tikopia, from the father only).

I use the term "godliness" to distinguish this entity from the more inclusive concept of "sanctity" (or "sacredness")—i.e., the state of anything regarded so by past or present contact with certain gods, a state that many Polynesian peoples called *tapu* (or *kapu*, etc.). In this usage, temples and god images were *tapu*, as were persons containing very large "amounts" of godliness. Also, in some societies, including especially those of Samoa and East Futuna, some titles themselves were imbued with sanctity, as were their current incumbents—which, after all, may also be said of such Western titles as bishop and rabbi.

Beliefs about inheritance of the more palpable entities are ambiguous, to say the least. Take "blood," for example: as noted earlier some peoples used the word for "genetic" relationships with relatives of both father and mother (in contrast to relatives by marriage or adoption). Yet some of those same peoples visualized conception as a blending of a father's semen and a mother's blood, thereby implying that one's blood came only from one's mother—an inference at odds with the characterization of the relationships with relatives of both mother and father as "blood." But then few folk beliefs of any society anywhere can stand the test of Western, scientifically semantic logic.

In summary, most peoples believed that a child inherited something(s) from one or both parents, but except for the entity herein called "godliness," no Polynesia-wide generalizations can be made concerning what those something(s) were.

The only contraceptive measure mentioned in sources known to me was coitus interruptus. Much more numerous were practices designed to assist conception when customary copulation had not worked—"customary" having meant, in most societies, several consecutive acts of copulation with the same male.

To begin with, it is notable (but not surprising in societies as "bilateral" as most of them were) that in cases of childlessness, (male) sterility was faulted almost as commonly as (female) barrenness. In some societies sterility was attributed to excessive orgasms (which "diluted" a male's supply of semen), or to a male's not having eaten enough fatty foods, especially coconuts—coconut oil having been equated in some respects with semen. As for barrenness, that was in some societies attributed to a "twisted" womb, in others to a womb made unreceptive as a result of a female having been too much alone—therefore likely to have engaged secretly in "wrongful" behaviors. And in a few societies barrenness was thought to be inflicted by malevolent gods whose specialty that was and who acted either gratuitously or upon the petition of a human enemy of the victim. Logically enough, one of the most common remedies for sterility was eating more coconuts, and for barrenness, reducing solitariness—plus, in all such cases, appealing to gods for cures.

Although offspring were in general welcomed in all societies, there were individuals here and there who sought to abort them, for reasons that will be listed in due course. The questions now are, How were abortions accomplished? and How often did they take place?

Abortion techniques practiced in one society or another included inserting into the vagina a supposedly poisonous herb or a sharp-ended stalk of grass or killing and expelling the fetus by heavy-handed kneading or by scalding steam. Speaking of which, there was a widespread distaste for and fear of an aborted fetus, whether deliberately aborted or not. Nevertheless, in the myths of several societies, aborted fetuses—so-called "shapeless clods"—survived to become powerful demigods, including (in some versions) the mischievous but beneficent culture hero Maui.

Turning to normal full-term pregnancies, the few behavioral restrictions that here or there accompanied them (and that were related mainly to the welfare of the fetus) applied mostly to the mother: for example, not to quarrel with her spouse, not to spend much time alone (and therefore be more likely to commit social or religious wrongs), and not to eat fetus-harming foods (such as crabs, which were thought to cause the child to have crablike limbs). Conversely, in some societies a pregnant woman's unusual craving for certain foods was construed as coming from the fetus and as being indicative of its character. In Hawai'i, for example, a craving for the "shy" *manini* fish foretold a shy and home-loving person, whereas hunger for the eye of a tiger shark (as was expressed by the mother of Kamehameha I) foretold a ferocious warrior (which that person truly turned out to be).

Reverting to pregnancy proscriptions: it is notable that, unlike the customs of many other Pacific Islanders, those of most Polynesian peoples set no limitations on copulation by or with a woman believed to be pregnant, some couples having continued up to the onset of labor.

Another particular aspect of pregnancy that typified some other general features about Polynesians was the practice, in many of their societies, of reciprocal gift-giving between the parents of the childbearing woman and those of the fetus's "official" father—another example of the bilateral structure of most Polynesian consanguinal social units.

CHILDBIRTH

"No where are children brought into the world with less pain or [physical] danger: the women submit to little or no confinement within doors, but rise and go about as usual" (Wilson

1799, 330). That statement, by the captain of the *Duff* (the ship that carried the first English missionaries to Polynesia, in 1797) referred specifically to Tahiti but would have been applicable to most other Polynesian peoples as well. Also, although the beliefs and cultural practices accompanying childbirth varied considerably from society to society, they were indicative of several broad social and religious tenets common to most of them. But before listing some of those a few facts need to be reported concerning the physical procedures of delivery itself.

In most societies the pregnant woman gave birth in a sitting or squatting position, with someone behind her to lean against, and if necessary help press out the child. In some cases she held onto a rope suspended from the ceiling or pressed her feet against someone sitting in front of her in order to assist ejection. Delivery was also "assisted" in some societies by prayer, or by the woman's eating of "slippery" foods. In a few societies the umbilicus cord was severed by biting, but in most of them by cutting with a sliver of bamboo—the prescribed tool even after the advent of metal knives. (Involuntary childbirth mortality doubtless occurred but I know of no credible evidence regarding its frequency. As for the practice of deliberate mortality—infanticide—see below.)

Turning now to the nonphysical aspects of childbirth practices: to most peoples it was mandatory for delivery to take place in a location other than the mother's usual sleeping-house—e.g., in a specially constructed shed (which was subsequently demolished) or in a secluded open-air place. The principal rationale for such practices was in some societies anxiety over the supposed dangerous, pollutive nature of afterbirth blood. On the other hand, delivery itself was in most societies anything but a restricted, sequestered affair. In many of them it was witnessed by several relatives. And in some of them—in sharp contrast to the practices of several non-Polynesian Pacific Islanders—the woman's husband not only witnessed but actively assisted with the birth.

Not surprisingly, births were considered to be critical events, and were therefore accompanied by religious measures, which ranged from mere prayers with or without offerings (in the case of some commoners) to tribe-wide restrictions and awesome rituals (in the case of the heir to a tribal chief). Moreover, such practices usually differed in

kind and magnitude according to the sex and birth-order of the child, with most elaboration reserved for firstborn males.

Another noteworthy set of practices accompanying childbirth had to do with disposal of the navel cord and afterbirth. Details of such practices varied from society to society, but underlying most of them were beliefs that those things continued to remain vital components of the living child and that the use made of them affected both the current existence and the subsequent life of the child. Thus, in several societies both cord and afterbirth were hidden in order to forestall attempts by ill-wishers to obtain and use them magically to harm the child. Or in Tongareva the afterbirth of a male child was buried on land in order to assure his productiveness as a landsman, or in the ocean to assure his skills as a boatman. And in Samoa the cord of a male was severed on a war club to make him a warrior, while that of a female was severed on a barkcloth anvil (for equally metaphoric reasons).

Regarding destinies in general, in some societies the events attending delivery itself or the circumstances accompanying a child's birth were believed to determine some aspects of its course of life. In Pukapuka, for example, a child delivered feet first was expected to have a very short life, as was one born during daylight. And in Hawai'i the season of a child's birth was believed to endow one or another of its potential temperaments; thus, one born in *kaelo* (January–February) would come to have much affection for his wife and offspring, and one born in *hinaia-eleele* (July–August) would turn out to be lazy, stupid and excessively pleasure-loving—unless, that is, he had a dark flat mole on the crown of his head, which signified that he would become learned and a diviner or counselor of a chief.

However, circumstances attending birth were not the only factors believed to influence a child's destiny. Less adventitiously, actions were taken in several societies not only to promote this or that career but also to endow, by ritual, the child with one or another kind of temperament (such as "vitality" or "courage").

Even more so than abortion, the topic of Polynesians' practice of infanticide has become controversial among present-day writers—not only because of its "immorality" (as charged by some critics, past and present) but because of uncertainties about its frequency (including the charge by present-day champions of Polynesian customs that the early accounts of the profuseness of infanticide and abortion were written by missionaries intent on capitalizing on the wickedness of their heathen clients—and therefore the difficulty of the task of Christianizing them).

Uncertainties aside, several Polynesian peoples did undoubtedly kill some of their newborns, for one reason or other—as will be listed below. In Tahiti, where the practice was perhaps most prevalent, the victim was killed mostly by strangling and soon after birth (on the premise that it was not yet fully "alive"). In Hawai'i, on the other hand, where the practice was perhaps less prevalent, some reports assert that some children were destroyed weeks or months or even years into life.

Early Western sojourners in Polynesia adduced several reasons for the practice of infanticide (and of abortion). One was the physical need recognized by some parents to limit the number of mouths to be fed during periodic famines—a situation that occurred mostly in the Marquesas and on atolls subject to devastating hurricanes. Another was the attitude best exemplified by Tikopians, who favored eliminating, by abortion or infanticide, a child of unknown paternity; in that emphatically patrilineal society a person without a father was disadvantaged in several crucial ways. (And corollary to that situation, custom mandated that when the identity of the seducer of an unmarried girl was known, or suspected, he was required to marry her and thereby "legitimate" their offspring.)

A third and less focused reason proposed for eliminating fetuses and infants—in this case one's own—was the wish to avoid the extra labor and sundry other responsibilities and restrictions that parenting usually entailed. Some of those influenced by this motivation were parents of extra-large broods, already stretched to the limit of their abilities to cope. (In this connection, there seems to have been in most societies a tendency to exempt more male newborns than females from infanticide; in the recorded words of one such parent: "There are already enough mat-makers in the family.")

There were also parents here or there who avoided having additional offspring because of what missionaries labeled "sheer laziness"—i.e., although physically and situationally capable of supporting more offspring, they declined to do so. (Note well that such an attitude differed widely from the one usually—and accurately, I think—attributed to most other Polynesians, namely, their wish for many offspring—as exemplified by the prevalence and ease of adoption.) Also, there were individuals here or there who avoided parenting solely in order to remain free of all family responsibility, including the usual limitations imposed by strict conjugality. Such individuals were to be found mostly in the more populous societies, such as those of Hawai'i and Tahiti, and the most conspicuous of them were young women intent on maintaining their sexual attractiveness and freedom. (Such "freedom" could be and often was maintained by relinquishing unwanted offspring by out-fostering them—there usually having been persons willing and eager to adopt them.)

Finally, in one society there was a religious cult whose members characteristically copulated promiscuously among themselves and with outsiders, but were required to eliminate all their offspring, by abortion or infanticide. Reference is to the Arioi cult of Tahiti, which was mentioned earlier and which will be described more fully in chapter 23.

Present-day scholarly—and unscholarly!—controversy about precontact infanticide focuses mainly on its frequency. There are few total denials as to its precontact occurrence but wide differences of opinion about its frequencies (partly for the reasons noted earlier). In reports by early Western sojourners the numbers ranged from "two thirds of all births" (as the Reverend William Ellis wrote about Tahiti) to "not practiced" (as ethnographers have asserted about present-day, but culturally conservative, Pukapuka). Undoubtedly, societies differed, perhaps widely, in frequency of infanticide relative to total population, and comparison of such differences would yield interesting generalizations—if (a big if) more credible numbers were available for such a comparison, which I judge not to be so.

The foregoing descriptions focused on practices attending the physical act of child delivery; for most Polynesian peoples, however, the neonate was not counted a member of its society until some other acts had been performed. That is to say, full social birth entailed other actions such as familial recognition and naming, and—in some societies—consecration to family gods as well.

In societies where a child's presumptive "father"—i.e., most effective progenitor—participated in its delivery, that in itself constituted "recognition." There were however some societies—i.e., the more rigidly class-stratified ones—in which an upper-class husband did not participate in delivery, but visited his wife and her newborn sometime after delivery and then formally accepted—or in some cases refused to "recognize" the child.

Turning now to naming, it is essential at the outset to distinguish personal names (those bestowed on individuals per se) from dynastic ones (those bestowed on successive holders of familial titles). The complicated nature of the latter will be described later on; present concern is with the former, which in some cases were even more complicated. As Bligh said of Tahitians: "Every chief has perhaps a dozen [personal] names in the course of 30 years, so the Man and Woman that has been spoken of by one Navigator under a particular name, will not be known by another, unless other causes lead to Discovery" (1789, I: 384, as quoted in Oliver 1974). It is questionable that such profusion prevailed with every people everywhere, but enough of it did to require some description of its more widespread features.

Every infant allowed to survive was given, soon after birth, a name, which in many societies derived from a set of them associated, sometimes exclusively, with its father's or mother's descent unit (clan). In some societies the choice was made by one or both parents, in others by a larger circle of consanguines, and in some by the infant itself—i.e., a list of names having been recited to the infant, who "chose" one of them by, say, moving an arm or blinking an eye. (In such cases it was believed by some peoples that a mystic bond was thereby established between the infant and some relative who had borne that name.) Another source of an infant's initial personal name was, in some societies, a peculiar feature of its appearance or behavior—say, a birthmark or continuous crying or an event coincident with its birth (for example, an earth tremor or an eclipse). In some societies an infant initially received two personal names—one of them public, for everyday use, the other secret and known to close relatives and used mainly in religious contexts.

As noted in the (frustrated) statement by Bligh

just quoted, for most persons the application of an initial personal name was just the beginning. At some time or times during life most persons were given, or themselves chose, a nickname—the sources of which varied widely: for example, Dark Skin, Constant Liar, Sweet Smelling, News Bringer, Fast Eater—such names having been appropriate in that they applied directly to some characteristic of the bearer. (Many other names could also be "translated," but their meanings had no more relevance to their present-day bearers than, say, such English-language names as "Carpenter" or "Armstrong" or "Fisher.") In some cases a person's nickname totally replaced his initial one; in others the two names were used interchangeably, or one was used, say, by close relatives, the other by mere acquaintances.[121] And in some cases nicknames not only replaced initial names but came to be applied to chiefly dynasties—one of the best-known cases having been that of northwest Tahiti Island, which during the late 1700s had come to be named Pomare (Night Cougher) because of that habit of its current incumbent.

Again, however, one nickname was only the beginning. During their lifetimes some individuals acquired several new nicknames, which either replaced or augmented the one or more already in use. And in addition there were at least two other widespread ways of acquiring new names. One was used by some victorious warriors, who adopted the names of enemies slain by them—a practice some (but not all) scholars interpret as intended to capture the "vitality," etc., of the slain. Another was the exchange of names between formally—i.e., ritually bonded—"friends"—an institution found in many Polynesian societies and one that in some cases involved not only name exchange but unlimited use of one another's goods—and wives—as well.

As noted above, some names came to be applied exclusively to whole families, and dynasties of families; the extreme of that exclusiveness was reached in cases where the subjects of a chief were forbidden to use not only his name but all words containing sound combinations more or less identical with his name. In Tahiti this custom, labeled *pi*, led not only to the invention of temporarily substitute words but, as was noted in chapter 7, in some cases to permanent vocabulary change (White 1967).

Pi and other customs relating to personal names raise a question of deeper implications: namely, What kind of connection was believed to exist between an individual and his (or her) name(s) beyond his more or less exclusive identification with that name? More specifically, Was an individual's personal name thought to be as much a part of him as, say, his navel cord, hair cuttings and spittle, when he was alive, or his bones, when he was dead? In other words, could an enemy use his name for sorcerizing him as effectively as using his physical exuviae? Or was his name used only indirectly, to direct the sorcerer's god-familiar to identify and then attack him? I do not know the answer to those questions, nor believe that they can be answered from available documents. In his remarkable reconstruction of indigenous Marquesan culture, E. S. C. Handy wrote: "[T]o the native the personal name, whether of a man, a thing, or a force of nature, is that person or object. In other words, the name is not attached to or descriptive of, but is identical with a person or thing" (1923, 85–86)—a bold and positive but otherwise cryptic assertion, for which, however, Handy provides no convincing evidence.

Turning, finally, to the more strictly venerative practices attending successful childbirth: those ranged from offhand prayers to the family's tutelar god to elaborate temple rites in which the infant was presented to, in some cases sanctified by, its family or tribal gods—or in at least one society desanctified.

Desanctification is exemplified by the Tahitian custom of *amo'a*, which meant, literally, "*a* (negative) *mo'a* (sanctity)." Its underlying rationale was that newborn infants were characterized by a certain amount of contagious dangerousness[122] (owing to their inherited godliness), and that that dangerousness had to be, so to speak, insulated, in order for others to interact safely with them.

LIFE STAGES

Polynesians everywhere were attuned to and their lives shaped by recurring sequences of natural events: solar, lunar and stellar cycles, well known changes in wind patterns, etc.—some of which determined the timing of their subsistence activities and travels, as well as some of their ceremonies and wars. Also, there were names for most of those natural sequences, including what Westerners call "year" (and in some cases "half a

year"). However, no Polynesians defined an individual's length of biological life in terms of number of "years."[123] Instead, most peoples chronologized a person's life span in terms of sequential changes in his (or her) bodily features or behaviors. During the earlier parts of a person's life phrases such as the following Hawaiian ones were used—in this case for a male:

- "big enough to carry a small gourd of water" (estimated by Westerners to be about two years old);
- "big enough to carry two [presumably unhusked] coconuts" (about four to six years old);
- "strong enough to carry a small member of the family on his back" (about ten years old).

(from Pukui et al. 1972, II: 50)

In addition, all or most Polynesian peoples labeled what they conceptualized as the major stages of a person's whole life: namely, infancy, childhood, youth, maturity, and old age. However, the labels for those stages—which served to characterize their referents' physical condition or behavior—varied somewhat from society to society, as did the signs or conditions marking the onset of each stage. Consider, for example, the differences between Tahitians and Hawaiians in this respect—first, those of the Tahitians:

- *'aiu* (*'ai*, to eat or drink; *u*, milk), a suckling child, affectionate term for a young person;
- *tama*, a child, male or female;
- *taure'are'a* (*tau*, time of; *re'are'a*, pleasure), the young, healthy, and vigorous of the people;
- *pa'ari*, mature, old, ripe, hard; wise, knowing, skillful, cunning;
- *ru'au*, old, stricken in years; an old man or woman.

(adopted from Davies 1851, the Tahitian-English dictionary compiled by missionaries of the London Mission Society)

The corresponding set of Hawaiian labels was in some respects closely similar, in others widely—significantly—different. The first stage—"infancy"—was identically labeled (i.e., *'aiwaiu*, eating breast milk. "Old age" was, as in Tahiti, labeled by words that also signify "physically worn and weak." And *kama* (Tahitian *tama*) meant not only "child" but, more generally, "native" (e.g., *kama'āina*, "person of the land"). However, whereas the Tahitian word for "youth," *taure'are'a*, translates literally as "time of engaging in pleasure," its

Hawaiian counterpart, *ka wā uʻi*, translates literally as "time of youthful beauty and vigor." And whereas the Tahitian label for "maturity" (*paʻari*) also signified "ripe" (said also of fruit), "hard" (said also of wood), "skillful" and "cunning," its counterpart in Hawaiian, *hoʻomakua*, meant "to act as a parent (*makua*), to become established or permanent" (adapted from Pukui and Elbert 1957).

An even wider and more significant life-stage difference between Tahitians and Hawaiians prevailed with respect to their apportionment of social worth. In both societies most respect was accorded to, and most socially important roles exercised by, individuals classified as "mature"; and while Hawaiians were generally considerate of the old-aged, the Tahitians tended to neglect and abuse them—or even to hasten their demise (Oliver, 2001).

Wider still were differences between Tahitians (or Hawaiians) and, say, Pukapukans in the apportionment of age-related social worth. For, among the latter, the *tupele* ("old, gray-haired men"), who were at the final stage of life, were not only served and respected but elevated to membership in each village's council, which governed both political and social affairs.

Another way Polynesians differentiated individuals according to temporal aspects of their lives was in terms of relative order of birth among siblings: with the partial exception of Samoa, in all societies the firstborn son, or the firstborn child of either sex, was accorded superiority over his or her siblings in one or more crucial respects. In most societies that differentiation was verbalized in appellations such as "first," "in front of," or "sacred." And in most of them the firstborn was singled out by some measure of recognition and privilege, ranging from an initial (though temporary) advantage over siblings in the control of family resources to absolute and religiously sanctioned command over all family property and services—a command that began, in principle, at the firstborn's birth and that lasted until the birth of his (or her) first son.

Examples of such practices will be given in a later chapter; suffice it to note here that the rationale for most of them constituted one aspect of the concept of godliness (which was delineated broadly in chapter 8). The aspect met with here was the belief that, inasmuch as most humans were descended originally from one or another god,[124]

they had thereby inherited, reproductively, a portion of that godliness—the "amount" (or intensity, or whatever) of one's portion having decreased relative to order of birth (i.e., among persons of recognized common descent the firstborn of a line of firstborns having had the "largest" amount, the last-born of a line of last-borns the least).

While in most societies the eldest offspring (or the eldest male offspring) of a couple usually inherited some advantages over his or her siblings with respect to rights of command and control, there existed in some societies institutionalized recognition that in many families some younger offspring was in fact the "apple"—more appositely, the "coconut"!—of its parents' (or in many cases, grandparents') eyes. This recognition was most highly institutionalized in Hawaiʻi, where such children (often but not necessarily firstborns) were labeled *pai punahele* (made, or pampered favorite). When young they were usually carried about long past walking stage, and when older they were excused from the tasks performed by other children and were provided with piles of mats or barkcloth for soft sitting.

Another factor that served to change the primogenitural pattern of succession was adoption, which took place throughout Polynesia.

Polynesians' penchant for fostering one another's progeny took many forms: from the temporary housing and feeding of others' children, to their total and permanent assimilation, including virtual severance of their natal ties. In several societies some transfers were arranged even before birth—the adopting family having taken possession of the child at or soon thereafter. Moreover, in some societies certain categories of relatives (e.g., grandparents, uncles and aunts) enjoyed overriding "demand" rights to do so, despite any contrary wishes of the child's parents (who, it should be added, were customarily attuned to the practice, which they themselves could also make use of). More about this salient feature of Polynesian social relations will be given in chapter 18; it is mentioned here in order to point up the fact that a large percentage of Polynesians lived, some of them from birth, in families other than their natal ones.

Other factors, such as differences in personality, often conspired in real life to alter the pattern of succession represented in the primogeniture model, but that model remained an important ideal almost everywhere.

INFANCY

In most societies the first stage of a person's life was conceptualized as lasting from birth to complete, or nearly complete, weaning—"nearly complete," inasmuch as some infants in some societies continued to suckle occasionally even after reaching the next conceptualized stage, of "childhood." The label applied to individuals in that first stage was in some societies "breast feeders," in others "sleeping child." Among many peoples, infants were started on other kinds of food (e.g., coconut cream, soft puddings, premasticated tubers, etc.) shortly after birth—partly to encourage weaning and partly (in some societies) to fatten them.

Substitute (i.e., "wet") nursing was resorted to mostly in two kinds of situations: when the natural mother became ill or conclusively pregnant, or when, in highly stratified societies, an upper-class mother was unable or unwilling to nurse. ("Unable" because of religious restrictions, "unwilling" because of her wish to remain unburdened.)

According to the few reports about this matter, weaning was in most societies deliberate, and ranged from gradual (as, for example, by slow substitutions of other foods) to abrupt. In only one society I know of was the infant itself given a "choice." That occurred in Hawai'i, where two objects, representing its mother's breasts, were placed in front of the infant and a request addressed to gods to induce it to give up its desire for milk. If the infant tossed away the objects, that signified its desire to nurse no more. And if not, nursing continued until another such test indicated the infant's willingness to be weaned (Handy and Pukui 1972, 88).

Meanwhile, in most societies an infant was left free of confining clothing,[125] and efforts were made to "develop" it, which consisted not of cultivating its behavior (e.g., in speaking or moving or holding things) but of perfecting its body. For males that included, here or there, flattening the occiput and molding the upper cranium into wedge shape (i.e., "to add to the terror of [its] aspect in warfare"). And for females it included rolling their fingertips to make them taper, of molding the nasal bridge in order to make it flatter (as in Tahiti) or sharper (as in Hawai'i), and either enlarging the vulva (as in Pukapuka and the Marquesas) or flattening the *mons veneris* (as in

some other societies)—all in the name of "comeliness."

"Comeliness" was also deliberately sought after in several societies through making infants fat (by frequent and virtually forced feeding), unblemished (by keeping their skins smooth and soft by frequent bathing and oiling), and light colored (by sheltering them from the sun).

While several Western observers commented on the apparent physical ease with which Polynesian women gave birth, for many Polynesian peoples the process itself and certain periods of time thereafter were thought to be fraught with danger—partly due to the perceived vulnerability of the neonate to recognized natural hazards and partly due to god-associated ones. Some of the latter were imagined to have come from human enemies acting through godly agents (e.g., by sorcery), others directly from gods themselves (e.g., from characteristically malign gods, or from tutelar gods resentful of insufficient homage). In any case, in several societies steps were taken to protect the newborn, or the newborn and mother, by sheltering them in a separate house rendered safe by human guards or religious devices. And it goes without saying that in societies where such practices prevailed, the elaborateness of them varied with the social status of the subjects—so that, in Mangareva (for example) the male heir of the island's paramount chief remained secluded for years in a remote mountain stronghold until about the time of puberty, when he emerged to be ceremonially presented to his future subjects.

In at least one society—that of Tahiti—the seclusion of high-rank infants was intended not only to protect them from persons intent on "harming" them—in this sense, physically or magically—but also to protect benevolent relatives from being "harmed" by them, contagiously. Reference here again is to "godliness," which, as previously noted, was believed by Tahitians (and, I conclude, by many other Polynesian peoples) to be an impalpable inherited component of most humans—the amount or intensity of which depended upon an individual's "genetic distance" from his (or her) ancestral god. (Bear in mind that a couple's firstborn was "closer" to them than were his siblings because of having inherited more of his parents' godliness than they.) Also note that while "large" amounts (or higher intensities, etc.)

of godliness entitled their inheritors to deference from those with much less, superiority (in godliness) was believed also to be contagiously harmful to persons with less (a concept that, doubtless, has led some scholars to liken *mana*, including godliness, to electricity).

In addition to beliefs about variation in godliness due to "procreative distance," it was believed, at least in Tahiti, that an individual's godliness was most efficacious at birth, but as noted earlier could be "insulated" by performance of rites of "desanctification" (*am'oa*), the first of which took place during an individual's infancy—partly for the purpose of allowing close relatives safe access to the child.[126]

Continuing with the custom of desanctification as practiced in Tahiti (with parallels in the Marquesas and elsewhere), the number of such rites varied according to the inherited rank (and therefore "amount" or "intensity" of godliness) of the subject. For most Tahitians there were only one or two such rites, which were completed during the subject's infancy. For a high-ranking male, however, the last of the series was performed much later and past childhood, when, according to one account, he "adopts a Friend [i.e., concludes a pact of bond-friendship]—which is the whole required to make his head Free, evry thing he toutches [prior thereto] being in his Minority or Sacred State is made Sacred by his toutch and rendered useless to any other" (Morrison 1935, 186, as quoted in Oliver 1974, 439). For a high-ranking female, however, the terminal *amo'a* rite took place at the time of her marriage, thereby enabling her and her husband to "eat out of the same dish" (Ibid.).[127]

CHILDHOOD

All Polynesian peoples conceptualized a distinct stage of a person's life between "infancy" and "youth," and by many of them a person at that stage was distinctively labeled "child" (e.g., *tama*, *kama*, etc.), in contrast to "infant" or "youth." Moreover, in most societies the beginning of that stage was delimited conceptually by weaning and habitual walking, but the criteria that marked the transition from "childhood" to "youth" differed somewhat among societies.

An example of a fairly abrupt transition (from "childhood" to "youth") prevailed in Hawai'i, where boys of six or seven (by Westerners' esti-

mates) who showed signs of being no longer a "dangler" (one so young that his penis dangled) moved ceremoniously from the family's *hale 'āina* (house-eating of women and children) to its *hale mua* (house in-front-of), where males past childhood ate and spent their daytime indoor hours.

Another example of abrupt transition from "childhood" to "youth" prevailed in Tongareva, and was signaled, for both boys and girls, by the appearance of pubic hair. For a boy this marked his introduction to copulation: a mature woman was appointed by his father to press back his foreskin over the glans and to instruct him, by actual demonstration, how to copulate. After that the boy began for the first time to wear a loincloth (i.e., to conceal his genitals) and was deemed to be a "youth," ready for actual (in contrast to playful) copulation and other activities of "youth." For a Tongarevan girl the transition was effected, first, by having her hymen digitally ruptured ("to clear the way for menstruation"—not to test her virginity) by a nonkinsman, and second, by clothing her for the first time with a skirt, which she thereafter wore to conceal her pubes.

In some other societies the transition took place upon the onset of menstruation, or upon the first appearance of pubic hair—and was also marked by the donning, for the first time, of clothing. And in still other societies, a boy's transition took place, whatever his physical signs of maturation, upon completion of his supercision or the beginning of his tattooing. Tattooing having been described in an earlier chapter, some discussion is now called for about the even more widespread Polynesian practice of supercision.

In many Melanesian societies the operation performed on a boy's penis was accompanied by harsh physical regimes and profound religious solemnities, and marked the most radical change of a male's whole life. Not so among Polynesians. Among most of them the accompanying practices were for most boys informal, and the operation itself consisted only of slitting the upper part of the foreskin, not of cutting and removing all of it (i.e., *super*cision, not *circum*cision). In some societies it happened to coincide with physiological signs of puberty, in others years before or after—or it took place opportunely (e.g., by young subjects in conjunction with the more ceremonious supercising of their chief's eldest son, when for their parents the operation was relatively costless).

It was usually done by experts (in many cases those who were also expert in tattooing), and usually for a fee.

Institutions of penis mutilation were and are worldwide: their current forms are numerous and their origins largely unknown. For many contact-era Polynesian peoples the most common explanation for the practice was that it rendered copulation cleaner and more pleasurable for females—one factor that led some females in several societies to refuse intercourse with unsuperincised males (another factor being, perhaps, that the latter lacked the hardihood and fortitude that accompanied the operation, i.e., traits required of postchildhood males). For some others, however, the practice was done "because it had always been done."

Turning now to the actions by and regarding individuals during their childhood, it is essential at the outset to distinguish two categories of children: those of chiefly and those of commoner families, inasmuch as some of the former—particularly those in highly stratified societies—led lives markedly different from those of the latter.

Beginning with the latter—i.e., commoners—the more credible accounts of their lives describe them as spending most of their days in play—including playful imitation of adult activities such as fishing and mock battling. Some pioneer missionaries reported that they did nothing but play. That may have been true of some commoner children in some societies, especially of certain explicitly "favored" ones (see below), but most of them, as well as some upper-class ones, doubtless spent some of their days helping, imitating, and following the instructions of older relatives in subsistence and craft activities—as was the case, for example, in Pukapuka:

All the child needs to know in later life is absorbed from his association with his elders in their everyday crafts and tasks. Boys and girls learn to climb coconut trees, and both accompany their elders to the *talo* [taro] beds where they learn *talo* culture. While the boy associates with his male elders and absorbs a knowledge of fish and fishing methods, the girl stays with her adult female relatives and learns the preparation of foods and the plaiting of baskets, food containers, mats, and clothing. No one particular relative is more concerned with the education of the boy or girl than any other relative.

Due to the vagaries of household membership and adoption, a child will learn from any related adults in the household. . . . In the more skilled crafts—the making of hooks, houses, canoes, nets, and fishlines—a boy learns today as he learned in the past, through watching and imitating an expert, either someone in the same household, often his grandfather, or one of the older men of the village group. The older men, being largely released from the necessities of daily fishing, have time for crafts. An interested boy ["child" or "youth"] watches the older person at work, and is given at first simple tasks, later graduating to the more difficult skills under the tutelage of the old master. (Beaglehole and Beaglehole 1938, 277–78)

Meanwhile, in Pukapuka as elsewhere in Polynesia, children were often required to take care of younger siblings while their parents were otherwise employed—"older" meaning in many cases only a year or two older than an infant charge.

Organized, explicit training of "youths," and perhaps also of some children, took place in only a few, highly class-stratified societies and was concerned mainly with intellectual occupations such as priestcraft and (chiefly) pedigree keeping. And while such schooling was undergone mainly by upper-class novices, it is likely that a few lower-class ones were also enrolled—thereby providing one of the few opportunities, in such societies, for upward mobility.

Another mark of "childhood" in many societies was the absence of clothing. In fact, one of the most widespread signs of the end of "childhood" was the donning of at least enough clothing to conceal a person's sexual organs.

As noted above, in the more highly class-stratified societies the "childhood" of upper-class persons differed considerably from that of commoners. The former, typically, were seldom required to work at subsistence chores, and some of them were so narrowly constrained in their movements and companionships that there were few opportunities for wide-ranging, freewheeling play. In Tahiti, for example, the "child"-age offspring of some tribal chiefs lived, with their servants, in separate compounds and were visited only occasionally by their parents. And the heir of the island's highest-ranking chiefs had to be carried when going outside his compound, lest his feet touch the ground, thereby rendering that area sacrosanct, and forbidden to others to reside or walk on.

Regarding the disciplining of individuals during their childhood, most reports about it by contact-era observers characterized it as "absent" to "light"—as for example the following one on Hawaiians: "Those [offspring] whom they did [let live] they utterly spoiled by allowing them uncontrolled liberty to correcting them, though the rebellious children often and unmercifully abused their parents" (Montgomery, 1831, 69). (It should be added that this report, like some others of similar judgment, was written by missionaries, whose own preference for child disciplining was doubtless "heavy.")

According to some reports about early Samoa, parents there were less lenient: "While it is true, as Wilkes noted during his visit to Tutuila in 1839, that parents are "extremely fond of their offspring," it is also true that from infancy onward Samoan children are subjected to quite stringent discipline. Thus, Samoan children, as Stair observed during this same period, are alternately "indulged in every wish" and "severely beaten for the most trivial offense" (Freeman 1983, 205). (Be it added that of the two only Stair was a missionary.)

Statements such as the above are, unfortunately, too brief and unequivocal to permit generalization. Fuller, therefore likely more accurate, descriptions of the matter—such as Raymond Firth's (about Tikopia) and Feinberg's (about Anuta) reveal some differences, both between and within societies, along with more similarities to the effect that children, on the average, were on some occasions indulged and on others restrained.[128]

YOUTH

As just noted, an individual's transition from "childhood" to "youth" differed somewhat from society to society in the criteria that distinguished them. The transition from "youth" to "maturity" also differed among societies in some respects. For, although being "married" was in most societies an important criterion for "maturity," it was not the only one. Moreover, as will be detailed in chapter 18, the state of being "married" was itself not the same everywhere. In most societies, commoner sex-partner couples were deemed to be "married" only if they resided together and, in

some societies, only after they had propagated or adopted offspring. On the other hand, in a few societies some or all "marriages" were established by performance of a nuptial rite alone, regardless of the couple's subsequent interactions.

Nor, as just stated, was postchildhood bachelorhood-spinsterhood the only criterion for "youth." In some societies some (heterosexual) males never "married"—mostly on account of disparity in sex ratio—but nevertheless attained "maturity" in all other respects, including abandonment of "youth-ful" diversions and engrossment in occupational and political affairs. Also, in at least one society—i.e., Pukapuka—all members of a specifically labeled age grade cohort "graduated" from "youth" to "maturity" (in terms of clothing and household-community activities) even if unmarried. And in Tahiti full membership in the Arioi cult—an organization characterized by its members' "youth-ful" activities such as dancing and sexual promiscuity—was limited to unmarried, nonparental postchildhood persons, male and female, whatever their physiological age.

Notwithstanding such variations concerning the perimeters of "youth," there were certain kinds of practices that characterized the actions of most "youth-ful" males, and of many "youth-ful" females, in most societies of tropical Polynesia, namely, a preoccupation with pleasure making—including dancing and more or less promiscuous copulating, and efforts toward self-beautification that served to enhance one's sexual attractiveness. In most societies "youth" was for males also the conventional period for more strenuous kinds of subsistence work, especially teamwork. And in many societies it was mainly their male youths who practiced for and engaged in war. The techniques involved in all such activities have already been described; there remain however a few "youth-ful" aspects of them that deserve further mention.

First of all, it is especially noteworthy how widespread, evidently fundamental, were the practices of "youth-ful" self-beautification (i.e., fattening, skin bleaching, and cosmetic ornamentation), many of which were carried out in groups and concluded with public exhibitions (which in some societies served also, explicitly, as marriage marts).

Also noteworthy is the fact (also mentioned earlier) that in several societies males in general achieved a certain éclat in deflowering virgins, and took evident pride in espousing them—i.e., in being the first, and thereafter the exclusive, possessor of their spouse's sexuality—which in some societies in many cases, and in many societies in some cases, was considered to be a valued social asset. In keeping with that attitude high-status males were usually honor-bound to marry only virgins, and high-status families to give only virgins in marriage—a consideration that moved some families to seclude their daughters until marriage. Such decorum prevailed especially in western Polynesia, where, as mentioned earlier, some families designated one of their daughters—usually the eldest—to be their "sacred maid" (taupoo, etc.), who thereby became a prized and well-guarded symbol of family honor. The acme of such attitudes and practices occurred in Samoa, as will be later described.

Turning to the productive and constructive practices of males' "youth-ful" lives, what distinguished them was their work in teams. Whereas older men tended to labor individually or in family-sized groups, "youth-ful" males did so with one another—in ground clearing, fishing, food collecting and building, and typically with the exuberance of play.[129]

One good example of such group activities prevailed in Pukapuka, where upon reaching "youthhood," all of a community's males were formed into a tanganga, which for periods lasting from six months to about two years—i.e., until superseded by the next-younger cohort, did most of the community's deep-sea fishing as a group, their catch having gone to the community's elders, who kept what they themselves ate and passed on the rest to other residents, including the fishermen.

MATURITY

In view of the role of what Westerners label "marriage" in helping to define "maturity," it will be useful to provide a few words about its Polynesian parallels. (More on this complex subject will be presented in chapter 18.)

Open, widely sanctioned and more or less durable sexual unions between male-female couples occurred in several forms. One extreme variant was a maritally ceremonialized but brief union, for political purposes, between, say, an elderly upper-class male and a preadolescent upper-class female, wherein the couple resided in separate households and between whom sexual relations were implied, and authorized, but seldom if ever realized. At the other extreme were couples who cohabited more or less exclusively for numbers of years and without the sanction of a marital ceremony but with community knowledge of and approval for their union.

Although both of those extreme types of union, and the several different ones between them, were considered "legitimate," only some of them appear to have qualified their partners as "mature." And while postulating that "marriage" was one requisite for what many Polynesian peoples defined as "maturity,"[130] it cannot be said that being "married" was the sole or indispensable condition for it. Thus, in some societies being "mature" also meant being and behaving as a parent (i.e., having and supporting one or more of one's own or foster children). And in some societies there were persons, no longer classified as "youths" and not yet classified as "old," who had never married nor supported children, but who were nevertheless labeled "mature." In other words, although not all Polynesian peoples had precise words for "maturity," it is probable that all of them conceptualized a life stage between "youth" and "old age," during which most but not all persons became married and supported children, and who behaved neither with the exuberance and irresponsibility of "youth" nor with the decrepitude of "old age." Moreover, it was during that interim but fairly lengthy stage of life that some of its members held most of their society's most skillful and influential roles. However, since most of the activities involving those roles have been described in previous chapters, or will be later on described, we can proceed to examine the more obscure topic of old age.

OLD AGE

How old was "old" among contact-era Polynesians? Also, what percentage of a society's members became "old," and having become so, how much longer did they, on the average, remain alive? Essential questions for an ethnographer, but questions that are unanswerable in measured chronological terms.

Basic to the above culturally framed questions is the actual demographic one of a population's average life span, as measured in solar years.

Some vanguard Western visitors gave estimates about the ages of certain natives, but they were only guesses, inasmuch as Polynesians did not count a person's age in solar years.[131] Thus, the only persuasive evidence—and that only approximate—on year age at death comes from pre-Western cemeteries. As described earlier, the largest of those so far excavated are in Hawai'i, where six cemeteries yielded a total of 2,288 bodies, of which 1,608 were judged to have been over about twenty years old. The mean age of those 1,608 bodies was calculated to have been about thirty-seven.[132] However, in considering the typicality of these figures it should be noted that not all Hawaiians were buried in cemeteries, some having drowned at sea and some, probably many, killed and their bones scattered on battlegrounds.

As noted earlier, the causes of death of the 1,608 excavated bodies can be determined in only a few cases, their deaths having occurred before the introduction, by outsiders, of such bone-marking diseases as syphilis and leprosy. Nor can post-contact evidence be relied upon to indicate pre-contact life spans. That alien diseases and other outsider influences shortened average precontact life spans is beyond doubt. Moreover, post-Western censuses provided little or no age-related data for several decades after contact.

Reverting to the culturally framed question How old was "old"? that question becomes, What criteria did Polynesians use for distinguishing "oldness"? Answers to that question, which are provided in some of the sources, are mostly in terms of physical characteristics (e.g., in men: white hair, sagging flesh, physical decrepitude; in women: those past reproductive age). In some places overall mental decline was also considered a typical characteristic of "old" age—but in others some or all "old" persons were credited with superior wisdom in general or in certain spheres of knowledge in particular (e.g., "history," cosmology, divination). And in some societies "oldness" was defined largely, or entirely, in terms of a person's age-grade cohort (as in Pukapuka) or familial generation (i.e., upon birth of a grandchild a person became ipso facto "old").

Nevertheless, however they defined it, all Polynesian peoples had words for "old" persons, along with distinctive attitudes toward and prescribed statuses for them. Some of those words were distinctively denominative (e.g., *ruau*), some

generational (i.e., grandparental [*tupuna, kupuna,* etc., which in many languages also meant "ancestral"]), and some depictive (e.g., "worn out," "faded," "eyelid drooping," "dilapidated," "wrinkled").

Within each society individuals doubtless varied in their attitudes toward particular "old" persons, ranging from affectionate nurturing to abusive irritation, but of more relevance to this study are whole peoples' institutionalized ways of thinking about and acting toward their "old" members. And in most societies for which information is recorded—unfortunately, only a few—those patterns are fairly similar. Thus, "old" persons were usually excused from most forms of productive labor—such as gardening, fishing, collecting, building—but were generally admired when they voluntarily participated, or sympathized with when circumstances forced them to. In fact, in many societies the task most "old" men performed, and that almost incessantly, was making sennit, alternating in many cases with mending fishnets—both of them indispensable rather than marginal contributions to their households' economy. As for "old" women, most of them continued, as long as physically able, to fabricate mats and barkcloth, and in several societies a few of them were the leading specialists in midwifery and in herbal and other kinds of healing. And in most societies the "old," both male and female, were called upon to look after young children, while the latters' parents were otherwise engaged.

"Old" men[133] were everywhere excused from warfare—but specially admired when they chose to fight. And although "old" persons were considered incapable of effective copulation, they were commended, usually with ribaldry, when they proved, or tried to prove, otherwise. Conversely, in some societies they were tacitly excluded from such "youthful" diversions as dancing, and regarded as silly when they tried to join in.

It was believed nearly everywhere that men increased in knowledge and wisdom with age—but only up to a point. Thus, while many, perhaps most, "old" men were respected as having those qualities, and were employed as councilors, teachers, priests, diviners and repositories of sacred knowledge, etc., it was also widely thought that with extreme "oldness," mentality-weakening senility invariably set in.

Likewise with authority—in families, in communities and in tribes. It was a fundamental precept of most peoples that relatively older men—"older" in terms of birth order—should govern and take precedence over younger ones, but only up to the point when the older ones became afflicted with physical and mental decrepitude. In some such cases the older incumbent came to acknowledge his (or her) condition and to voluntarily "retire." In others, however, the younger aspirant was left to seize control by force or politics. In this connection, the precept of "older over younger" fails to apply in some polities structured by hierarchically positioned kin titles, such as Samoa. In those, the holder of the higher-ranking kin title took precedence over the lower-ranked titleholder whatever their respective ages. (Readers will note that the statements in this paragraph apply mainly to males. In some polities, such as Hawai'i and Tahiti, some titular authority was also held and exercised by women. And in many families women exercised much authority despite, or along with, the unit's titular male head.)

The most extreme (reported) exception to Polynesians' generally respectful and benevolent attitude toward the "old" prevailed in Tahiti, where they were comprehensively disvalued. Except for a few individuals of high office (and forceful personality) they were ignored, neglected, and depreciated—and not infrequently considered to be so burdensome that they were assisted to die (e.g., by isolation and lack of feeding, and in some case by live burial). The original cause of this disvaluation is undiscoverable, but it was reinforced by Tahitians' predilection for "youthfulness" and by their practice of transferring a kin title to an heir at its birth (Oliver, 2001).

What percentage of Tahitians, and of other Polynesians, reached "old age" cannot now be known, but eventually they and all of them attained the final life stage, of ghosthood, which followed mortal "death," to which we now turn.

DEATH

Most Polynesian peoples devoted more institutionalized thought and action to a person's biological death than to any other culturally defined threshold of his (or her) life—for to them "death" meant not an end to a person's existence but passage into a different realm: from *ao* to *po*, from the realm of daylight and palpable beings and objects to that of nocturnal darkness and of beings that were in most cases incorporeal, longer lasting, and more versatile and powerful than living humans. The ideas and practices concerning that realm will be summarized later, but first, some of their beliefs and practices concerning and accompanying "death."

All Polynesian languages had words approximating what Anglophones mean by "alive" (e.g., *ora*) and "dead" (*mate, pohe*, etc.). Those words were sometimes used for other conditions as well (*ora*, for "physical well-being," etc.; *mate*, for "injury," "sickness," "jealousy," "loss of argument," etc.)—as, indeed, is also true of Anglophones, for whom however such usages are in most or all cases consciously metaphorical (which may or may not have been true of Polynesians). Words aside, most or all Polynesian peoples judged a human's "aliveness" to be irreversibly terminated and his "death" immutably begun when his spirit (*varua, uhane*, etc.) left his body (e.g., via mouth or tear duct, etc.) and remained outside it too long—"too long" usually indicated by signs of physical decay. (However, there were legends about spirits being recovered, and life thereby restored, days after decay had begun—although such persons usually bore thereafter the mottled marks of decay.)

Polynesians had evidently learned by observation that individuals died—how could they not have?—and concluded that they did so as a result either of "fate" or of accidents (e.g., falling from trees, drowning) or of wounds or of various kinds of bodily disorders, including senile decrepitude. Concerning death by "fate," it was believed by some peoples that, unless forced to leave by accident, homicide, sickness, etc., the spirit remained in the body, or outside it only temporarily, until a predestined time—presumably set by some god. The question then becomes, Which of those other, "premature" causes of "death" were "natural" and which were believed to be initiated or executed by gods?

Some ailments, fatal or otherwise, were considered, axiomatically, due to godly intervention: for example, those caused directly by malevolent gods acting gratuitously or by otherwise "neutral" ones, to punish violations of religious rules. Other such interventions included those of gods acting at the behest of sorcerers or those enlisted to effectuate weapons or poisons or curses. In connection with punishment for rule breaking, it needs adding that the objective was sometimes accomplished not necessarily by killing the rule breaker himself but by killing one or more of his close kin.

More problematic are the causes of drownings and other fatal (real) accidents. However, many reports state or imply that they too were attributed to gods, who, for example, dislodged the victim from the top of a palm or pushed him overboard or raised the storm that swamped the canoe.

Even more problematic are deaths by homicide or suicide. Some instances of murder, including infanticide, were explained as having been carried out at the behest of or assisted by gods in order to uphold god-sanctioned rules or to avenge violations of them. However, it is difficult for me to accept that Polynesians attributed godly intervention to, for example, all murders committed by jealous husbands or to acts of infanticide committed by women in order to spare themselves the burden of child rearing.

And then there was suicide, by both males and females, which occurred in most societies, and in some societies with fairly high frequency. Causes included anger, jealousy, unrequited desire and, sometimes, loss of power or prestige. In Mangareva, for example, the preferred method was jumping off a cliff—and to add a characteristically Polynesian touch, women of high rank jumped off one cliff, lower ranking women another (Buck 1938a, 472). Elsewhere, preferred methods included jumping from high trees, paddling off into the empty ocean or having relatives bury oneself alive—the latter in Pukapuka, a method voluntarily taken by some men defeated in battle. It is difficult to detect beliefs that were directly involved in most such deaths—although it could be argued that even suicide was believed to be caused indirectly by one or another god.

In view of their beliefs about the causes of death it is not surprising that Polynesians had recourse to measures for preventing it. (For, as will presently be described, their beliefs about their spirits' destinies in the *po* cannot have made more than a few of them eager to be there. As will be suggested below, few pagan Polynesians would have yearned for "The Sweet Bye and Bye, when [they would] meet on that Beautiful Shore.") Preventive measures included actual weapons (against potential human enemies), god-supported

devices (amulets, etc.), concealment of one's sorcery-vulnerable exuviae and—of course—avoidance of actions that provoked godly punishment. Moreover, it was customary to offer prayers, and sometimes material sacrifices, before numerous kinds of undertakings—not only to secure godly assistance for success but also to safeguard the lives of participants. (As was suggested earlier, Polynesian prayers were carried out more often in the spirit of prophylaxis than of gratitude.)

In cases of sudden and irreversible death, actions were sometimes taken to discover the god-related cause—in order either to prevent recurrences or to wreak revenge on the revealed human culprit, or both. Even in circumstances such as falling from a tree, where the immediate physical fact of hitting the ground was understood, efforts were often made to discover what god-related factor had caused the victim to fall.

Likewise with the occurrence of what was considered to be a life-threatening condition, from accident or disease. In cases where the proximate causes were believed to be known, the patient's relatives sometimes proceeded forthwith to employ a curer who specialized in the particular ailment. Otherwise, a diagnostician was employed to determine the cause and the type of treatment needed—and often to carry out the treatment as well.

Some ailments were believed to require treatment by mainly physical measures, with little (or no?) godly intervention: fractures, strained muscles, open sores and wounds, partial drownings, digestive disorders, overimbibing of kava, etc. A large—and largely unconvincing—literature has accumulated, from native legends and marveling Western visitors, about the "astounding," even "miraculous" cures effected by some of those measures, including the healing of cavernous wounds, the setting of disjointed bones, the reshaping of crushed skulls, the rejoining of severed limbs, etc. Be that as it may, more credible are accounts of the highly effective skill evinced by some practitioners of the widespread custom of massage (*lomilomi, rumirumi*, etc.).

Ailments believed caused by direct godly intervention required—logically—therapies to persuade or force the relevant god to intervene—therapies that ranged from reverent petitions to exorcism (and sometimes destruction) of malevolent demon-gods, including those acting on instructions from a human sorcerer.

The expertise practiced in one or another kind of therapy included surgery, bone setting, massage, vulnerary medicine (mainly using plants), diagnostics, magic (both curing and harming) and priestcraft. Some specialists were adept in only one of these skills, some in two or more. The methods used in some of them and the places in society of these and other specialists are described elsewhere in this book.

FUNERALS

When "death" occurred—i.e., when it was believed that a person's spirit had left his body finally and irreversibly—Polynesians did some or all of the following: engaged in genuine or conventional grieving; sought information concerning the cause of that death and acted to redress it and, when relevant, to revenge it; took steps to secure the goodwill and safe passage of the departed spirit; and preserved some parts of the remaining body, while disposing of the rest. The amount of activity and goods devoted to those actions varied widely, according to the social status (including life stage) of the deceased—most commoner infants having occasioned little or none (the same having been true, in some societies, with burdensome commoners of "old" age). In contrast, in many societies the death of a ruling chief gave rise to tribe-shaking paroxysms of "grief," including sacrifices (in some cases of humans), factional strife, etc.

Grieving was expressed most usually in the form of wailing dirges conventionalized for particular relationships, such as "Alas, my husband (or wife or mother, etc.), when will I see your brave (or beautiful or caring, etc.) self again?" In addition, the "grieving" was on some occasions accompanied by cutting one's hair or knocking out a tooth or, most drastically, by gashing one's head and breast to induce the flow of blood—the latter also having been practiced in some societies, mainly by women, to express great joy—e.g., upon the return of a long-absent relative.

Some Western observers questioned whether those and other such expressions were "sincere"—having noted that many grievers interrupted their wailing or self-mortification, etc., now and then with laughter-laced conversation. (However, it would be just as irrelevant to question the sincerity of Westerners attending the funeral of, say, their firm's president or their town's mayor.)

Other conventionalized expressions of "grief" that occurred, here or there, included unusually frenzied dancing (sometimes nakedly); realistic

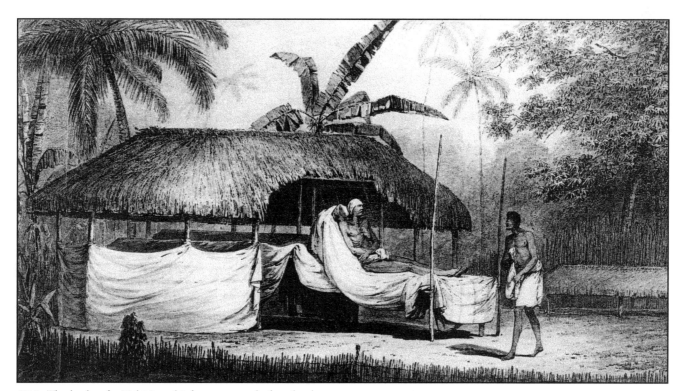

17.1. The body of a Tahitian chief as preserved after death

17.2. A chief mourner of Tahiti (on left) beside the bier of an embalmed high-rank man

dueling (supposedly induced by "anger" over the death); and anarchic self-induced "madness," either individual or general—the latter having taken place in some of the larger and more hierarchical politics upon the death of their chief. (Moreover, such behaviors were quite fitting, since in some societies the death of a tribe's chief did indeed result in devastating wars of succession—or opportunistic attacks from outside.

Mention was made earlier of the measures taken to discover the causes of death; it is enough to add here that the actions taken to redress the death of a chief sometimes included outright warfare against the tribe believed magically responsible for it.

Other actions taken on the occasion of a person's death were intended to secure the goodwill of the deceased's spirit and secure its safe passage to the society's version of a desirable—or less undesirable—sphere of the afterworld. One such measure, already mentioned, consisted of conspicuous grieving. Another was the donation of food and other offerings to the spirit. (When done by nonrelatives, both of these actions doubtless had the additional purpose of displaying support for,

17.3. Close-up of a Tahitian chief mourner in mourning dress

17.4. Chiefly burial pyramid at Tongatabu

17.5. The Tongan Ha'mongaamaui monument

or obtaining the goodwill of, the deceased's close relatives.) In many Polynesian eschatologies a spirit's passage to an agreeable sphere of the afterworld could be obstructed by intrinsically malevolent gods or by the god-familiars of malevolent sorcerers; hence measures were sometimes taken to avoid or frustrate such dangers, by means of soliciting the protection of friendly gods.

Finally, all Polynesian peoples had some conventional methods for dealing with human bodies after departure of the spirit. In a few places some or most bodies were disposed of whole, and soon after the funeral, by burying them nearby, or in the place the deceased's family-tutelar god was believed to frequent. In most societies, however, a body's bones and soft parts were dealt with separately—the latter cut away or allowed to rot away from the bones—and buried forthwith (as being without further significance), some or all of the bones cleaned and retained (as having a continuing association with the departed spirit).

In some societies and in the case of important persons, the separation of soft parts from bones was postponed for weeks or even months by one or another method of embalming (e.g., extraction of intestines followed by oiling or sun drying the corpse)—the main purpose having been to extend the period of mourning in order to prolong respect for the deceased's memory (plus allegiance to his heir). Eventually, however, some or all of the bones were kept by relatives or buried in one or another kind of grave (e.g., at a temple, under a mound) or were hidden in a cave—i.e., to keep them out of the hands of enemies, who might attempt to use them to dishonor the memory of the deceased by, for example, making fishhooks of them, or to harm his spirit by means of sorcery. As for bones retained by relatives, two purposes were thereby served. In some cases, single bones were kept and worn by relatives, or whole packets of them stored in their houses, with what seems to have been genuine wishes to retain mementos of a loved one. In addition, some bones—particularly crania—were also retained as being the most suitable resting place for the deceased's spirit on its voluntary, or petitioned, visitations. This leads to consideration of a spirit's imagined existence after death.

AFTERLIFE

In many, perhaps most, Polynesian eschatologies the spirits[134] of most dead persons embarked forthwith on their journeys to the afterworld.[135] Those that did not remained nearby for one of four causes: they were captured by some human sorcerer and used by him for malignant purposes; they were destroyed by some demonic spirit; they tarried voluntarily in order to be near or assist some beloved person (a rare occurrence); or they remained, also voluntarily, to haunt those of their close survivors who had failed to do enough for them—i.e., to conduct proper funerals, including prayers and offerings, to protect them on their journeys to and existence in the afterworld.

Beliefs regarding that journey, and of the spirit's final destination, had many versions, not only from society to society but within some societies as well; even within some tribes there seems to have been no "official," dogmatic version. And even though a tribal chief may have subscribed to one version, there appears to have been no sanction-backed effort to impose it on his subjects. Therefore, instead of attempting to reproduce that multiplicity—which would require scores of pages—a few paragraphs will be offered to list some of their more common features.[136]

First, regarding destinations: One of the most widespread tenets was that the final destination was located westward (which in the case of many peoples was linked with the setting—i.e., departing—sun), or downwind (during the prevailing easterlies), or in memory of their pioneer ancestors having come from the west (corollary to which was the belief in some societies that spirits endeavored to return to their ancestors after death). In a version similar to the above the destination was *i raro*, which meant both "far westward" and "far below," and "long ago" as well (another example of the ambiguities involved in translating Polynesian texts into concrete Anglophonic meanings).

Another widespread tenet was that the destination, as part of the cosmos, consisted of several "levels," each of which was the abode of a distinct type of (hierarchically stratified) god, with the most universal and powerful at the top. In line with this concept, the spirits of humans were able to attain no higher than one of the lower levels—which one having depended upon factors to be described below.

Somewhat different was the cosmic geography represented in some Tahitian versions of afterlife. According to those there were not just stratified but markedly dissimilar destinations. Using Anglophonic analogies: one was a paradise, the second a purgatory (for unpurged wrong-doers—i.e., those who had broken religious or chief-made rules without expiation), and the third a limbo (for purged wrongdoers and those not otherwise eligible for paradise). Particularly interesting are some characterizations of that paradise. According to one observer it was an Elysium of a place: "where the air was remarkably salubrious [and] flowers abundant, highly odoriferous, and in perpetual blossom. Here [those] raised to this [privileged situation] followed all the amusements and pursuits to which they had been accustomed in the world, without intermission or end. Here was food in abundance, and every indulgence" (Ellis 1829, I: 517). And "here there was no sickness and no aging, and all women remained eternally beautiful" (Moerenhout 1837, I: 434— in other words, a highly suggestive commentary on the Tahitians' "youth"-fully oriented life goals.

Also significant were the beliefs about the kinds of persons whose spirits were admitted to that Tahitian paradise. According to another observer, those most eligible were former active members of the Arioi cult, whose fate it was to enter into "the full enjoyment of their paradise, where it was believed that no children existed to mar their pleasure" (Henry 1928, 242). And again according to Moerenhout, paradise was also accessible to chiefs and "to the friends of chiefs and to other such individuals affluent enough to [have provided] the gods with enough sacrifices, and the priests with enough gifts, to induce the latter to pray so as to bring about, eventually, the transfer of the donor's souls [from limbo] to the abode of light and pleasure" (1837, 435). He added, however, that such donations required so much wealth that most people entertained no hope of ever tasting the delights of that heavenly abode.

In contrast to the complexities exemplified in Tahitian eschatologies, some other conceptualized destinations were—or were reported as having been[137]—simply at the abode of one's ancestral god (for example, in the ocean if that god was a shark, into a crater if a volcano god). Or simpler still were those eschatologies, mentioned earlier, which portrayed that, upon death, the spirit went "west" or "up" or "down" or into the *po*.

As to the spirit's journey, here again the recorded accounts vary widely in detail. Some state that it simply "went" to its destination, others that it traveled thence with the assistance of its ancestral god(s), and still others reported itineraries of labyrinthine complexity studded with hazards. In line with the widespread notion of the destination being "westward," many eschatologies included a tenet that the spirit embarked on its journey by leaping off its home island's westernmost cape. As for the hazards that were included in many journey versions, some were quite comprehensible (by Western logic) but others both bizarre and unreasonable (also by Western logic, but revelatory of some Polynesians' views regarding punishment and reward). Also comprehensible is the tenet, included in some eschatologies, that the journeying spirit was confronted with malevolent demons that sought to destroy it and sometimes succeeded in doing so. The events that seem "unreasonable" may again be exemplified by incidents in one Tahitian version.

In this version the journeying spirit, now become blind, reached two stones just after the take-off from its home island's westernmost cape. If it happened, entirely by chance, to step onto Stone A it survived and continued on its journey; if however onto Stone B, it was exterminated forthwith. Then somewhat farther the Stone A spirit passed through a patch of gardenia blossoms, whereupon, if it (still unknowingly) picked any of those highly favored decorations, it perished then and there. (What may strike a reader steeped in the reward-and-punishment doctrine of most Western religions is the utter fortuitousness and seeming triviality of such events.)

Such fortuity, when added to beliefs about "Who gets to heaven," serves to underscore a judgment that among many if not most Polynesian peoples a human's conduct toward other humans had less effect upon his fate in the afterlife than did his conduct toward gods. Or, in some situations his purposeful conduct, in contrast to pure chance, had no effect upon his afterlife at all. Of course, a case might be made that in some situations a spirit's "salvation" did, in part at least, depend upon the amounts of funeral offerings contributed by his survivors—and that those amounts depended, in turn, on his lifetime conduct toward them. That however is my rationalization; I know of no reported instances of Polynesians having expressed such a judgment.

18

HOUSEHOLDS AND FAMILIES

I turn now to the large and thorny topic of (tropical) Polynesians' social relationships ("thorny" not only because of the topic's inherent complexities but also because of the superficialities and obscurities about it contained in much of the literature—most contact-era descriptions of it having been piecemeal and focused on the relationships of a few chiefly personages). Also, with a few exceptions, comprehensive studies of the topic by competent observers were made decades later, after Western-induced changes in some of those social relationships had taken place. Nevertheless, some area-wide generalities on the topic can be inferred, or salvaged, beginning with some about all Polynesian peoples' most basic types of social groups—namely, families and households.

What is here called a "social group" is any kind of aggregate of persons who interact with one another, directly or seriatim, with some regularity and at the time more or less distinct from all other persons. In addition to families and households, Polynesian groups included, for example, deep-sea fishing crews, religious sects, dance troupes and tribes. As such, a social group differs from a social category—the latter having been all persons in a society who shared one or more specific attributes considered distinctive by members of that society, such as "priests," "warriors," "skilled carpenters," "navigators," "males" and "females." In some cases all of a tribe's priests or warriors or skilled carpenters, etc., did constitute groups—but rarely did all its "males" or all its "females."

Polynesian households were made up of persons who resided together in a discrete set of buildings and who pool-shared[138] in the production and consumption of food. In addition, many if not most members of a household shared in the maintenance of their common buildings, tended one another's infants and children, nursed one another's ailments, and worshiped together—in many cases a particular god of their own. On the

other hand, very infrequently if at all did a household unit per se, as distinct from its core family, own any territory, terrestrial or marine. (The complex topic of property ownership will be considered in chapter 19.) The core members of the residents of nearly every household were a family, either nuclear, polygamous or extended, added to which in many cases were one or more other relatives. I return to the activities, etc., shared by all members of any household after some details about their constituent families.

A family is herein labeled "nuclear" if composed of a "married" couple, plus—if any—their offspring, biological or adopted. Or it is "polygamous" if composed of a man with two or more of his wives,[139] or "extended" if multigenerational or composed of more than one nuclear family—say, two siblings and their spouses and offspring (if any). "Nuclear" is also applied to families composed of a single or widowed parent and his or her own or adopted offspring—but not to a single or widowed parent alone, since in Polynesia such persons nearly always resided with another family.

In Polynesia some "marriages" were instituted without formality—by one person simply moving into the household of his or her sexual partner—or rarely, by a sexually mated couple setting up a separate household of their own. In other cases a marriage was formalized—socially legitimized—by ceremony and by exchanges of goods between the couple's respective families. In most societies both ways of marrying prevailed, with nuptial ceremonies mainly limited to upper-class couples—i.e., those whose prospective offspring would become recipients of the titles and other assets of the couple's respective families.

However, despite differences in ways of marrying, all Polynesian marriages shared certain other features that distinguished them from other forms of social relationships—beginning with who could marry whom.

18.1. Hamlet scene in Hawai'i

All peoples everywhere, including the Polynesians, have, and have had, such rules, and all of them, with a few partial exceptions, proscribe marriage between father and daughter, mother and son, and brother and sister.[140] The most noteworthy Polynesian exception to this rule, and the actual practice of it, occurred in Hawai'i, where brother-sister marriage was not only permitted but encouraged between persons of highest rank, in order to preserve and even augment their respective quotas of the godliness passed on to their offspring.[141] But even in Hawai'i sexual relations were frowned upon, and marriage forbidden, between brothers and sisters among the society's commoners.

Most peoples, everywhere, also proscribe marriage between other "close" consanguines as well—"close" being defined somewhat differently from society to society. In most human societies "closeness" includes those within three degrees of consanguinity (i.e., in Anglophonic terms, for example, between first cousins), in other societies four such degrees, and in a few societies all those with whom a consanguineous link is believed to exist. On the other hand, there are a few societies in which marriage between a person and his or her parallel cousin (i.e., the offspring of a father's brother or a mother's sister) is proscribed, while marriage between cross cousins (i.e., offspring of a father's sister or mother's brother) is not only permitted but favored. However a people define

"closeness," their rules against violations of it usually include both social and supernatural sanctions—which vary in kind and severity from society to society. As for native explanations for those rules—i.e., for their particular concept of "incest"—the most common one is that such rules were established by god(s).[142]

Focusing again on Polynesia: reaching back in time it is quite certain that the ancestors of the peoples now called "Polynesian" also had rules regarding the boundaries of "incest," but those rules must have been flexible enough to permit their descendants to waive them in order to adjust to the changes in population size that surely occurred during their eras of migration and pioneer settlement. Thus, a pioneer population of three or four closely related families (e.g., the members of a single migratory canoe) could not have survived and proliferated without narrowing the bounds of permissible marriage. And while such pragmatically founded norms might have changed in most societies as their numbers increased, there were some other societies in which the narrower pioneer-era bounds were retained due to the weight of tradition.

One final word about rules of "incest": studies of recent Polynesian marriages reveal that violations of those rules were sometimes winked at after the fact, because of "circumstances"—which suggests that such was also the case in precontact times.

Among Polynesians, consanguinity was not the only widely prevalent kind of restriction on choice of spouse. In most of the highly class-stratified societies there was preference among upper-class persons for upper-class spouses, for themselves and for their offspring. And in some of those societies (e.g., Tahiti, Hawai'i and Tonga) that preference was rigidified into inflexible rules. Such rules did not, and perhaps were not intended to, prevent upper-class men (and in some societies upper-class women) from dallying sexually with lower-class persons, but they served to preclude wholly approved marriage of such pairs.

Turning from society-wide restrictions to more personal preferences in choosing a spouse: most young persons appear to have preferred someone near their own age—a corollary of the high value placed on physical beauty (i.e., as locally defined). However, marriages between a male and a much younger female were not unusual; indeed, some young females were reported as having preferred to marry a much older male—i.e., because of the latter's proven dependability and greater social worth. And whereas males in some societies (mainly those in westen Polynesia) preferred, or would accept, only a virginal bride, many females in those and other societies showed preference for sexually experienced males.

Another mode of spouse selection—a combination of personal preference and expedience—was the widespread custom, called by scholars the "sororate" (from Latin *soror*, "sister"), of a man having a marital relationship with a pair of sisters at the same time or of marrying a wife's sister upon the death of the wife. Conversely, it was not unusual for a widow to become married to a brother of her late husband (a worldwide custom called the "levirate"), although I know of no Polynesian practice of a female being married simultaneously to two living brothers—except possibly (?) in the Marquesas.

As noted earlier, not all Polynesian marriages were the outcome of a couple's personal choice. In many societies some marriages, varying from a few to nearly all, were match-mated by the couple's parents, with little or no consideration of the couple's preferences and regardless of their ages at the time. In fact, some betrothals were arranged during a couple's infancy, or even before the birth of one or both of them (contingent of course upon their being of different gender). In the case of upper-class parents such arranged matches were made, typically, for considerations of a political nature. Or, in many other instances, parents chose for their offspring mates who were known to be industrious and reliable. And, not surprisingly, oral "literature" included stories of young persons who, upon being forced by parents to abandon their personal choices, resorted to desperate measures, including even suicide.

Finally, in some societies some marriages were the Polynesian equivalent of "shotgun weddings"—reluctant Don Juans having been coerced into marrying pregnant maidens known, by process of elimination, to have been impregnated by them.

Focusing now on avenues to marriage: the range of them was very wide. At one extreme a pair of sex partners, having found one another more satisfying and congenial than other casual partners, simply began dwelling together, either in one of their parental households or, less frequently, in a new one of their own. In most such cases no ceremony was held to legitimize or celebrate the union; as was said in Hawai'i of such (socially inconsequential) a marriage: "It was just a pebble to pelt a rat" (Beckwith 1932, 166). At the other extreme were parentally arranged unions with formal contractual betrothals, including exchanges of goods, lengthy periods of engagement (in some cases from birth onward) and close watch over the chastity of the female (but not over that of the male), culminating in elaborate nuptial ceremonies including religious rites, feasts and additional interfamilial exchanges of goods—plus, in at least one society, a ceremonious testing of the bride's virginity.

Virginity testing was most elaborate in Samoa, where at the weddings of high-ranking persons, the groom or his representative digitally tested the bride's hymen. If blood flowed, thereby indicating that the hymen had been intact and the bride a virgin, it was exhibited publicly, to general rejoicing and to the honor of the bride and her family. If, however, no blood flowed, the wedding was usually called off and the bride punished by her disgraced relatives, in some cases by death.[143]

In several societies the ceremonious weddings held to celebrate the unions of high-ranking persons, and especially of firstborn heirs, served not only to link the couple's families politically but also to assure the high-rank status of their offspring.

One noteworthy variant on avenues to marrying was the Tikopians' custom of "bride-capture," in which a youth's relatives (with or without his concurrence) went in a body to the house of a maiden (of the youth's or his relatives' choosing), abducted her—to the accompaniment of actual or feigned resistance by her relatives—and took her to the house of the youth, who copulated with her then and there, thereby finalizing the marriage. In some cases the bride was a willing, even cooperative, partner in the action; in others she fought against it and had to be raped by the groom with the help of his relatives. In either case most such unions were eventually legitimized by peaceful exchanges of goods between relatives of the pair.

A different version of the above occurred on Samoa, where, in one form of marrying, a youth "abducted" a (willing) maiden, who after one night with him was recognized, pragmatically, by both their families as having become his wife.

Before addressing the large and misty topic of husband:wife relations, something needs stating about Polynesian varieties of polygamy, beginning with polygyny—i.e., unions of one husband and two or more wives.

A Polynesia-wide fact about polygyny is that, while it was in no society forbidden, it was practiced quite spottily and mainly by men well-situated enough to subsist more than one wife—and in some cases forceful enough to impose such an arrangement upon them. For, although some women were agreeable, even desirous, to have one or more cowives—i.e., to share domestic chores and child care—there were others who for jealousy or other reasons objected (except, usually, when a cowife was a sister, which in many cases was the pattern). And although the cowives of high-ranking men in societies such as Tahiti and Hawai'i appear to have accepted their positions, they do not seem to have been submissively haremlike in their attitudes and actions.

Polyandry, the concurrent marriages of one female with two or more males, occurred in two or more Polynesian societies but was most firmly institutionalized in the Marquesas. Polygyny also occurred in the Marquesas, but only rarely—a circumstance, along with the incidence of polyandry, which some writers attribute to the society's large preponderance of males.

One kind of situation that led to Marquesan polyandry appears in Melville's fictionalized but partly authentic *Typee*: "The girls are first wooed and won, at a very tender age, by some stripling in the household in which they [both] reside. This, however, is a mere frolic of the affections, and no formal engagement is contracted. By the time this first love has a little subsided, a second suitor presents himself, of graver years, and carries both boy and girl away to his own habitation. This disinterested and generous-hearted fellow now weds the young couple—marrying damsel and lover at the same time—and all three thenceforth live together as harmoniously as so many turtles."

More convolute—and probably more authentic, was the kind of Marquesan situation reconstructed by Handy:

A boy (A) and a girl (B) would be betrothed when children, thus becoming *tuia*. When they grew up, the woman might marry another man, who would then be called *ahana pekio* [husband-secondary] in relationship to both A and B. The affianced [*tuia*] man might marry some other woman. She would be *vehine pekio* [wife-secondary] for both A and B. The two *tuia*, A and B, might never live together, but the man had a right to claim the woman at any time. The two *tuia* might be forced to come together by their relatives who had expended much wealth on the betrothal rites. The first child of the *vehine tuia*, no matter what father, belonged to the *ahana tuia*, came to live with him, and took the position in his establishment of his first-born, even though the man might have had children by another woman with whom he was living. The child was called *hamua*, first-born. (E. S. C. Handy 1923, 102)

The sources I have consulted say little or nothing about the status of non–"firstborn" children in a Marquesan family, but that of most wives, whether *tuia* or *pekio*, was, according to Handy, unambiguous: "When a woman undertook to live with a man, she placed herself under his authority. If she cohabited with another man without his permission, she was beaten or, if her husband's jealousy was sufficiently aroused, killed" (Ibid., 100). (I interject at this point the definition employed in this book of the sociological concept of "status," which herein refers to the normative rights entailed in a person's conventional office vis-à-vis those of other offices of the social unit under consideration. By "office" is meant the conventionalized role played by a person in a unit—such as "father" or "eldest son" in a family or such as "senior" in a clan or "chief" in a tribe); by "rights" is meant, for example, precedence, privilege and authority; and by "normative" is meant a society's consensual or most authoritative opinion concerning what incumbents of the office ought to do and be done to. In other words, this particular usage of the word "status"[144] is concerned with a people's social categories of, say, "eldest sons" or clan "seniors" or tribal "chiefs" in general, and not with, say, Malama as eldest son of a particular family or as senior of a particular clan or as chief of a particular tribe, wherein, while nominally occupying such offices, he might have exercised less authority, etc., say, than a younger son or a clan- or tribe-mate.)

(Another feature of the present book's usage of "status" is its comparability: within each type of social unit its component statuses may be compared one with the other in terms of more or fewer rights—or, as expressed herein, as being "higher" or "lower" than the other. Thus, in family units of the Marquesans—indeed, in those of most other Polynesians as well—the status of "husband" was generalized as being "higher" than that of his "wife," and in most Polynesian societies the generalized status of "father" was higher than those of his "sons" and "daughters.")

Resuming our survey of Polynesian forms of marriage, and turning—with some relief!—from the Marquesans' labyrinthine institution of polyandry to other, Polynesia-wide, aspects of marriage: It is a fact that some of them in every society ended in divorce, a matter that, mercifully, can be dealt with in very few words. According to most writings touching on the subject, divorce was finalized by either spouse simply by quitting their shared household. In a few cases, however, it resulted in vengeful actions, based on jealousy and affronted pride, or on demands of the injured party for restitution of his or her wedding "gift," if any. Also, the divorce of a couple whose marriage had constituted a purposeful alliance between two powerful families or tribes resulted sometimes in serious enmities. And even for less consequential couples divorce sometimes created family difficulties, such as one-sided separation from dependent children. Notwithstanding the complexities resulting from some divorces, the act itself, as just noted, was effected simply by the permanent exiting of one or the other spouse.[145]

Now back to households, the type of residential social group that contained one or more of the kinds of families just characterized—plus, in some cases more "distant" relatives (and in a very few cases, nonkin servants). We begin with what members of a common household did as such for their common good, namely, feed, house, clothe, doctor, child tend, and protect one another, and support the group's position in wider community affairs. Note, however, that Polynesian societies differed somewhat in the extent to which some of those functions were performed by households per se in comparison with the wider communities in which they formed parts. Thus, in some societies all of a community's men cooperated, for example, in building each of its household's dwellings or in clearing each one's garden sites or in operating a large seine. Also societies differed in the degree to which their households owned rights in the land on which they resided or gardened—a matter that will be touched on below. Those differences aside, there were nevertheless some activities done by or for households that followed conventional (but not inflexible) gender lines. Thus, the care of young children, the fabrication of mats and barkcloth and the collection of inshore shellfish were usually done by females, whereas sennit making, house building and the heavier work of gardening and food collecting were usually done by males. Some of that job allocation was based, reasonably enough, on some more or less inherent physical differences between males and females, but there were some other aspects of the gender division of labor that require elucidation.

In an earlier chapter the point was made that in some societies its females, having been characteristically engaged in, and consequently identified with, secular domestic activities—all of which were classified as *noa* (i.e., everyday, nongodly)— were mostly barred from activities involving interaction with gods (which activities were "sacred" and therefore antithetical and even mutually inimical to persons identified with *noa*). Some writers attribute that circumstance to a "deeper" cause, namely, to the occurrence of menstruation— which, such reasoning goes, was repulsive to human males and therefore to the (mostly male) gods as well. Among Polynesians, menstruation was indeed more or less—in some societies much less—repulsive to males, but that, according to some writers, did not necessarily lead to the above-stated conclusion. As one of them wrote: "The usual interpretation is that the gods found women to be repugnant, because of their connection with menstrual blood. . . . Hence the gods would withdraw upon the appearance of a woman, taking their *tapu* [sacredness] with them. An alternative view is that the gods were attracted to women rather than repelled by them, and that women therefore terminated *tapu* by absorbing the godly influence into themselves. On this interpretation the female is understood . . . to represent a passageway between the godly and human realms of existence" (Hanson 1987, 430). All of this raises questions about statements encountered in the literature to the effect that in Polynesia females were considered "inferior" to males.

It was doubtless true in Polynesia (as in most other societies elsewhere) that females were on the average physically weaker than males. In Polynesia, however, physical strength per se was not valued as highly as certain kinds of expertise, few of which were based weightily on physical strength alone. Moreover, two of the objects most highly valued everywhere, both as tokens of exchange and as symbols of affluence, were fine mats and barkcloth, which were fabricated mostly by females. And while it is true that "women's activities [were] conceived as confined and sedentary, men's as expansive and active" (Howard and Kirkpatrick, in Howard and Borofsky 1989, 78), to conclude ipso facto that women were considered socially "inferior" would require proof that sedentariness per se was "inferior" to movement—a conclusion belied in several Polynesian societies by the value attributed to inactivity-enhanced plumpness in both females and upper-class males. Finally, females' alleged "inferiority" might be attributed to the circumstance that males had more direct communication with gods than did females, but that argument is not only circular, but inapplicable to, say, Tonga (of which more later). But let us resign from this fruitless search for Polynesia-wide equivalents of Anglophonic "gender inferiority" and focus on male-female relations in specific familial contexts, starting with those between husbands and wives.

HUSBAND:WIFE

Most of the comprehensive ethnographies about Polynesia provide detailed coverage on who can marry whom, and on nuptial rites and exchanges, but little if anything on everyday relations between spouses—save for a few anecdotal specifics, and for clipped statements such as "[W]hen a [Marquesan] woman undertook to live with a man, she placed herself under his authority" (E. S. C. Handy 1923, 100), or "[A]fter marriage a [Samoan] woman's life was a long series of daily tasks, periodic pregnancies and confinements" (Mead 1930, 96–97),[146] in contrast with the lengthy descriptions devoted to, say, relations between opposite-sex siblings, or between chiefs and subjects. Nevertheless, it is possible to glean some generalities such as the following.

One important factor in husband:wife relations was the couple's place of residence. In most societies it was largely but not wholly virilocal—i.e., a couple resided more or less permanently in the place of the husband, either in the household of his own parents or in a separate one nearby. The most notable uxorilocal arrangement (i.e., residing in the place of the wife) prevailed on Tokelau, where males had productive but females had residential rights over their clan (i.e., descent-unit) land. As was said in that society: "The sister stays [in the natal home]; the brother goes on the path [i.e., to his wife's home]" (Huntsman and Hooper 1996, 110). However, elsewhere in Polynesia, even in societies that were preponderantly virilocal, some men "went on the path"—typically, when a wife's material or social assets exceeded theirs (as, for example, in the case of younger brothers). Also, there were in many societies cases of couples, especially young ones, alternating residence between his and her natal places. On the other hand, it was very unusual for a newly married couple to reside neolocally, i.e., in households of their own or in communities where neither of them had previously resided—in most cases, use-rights to life-supporting land having been inherited only through one or both parents.

Turning now to the locational aspect of husband:wife relations—i.e., to where spouses spent their days and nights in relation to one another—the sources provide little direct information on the matter, but some generalizations about it can be inferred. First, whatever conventions or circumstance may have separated them in daytime, other conventions permitted them to be together most nights. For even in more populous households each married couple, and their children, were usually allotted their own exclusive sleeping space (and not only to accommodate their sexual inter-actions, some of which took place during daytime in secluded spots outdoors).

Except for such nighttime interaction, however, there were in most societies circumstances or explicit conventions that tended to or required males and females in general, and husbands and wives in particular, to spend their daytime hours apart. To begin with, some of the everyday sub-sistence activities, such as gardening and fishing, were allocated along gender lines. Or, in some societies, there were extrahousehold buildings—such as canoe sheds or men's working and loung-ing quarters or fishermen's shacks—where many men spent much of their daytime hours and which, here or there, were more or less off-limits to females. And in many societies even the build-ings or sections of buildings of unitary households were subdivided in daytime along gender lines. Moreover, in many societies, including some of those without separate males-only buildings, or separate cooking facilities for males and females, it was customary for males and female adults to eat separately. And finally, on the few occasions when a husband and wife went anywhere togeth-er it was customary for the former to walk ahead.

Concerning cooking and eating: in every Polynesian society reported on in this respect females were forbidden certain foods—including, in most cases, pork. And with respect to gover-nance: reverting to the earlier statement about Marquesan couples, that "when a woman under-took to live with a man, she placed herself under his authority," a perusal of other ethnographies reveals that that arrangement did in fact prevail throughout much of Polynesia, even in marriages in which the wife was superior to her husband in (genealogical) rank. However, that is not to say that all wives everywhere submitted unquestion-ingly to their subordinancy. Anecdotes abound about husbands beating their wives for this or that, but reported instances of the reverse are not altogether lacking. Moreover, the sources contain both anecdotes and generalities about physically abused or merely discontented wives returning to their natal families—and even, in some cases, of their families inflicting upon brutal husbands some kind of revenge.

Finally, while societal rules may have placed a husband in command of his wife (and offspring), they did not discourage mutual affection.

Scattered throughout the sources are several anec-dotes and legends that reveal a sharing of solici-tude and fondness—in some cases deep enough to have led a bereaved spouse to suicide. And there are myths, noted in chapter 11, about men who turned themselves into food plants to save their wives (and children) from starvation.

The foregoing examples concerning hus-band:wife relations refer mostly to members of less stratified societies and to lower-class members of highly stratified ones. In the latter some mar-riages between highest-ranking persons differed markedly from those just described. In some cases, for example, such unions were entirely "politi-cal"—i.e., between top-ranking persons of differ-ent tribal dynasties made for the purpose of con-solidating or augmenting intertribal alliances. In some such unions the couples resided together only long enough to produce an heir. And even in cases of longer-lasting coresidence some upper-class wives maintained separate households, with their own retainers, and played separate and important roles in tribal and even intertribal affairs. More about such matters will be touched on later; mention of them is now made in order to establish that not all Polynesian wives "placed themselves under the authority" of their husbands.

PARENT:CHILD

Generalizing about parent:child relations in early-contact Polynesia is frustrated by lack of detailed first-hand observations. Several accounts note, say, the prevalence of adoption, the absence of formalized schooling (except, here and there, in priestcraft), and the privileges enjoyed by child "favorites." But as for the everyday interaction of parents and children there were only a very few societies that were looked at and written about with anything more than glances and brief off-hand judgments (such as those by missionaries, quoted earlier, regarding children's' unruliness). One reason for such omission on the part of most early observers was perhaps their view that such relationships were so generically familiar, so nonexotic, as to be uninteresting and therefore unimportant.[147] Another was the paucity of explic-it, solemnly stated, society-wide rules governing the relationship—such as those concerning a father's authority and sometime mentor role.

One aspect of parent:child relationships that needs airing at the outset is the situation, noted by several contemporary writers, that they were not exclusive—that because of the extended-family composition of most households, including parental siblings, the children in those households had two or more fatherlike and motherlike nurturers—a circumstance that was conventionalized by kin terminology (i.e., by the practice in all societies of referring to a (real) father's brothers as "fathers" and to a real mother's sisters as "mothers," a practice which in most of eastern Polynesia was extended to include mother's brothers and father's sisters as well).[148] Another factor that minimized the "exclusiveness" of the parent-child relationship was the frequency of fosterage, both temporary and permanent, whereby many children had two sets of "parents."

Speaking of adoption—the permanent form of fosterage—that type of transfer did in fact occur in all Polynesian societies, and in fairly large numbers,[149] including in many cases adoption by parents who had children of their own and still residing with them. In some instances children were asked for before birth, many more at the time of birth or during infancy, and a few during childhood or youth. The immediate personal reasons for adoption varied, from love of children to desire or need for an heir—and perhaps in some cases a wish to augment or balance a household's labor force or to provide some support for old age. As for the donor parents, in a few reported cases they released a child because of inability or unwillingness to nurture it, but more often out of affection or sympathy for or obedience to the adopting parent(s)—and in keeping with their society's positive valuation of adoption, not just as permissible but as a proper alternative way of nurturing children.

Whatever may have been the personal reasons for releasing or adopting, it goes without saying— but will be said anyway!—that in many cases the practice doubtless served to strengthen social ties between the true and adopting parents—although in some other cases the reverse may have occurred. Thus, the very high-status Tahitian clan senior and tribal chief Pomare II had been as a child adopted by a relative only ten years older than himself, but came in time to depend upon his adoptive "father" for help in driving his avowed father from office (i.e., the latter having been reluctant, in contravention to the usual Tahitian practice, to retire earlier from his tribal chieftainship).

In addition, at a higher (or lower?) level of analysis of present-day Polynesian societies, the pervasiveness of adoption has been described as "a powerful adaptive mechanism for equitably distributing people relative to resources, including land" (Howard and Kirkpatrick 1989, 76); or "[A]doption seems to communicate to children, and indeed to everyone in the community, that all relationships, even those of mother and child, are contingent and problematic . . . [and therefore fosters] a tendency to avoid strong emotional attachments to anyone" (Levy 1970); or "[A]doption conveys the message that persons must have ties beyond the domestic [and] therefore constitutes a form of social meaning that complements physiological weaning" (Firth 1936, 192–93)—all of which may be true.[150]

Adoption was, however, only part of the story. Short of it, during their childhood most if not all Polynesians spent periods, ranging from a few days to several years, residing in—not just visiting—households other their parents', a process labeled by anthropologists as "fostering" (and by the members of some Polynesian societies as "feeding") a child. The reasons for such episodes were varied: in some cases the child's unhappiness at home, in others its parents' altruistic wish to help the fostering family—or their wish to better themselves or their child socially, etc. And in some cases, what began as "fostering" ended as "adoption"—there having been no explicit rules to define or enforce a distinction between the two.

As will be described, in nearly all societies the relationship between parents and their children was influenced in some ways by the order of birth of the latter. Before that, however, a few words need be said about the widespread and in many societies institutionalized status of "favorite child"—a status often but not necessarily associated with order of birth. Hawai'i offers the best example of this status. There, one child of a family, usually but not invariably a firstborn, was selected and trained for the duties he or she would eventually be called upon to perform, as senior adviser-leader-steward-historian-etc. of the family. As such the trainee was known as *punahele* (favorite). The status also entailed privileges of several kinds—but privileges that were supposed to be largely earned. Quite different was the meaning of *pa'i punahele* (made or pampered favorite), the label conferred upon a child who was especially favored by adoring parents or grandparents. Such children, often but not necessarily firstborns, were not allowed to do any work—to plant or fish or make barkcloth, etc. They were provided with piles of mats or barkcloth for soft sitting, or sat on someone's lap. When very young they were fed by hand, including even premasticated food, and they continued to be carried about long past walking stage (Kamakau 1964, I: 26–27). In the case of high-rank ones, some of them were guarded—encumbered—with enough taboos to delay or even interdict sexual, parental and other normal activities. And in some places their elders, especially grandparental ones, held periodic *ho'okelakela* (beauty contests) to exhibit, competitively, their little darlings.

SIBLINGS

The two most noteworthy status-structuring aspects of Polynesian siblingship were birth order and gender, both of which involved not only the relations among full siblings (i.e., the offspring of same parents) but among larger groups and categories of consanguines as well.

As described earlier, the rule in most societies was that a couple's firstborn had authority in some matters over his or her siblings and was principal heir to most of the parents' separate and joint entitlements.[151] Note, however, that in most societies that rule was qualified to mean firstborn male. Note also that in several societies the rule was sometimes disregarded in favor of a more competent younger sibling. (Moreover, in at least one society, that of Samoa, rules regarding primogeniture were almost entirely disregarded.) Also, a distinction needs to be drawn between the kinds of rights just alluded to and the pampering enjoyed in some societies by a specifically labeled "favorite-child," inasmuch as the two statuses were not requisitely, and evidently not usually, linked.

Birth order among siblings was also reflected in kinship terminology—not necessarily in words of address (i.e., those used in speaking to a relative, such as "Tom" or "Mary") but in words of reference (i.e., those used to designate a relative's kinship connection, such as "grandfather" or "cousin"). Thus, in most Polynesian societies,[152] while one term was used to designate any sister of a male and another to designate any brother of a female, a distinction was made terminologically between the older and younger brothers of a male and between the older and younger sisters of a female.

The above generalizations refer specifically to full siblings, but there is evidence for concluding that the rule of primogeniture and the distinctions in terminology applied in most respects to half-siblings as well (although it is likely that the firstborn of an aristocratic second wife would have inherited, separately, some of his or her mother's entitlements).

While a firstborn male was entitled to exercise some authority over his male siblings, he and they were in other respects supposed, normatively, to act (in Anglophonic terms) "brotherly" toward one another (i.e., amicably, cooperatively, etc.) and in most reported cases they did so. On the other hand, native chronicles contain many accounts of discord among them. This was especially so among upper-class brothers, many of whom vied, sometimes fratricidally, for positions of power in tribal affairs.

As just mentioned, the rule of primogeniture served to differentiate not only siblings but larger groups and categories of relatives as well. That is to say, in several societies the descendants of a firstborn took precedence in some matters over those of his (or her) younger siblings. What those matters were, however, will be amplified in chapter 19, where those and other features of descent units (i.e., clans) are described.

Turning now to the function of gender in shaping relations among siblings, mention was just made of the bias of many peoples toward allocating most primogenitural rights to a firstborn male even when he was born after his elder sister. Such was indeed the case in most of the societies of eastern Polynesia,[153] but in those of the west, especially Tonga and Samoa, the division of rights between brothers and sisters was more complex and more explicitly institutionalized. Thus, in Tonga especially, while a firstborn male became heir to his father's quota of authority over secular family affairs, he was deemed inferior in certain sacred matters to his sister, who, in the words of one scholar, "represents sacred forces which impose moral order on [her brothers]" (Schoeffel 1978, as quoted in Howard and Kirkpatrick 1989).

The concept of sororal "moral" superiority was most highly institutionalized in Tonga, where all sisters were deemed "superior" to all their brothers regardless of relative age—their superiority having consisted of their right to be treated with honor and respect—which, among other things, meant avoidance of familiarity (i.e., of sleeping in the same house, of eating together, of playing together as children, etc.), and of "intimate" behavior in general (i.e., of engaging in or talking about sex). Almost as far-reaching were such conventions in Samoa, where, in addition, a sister's "moral" superiority over her brother was sanctioned by her inherent power of placing upon him a curse (e.g., to render him sterile) in case he acted against her wishes in family matters. And, as will be described, both in Tonga and Samoa the descendants of a sister possessed authority over those of her brother in certain matters, including some relating to their common clan.

In attempting to evaluate the status of females it is essential to note two seemingly paradoxical characterizations of them. One is the fact that in most societies they were, by their gender alone, forbidden access to most sacred places, including participation in formalized religious events there. Nevertheless, in many societies some women played important decision-making roles in household, community and even tribal affairs. A second fact to bear in mind is that most women occupied two statuses that were seemingly self-contradictory: one as a wife (and conventionally subservient to her husband); the other as a sister—who, as just noted, in some western Polynesian societies possessed "moral" authority over her brother no matter how powerful he was otherwise.[154]

Some Polynesian conventions regarding siblingship were extended to include certain relatives that Anglophones label "cousins"—i.e., they extended collaterally one or more degrees beyond the boundaries of a family. That is not to assert that individuals actually felt about or acted toward same-generation cousins as they did about full- or half-siblings, but in some societies they were labeled (in referential terms) "siblings" and to varying degrees were required, ideally, to relate to them in some of the ways applicable to (true) siblings. Moreover, in most if not all societies sibling terms were also used even for those nonconsanguines who behaved in "brotherly" or "sisterly" ways. (See chapter 20.)

RELATIONS WITH UNCLES AND AUNTS

In most eastern Polynesian societies the siblings of one's parents were looked upon, ideally, as coparents, and were correspondingly labeled (or perhaps it was the other way round!)—although, in some societies, they were distinguished with qualifying terms such as "little" father or mother. Conversely, in such societies nephews were called, referentially, "sons," and nieces, "daughters." That is not to say that actual relations between such pairs were necessarily as "close," etc., as those between own parents and offspring—although in many cases they doubtless were, inasmuch as they often resided in the same household or neighborhood. Nor did nephews or nieces necessarily inherit goods from their "coparents," although in some cases they were adopted by the latter and doubtless did so.

In most societies of western Polynesia a strikingly different pattern prevailed. There, the division of rights between brothers and sisters, noted earlier, carried over to their progeny—i.e., the progeny of a woman possessed some similar rights not only over their mother's brother but over his progeny as well—an ascendancy that attained its sharpest form in the Tongan custom of *fahu*, which was described by Gifford as follows: "As the sister is superior in rank [i.e., moral matters] to the brother, so also are her children. The sister's children are *fahu* . . . to their mother's brother. They have the privilege of taking their uncle's goods, also the goods of his children, either during his life or after his death. Even one of the uncle's wives might be appropriated. At the wedding of a man's child, his sister's children may help themselves to the presents. The brother's children must show respect (*fakaapaapa*) to the sister's children. The institution of *fahu* is a one-sided, nonreciprocal affair. The victims never have a chance to retaliate, but they exercise similar privilege toward their own mother's brother and his offspring" (Gifford 1929, 22–23). To which Radcliffe-Brown added: "[W]hen the uncle makes a sacrifice, the sister's son [sometimes?] takes away the sacred portion offered to the gods, and may eat it" (1924).

Moreover, as will be amplified below, in both Tonga and Samoa the principle of sororal ascendancy continued for generations to shape some relations between the descendants of a brother and of a sister—although in most cases to a diminishing degree.

GRANDPARENT: GRANDCHILD

Throughout Polynesia grandparents played an important role in the lives of their grandchildren—at least during the latters' infancy and childhood. (In consequence of the relatively short lives of most Polynesians not many grandparents would have survived long enough, or would have remained capable enough, to play active roles vis à vis their grandchildren during the latter's postchildhood period of "youth.") In many cases grandparents and grandchildren resided together in the same (extended family) household, whereby the former, having "retired" from heavier subsistence activities, served as substitute parents while the actual parents were otherwise occupied. And even when the actual parents were nearby, grandparents typically undertook to educate their grandchildren in matters such as craftsmanship and oral tradition, in which they usually excelled as a result of their longer lives and practice.

In cases where grandparents and grandchildren resided in separate households, it often happened that the former would not only feed and shelter the latter for long periods but would adopt them outright. And in at least one society a grandparent's right to adopt a grandchild outweighed its parents' wish to retain it.

Everyday relations between particular grandparents and grandchildren doubtless varied, from "bitter" to "sweet," but a gleaning of published accounts leaves the impression that they averaged "sweet." As was mentioned earlier, in at least one society grandmothers vied with one another by displaying their little darlings in public "beauty" contests. In Tonga, however, something similar to the *fahu* relationship also occurred between grandparent and grandchild: "The daughter's son must be honored by his grandfather. He is 'chief' to him. He may take his grandfather's property, and he may take away the offering that his grandfather makes to the gods at a kava ceremony. The mother's father and the mother's brother are the objects of very similar behavior patterns, of which the outstanding feature is the indulgence on the one side and the liberty permitted on the other" (Radcliffe-Brown 1924, 550).

Reverting to kinship terminology, those terms used in referring to grandparents are significant in at least two ways. One is that in most societies the same term was used for both grandfather and grandmother—an exception having prevailed in

Samoa. Conversely, a similar uniformity prevailed nearly everywhere with respect to the term *mokopuna*, and cognates of it, which was used to refer to a male or female grandchild. A second significant feature of kin terminology was the usage, nearly everywhere, of applying the same term to both grandparents and (dead) ancestors—who, it was believed, after death continued in most cases to act beneficently—i.e., grandparently—toward their living descendants.

AFFINITY

In terms of their wider societal ramifications Polynesian marriages ranged from insignificant (e.g., "a pebble to pelt a rat"—i.e., of consequence only to the principals themselves) to some that were momentous enough to affect congeries of tribes. In a book such as this one it is not feasible to sample the entire range of affinal ties, but here are a few generalities that apply to most of them.

First, because most marriages, at least among commoners, took place between persons residing near one another, many if not most of them served to transform some of each spouse's consanguines into affines—a transformation not only in terminology but in behavior prescriptions as well. Thus, in Tikopia, when a man's marriage changed a distant "brother" into a distant "brother-in-law," it transformed their prescribed relationship from one of familiarity to one of formality and restraint. Note however the emphasis on "some," inasmuch as a transformation often depended upon circumstances—upon the pragmatic needs of the principals to adapt to or ignore the consequences of its potential, but not obligatory, change.

Second, most ceremonialized marriages involved a reciprocal and more or less balanced nuptial exchange of goods, and in some societies services, between the families of the couple. (The significance of this practice lies in the fact that such exchanges were in most Polynesian societies not only reciprocal but balanced, a fact that distinguished them from marital exchanges in much of Melanesia, where bride-price was typically larger in value than dowry.) The classic example of such exchanges occurred in Samoa, where according to some early observers, the family of the bride exchanged *toga* (i.e., goods, such as fine mats, produced by females) for *'oloa* (goods, such as foods, produced mainly by males). Moreover, such exchanges were periodically repeated on ceremonious occasions for as long as the marriage endured. Another well-documented example of marriage-based interfamilial exchange prevailed on Tikopia. There it was the duty of male members of a husband's family to assist his in-laws by serving as cooks whenever they held a feast (Firth 1957, 305).

And third, it should be obvious by now that the general interfamilial bonds created by a marriage were strengthened and particularized by a couple's procreation—there having existed in most societies specific prescriptions governing the relations between, say, a man's son and his wife's brother, or a woman's son and her husband's sister.

The widest societal ramification occurred when marriages involved chiefly members of sep-

arate tribes. Most such unions were purposely designed, and actually served, to establish or strengthen intertribal bonds. As Handy reported of the Marquesas: "The festivals and rites connected with formal betrothal and marriage of two scions of chiefly or wealthy families of different tribes were among the most elaborate of all public festivals . . . . In fact, such alliances by marriage marked in the most thorough manner the alliance of tribes" (Handy 1923, 102–3). While bonds, in the Marquesas and elsewhere, were created or strengthened by the marriage itself, it is likely that they were further strengthened by the couple's procreation of an heir—who, in some cases, would come to rule both tribes. Indeed, such an outcome was in many cases the purpose of the marriage itself.

19

CLANS

We go next to clans,[155] a topic which, with long-voyaging, social stratification and political "evolution," has in recent decades attracted most scholarly attention to ancient Polynesia.

What is herein labeled a clan was, among Polynesians, a social unit—either a social group or a social category—composed of persons believed by themselves to have descended from some common and in most cases remote ancestor, along with persons fully adopted by or otherwise kin-assimilated to such descendants (as for example a castaway or a bond friend from a different tribe). In terms of gender-lines of descent there were three types of clans: patriclans (from patri-, paternal), composed of persons descended from the same genealogical line of males; matriclans (from matri-, maternal), composed of persons descended from the same genealogical line of females; and ambiclans (from ambi-, both), composed of persons descended from the same ancestor through a genealogical line that could and sometimes did include females as well as males.[156] Patriclans existed in only a few Polynesian societies and matriclans in only two, the most widespread type by far having been ambiclans.

AMBICLANS

(Ambiclans are also labeled "cognatic stocks," nonunilineal or utrolineal descent units.) As a corollary to the widespread Polynesian tenet that a person, male or female, was the genetic product of both parents—that he (or she) descended from both—so could he (or she) claim membership in both their clans (if mother and father belonged to different clans, which was frequently but not necessarily the case, inasmuch as Polynesian ambiclans per se were not exogamous). And if his parents' parents had belonged to different clans he could claim membership in their clans as well, and so on. However (and this is a big "however") most persons actually exercised those rights in only one or two clans—i.e., in those where they resided or in which they participated actively in clan affairs. Without that residence or active participation, after a while their ties became weak and eventually extinct. Therefore, actual membership in an ambiclan derived not only from descent, or from adoption by or kin assimilation[157] to a clan member, but from active sharing in clan affairs as well.

In what follows, ambiclans will be characterized with respect to several of their features: their depth and span, their social structure, their property (both material and nonmaterial), their shared activities and, in the following chapter, their place in tribal life.

A clan's "depth" includes its heritage in terms of its age and repute, as measured by the number and fame of the persons listed sequentially in its "official" genealogy, i.e., those who usually had been seniors of the clan ("senior" being the label given herein for a clan's superior officer).[158] Among the commoners of some highly stratified societies their remembered genealogies were so shallow—i.e., three or four generations—the numbers of persons sharing any one of them so small, and the commonly owned goods of the latter so few, that they cannot be said to constitute "clans" as that label is herein used. In contrast, in many societies, especially the highly stratified ones, the genealogies of some clans containing upper-class members were asserted to reach back thirty and more generations (of clan seniors) and to have originated in either a (subsequently apotheosized) human ancestor or a never-human god. And while most such genealogies included only males, a few female names did occur in some of them. Generally speaking, the longer the genealogy the more honorable the clan—a circumstance that doubtless led to some padding. In addition to the names of godly forebears, some genealogies began with cosmological entities, such as "Giant Stratum Stone," or with the names of plants and animals in evolutionary sequence (as, for example, in the *kumulipo* chant mentioned in chapter 7), some of which, perhaps, were included more for religious and aesthetic effect than as genealogical doctrine. Indeed, the recitation, usually public, of such genealogies was clearly intended not only to reaffirm and thereby celebrate the superiority of a clan (or of its current senior), but also to invite godly support for its perpetuity—and all done with a solemn sonority that was evidently much appreciated.

The "span" of a clan includes the number and spread of its branches and subbranches. Those with most branches were usually located on large and topographically complex high islands, those with least usually on small and isolated atoll islets—indicating that branching was promoted by an abundance of arable land subdivided by palpable natural borders, and suggesting that when the membership of a unified high-island clan proliferated beyond the capacity of their neighboring lands to support them comfortably, some members—most likely, younger brothers—colonized a nearby area (say, an adjoining valley or nearby island). Thereafter, according to this suggestion, the colonial, "junior" branch remained such if communications with its "homeland" or "senior" unit could and did continue. Or the junior branch became, eventually, a separate and autonomous clan if communications with the senior unit ceased—because of, say, natural barriers or intraclan enmity.

A different kind of development transpired in Hawai'i and in Tonga. There, while clanship continued among members of the upper class, by the time of contact the very concept of it had almost evaporated among commoners, leaving the core members of an extended family to constitute the "deepest" and "widest" form of common-descent unit. The likeliest cause of that change was the disenfranchisement, and in some cases actual dislodgment, by tribal chiefs, of commoners' traditional clan rights in land. Similar trends took place in a few other highly stratified societies, but nowhere did they reach as far as in Hawai'i and Tonga.

Yet another kind of development took place in Samoa, whose people, at time of contact, resided in nucleated villages made up of several clans or clan branches, many of whose functions were exercised by a village council (*fono*), made up of the seniors (*matai*) of the village's constituent clans.

Picture now, at the other extreme, a small island, unpartitioned by natural barriers. On such islands branching also took place—virtually inevitably, given an increase in population and a diverging of family interests and ambitions. However, short of the development of destructive intraclan enmities it was seldom that the branches would have attained full autonomy.

Branching, however, was not the only process undergone by clans. Assuming the inevitability of demographic variability among subclans, some of them experienced such decrease in membership that they became extinct—or their few surviving members ended up associating themselves, and the land they were using, with a nearby branch of their clan: not a difficult step in view of the likelihood that some members of the joining branch could claim potential but up to then unutilized, membership rights in the joining branch. It is also likely that in some cases whole clans became extinct or that their remnants joined a neighboring but entirely separate clan.

Nor was demographic variability the only factor leading to the reuniting of some of a clan's branches. Particularly in situations in which a branch senior happened also to be an especially powerful chief of their common encompassing tribe, it was not unusual for some or all members of a related branch to flock to him—i.e., to unite with his branch, bringing with them their branch's land. Thus, in Tonga: "Everything points to the necessity of a line of powerful [seniors] for a nucleus about which the [clan] groups itself. Without such [a senior] it appears to wilt and die and its membership gradually aligns itself with other rising [clans] (Gifford 1929, 30).[159]

One characteristic of all Polynesian clans, of whatever lineality, was their corporate ownership of property, full or residual, material or immaterial, including bounded units of territory—dry land and marine, specific trees (in some cases distinct from the underlying land), houses and other buildings, tools, etc., as well as specialized services and knowledge of several kinds—occupational, magical, etc. For present purposes it will be sufficient to distinguish three types of ownership: full, provisional and residual.

By "full" ownership is meant sole (i.e., exclusive) rights of use and alienation, without qualifications. Provisional ownership means tenancy use-rights only in a property, subject to limitation of time (and sometimes of type of use as well). And "residual" ownership refers to the reversionary rights in a property held by its full owners during its tenancy by others.

In those societies of tropical Polynesia where clans existed, most territory—dry land and wet areas (i.e., rivers, lagoons, etc.)—was owned, fully or residually, by one or another clan or clan branch. In most societies some parts of a clan's territory were used (i.e., in full ownership) by any and all of the members of a clan or clan branch—say, for fishing or logging or gathering wild foods—while most of the arable land or fishable waters of the territory were owned, and used, provisionally by one or another of the resident families of the clan's members, who in most cases were not empowered to dispose of it to outsiders but who held more or less indissoluble use rights in it subject to, or not opposed by, the clan's senior. Also, in most societies ownership of the territories of a subclan reverted to the clan as a whole when all of its members expired.[160]

While in most societies all territory was owned, fully or residually, by one or another of its clans, there were some in which multiclan communities owned some parts of it, for use by all their residents—one such society having been that of Tokelau. And there were a few societies in which the chiefs of multiclan tribes had usurped full or residual ownership rights in nearly all territory—rights so coercively powerful that they could and sometimes did deny some subjects the use of their traditional clan lands. The most extreme example of this development occurred in Hawai'i, but moves in that direction had been made in some other societies as well.

Another kind of clan property had to do with religion, and included the patronage of a clan's ancestral and other tutelar gods (and more or less exclusive rights to communicate with them); images, both anthropomorphic and nonanthropomorphic, of those gods; sacred "props" (e.g., feather girdles and other objects believed attractive to its gods); and edifices (temples and shrines) in which those gods resided when visiting.

In addition, many clans in many societies owned exclusive appellations, herein called "clan titles," which were similar to, say, England's Windsor, or Germany's Hohenzollern, in having

been applied to the officials of a clan either automatically (say, at birth or maturity) or by election by the clan's elders. In some societies such clan titles were applicable only to the office of a clan senior; in some other societies some clans owned two or more additional titles, which were assigned to, say, its principal priest and to its principal orator. And, although many such clan titles devolved in hereditary lines (say, from a father to his eldest son), in some societies they were contested for by intraclan rivals, inasmuch as they usually entailed special authorities and privileges.

The practice of clan titleholding reached its culmination in Samoa. There, the (elected) senior (*matai*) of each clan branch held a clan title, which entitled its incumbent to one or another (rank-graded) seat among the members of his village's governing council (*fono*). Some of those clan titles also entitled its incumbent to a (likewise graded) seat in the multivillage (i.e., tribal) *fono*, and a few of them to an all-islands *fono*—which, however, seldom if ever convened but in which membership was highly prized. The intravillage and intratribal grading of clan titles was fixed, ideally, but in fact changed over time along with the relative importance—in numbers and affluence, etc.—of their respective clans or clan branches. In addition, in some cases military ascendancy resulted in exalting the paramount clan title of the victorious tribe over those of his opponents. However, that ascendancy pertained mainly to the grading of those clan titles in ceremonial precedence; seldom did it result in the subjection of the losers or in the seizure of their lands.[161] For in Samoa there was enough fertile land to support all its people, and political rivalries had to do mainly with precedence in ceremonial affairs—i.e., with which person (or rather, with the holder of which clan title) sat in a *fono*'s most honorable seat, was served first with kava, etc.

Next to be noted are the kinds of activities engaged in by persons as clanmates—an assignment easier to frame than to fulfill, inasmuch as clan members were also members of households, and in many cases multiclan tribes, and the sources often do not specify which activities pertained to which. Thus, while individuals may have gardened on land belonging to their clan, the food they produced was consumed mostly or totally by members of their own household. And even when several men cooperated in clearing large tracts in order to prepare garden sites for their respective households, the sources rarely specify whether such cooperation was undertaken as clan projects or as works of cooperation among their several households.

There was, however, at least one kind of activity, engaged in nearly everywhere, that was unmistakably and exclusively related to clans, namely, religious services devoted to celebration or supplication of a clan's tutelar gods. Also, while gatherings accompanying a person's rites of passage (e.g., marriage, death, etc.) were usually attended by other neighbors and relatives as well, his clanmates were usually more likely than others to attend, and figured more conspicuously in the proceedings.

Turning now to the social structure of ambiclans, there were doubtless some that were unsegmented at time of contact—i.e., ones that had never branched or had branched off much earlier and had severed all but vague legendary ties with other branches. However, at contact times, most ambiclans were segmented, some of them numerously so—not just branches but subbranches, subsubbranches and so on. And because of widespread commitment to the principle of primogeniture, the usual point of segmentation had been a younger brother, whose seniority in his new branch passed eventually to his child, most usually to his eldest son—and so on down the generations. This leads to consideration of the roles of clan seniors.

First and foremost, a clan senior was in most cases his clan's top manager and final arbiter in secular clan affairs, as well as its titular representative to its gods. In many clan branches, especially the more populous ones, the role of conducting religious services—of communicating with gods—was delegated to specially trained priests, but even in most such cases it was understood that the priests were acting on behalf of and not in preference to the unit's senior. Another scenario, followed here and there, was for a clan senior to transfer—not just delegate—all of his nonreligious functions to, say, a younger brother, thereby establishing what would become a second and separate dynasty, with authority over secular matters of the whole clan—an arrangement that sometimes resulted, after a few generations, in reducing the senior of the senior dynasty to figurehead priestly status. The most notable example

of that scenario took place in Tonga, where the Tuʻi Tonga, the senior of the society's preeminent clan and chief of its most powerful tribe, transferred secular authority (*hau*) to a younger brother, thereby retaining for himself the office of high priest—a split rulership that was maintained by their respective successors for several generations thereafter, and one described by a European as follows: "[T]here were in Tonga a spiritual and a temporal king [sic]. The former—the Tui Tonga—was lord of the soil, and enjoyed divine honours in virtue of his immortal origin; but he had an ever-diminishing share in the government . . . . The temporal king [*hau*]—the Tui Kanokubolu—was the irresponsible sovereign of the people, wielding absolute power of life and death over his subjects, and was charged with the burden of the civil government and the ordering of the tribute to the gods and their earthly representative, the Tui Tonga" (Basil Thomson, as quoted in Kirch 1984, 225).[162]

A second role played by a senior in his clan's affairs was to exercise control over use of the unit's territory, both land and inshore waters. Ideally, he was in most societies principal steward, not absolute owner, of such territory—i.e., he held authority to allocate use rights in it to his clanmates but not to monopolize use of it, nor to transfer control of it to outsiders. Practically, however, in most societies the use rights to particular portions of the territory became so perpetuated that the only managerial role played by the senior was to refrain from revoking them. Nevertheless, a senior's jurisdiction over his unit's territory was substantial enough to entitle him to some share of its produce, both in the form of seasonal first-fruits and of occasional special levies. On his part, a senior undertook to assure the fecundity of the whole territory by prayers and offerings to its gods. Indeed, in some societies that fecundity was believed to be associated, magically, with the senior's own—a belief that was exemplified in some societies by, e.g., the practice of warriors crawling through the straddled legs of a senior (i.e., close to his genitals) in order to strengthen themselves for battle. And in at least one society (i.e., Ontong Java) a clan's welfare was identified so closely with that of its senior that he was required to vacate the office, by suicide or public execution, if that welfare declined (Hogbin 1934, 177–78).

A senior's right to levy produce extended to services as well—e.g., for constructing edifices for use of the whole unit (and for his own family), for large-scale fish drives, for entertaining—including feeding—important guests, and for celebrating passage rites for his heir. There were also occasions on which seniors conscripted their clanmates for warfare—in some cases for a clan's own battles, more commonly as part of the forces of its encompassing tribe.

Note well that in playing the roles in all the above a clan senior was, ideally, supposed to do so as a kinsman of all his clanmates—which in fact he was. And while his position as senior, and therefore superior, kinsman was generally recognized and duly respected in these pervasively nonegalitarian societies, the factor of kinship was expected to soften somewhat the inequalities of hierarchy—as it doubtless did in many if not most instances. However, there is evidence aplenty, both legendary and eyewitness, that some seniors were despotic enough to have been removed from office by clanmates.

While Tikopia clans were patrilineal rather than ambilineal, and while the behavior of its clan seniors cannot be considered typical for all or most Polynesian societies, Firth's characterization of one of them merits quoting: "Normally the [senior] does not interfere with the conduct of members of his clan; he expresses his displeasure in private grumbling, and this acts as a check upon too excessive disregard of his authority and wishes . . . . There may come a time, however, when the [senior] thinks that his wishes have been flouted far enough. Then the situation changes with amazing rapidity. The lightning of his anger flashes, and all abase themselves before it. The easy carelessness of his people is replaced by a vivid concern, and with anxious demeanour they hasten to do his bidding, or try with soft words to pacify him. As one sees his fury and hears the thunder of his voice, notices the solemn faces and hushed tones of those who discuss the situation, one is left in no doubt as to who in the last resort rules the clan" (Firth 1957b, 379–80).

In many societies the titular office of clan senior was labeled *ariki* or some cognate thereof (e.g., *ari'i, ali'i, ariki, 'eiki*, etc.), a label sometimes applied referentially to a society's aristocrats as well. (And, as will be described, in some societies the same label was also applied to a tribe's chief,

whether or not he was senior of his clan.)

As noted earlier, in addition to a generic title of seniority (e.g., *ali'i, ariki*, etc.) held by clan seniors, in some societies clans owned other particular and distinctively named titles (i.e., offices) that defined their incumbents' specialized roles in clan affairs, such as high priest and war leader—some of them heritable in family lines, others filled by appointment or election. In Samoa, for example, there was in many clans an office labeled *tulafale*, whose incumbent served as executive officer-spokesman[163] for a clan's senior and who in some cases came to surpass the latter in effective political power—deliberately or by default of the senior. In addition, most or all Samoan communities included an office of *taupo* (sacred maiden), whose incumbent served as ceremonial "ornament" of the community's highest-ranking senior—and therefore of the community itself. As was noted earlier, she was usually a close relative of that senior and was required to remain virginal while in office—which, consequently, made of her a highly prized and sought-after bride.

In most societies, and particularly in those of eastern Polynesia, succession to clan seniorship was based on (male) primogeniture, but even in those the office was sometimes awarded to a younger son of the former senior, or even to a collateral kinsman if the clan's elders judged the eldest son to be unfit. (And, not surprisingly, in the cases of clans whose seniorship entailed weighty authority and numerous privileges, deadly fights sometimes occurred between rival claimants.) In a few other societies, however, seniorship was awarded to a clan's eldest and still competent member, regardless of his relationship to the former senior.

Societies also differed with respect to the time of seniorship transfer. In most cases it took place only at an incumbent's death, or when he vacated the office (either voluntarily or by demand of the clan's influential elders). However, in at least one society (i.e., Tahiti), the title, with most of its religious powers and ceremonial privileges, was transferred to its incumbent's eldest son upon his birth—leaving its political authority with the father until he himself transferred it voluntarily—or was forced to do so by his heir.

Reverting to clan structuring, a different form of it prevailed in Samoa. There, it will be recalled, a man's sister possessed some control over him in his management of family property, even when at marriage she had moved to her husband's community elsewhere (and when subsequently only few if any of her descendants tended to move back to her natal community). In other words, while most male members of a branch resided together and on its corporately held land, its married female members and their descendants tended to reside elsewhere. Nevertheless, the latter continued for a few generations to possess some membership rights in the branch unit of their female progenitor, and as such were known as the unit's *tama fafine* (child [of] female—i.e., offspring of the distaff side of the unit), in contrast to the *tama tane* (child [of] male). And although particular groups of *tama fafine* tended to remain cohesive for only a few generations, while they were so they retained some kind of control over the unit's *tama tane*, as their common ancestress had over her brothers.

Turning again to Tonga, where—it will be recalled—relations among family members were hierarchized both by age and gender, a person's relationships with other consanguines were graded, hierarchically, by yet another principle—as described by Adrienne Kaeppler:

An individual's [extra-familial] kinsmen are divided into two classes—the paternal kinsmen [kinpersons] who rank higher than ego, and the maternal kinsmen [kinspersons] who rank lower than ego. Thus in the parental generation, the highest kinsman [kinperson] is father's eldest sister, and of only slightly lesser status are other sisters of the father. Following these, father's brothers are distinguished in status according to age. Continuing with these principles, we see that the lowest in status are mother's brothers and only slightly higher are the mother's sisters. The relationships of ego to members of the generation below him depend primarily on whether they are related through his sisters or his brothers. Sister's children are higher in status than ego, and this is reflected in the special term he uses for them (*ilamutu*), the highest of this group being his sister's eldest daughter. These kinsmen [kinspersons] are *fahu* (i.e., "above the law") to ego and can take any of his possessions. Ego is also expected to make ceremonial presentations, such as first fruits, to his *fahu* throughout his life. Ego's brother's children, on the other hand, are classified with his own children (*'ofefine* and *foha*) and are therefore lower than ego. (1971, 207)

As Kaeppler puts it: "The most crucial concept for any understanding of Tongan culture, in Captain Cook's time or today, is that of hierarchichal ranking. All interpersonal relationships in this island kingdom are governed by principles of rank, and language, food and material culture reflect this pattern" (Ibid., 206).

Clan structures like those of Tonga and Samoa just described existed also on East Uvea, East Futuna and Tokelau, but to less institutionalized degrees.

Up to now our focus has been upon clan segments (or upon unsegmented clans)—in other words, upon cohesive, and mostly localized, groups of clanmates. Next to consider are the kinds of relationships that prevailed among the various branches of a segmented clan. Most of the information touching on this matter concerns relations among subtribes, and not among the branches of single clans. What information there is, however, suggests that in most societies it was the ideal that a "senior" segment retained some prerogatives over its branches—such as periodic levies of goods and services, especially for clan-wide religious purposes. In practice, however, the actual delivery of those goods and services depended largely upon geographic distances between the units and the attitudes of their respective seniors. Also ideally, a senior segment retained residual rights over its branch's land—i.e., if a branch became extinct, its land reverted automatically to its senior. But again, there is not enough information to permit generalization about what actually happened in such situations.

Nevertheless, however attenuated the relationships actually were among a clan's branches, their members would have been reminded of those relationships through their orally transmitted and more or less historically accurate traditions. And in at least one society, Tahiti, the links among a clan's branches were preserved, literally, in stone. Reference here is to the custom of including in the walls of a new branch's temple a stone from the temple of its senior clan unit.

Finally, although the inhabitants of ambiclan societies could claim membership in the clans of both of their parents, most persons in most of those societies appear to have had stronger ties with their father's clan—a consequence of and cause of the preponderance of virilocal residence. That circumstance, together with the larger number of (names of) males in the official genealogies of virtually all ambiclans everywhere, serves to indicate that they were in fact more patrilineal than ambilineal. Nevertheless, true patriclans—i.e., those in which a person belonged categorically, by birth, only to the clan of his or her father, existed only in Pukapuka (within the "Polynesian Triangle") and in a few of the small Outlier societies west of it, the most fully described of the latter having been Tikopia.

PATRI– AND MATRICLANS

On Tikopia patriclans were the only type of clan; on Pukapuka they coexisted with matriclans, every person having been a member of one or another segment of both.

On Tikopia the nuclear unit of patriclan organization was the *paito* ("house"), a unit composed of two or more localized branches, whose members traced descent, through males only, from a common (male) ancestor, whose household site served as the unit's ritual center. Most founders of *paito* had been members of older Tikopian *paito* but had for some reason or another established a separate one of their own. Other founders had been immigrants (including castaways) who had married Tikopian women, thereby establishing new *paito*. Among the locally born founders some had been members of older high-ranking *paito*, a status retained by their *paito* descendants for several generations thereafter. In terms of property ownership, of activities, and of social structure, Tikopia's *paito* resembled in some respects Polynesian ambiclans, but differed from many of them in having been aggregated into "super" patriclans (*kainanga*), of which there were four. In the words of their ethnographer: "The majority of members of each *kainanga* are of common descent, their *paito* having been offshoots in various generations from the common stock. . . . Other *paito* have been incorporated into the [*kainanga*] by assimilation, usually through the marriage of an orphan or immigrant from another island with a daughter of the reigning [*kainanga* senior]" (Firth 1936, 362).

The seniors of the four *kainanga* (who were themselves interrelated by known ties of kinship) were in effect also the society's high priests, each having been responsible for assuring the fruitfulness of one of the island's four main food plants, by ritual obeisance to each crop's guardian god.

And although they were equal in status in other ways, one of the seniors was considered superior, in having had stewardship over all of the island's canoes and over use of its central crater lake.

Neither *paito* nor *kainanga* was jurally exogamous. *Paito* tended to be so in fact, but due to general rules against marriage between "close" consanguines (as locally defined).

In a few other societies, such as East Futuna, clan membership was in fact as invariably patrilineal as in Tikopia, but unlike in Tikopia that membership was not backed by a concurring theory of paternal-only conception.

Another variant of patriliny prevailed on Anuta, a small (.15 square mile) high island about eighty-five miles northeast of Tikopia. Its two hundred or so residents (in modern times) were divided into four clans (*kainanga*)—or rather, four branches of a single clan, whose legendary (and historical?) founder had lived about eight or nine generations prior to the time, in 1972–73, when the island's first comprehensive ethnography was carried out (by Richard Feinberg). Each branch was composed of from one to twenty households (*patongia*), which the ethnographer describes as a "patrilateral extended family"— marital residence having been mostly virilocal. The core members of most *patongia* were indeed related by common partilineal descent, and all of them included one or more individuals from other islands (mostly from Tikopia), including some married to Anutan women and one or more "bond friends" (*tau toa*) of *patongia* core members—for, as the ethnographer emphasizes, although the seniors of Anuta's clan branches were interrelated by ties of common (patrilineal) descent, the criteria for membership in a branch consisted of patrilineal kinship or other kinds of behavior ideally characteristic of patrilineal kinship, namely, "pity," "sympathy," "affection," etc., as exemplified in the sharing of material goods—i.e., sentiments and behavior included in *aropa* (the Anuta cognate of and meanings attached to that Polynesia-wide concept known in Hawai'i as *aloha*). In other words, although the framework of an Anuta clan was common (patrilineal) descent, actual membership in any one of its *patongia*—and therefore in the clan as a whole—was attainable even to outsiders by performance of what the ethnographer calls "appropriate [clanmate] behavior."[164]

As an aside: "appropriate behavior" was also an important qualification for active membership in Polynesian ambilineal clans, inasmuch as the offspring of parents of different clans could in many cases choose which one to affiliate with—"appropriate behavior" under such circumstances having consisted mainly of residing and behaving "appropriately" with the group chosen.

Turning to Pukapuka: when the three atoll islets comprising that atoll were first systematically studied, in 1934–35,[165] their 632 inhabitants were divided into seven patriclans and two matriclans, each of which was divided into branches (and each person belonged to a branch of both a patriclan and a matriclan). I begin with patriclans.

The word for patriclan was *po* ("cemetery"; also "night" and "underworld"), a reference to each patriclan's own, exclusive cemetery, where every member of that clan was eventually buried,[166] and in that section reserved for members of his (or her) branch. As the label "patriclan" signifies, a person became a member of his father's branch at birth—although some exceptions occurred through adoption, and also in a few cases by a person's deliberately changing membership.

Pukapuka patriclans were neither exogamous nor endogamous, "closeness" of consanguinity having been the basis for choice of spouse. Thus, marriages sometimes occurred between members of branches of the same clan, but seldom if ever between members of the same clan branch.

In addition to its cemetery, each *po* held corporate ownership of the section of land on which most of its male, and unmarried female, members resided—residence having been virilocal. Some of the coconut palms, taro beds and timber trees on the section were owned individually by its members and were passed on down paternal lines, but the rest of the section was owned corporately by the *po*.

Anciently—i.e., before the introduction of Christianity and other Western institutions—each *po* included priests, who represented it in communications with its gods in religious edifices built on the *po*'s land. Also, each *po* had a senior and each branch its own (sub) senior—but beyond that general information nothing is known. By 1934, according to the Beagleholes, the *po* possessed no "formal structural organization," not even a "council of the men of the group" (Beaglehole 1938, 231).

Every Pukapukan also belonged to one or another subbranch of one of the island's two matriclans (*wua*, meaning also "life-generating female organs"). Each *wua* was divided into two branches and each of those into three or more subbranches. In 1934 every branch was exogamous, which however was not the case with *wua* as a whole. An individual belonged to the subbranch (and therefore branch and *wua*) of his or her "mother," true or adoptive.

Unlike the society's patriclans, its matriclans had no religious functions, and because of the preponderance in the society of virilocal marital residence there was no residential cohesion among its members. And while the membership as a whole of each matriclan often acted as a group in fishing and sporting contests, it was its branches that were corporate in economic and other ways. Thus each branch owned residual rights to certain taro beds; and although portions of these were allotted to its subbranches for cultivation, they returned to the branch for reallotting when a subbranch became extinct. However, it was the subbranches that assumed collective responsibility for antisocial actions by its members.

During the time of the Beagleholes' study each branch was headed by its eldest member, male or female, whose functions are described as "light," and whose position within the branch gave him (or her) "no special status in the community" as a whole (Ibid., 227).

There were (of course) fabulous myths regarding the primal origin of this (for Polynesia, nearly anomalous) type of clan, but, as proposed by Marshall Sahlin in his influential *Social Stratification in Polynesia*, it may have been invented locally as a way for assuring equitable distribution—in this case periodic redistribution—of food-production resources among a people who (like all peoples everywhere) were subject to demographic variability among individual families, but who were in addition confined to a very limited area of land that was vulnerable to severe natural disasters such as hurricanes and tidal waves.

Social units resembling matriclans also existed on the Outlier atoll of Ontong Java (Hogbin 1930, 1934), but too little has been reported about them to permit summarizing here.

Two other Outlier societies well studied enough to include in this survey are those of

Kapingamarangi and Nukuoro, both of them located on atolls closer to peoples of the (Micronesian) Caroline Islands than to any of Polynesia. Of the two, Kapingamarangi was divided into ambilineal clans, which, however, were relatively shallow in generational depth and relatively limited in collective functions—the three-generation ones having functioned as corporate land-owning units, the five- and six-generation ones also as collective sponsors of a member's wedding feast. In addition, there was at one time a division of the whole populace into two categories: *tangata tauihora* ("wrong servers") and *tangata tautonu* ("true servers"), membership in each having been traced through one's maternal line. However, the only difference between the two units was that only "true servers" could play leading roles in religious activities (Emory 1965; Lieber 1970, 1974).

As for Nukuoro, its ethnographer reported that there were no common-descent units there larger than "families" (Carroll 1970).

KINSHIP AND FRIENDSHIP

For Anglophones the more authoritative (i.e., dictionary) definitions of "kinship" limit it to consanguinity (relationships by blood)—i.e., common biogenetic descent from some particular male or female ("blood" in this usage being more metaphorical than physiological). In everyday Anglophonic conversation, however, "kinship" often includes adoptees (i.e., "legalized consanguinity") as well as spouses and other affines. The closest and most widespread Polynesian gloss to the English word "kinship" was—still is—*kaaiga* (and cognate forms). Like "kinship" its primary referent was relationship by common descent, and like "kinship" it included other referents—which, however, were unlike those of Anglophonic "kinship" in some particulars. Anthropologists in general strive to be nonethnocentric when studying and writing about peoples of different cultures (including languages) but English-speaking ones nevertheless categorize and label many of those peoples' interrelationships as "kinship." And while most Anglophonic anthropologists are at pains to indicate how, say, Navaho or Nuer or Maori, etc., concepts of "kinship" differ from their own English-language ones, the very use of the word tends to imply that most of the beliefs and sentiments and values and practices so labeled are broadly similar to those included under that English-language label. In many cases they may have been—but not necessarily so.

Writings by anthropologists about Polynesian "kinship" are profuse, multifarious and complex. Whole books have been devoted to describing and analyzing a single people's behavioral variants of that Anglophonic category of relationships, and another large one would be required just to summarize Polynesians' ways of defining and classifying "kinfolk" and their rules concerning how "kinfolk" ought to interact. The most pithy statement I have come across about how Polynesians in general define "kinfolk" is as follows: "The notion of *kinship* as *shared substance* [italics added] is richer and more ambiguous than analysts' conventional definition of kinship in terms of genealogy. Substance may derive from filiative links, from shared involvement in land (that most precious of commodities), or from shared consumption of produce. In particular, those who regularly shared food are seen in Polynesia as acting like kinsmen, regardless of their blood ties. Thus behavior is treated as an index of kinship, as a basis for affirming or denying it. Furthermore, acting like kinsmen is a means to creating kinship bonds between persons previously unrelated" (Howard and Kirkpatrick 1989, 67). All very true. Some examples of such behavior have already been given in generalizations about families and clans, but to explicate that concise statement satisfactorily would require much more space than allowable in this introductory text. Instead, it may be most useful to list, briefly, some of the more noteworthy ways in which the "kinship" terms of Polynesian peoples, and their corresponding normative patterns of behavior, resembled or differed from those now common to many—perhaps most?—Anglophones.

Like Anglophones, Polynesians categorized "kinfolk" by labeling them with generic referential terms,[167] such as "father," "daughter," etc. And while such terms likely referred primarily to actual relationships based on obvious or surmised common descent, Polynesians, like Anglophones, occasionally used such terms as behavioral metaphor (e.g., when speaking of "brotherly" behavior). Moreover, in some Polynesian societies persons believed to be related by ties of common biogenetic descent—say, distant "brothers" or "fathers"—were not considered to be "kin" unless they behaved in a society's prescriptions for "brotherly" or "fatherly" ways. Conversely, in many societies persons who did behave, say, "brotherly" or "fatherly" were labeled "brother" or "father" even in the absence of known or supposed genetic links.[168] For Anglophones the latter practice is considered, consciously, to be metaphorical (as for example, in the case of "brotherly love," or of "our Father who art in Heaven"), but it is not at all certain that Polynesians would have distinguished so sharply between genetic and connotative "kinship."

To broaden and diversify the concept(s) even further, some Polynesian peoples applied the same word not only to genetically linked persons but also to those who shared, say, periodic participation in food exchanges or ownership of a particular plot of land (as noted in the statement from Howard and Kirkpatrick, above). In other words, even when translating words of a single Polynesian language it is in many cases inapposite to use a single word, such as "kinship," for a variety—in Anglophonic meanings—of referents. Moreover, the use of a single English word, such as "kinship," to link and summarize postulatedly related concepts in most or all Polynesian languages cannot possibly be accurate—"cannot possibly" on account of the scores or hundreds of years during which the different peoples, and their languages, had been partially or completely separate.[169]

Bearing in mind the caution against identifying a "kin" term too literally with genealogical connection, it is nevertheless worth reiterating some of the more noteworthy ways in which many or most Polynesians used such terms differently from common present-day Anglophonic usage.

First, with respect to "grandparents"—i.e., to a person's parents' parents, it is noteworthy that among most Polynesian peoples the very same term was used for both mother's and father's parents as well as for those grandparents' siblings and same-grade collaterals. In most Polynesian languages the term was *tupuna* (or cognates thereof), which was applied also to ancestors in general—not surprising, since in most cases a person's own parents' parents had died by the time he or she had reached "maturity."

Also noteworthy is the fact that in most Polynesian societies the term for "father" was applied to the latter's male siblings and male same-grade collaterals (in English, his "first cousins") as well, and the term for "mother" to her female siblings and female same-grade collaterals. And while in some societies—mainly those of the east—the term "father" was also applied to

a person's mother's brothers (and to their male same-grade collaterals), and "mother" also to a person's father's sisters (and their female same-grade collaterals), there were some other societies—mostly in western Polynesia—where terms separate from the above were applied to one's father's sisters and to one's mother's brothers—verbal practices that corresponded to the distinctive behaviors prescribed for those relationships.

Regarding a person's own siblings: a practice, followed in most Polynesian societies, was that of distinguishing terminologically between a person's same-sex siblings in terms of birth order. Thus, in such societies, for a male there was no single term for "brother," but only for "older brother" or for "younger brother"—the same having applied with respect to a female's sisters. In addition, as with most other Polynesian kin terms, those referring to siblings were in some societies extended—in this case to same-grade collaterals.

As for a person's own offspring and their same-grade collaterals, the terminological identities and distinctions applied to the latter were in most societies derivative—i.e., where their parents were classified as "mother" and "father" they were referred to in siblings terms, but where their parents were classified as "aunt" and "uncle" they were referred to in distinctive "cousinlike" terms.

And with respect to a person's offsprings' offspring (and the latter's same-grade collaterals): as with "grandparents" a single term (e.g., *motopuna* or cognates thereof) was in most societies applied to all of them regardless of gender and of "distance" of collaterality.

Concerning all the above: it should be noted that in most communities, or even some entire tribes, many members were believed to be "kin" related through more than one genealogical link. In consequence, and with respect to more "distant" kin ties, it was possible for many pairs of individuals to opt for the kinds of ties that best suited their interests at the time—an option that many of them doubtless availed themselves of. Moreover, as noted earlier, in most Polynesian societies many persons were, or were believed to be, interrelated by both genealogical and affinal ties. Here, as in the case of multiple ties of common descent, in some societies pairs of individuals had the option of choosing which of the two kinds of relationships to activate if both were of about equal "distance."[170]

FRIENDSHIP

"Friendship," in the English-language sense, surely occurred in all Polynesian societies between innumerable pairs of individuals: male and male, female and female, even male and female, within and outside the contexts of kinship and affinity, and in some societies the relationship was explicitly institutionalized.

In Tahiti, for example, three terms were used to characterize "friendly" relationships between individuals: *hoa* (companions?), *tau'a* (friends) and *taio*—only the latter having applied to the formalized type of relationship hereunder described. The term *taio* was also used to label the kind of political, usually short-lived, relationship involved in the exchange of civilities between currently nonwarring chiefs when meeting one another. But the *taio*ship now under consideration was much more comprehensive in commitment and was intended to be permanent. All known recorded instances of it involved males, and mostly males who were unmarried when their relationships—their pacts—were first instituted. In some cases the pacts were arranged and sponsored by one or both of the principals' father(s), for purposes that were at least partly political—e.g., to solidify interfamilial ties. But in other cases the pacts were initiated by the principals themselves, to celebrate and formalize their own friendship. There are no recorded estimates of the frequency of such pacts, but the formalities and commitments attending them suggest that they involved mainly middle- and upper-class youths, and were therefore few in number relative to size of population.

The fullest description of the institution was provided by James Morrison, boatswain's mate of the *Bounty*, and one of its allegedly unwilling mutineers, who lived in close contact with Tahitians for about six months before his capture and return to England:

> When a Man adopts a Friend for his Son the Ceremonie is the same [as a nuptial rite], only placing the Boy in the place of the Woman, the Ceremonie is ratified, and the boy & his friends exchange Names and are ever after looked as one of the Family, the New Friend becoming the adopted son of the Boys Father—this Friendship is most religiously kept, and never dissolves till Death, tho they may separate, and make [other,] temporary [,] Friends while absent, but when they meet always acknowledge each. And should a Brother or one who is an adopted friend become poor or lose his land in War, he has nothing more to do but go to his Brother, or Friend, and live with him partaking of all he possesses as long as he lives & his wife and Family with him if he has any . . . . (quoted in Oliver 1974, 843)

Elsewhere in his *Journal* Morrison added: "No man ever Claims a right to any land but his own, or his adopted Friends, which he may Use during his Friends life, and should his Friend die without any other Heir the Adopted friend is always considered as the right owner and no man disputes his right" (as quoted in Oliver 1974, 847).

In addition, while sexual relations were proscribed between a man's sister and his pact partner, a friendship pact appears to have licensed and even encouraged sexual relations with a partner's wife—she having been considered (in the words of another early visitor): "a common property for his *tayo*" (Wilson 1799, 346). However, according to Morrison, the woman herself had a choice in the matter: "[I]t is looked upon [as] a Great friendship for a Man to Cohabit with the Wife of His adopted friend if She is agreeable: the Adopted friend being always accounted as a brother" (quoted in Oliver 1974, 846).

Finally, while the early reports imply that pact-friends became identified with one another in relations with the members of each other's (nuclear) family—i.e., with respect to land property and sexual relations—there is nothing in print to indicate how far, if at all, that identity extended to other kin.

Institutions closely similar to Tahitian bond-friendship existed in several other Polynesian societies, one of the fullest described having been that of Anuta Island (mentioned in chapter 19), where, in addition to the institutionalized adoption of someone by an individual or by a whole clan, there was another type of formalized relationship that served to establish a close fraternal tie between two males. Such relationships were usually instituted by the parents of the pair during the latter's infancy or childhood, and although it entailed lifelong close friendship and cooperation, it involved only the pair themselves (Feinberg 1981).

21

COMMUNITIES AND TRIBES

Having considered how Polynesians structured their social relationships in terms of gender, "consanguinity" (including birth-order seniority), affinity, occupation and friendship, we turn now to the part played by residential proximity (combined with collective activity) in shaping them. As we saw, families and households constituted coresidential units, as did the core members of clan branches. In all societies, moreover, such units were also parts of larger groups—i.e., of "communities," which are herein defined as all persons who resided near one another in a discrete cluster of households and who on occasion interacted with one another in institutionalized cooperative ways.

Beginning with the spatial aspect of communities: it can be said at the outset that few (tropical) Polynesian peoples built their residences in the form of compact—i.e., "nucleated"—villages, the main exceptions having existed on the high islands of Samoa, Rurutu and Rapanui (Easter Island), and on some atoll islets (where the scarcity of land rendered propinquity unavoidable).[171] Elsewhere, a community's residences were strung out in thin lines near (but rarely directly on) shorelines, or were scattered throughout the lower and middle sections of valleys. Along with that scattering, however, most communities contained their own common social center, usually consisting of a religious edifice or a secular meeting place. In some societies a community's social center was separate from all residences; in others it was adjacent to the household of the community's headman (an office to be distinguished from a tribe's—although in many cases a community's headman was a clan senior or a tribal chief as well).

In many societies their communities were composed of members of branches of two or more clans,[172] whose respective landholdings remained separate. But even in communities containing branches of different clans the local members of all of them would combine on occasion to do something together—such as participate in large-scale fish drives or building-bees or dance fests or sporting events. (Otherwise they would not have been "communities" as herein defined!) Also, some communities per se shared corporate rights of ownership of land not otherwise owned by any of their constituent clans—land that could be used by any and everyone residing there. And—an important and virtually indispensable feature—most if not all communities had an overall government, which consisted of either the senior of its most populous clan branch or, as in Samoa, a council of all of its clan seniors[173] or all of a community's elderly men—or, as in Hawai'i, a representative of the chief of the community's encompassing tribe—which brings us to consideration of the Polynesian form of that worldwide type of social group.

A Polynesian "tribe," as herein defined, was a territorially bounded social group composed of one or more communities under the overall authority of a chief, or combination of chiefs, who was (or were) under the political authority of no one else anywhere.[174] (By "authority" is meant ability to compel someone to do something, by threat of or actual use of institutionalized sanctions, including physical force. As such, authority differs from "prestige" (i.e., being or having something that others admire or praise). It also differs from "influence" and "leadership" (i.e., ability to persuade, without coercion, others to do something they might otherwise not do). In most cases, perhaps, Polynesian chiefs also possessed prestige and occasionally displayed leadership, but for the sake of clarity the three qualities will be differentiated in this book.

Polynesian tribes differed widely in number of members and in degree of segmentation: from a hundred or so members to many thousands, from a single community to scores of them (which were

21.1. Portrait of the Tahitian chief Pomare

21.2. A chief of Hawai'i leading his party to battle

21.3. Portrait of a Marquesan chief

21.4. Portrait of the Tongan "king"

in many cases combined into subtribes, sub-sub-tribes, and so on). On Anuta Island, the entire population of about two hundred persons constituted a single tribe. In Hawai'i, at the time of first contact its two hundred thousand or so inhabitants were grouped into countless subtribes and sub-subtribes, making up about thirty-four tribes (*moku*)—which, off and on, were themselves combined, usually coercively, into still larger tribal units, called *moi* (and which, after Western contact and with the use of some European weapons, were united by one chief, by conquest or threat of conquest, into a single so-called "kingdom"). Note well the adverbial "off and on": the tribal boundaries of precontact Hawai'i (and of several other Polynesian societies) were far from immutable.

If indigenous accounts of their recent precontact past were credible—which many of them were, aside from detours into legend and myth—tribal boundaries nearly everywhere in Polynesia changed intermittently, but, over the long run, in the direction of fewer and larger tribes. Some of those changes were effected by the purposeful marriage of the scions of different chiefly dynasties, but most were brought about by warfare (and in some cases were then "ratified" by such marriages).

Tribes varied considerably in structure. One of the most complex was that of Tonga—not surprising in view of that society's great age (i.e., about three thousand years). In addition to its split rulership, mentioned in chapter 19, its rulers (whose clan territory was originally in central Tongatapu Island) succeeded after a time to extend their rule not only over all of the Tongan archipelago but also, in some measure, over the distant islands of Niuatoputapu, Niuafo'ou, and East Uvea (the last about 500 miles from Tongatapu)—a veritable Empire, made possible by the Tongans' fleets of large sailing canoes. And that was not all. At one point Tongans established centuries-long rulership over parts of Samoa (and thereafter conducted occasional trade exchanges and marriages with Samoans, over a distance of about 550 miles from Tongatapu). They also maintained relations with Fiji, having gone there in numbers to fight as mercenaries in local wars, and to build their larger canoes (there having been little of preferred kinds of timber in Tonga itself). Unlike Hawai'i, where all its tribes became united

only after contact with Westerners, the precontact Tongan supertribe broke up into several interwarring tribes after contact and were not reunited until 1865 into an archipelago-wide tribe (which survives today as an autonomous "kingdom").[175]

A different kind of complexity prevailed in Tikopia. As described in chapter 19, the Tikopians were divided into four patrilineal clans (*kainanga*), whose respective members were, however, interspersed throughout the island, which itself was divided into several communities (*kainga*), and those grouped into one or other of the island's two districts (*fasi*). Thus, while most individuals were subject to their own clan senior in certain matters, they were also subject to their community headman in others, and in still others to whichever of the island's four clan seniors resided in their district. And although those four were ranked among themselves in terms of religious responsibilities and social precedence, and acted conjointly in many matters of islandwide concern, no one of them held authority over the others. In other words, Tikopia did not constitute a single tribe, nor was it divided into (geographically separate) autonomous tribes: a structural situation that might be rationalized as being "anomalous," but which is very likely to occur when, as in this book, an attempt is being made to generalize about peoples, even historically interrelated peoples, as widely scattered as the Polynesians. Situations as "anomalous" as those of Tikopia may have prevailed in some other small Polynesian societies, but none has been recorded as fully as that of Tikopia.

Leaving aside the anomalies, the question arises, What were the motives that led chiefs to attempt to expand their domains?

There were cases in which the dire need for more fruitful land to support an increasing population led a chief to conquest. One such well-documented case was the successful campaign, in the Society Islands, of Boraborans to invade and conquer nearby Raiatea and Tahaa. Another was the successful campaigns of some Tikopians to expel from that small and overpopulated island a large number of people in order to obtain their food-producing resources. But perhaps the most telling example occurred—and often recurred—on Mangaia (Cook Islands), where its tribes periodically fought one another for occupation of the island's most fruitful area, and where its current

21.5. A young woman of Tahiti wearing presents of barkcloth and gorgets

occupants, if defeated, had to retire to less fruitful areas until strong enough to retaliate and regain the better lands.

Somewhat similar were the efforts of immigrant bands to gain and expand footholds on already inhabited islands—a scenario that doubtless occurred numerous times during the centuries of dispersion and colonization (including such well-documented ones as Rarotongans' conquest of Mangaia, and Tongans' of East Uvea).

In many other cases the motivation for tribal expansion originated in a chief's personal desire to enlarge his domain: to acquire more subjects, more tribute and more honor (including super clan titles) vis-à-vis other chiefs. For, as Irving Goldman recorded in his frontispiece quotation (from Balzac): "The noble of every age has done his best to invent a life which he, and he only, can live" (1970). The proclaimed causes of many such conflicts were revenge—to retaliate for the killing of a fellow tribesman or to avenge publicized insults to a chief's honor—but in many cases those were only pretexts, used by a chief to undertake personally enhancing conquests.

In some respects Polynesian warfare resembled that of modern nations: whole tribes fighting other whole tribes. There were, however, two other features of Polynesian tribes that were more distinctive. One was the occurrence—in some tribes of some societies—of one of its subtribes fighting another without intervention of their common chief. Second was the occurrence in some places of one subtribe waging warfare against another tribe, or part of another tribe—as if the state of Maine waged warfare against all Canada, or against Quebec Province only.

Warfare was perhaps the most characteristic but not the only kind of activity engaged in by Polynesian tribes. In fact, except for warfare, tribal activities were the same as those of many clans writ large. Included in those were entertaining (and of course banqueting) visiting notables from other tribes—and making visits and being visited and entertained in turn. In some societies such visiting was so frequent and large in scale that the hosts—or more often the host chief's subjects—were perennially impoverished by food levies for such occasions.

In addition, some chiefs in some societies—typically the highly stratified ones—also levied food and other objects in order to support, or help support, themselves, their families, their staffs, etc. In some cases, such as Hawai'i and Tonga, some chiefs relied almost entirely on such support; in many other cases, they (like most clan seniors) obtained their everyday food, etc., from their own gardens and groves.

As with clans, tribemates also engaged occasionally in work projects for the benefit of their unit—their tribe—as a whole or, more often, for the benefit of its chief. On the average such projects exceeded those of clans by far—in many cases very far. Thus, on Easter Island one large statue destined for a tribal temple, and weighing about eighty-four tons, is estimated to have taken thirty men one year to carve, ninety men two months to move it the four miles from quarry to temple site, and ninety men three months to erect it there—a total of about twenty-five thousand man-days (Mulloy 1970).[176] And in Tahiti the stone structure on Mahaite *marae* (temple) measured about eighty-five by twenty-four yards at the base and rose as a pyramid of ten steps to a height of about fifteen yards. No counts were recorded of the amount of labor involved in its construction, but it must have been a calamitous drain on the manpower of its tribe, which at that time had a total membership of about seventy-two hundred.

Also like clans, tribes as such engaged in religious activities of several kinds, including petitions to tribal tutelar gods for assistance and thanks for help received. In some cases the tutelar god(s) and temple of the chief's own clan became, "officially," those of his entire tribe (as in the case of the Church of England!); in others the tribe as such had its own distinct tutelary god(s) and temple(s). Ceremonies celebrated at tribal temple(s) included passage rites for its chief and his heir, petitions for good harvests, and the beginning and end of intertribal warfare. Regarding a chief's passage rites, I know of no cases in which the death of a clan's (nonchief) senior as such excited as much public commotion as that of some chiefs, whose deaths were sometimes followed by months of tribewide "grieving" or periods of anarchic liminality. And with respect to warfare, nearly all religious actions connected with it were tribal affairs—including omen-seeking regarding outcomes, the magical empowering of warriors and weapons, and the magical weakening of enemies. Also, in some societies attempts were made by both sides to obtain the exclusive support of their society-wide god(s) of warfare—a practice common to warfare between Christian nations as well.

Focusing now on the kinds of property associated with tribes, it would be useful to differentiate those belonging corporately to whole tribes from the personal belongings of their chief—useful but not always possible, inasmuch as chiefs in some societies considered their tribes' property to be their own, to use or dispose of as they wished. Thus, in Hawai'i, upon his inheritance or seizure of a chieftainship, the new incumbent—now sole residual owner of all lands within the tribe's boundaries—reallocated management of them to some of his followers, who in turn confirmed or reallocated use-rights in them to proprietors of their own choice (which eventuated often in numerous expropriations and dislodgments). At the other extreme, there were some societies whose chiefs obtained all of their household's food, etc., from their own family or clan lands, and whose ownership, or rather stewardship, over other lands within the tribal boundaries were only connoted, and that by token amounts of "first-fruits" offerings from the provisional but well-entrenched users of those lands.

Another aspect of the relationship between a tribe and its territory had to do with its chief's authority to impose temporary restrictions on the consumption of specific resources of that territory, including fish and coconuts. Some such restrictions were imposed for tribewide purposes—including the conservation and accumulation of food for tribewide celebrations, but others were imposed for the sole benefit of the chief himself. Speaking of which, in many societies certain of its resources were reserved exclusively for chiefs; the most prized of these, nearly everywhere, having been turtles, the eating of which by others was punished, in some tribes by death.

Another kind of asset owned, possibly, by the tribe as a whole, and therefore specifically by its chief, was the services of its residents—and not only the occasional services required for, say, fish drives and large-scale construction, but also for waging war, including dying on behalf of the tribe and of its chief. Note however the word "possibly," there being some uncertainty about the nature of that "ownership." That is to say, while modern states manifest clearly their "ownership" of their citizens through powers of universal conscription, it is unclear whether such powers rested

in all or most Polynesian tribal polities. Certainly, while the chiefs of some of them were powerful enough to coerce all of their subjects into doing something for them, including fighting, that is not quite the same, conceptually, as a modern state's conscription laws.

The larger size and more heterogeneous composition of some tribes, along with the personal indulgences and aspirations of their chiefs, required large staffs. In Hawai'i, for example, the typical "headquarters" staff included "a [principal] counselor, a [principal] priest, a war leader, a council of military strategists, common warriors, historians, and readers of omens." In addition to which were "guardians, foster parents, wet nurses, all *kahu* [caretakers], a keeper of household goods, a chief executioner, night guards, a chief steward, a treasurer, a reader of signs, an orator, a guardian of the royal genitals, and massagers" (Goldman 1970, 224, after Kepelino in Beckwith 1932). And to which may be added, for some chiefs, a keeper of his spittoon—a gourd container in which his spittle was guarded against theft by some sorcerer bent on murdering him by use of the spittle as "bait." In addition, in some societies a chief's household included "court" musicians, dancers and concubines, plus assorted hangers-on, both kin and nonkin. Hence the need for frequent and copious levies of food, and hence the plague-like effects of their presence when accompanying their chief on his peregrinations, which in some societies were almost continuous.

I turn now to the characteristics of the office (i.e., status) of chief.

Like the office of most clan seniors, that of the chieftainship of many tribes had two sides: sacred and secular,[177] the one priestly, the other managerial; the one consisting of communicating with gods on behalf of tribal welfare (including that of the chief himself), the other administering tribal mundane affairs—although, it should be added, for Polynesians the antithesis between the two spheres of action was far from sharp.

The "sacred" side of many if not most chieftainships derived, likely, from the circumstance that most tribes were at one time ruled by seniors of their most populous clans, who, by convention, were their most "sacred" members, i.e., those in "closest" relationship with their units' tutelar god(s). Some persons became "close" to a god by being occasionally or permanently "possessed" by him, thereby becoming his "medium" for communicating with other humans. Or some chiefs, here or there, were believed to *be* gods.[178] But it is my (undocumentable) surmise that many chiefs held their office by virtue of their seniority in a clan—i.e., by their inherent, inherited godliness—godliness (as postulated earlier) being a substance, corporeal or incorporeal, inherited through one's parent(s) from some primordial ancestor-god.

Doubtless, there were some chiefs, here or there, who had achieved that office through other routes, including forceful usurpation or political maneuver, but even in such cases some of them added more godliness to their successors by marrying women endowed by birth with superior degrees of godliness. Or, in some cases, there were individuals who, having achieved chieftainship by routes other than birth, were popularly endowed with "sacredness" because of their achievements: for, along with the pervasive, Polynesia-wide reverence for inherited "sacredness," there was also admiration for individual efficacy, based on the belief that manifest ability was also a sign of god-given superiority (a thesis proposed and convincingly documented by Irving Goldman in his monumental *Ancient Polynesian Society).*

Turning to the "secular" side of chieftainship, which in many languages was labeled *hau,* the degree to which it was exercised varied not only between societies in general but between tribes (i.e., chiefs) of the same society as well. At one pole were chiefs, such as many in Hawai'i, who delegated most of their "sacred" duties to priests, and engaged actively, in some cases tyrannically, in the management of mundane tribal affairs, including intertribal warfare. At the other pole were chiefs, such as many in Samoa, who delegated tribal administration to executive officers (called *tulafale* in Samoa) while maintaining a Buddha-like passivity. Or an even greater extreme was exemplified in Tonga, where a chief retained the sacredness function for himself and his successors but gave up his *hau* to a brother and his successors (in order to avoid assassination, according to some traditions).

Speaking of assassination: While Polynesians in general held their chiefs in reverential awe, and considered them privileged to behave toward their subjects in ways beyond the normative limits of other kinds of intratribal relationships, there were exceptions. Thus, in many instances a sibling or

other relative of a chief looked upon him with envy or contempt, even to the extent of deposing or assassinating him in order to take his place. Also, among the other subjects of some chiefs there were doubtless many who bore them malice because of perceptions of egregious injustices inflicted upon themselves.

Reverting to the "normative" limits of most intratribal[179] relationships, a few words are in order concerning those norms and the penalties prescribed for infringing them—but only a few, since many of those norms have already been touched on in this and previous chapters. Also, because the topic is too large, varied and complex for comprehensive treatment in this book, only a few broad generalities will have to suffice.

First and foremost, in line with the intrinsically, even gods-given hierarchical nature of Polynesian societies, the concept of "equality under the law" was utterly alien to them—and not only with respect to relations between a chief and his subjects but among his subjects as well, for Polynesian societies were pervasively hierarchic: in relationships between individuals of different statuses those of higher status were comprehensively more privileged than those of lower status. Thus, a close kinsman of a chief could with some impunity commit "wrongs" against a commoner—say, seduce his wife or appropriate some of his coconuts—whereas such acts by another commoner could and often did lead to conventionally sanctioned violent retaliation.

Second, most interpersonal "wrongs" among equals were adjudged to be so, and were punished by, the sufferer himself or his close relatives; except in the few kinds of situations in which a whole community "suffered" there were no official courts to adjudge acts to be "wrong" or to apply punishment for them.

And third, with regard to the nature of "wrongs," they varied widely from society to society, as did their penalties (which also varied according to statuses of their sufferers).[180] Nevertheless, along with acts of *lèse majesté* and, in some cases, homicide, theft was everywhere considered to be a very serious "wrong," with penalties for it ranging from property destruction to exile or death—this along with the fact that in at least one society (i.e., Tahiti) successful (i.e., undetected) thieves were widely admired and their patron god revered.

22

SOCIAL STRATIFICATION

Since the beginnings of Western contact, explorers, missionaries, other early visitors, and more recently scholars have declared social stratification to be one of the most salient and distinctive features of Polynesian societies—salient on account of its conspicuous manifestations and distinctive on account of its contrast with features of the more egalitarian societies of most of neighboring Melanesia. Most studies of the subject have focused on how it came to exist; that is indeed an interesting question that invites answers, but first, a clearer understanding is needed about its shapes, and about the two types of status, hereditary and achieved, that it comprised.

I begin with stratification in clans, because of my judgment that a person's hereditary status in a clan, and the normative relationships among a clan's branches, served most weightily to stratify the statuses among members of a tribe—and, by extension, among all members of their encompassing society.

In most Polynesian societies commitment to the principle of primogeniture—qualified in most of them by some bias toward males—was the most basic stratifying criterion, not only among siblings but among the constituent families of a clan branch and, up to a point, between the branches of a clan. Thus, within a branch, the statuses of the offspring of its senior were usually higher than those of the senior's younger siblings and their offspring. And, among a clan's branches, the statuses of offspring of the senior of the senior branch tended to be higher than those of all of the members of the junior branches as well. However, except in a few cases, that superiority did not extend to the senior branch as a whole—i.e., all members of the senior branch were not as a whole higher in status than all members of other branches of a clan.

As proposed earlier, the status-structuring tenet of primogeniture derived from belief in the procreational aspect of godliness—i.e., the belief that most of a parent's quantum (or whatever) of godliness went into its firstborn—of both parents in ambiclans, of fathers only in patriclans.[181] Supplementing those beliefs was the conviction that a large quantum of godliness was indispensable for attaining high hereditary status (and the many rights included in it). Put together, those beliefs motivated persons of high hereditary status to procreate successors with as "much" or "more" godliness than their own. In the context of patriclans, inasmuch as only a father's godliness was transmitted, that did not call for a high–ascriptive-status wife-mother as well. But in the context of ambiclans, to reach that objective required parental mates of equal or near-equal hereditary status, hence the eugenic rules regarding choice of mate—rules which prevailed among high-status members in many ambiclan societies and which resulted, in some societies, in the formation of stratified marriage classes. In a few such societies, notably those of Tonga, Hawai'i and Tahiti, the upper marriage classes became prescriptively endogamous—in Tonga and Hawai'i so exclusively so that clan-based relationships with the rest of the populace had nearly ceased to exist.

In light of the above developments, the question arises, Why did they not take place in all ambiclan societies to similar degrees? Why was it that in some ambiclan societies many high-status men, including clan seniors, were content to marry—to produce successors with—lower status women? Answers to that question are doubtless multiple. One is that their populations, being smaller, could not provide a large enough "pool" of potential high-status wives. And under such conditions (I suggest) expedience replaced beliefs about ambilineality and shifted toward contentment with or preference for patriliny—which in fact may have been the personal preference of most Polynesian males anyway!

The discussion so far has focused on (hereditary) status differences within clans—within each of a clan's branches and between branches of the same clan. Also, as just noted, in several societies the higher heredity-status members of some or all of a society's clans constituted a more or less endogamous upper class. And finally, in a few societies clans themselves were ranked vis à vis one another, due (among other causes) to a clan's own vicissitudes or to those undergone by its encompassing tribe—a notable example of which occurred in the Society Islands, where one clan based originally on Raiatea Island came in time to ramify throughout the archipelago and outrank all other clans.

Like clans, all Polynesian tribes, everywhere, were socially stratified: each of them had a chief (or, as in Tikopia, conjointly ruling clan seniors), who ranked higher, socially, than all other members. Unlike clans, however, tribes varied widely in number of distinctive offices, both hereditary and achieved, and in the ways those offices were stratified. The number of tribal offices was correlative, roughly, with a tribe's size; i.e., in the case of some small tribes the only such office was that of chief, by heredity or achievement, whereas in some very large tribes there were many others, both hereditary and achieved, including, for example, heir to chieftainship, high (tribal) priest, war leader, messenger, etc.—which however were not everywhere stratified in the same way.

Tribes also differed from clans in that more tribal offices were reached by means other than birth. That is to say, although some offices were hereditary, in family lines, others were attainable by personal achievement.

In addition to the above, in many tribes occupations were also stratified *inter se*—e.g., fishing above (or below) farming, or carpentry above (or below) tattooing, and in nearly all such cases this pattern of ranking prevailed throughout a tribe's encompassing society as well.

The most comprehensive treatments of society-wide stratification are those of Marshall Sahlins, in his *Social Stratification in Polynesia* (1958), Irving Goldman, in his *Ancient Polynesian Society* (1970), and Patrick Kirch, in his *The Evolution of Polynesian Chiefdoms* (1984).[182]

Sahlins classified the fourteen societies in his sample into four "status levels":

Level I: Hawai'i, Tonga, Samoa and Tahiti
Level IIA: Mangareva, Mangaia, Easter Island and East Uvea
Level IIB: Marquesas, Tikopia and East Futuna
Level III: Pukapuka, Ontong Java and Tokelau

He then went on to explain a society's position in this gradient as having been correlative with its "productivity": "Strategic goods not consumed by the producers were often accumulated by chiefs and periodically redistributed among producers of the goods, and as well among specialized and communal laborers. The distinction between chief and nonchief in distribution function further implies social differentiation in other aspects of the economy and society. It was suggested, therefore, that stratification is directly related to productivity, if productivity be considered to mean the ability of the wielders of the technology to produce strategic goods beyond their consumption needs. The greater the productivity, the greater the differentiation between distributors (chiefs) and producers (nonchiefs) and the greater the tendency for this distinction to extend itself into other aspects of culture" (1958, 248–49).

He then proceeded to measure that "productivity" by size of a "chief's" "redistribution systems" and their frequency of occurrence:

It was posited that in any given group, other factors being constant, the greater the surplus producible by the producers the greater would be the range of distribution, and productivity was measured by considering the number of people embraced in the largest redistributive network of food and how frequently this overall network was utilized. As a check on productivity derived by this measure, the Polynesian groups [societies] were also examined with respect to the amount of non–food-producing specialists they contained and the particular types of technology and environment present. In the former case, it was assumed that the greater the productivity the greater the proportion of people who might be divorced from food production. The particular ecologies were rated according to other assumptions: e.g., other things being constant, agriculture is more productive than hunting and gathering; specialized techniques of domestication, such as irrigation, agriculture and selection of crop varieties, are more productive than the lack of specialized techniques; the

greater the diversity of environmental opportunities
the more likely that productivity will be greater; etc.
(Ibid.)

The other aspects of "culture" referred to had to
do mainly with the authority and prerogatives of
"chiefs"—whether clan seniors or tribal chiefs or
both is not clear.

Sahlin's study has been criticized, with some
justification, for its characterization of certain of
the societies in his sample, and for its almost
preclusive emphasis on technology and productivity, but it deserves great credit for its pioneering
attempt to account for, by systematic comparison,
social-structural differences among the numerous
species of the Polynesians' cultural genus.

Goldman's study is more difficult to summarize. It provides a panoramic view of social relationships in eighteen of Polynesia's societies and
many insights into several social processes prevalent in them. Also, it emphasizes, almost for the
first time, the role played by status rivalry in
changing social relationships that have been characterized in most earlier studies as having been
fixed inflexibly by birth. And the study was the
first to draw attention to intrasocietal differences,
throughout much of Polynesia, between the sub-
cultures of high- and low-status persons. On the
other hand, it minimizes or even ignores the influence exerted by environmental and technological
factors upon social relationships. And it falls short
of the lucid succinctness that characterizes Sahlin's
study. Nevertheless, Goldman's classification of
Polynesian societies in terms of "development
sequence" of what he calls their "status systems"
is very noteworthy.

At the beginning of his developmental
sequence are those societies that he labels
"Traditional," i.e., those which he considers to
have been nearer the supposedly ancestral form of
all Polynesian societies (i.e., those in which "the
logic of seniority through males is most fully carried out") (1970, 25). He includes in this category
Tikopia, Maori, Manihiki-Rakahanga, Tongareva,
East Uvea, East Futuna, Pukapuka and Ontong
Java.

Next in the developmental sequence are societies that he labels "Open" (Mangaia, Easter,
Marquesas, Samoa and Niue)—i.e., those in
which the "Traditional" values and forces contended with those in which "seniority has been

modified to allow military and political control"
(20). And, while the Traditional system was
"essentially a religious system headed by a sacred
chief and given stability by a religiously sanctioned gradation of worth," the Open system is
"more strongly military and political than religious, and stability in it must be maintained
more directly by the exercise of secular powers"
(Ibid.).

Finally, at the summit of Goldman's developmental sequence are the "Stratified" societies—
Mangareva, Tahiti, Hawai'i and Tonga, in which
"status differences are economic and political,
High ranks hold the rule and possess the land
titles; the commoners are subjects and are landless"[183] (Ibid.). And in Tonga, as reported by
Goldman (drawing upon Mariner), commoners
were so inferior as to have had no "souls"—i.e., to
have possessed no component that survived after
biological death.

Kirch's study differs from those of Sahlins and
Goldman in having had a larger topical objective
(i.e., larger than "social stratification" alone), and
in having included information from recent
archaeological researches (many conducted by
Kirch himself)—researches that postdated the
studies of Sahlins and Goldman. It also differs
from theirs in having considered a wider range of
causative factors, including (1) the circumstance
that Polynesians themselves had altered their
pristine environments, either to increase their productivity (e.g., by irrigation and fishponds) or,
unwittingly, to decrease their productivity (e.g.,
through deforestation and overuse); and (2) the
fact of slow but sure population increases—not
themselves a direct and independent cause, but, in
the context of regional differences in per capita
productivity, as having spurred "chiefs," who
were allegedly so inclined by temperament and
tradition, to intertribal rivalry and conquest.

I will not attempt to propose a new and "better" explanation for societal stratification than
those championed by Sahlins, Goldman, and
Kirch, but can point out some aspects of the phe-
nomenon not sufficiently emphasized in their
schemes.

First, it should be emphasized that Polynesian
societies differed in the ways in which class (i.e.,
stratum) boundaries were delimited, behaviorally.
At one pole were those in which the only distinction
was in terms of respect behavior—i.e., those of

lower-class status having been required to be more "respectful" in their interactions with upper-class persons than with members of their own class. At the other pole were societies with rules that also prohibited marriage between upper- and lower- (marriage) class persons, including nonmarital sexual relations that produced surviving offspring—proscriptions that were, however, sometimes ignored, as evidenced by the existence of "half-castes" in many of those societies. Or an even greater extreme was exemplified in Hawai'i, where the *kauwā*, the lowest stratum, were deemed to be so inferior that their very propinquity was believed to be polluting to members of all other strata, and in Tonga, where, as noted earlier, members of the lowest stratum were deemed to lack (death-surviving) souls.

Next to be noted is the fact that the otherwise admirable taxonomic schemes of both Sahlins and Goldman obscure some important differences between the societies in their samples. For example, while joining Hawai'i with Tahiti in the "most highly stratified" level is quite accurate, it blurs some significant dissimilarities between the two. Thus, although both Hawaiians and Tahitians were divided into three major strata—of *ali'i*, *maka'āinana*, and *kauwā* in Hawai'i, of *ari'i*, *ra'atira*, and *manehune* in Tahiti—Tahiti's *ali'i* were relatively few in number and composed of only two or three substrata, while Hawai'i's *ali'i* were relatively numerous and divided into eleven substrata. And, while Tahiti's lowest stratum (*manehune*) constituted the bulk of the population and contained some members who played essential roles in Tahitian society, Hawai'i's *kauwā* were relatively few in number and (as noted above) were deemed so inferior as to be outcastes, whose very propinquity was believed to be polluting to both *ali'i* and *maka'āinana*.

Drawing on the works of Sahlins, Goldman, and Kirch and on many single-society Polynesian ethnographies leads to the following amended explanations for intersocietal differences in kinds and degrees of social stratification.

The underlying and foremost basis for all forms of Polynesians' social stratification was their common ancestral heritage of a hereditary hierarchic ranking among members of each clan, based largely (as Goldman states) on male-biased primogeniture and, derivatively, on seniority-ranking among collateral lines of consanguines. (It

is my rationale that such ranking derived from their concept of the inheritance of "godliness"—specifically, that the "amount" of godliness inherited by a child from his or her parent diminished with order of birth. However, it is quite possible that such ranking may have been based on some other, less mystical, rationale.)

A less influential but nevertheless weighty factor in Polynesians' thinking about social status was their respect for achievement in certain spheres of activity—including especially achievement in leading or fighting battles, in certain kinds of occupations and in skills concerned with relations with gods, and—not least—success in accumulating and distributing large quantities of food and other high-value goods. Achievements in these spheres of activities doubtless led many individuals to rise in status (i.e., above their birth-given one) in their own tribe, but also served to create new tribe-wide social strata (such as guilds of builders or navigators, corps of warriors, and holy orders of priests)—strata that were in some societies graded, in terms of rights, below those of chiefs and their close relatives but higher than those of the rest of their tribemates.

In this connection it is reasonable to conclude that the larger the tribe the more likely it was to have contained individuals with better-than-average mental or physical capabilities, and therefore likely to have achieved statuses higher than the one born with.

A tribe's physical environment might also have affected its degree of social stratification. That is to say, in cases where a tribe's territory included both fertile and relatively infertile areas, those living in the former were enabled to be more productive, etc., than those of less favored tribemates—which leads to the hypothesis that tribes whose members occupied widely dissimilar landscapes were more subject than others to this form of stratification.

Carrying this reasoning even further, it would be logical to conclude that in the event of warfare between two tribes, victory would have gone in most cases to the one with the larger population (including more warriors) and more fertile environment (i.e., more supplies of food, etc.). And in cases in which victory resulted in the incorporation of the defeated into the tribe of the victors—a not-unusual consequence—it sometimes led to an increase in the resulting tribe's degree of stratification through subordination of some or all of the defeated into a distinct underclass.

Finally, a word about another somewhat related but nowadays less fashionable explanation for the social stratification of whole societies.

Until about 1930 some explanations of society-wide stratification in Polynesia attributed it to the arrival of more "advanced" groups of immigrants onto islands already inhabited by less "advanced" settlers, followed by the overwhelming and subordination of the latter. The outstanding expositor of this so-called "wave" theory was E. S. C. Handy, whose view was nourished by decades of field and library research but who underestimated or ignored other possible explanations. Then followed a period during which the "wave" theory itself was widely, and totally, rejected—based partly on skepticism about Polynesians' ability to carry out deliberate, nonaccidental, long-distance colonization voyages, and partly on deeper, functionally oriented and archaeologically documented understandings of their cultures. Now, however, as a result of recent demonstrations of the feasibility of such voyaging, and the historically documented actuality of some shorter-distance incursions (such as those of Tongans upon Samoa and of Rarotongans upon Mangaians), it is time to reconsider the possibilities and consequences of "second-wave" immigrations—if not always of the magnitude of socially stratifying tsunami-like size (such as those imposed by Tongans upon East Uvea), then at least of the size of culture-enriching ripples. (In fact, there are several well-documented examples of ripple-sized contacts between Tahiti and the Tuamotus.) In this connection, some scholars have maintained that one or more landings by Tahitians (which may in fact have occurred) served to produce tsunami-sized changes in the lives of Hawaiians—an opinion, however, that has been persuasively refuted by the archaeologist Ross Cordy—not the possibility of such landings but the size of their effects (Cordy 2000).

Postscript: The more recent work by Alfred Gell, referred to at the end of chapter 10, includes a classification of Polynesian societies formulated for the purpose of seeking correlations between the "intensity" of a people's tattooing practices with their overall sociopolitical institutions. In doing so, Gell categorized their social "systems" into four types: "conical," "feudal," "devolved," and "mixed." His "conical" type corresponds closely with those of Goldman's "traditional" ones, his "devolved" with Goldman's "open" ones, and his "feudal" with Goldman's "stratified" ones—except for his classification of the Society Islands society as "mixed." The product of and reasoning behind Gell's classification are summarized in a few pages (289–95), and are well worth reading—with dictionary handy!—but add little to the formulations of Sahlins, Goldman, and Kirch.

23

SOCIETIES

Up to now this text has focused on social units that differentiated the statuses of individual Polynesians—i.e., into members of families, clans, communities, occupations, tribes, and stratified social classes. We turn now to the institutions that in some cases served to unite them, at least temporarily, into whole societies. As previously noted, there were a few (numerically) small societies that consisted of a single tribe—wherein all tribe-wide practices (such as tribute-paying and the joint observance of tribal religious rites) were therefore also society-wide. In the case of multi-tribal societies, however, intertribal unity was either never reached or was reached only temporarily—albeit, in some societies, periodically. Needless to say, all such occasions contained explicit religious elements, and most of them had political aspects as well. Among the best documented of them were the Bird-man cult of Easter Island, the 'Oro cult of Tahiti and the Lono cult of Hawai'i.

BIRD-MAN CULT OF EASTER ISLAND

Easter Island was colonized from the Mangarevan-Pitcairn-Henderson region circa 800 A.D. (Green 1998). Its colonizers succeeded in transplanting a few of their root crops but neither coconuts nor breadfruit. And of the Polynesian triad of domestic animals only chickens were to survive the long colonizing voyage(s) and thereafter to multiply. There is no knowing how many humans endured those voyages—but enough, evidently, to increase to a population of between four thousand and seven thousand by time of contact (in 1774). It can be assumed that most or all of the pioneer colonizers were kinfolk—perhaps members of a single (ambi) clan. In any case the pioneer clan (*mata*) or clans eventually segmented into numerous branches—and ultimately into separate clans, each of them occupying its own territory, which contained the residences of at least its

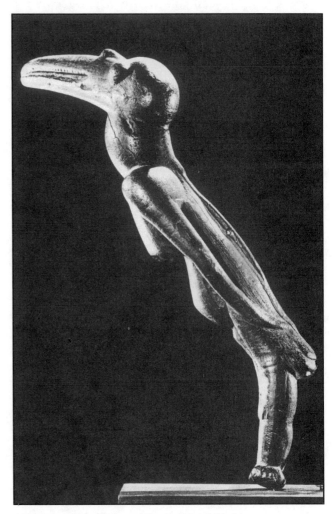

23.1. Wooden carving of Easter Island Bird-man

higher-ranking members along with an open-air temple devoted to communicating with the clan's deified ancestors (and on which were erected the giant stone statues that have made the island famous worldwide).

Meanwhile, the expanding population pressed so heavily upon the island's scant food-growing capacity that people turned to fighting for land, which eventuated in the formation of ten autonomous and bellicose tribes, whose chiefs—

who were mainly warriors—came to supersede traditional clan seniors. And over the centuries there was "invented" a new god, whose worship eventually replaced that of the traditional ones (such as Ta'aroa, 'Oro, and Tane, to give them their Tahitian names). His name was Makemake, and one of his most active personifications was that of patron god of birds.

As the island's land-based food shortages worsened—through increase of population and degradation of soil—intertribal warfare increased so greatly that most of the hundreds of temple images were toppled by enemy action and many of the defeated were forced to find temporary refuge in caves. Nevertheless, the annual Makemake-honoring festival continued to flourish, until it and most other native religious practices were supplanted by Christianity.

As mentioned earlier, the only domestic animal that survived the island's colonization was the chicken, and the only indigenous terrestrial vertebrates already there were lizards and, possibly, rats. On the other hand, the island and its nearby islets were resting and nesting places for swarms of seabirds (e.g., petrels, boobies, frigates, tropics and several species of terns), whose eggs were prized highly as food. So important were those birds and their eggs to the islanders that they figured prominently in their myths and religious practices—Makemake himself having been represented in carvings and petroglyphs, most typically by a bird head attached to a human body. As principal god he was the regular recipient of first-fruits offerings—including the first egg to be obtained each year from the thousands laid by a huge flock of sooty terns, an event around which was constructed the islanders' grandest, society-wide ceremony.

Those eggs were laid on a small uninhabited islet about a mile and a quarter off the main island. At the predictable time several men swam to the island and waited—sometimes for many days—until one of them had found an undamaged egg. Thereupon, the finder, accompanied by all the other searchers, swam with the egg back to the main island and delivered it to his own chief—each of the island's leading chiefs having been represented by one searcher in the contest. The chief of the successful searcher thereby became Bird-man of the island for the ensuing year, a position that was hedged about with food taboos and restrictions on his interpersonal contacts but one that entailed many privileges as well, including religious sanctity and rights (carried out by his followers) of island-wide social license and of vandalism and appropriation. Some early European visitors reported that the Bird-man was also the society's supreme secular authority during his incumbency, but that cannot be confirmed. What does appear likely is that the Bird-man was regarded as the avatar of the god Makemake, who is said to have actually chosen his human vessel in advance and then empowered the latter's servant-searcher to discover and deliver the prize egg.

The annual egg search was surrounded by months-long society-wide ceremonies, including feasting and Makemake worshiping. In fact the prize of being Bird-man was valued highly enough to kindle fierce intertribal rivalry before the contest (i.e., in efforts to win Makemake's favor) and bitter recriminations afterward (that were exacerbated by the licensed depredations of the followers of the victorious chief). However, during the ceremonies that accompanied the contest itself and its immediate aftermath there prevailed a society-wide pause in the chronic intertribal wars.

It has been suggested that the ceremony was a kind of rite of increase (specifically of bird eggs, or more generally of other kinds of food as well), but that is speculation that can now be neither proved nor disproved.[184]

'ORO CULT OF TAHITI

The principal, though not the sole function of the Tahitians' god 'Oro was as god of war. 'Oro's original and capital congregation was either on Borobora or at Opoa, on Rai'atea Island, whose clan seniors—and tribal chiefs—succeeded over the years in establishing religious and political outposts throughout the Society Islands. They did so through a combination of proselytization and force, solidified by marriages with local aristocrats. In the process the name of their original Opoan temple, Taputapuatea, was applied to each one of the outpost temples, whose religious and political importance increased with spread of belief in the martial powers of 'Oro. For it was only at a Taputapuatea temple that the assistance of 'Oro could be effectively enlisted—and that with the offering of human sacrifices (which at time of contact took place only at such temples).

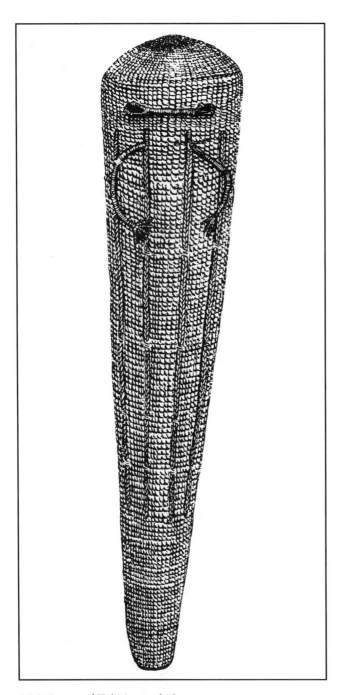

23.2. Image of Tahitian god 'Oro

ety-wide sect devoted to his worship—namely, the Arioi, whose members were divided into local chapters, one to nearly every tribal district throughout the archipelago.

For its local clerics—i.e., there were several in each tribal chapter—the sect was a full-time and in some cases a lifelong vocation, most other (i.e., lay) members having spent up to several weeks of each year in cult activities and the rest of their time at home in their ordinary pursuits.

Cult activities consisted mostly in traveling about from district to district, intra- and interisland, and performing religious ceremonies and secular entertainments, in exchange for lavish hospitality, and within the context of 'Oro worship. In some cases a single (tribal) chapter went on tour by itself; more typically the chapters of several neighboring tribes assembled and traveled together. Before arriving at some place, usually near the residence of the host chief, they dressed in their distinctive costumes and approached their destination with great clamor. They proceeded to a temple, one dedicated to 'Oro, if nearby, paid their respects to their tutelary, and then settled down to several days of dancing, theatrics, feasting—and sampling the sexual wares of their hostesses and hosts (there having been female Arioi as well as male). While many other types of dancing and theatrics of the Tahitians contained sexual allusion, those performed by the Arioi were especially explicit in this respect. Also, some of their plays were farcical satires containing biting social critique, including mockery of the foibles and tyrannies of their chiefly hosts—a remarkable license in this society, where acts of *lèse majesté* were at most other times sternly punished. A visit by a throng of Arioi was a drain on the food supplies of a host community, and perhaps a strain on some marital relationships as well, but at the same time such visits were regarded by many in the host communities as pleasurable breaks in their ordinary day-to-day routines.

Because of the lasciviousness of many of their performances, the sexual license that attended their visits, and the promiscuity that obtained among the Arioi themselves, some writers have characterized the practices as a fertility cult—a grandiose rite of sympathetic magic designed to encourage natural fertility, of humans and of supplies of food. Be that as it may, the sect also served to "unify" Tahitian society at least temporarily,

Eventually warfare became so widely prevalent, and 'Oro's assistance so sought after, that his cult came to overshadow those of other gods. In addition, the clan titles associated with Opoa, 'Oro's legendary place of origin, came to rank higher than most others in the Society Islands in religious and social importance (but not in political power, which, however, was attained after contact with the help of Europeans). Indeed, so exalted did 'Oro himself become that there came to be a soci-

fighting having been interdicted at any place where Arioi performances were taking place. Also, when on tour the Arioi themselves were immune to attack. And while the sect's principal tutelary was the war god 'Oro, that personification of him specifically worshiped, but not otherwise imitated, by the Arioi was "'Oro-of-the-laid-down-spear"—in other words, the fight-ending, peacemaking aspect of the god. (As elsewhere in Polynesia some high-order gods had two or more functionally different personalities.)

There are no credible head counts of Arioi members, but during the contact era there were certainly hundreds and possibly thousands of them, males having outnumbered female members by about five to one. As noted, nearly every tribe had its own chapter, headed by a "master," and in some cases by a "mistress" as well. Of the other members there were three types: active, "parented" and retired. The distinction between active and other members was based on the fundamental requirement that full participation in the sect's activities was dependent upon a person's having no live offspring. However, constraints were not placed on copulation—far from it. In fact, active Arioi were notoriously avid and promiscuous, among themselves and with nonmembers; the rule was against allowing a member's known progeny to survive, which was accomplished by abortion or infanticide. (Whatever may have been the basic reason, or rationale, for this rule, it had the practical effect of enabling members to carry out their sect activities free of domestic responsibilities.) If, then, an active member did bear or sire a child that for some cause or other happened to survive, the guilty parent (thereafter called "parent-ed") was thenceforth forbidden full participation in cult activities. The status of "retiree" was, however, entirely honorable; it was reserved for members who had spent years as active members and then, upon reaching "maturity," had deliberately dropped out of touring, etc., and had married and settled down to domesticity.

Active members were divided into seven or eight grades (observers differed concerning the number), from novice (*po'o*) to "black leg" (*avae parai*). In most cases an individual became a novice by "application": he (or she) attended a cult performance, and in a state of *nevaneva* (spirit-possession, presumably by 'Oro himself, who thereby selected the applicant for potential membership), proceeded to dance and sing along with the performing members. If the applicant's dancing, etc., revealed sufficient talent, and—most crucial—if he (or she) was physically well-formed and unblemished, he was invited by the chapter's "master" to apply for membership (physical perfection having been a hallmark of Arioihood, along with such other aspects of youthfulness as skill and ardor in dancing, singing and sex—and as noted above, freedom from parenthood and its associated burdens). At the end of the period of novitiate the novices were tested—in dancing, etc.—and either accepted into active membership or turned down. After that, members were promoted to higher grades according to progress revealed in Arioi skills (including—say some sources—deepening knowledge of (unspecified) sect "secrets"). Advance up the grades was marked by changes in costume and by different designs and body placements of tattoos. Thus, the lowest-grade member wore a headdress of colored leaves and bore a single small tattoo, while the highest-grade members (the "Black Leg," a status achieved by very few) wore a red-dyed barkcloth loin-girdle and were tattooed solidly from foot to groin (including the torso and arm tattoo marks acquired in the intervening grades). And—as to be expected in this Polynesian society—rise in grade-level was rewarded with increases in privileges, including command over the services of lower-grade members.

As previously mentioned, each local chapter was headed by a master and in some cases by a mistress as well—both of these having been appointed to their offices by their tribal chief. In addition, the offices of master of the separate chapters were graded in terms of ceremonial precedence, etc., for those not infrequent occasions on which two or more chapters joined together on tour. (And, not surprisingly, the highest-grade office was that of the master of the founding chapter at Opoa.) As for the general membership: when they were not trying to kill one another as members of separate and frequently warring tribes, all Arioi were supposed to behave toward one another amicably and hospitably; to do otherwise was to court expulsion.

Finally, membership in the cult was not limited to persons of upper-class status; even commoners (*manahune*) were admitted if they were otherwise acceptable, a remarkable flexibility in this class-stratified population. Nevertheless, it transpired that when young persons of upper-class status joined the cult (which many of them did) they were excused from the novitiate and admitted directly into a higher grade.[185]

THE LONO CULT OF HAWAI'I

As noted earlier, the native inhabitants of the Hawaiian Islands were for centuries before contact divided into numerous, more or less independent, chiefdoms (*mō'ī*), many of whose boundaries, however, changed over time—either by conquest and amalgamation or by warring partition. Also, whereas the office of chieftainship normatively devolved to an incumbent's eldest son, it was often contested, militantly, by some other kinsman or by a nonkinsman. In other words, warfare, both large-and small-scale, was a typical characteristic of Hawaiian culture. In fact, the only known widespread and institutionalized suspension of warfare, intra- and interchiefdoms—as well as individual acts of homicide and rituals involving human sacrifice—occurred during the annual Makahiki (New Year) Festival, which was dedicated to the god Lono.[186]

Lono was one of the Hawaiians' major gods, his principal and distinctive attribute having been rainfall—and thereby the generation of useful nonirrigated plants such as sweet potatoes, gourds and candlenuts, in contrast to irrigated ones such as taro. The other major gods were Kāne (patron of irrigated plants, of human sperm, of spring water, of fishponds, etc.), Kanaloa (patron of the ocean, of death, etc.), and Kū (patron of cultivated and forest trees, of canoe building, of fishing and of war. Kū in particular figured in opposition to Lono, having been associated with rites of human sacrifice (which were suspended during the latter's earthly sojourn).

As the reader will have deduced, the above four gods had cognomen parallels in some other Polynesian pantheons—e.g., Kanaloa with Samoan Tangaloa and Tahitian Ta'aroa; Kū with Marquesan and Samoan Tu; etc.—some of which name parallels were matched by functional attributes as well. In the case of Lono the closest parallels, both in name and in function, were with the Maori and Mangaian Rongo. And in Tahiti, while the god 'Oro—featured earlier in this chapter—was patron of the festive Arioi, and thereby associated with the suspension of war making

during their periodic tours, his name seems not to have been etymologically parallel to Lono; moreover, he was also patron of human sacrifice and war, actions that were contrary to Lono's attributes.

The rain-bearing Lono visited the Hawaiian Islands annually during the Makahiki season, which began with the first after-sunset rising of the Pleiades and lasted about four lunar months—by Gregorian calendar reckoning from about mid-November to about early March. (Be it noted, however, that the native missionized scholars—Malo, Kamakau, I'I, etc., writing many years after termination of the events marking those "visits," differed rather widely concerning their timing.) During that season the actual visitation of the god, encased in a wooden image, lasted twenty-three days, during which it was transported ceremonially around each (?) island, pausing at certain places to receive "offerings" and to usher in several days and nights of festivities. Upon completion of the circuit, which began and ended at the principal *luakini* of the area's chief (the temple at which the chief consecrated sacrifices, including humans), the god himself departed and returned to his celestial homeland, his image having been stored in the *luakini*.

The mythical rationale for Lono's visit was that in ancient times he, in Handy's words, being "animated by jealousy [had] killed his [beautiful] wife; then, overcome by grief, he had rushed about the island boxing all those whom he met, and afterward departed for some foreign land, promising that he would return" (1927, 296)—bringing with him the fertilizing blessings of food-producing rain. But before expatiation of the main features of Lono's visitation, I must interpose my difficulties in accepting the "logic" of the basic accounts of some of them.

My principal difficulty has to do with geography—i.e., which islands in the Hawaiian chain did Lono " visit," and how could the bearers of his image have circumambulated the larger of them in the prescribed twenty-three days? This is especially questionable in the case of the island of Hawai'i, the largest of those islands, whose shoreline circumference is over three hundred miles and upon which most of the basic sources focused. Closely related to that difficulty is the question of the boundaries of the islands' several chiefdoms: during the period—the eighteenth and early nine-

23.3. Image of the Hawaiian god Kūkā'ilimoku

which Lono was transported during his circuit. Paraphrasing Valeri (205), it consisted of a pole of *kauila* wood (*Alphitonia ponderosa*) about three inches thick and eleven to eighteen feet long, the top of which was carved to form an image, either of a whole body or of only its head. Near the top was fastened a crosspiece of wood to which were attached pieces of maidenhair fern (a famine food and medicinal plant, the latter signaling, I suppose, the god's therapeutic attitude), feather wreaths, skins of albatrosses and pieces of bark-cloth. (Needless to add, the fabrication of the image was accompanied by religious rites—as were most other formalized events of the god's arrival, circuit and departure.)

Accompanying the god on his circuit were the images of other gods, the most noteworthy having been a god of games, who presided over the boxing and other sports that took place in honor of Lono throughout his circuit.

Just prior to the circuit, Lono was honored by a ceremonious party that lasted four days and included a mass bathing in the ocean—by both aristocrats (*ali'i*) and commoners (*maka'āinana*), males and females, an orgy of feasting, of reviling and blasphemous singing, and of indiscriminate copulation. During that time, all productive work was suspended, as was fighting, homicide and human sacrifice. And to avoid witnessing the blasphemy and other religious taboos, the priests blindfolded and secluded themselves. Except for the mass ocean bathing, similar four-day-long activities and freedoms and restrictions prevailed at each of the god's halting places during his circuit—although (I suppose) in somewhat less orgiastic forms.

Also just prior to its circuit, Lono's image was ceremonially, and affectionately, greeted, feted, decorated and generally honored by the tribe's (or subtribe's) chief. Following this, the image was introduced into the chief's *hale mua* (house in front of, the house reserved for "adult" males)—an action that on other occasions ritualized the initiation of boys into "youth" (see page 136).

The tour of the god's procession is described as having taken twenty-three days and as having proceeded around the perimeter of an island (or a single chiefdom?) and in a clockwise direction—how close to its actual boundary is not noted. The clockwise direction kept the image's right-hand side pointing toward the center of the island, or

teenth centuries—implicitly included in the accounts, not all islands consisted of a single chiefdom (or "kingdom," as some of their describers labeled them). Not to worry: however narrow their relevance, the events composing Lono's annual visits nevertheless merit attention, which I now continue to outline.

First to consider is the nature of the image in

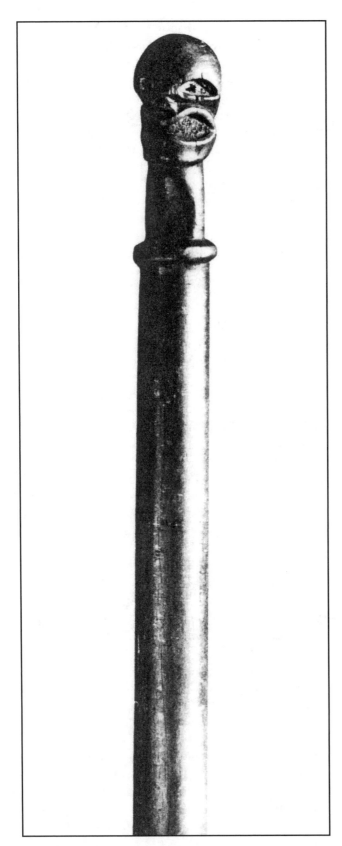

23.4. Image of Hawaiian god Lono

chiefdom, signifying the god's temporary possession of it. (Meanwhile, the image of a lesser god was transported along the perimeter of each subchief's district in a counterclockwise direction, signifying that subchief's temporary loss of it.

The carriers of the Lono image, along with the crowd of boxers, etc., accompanying them, halted at the altar, the *ahupua'a* ("altar pig") that marked the boundary of each basic land division, also called *ahupua'a*, where that division's residents had assembled and deposited food and other goods required for the occasion. This leads up to some discussion of the formalized material transactions that occurred throughout a Makahiki.

There were at least three types of such transactions, one of small scale and two of very large scale. The small-scale ones, which took place randomly, consisted of women donating goods directly to the Lono image with the plea that the god exert his fertilizing powers to assist them to bear children. One of the very large-scale ones occurred just prior to the circuit, and although timed to take place in conjunction with Lono's visit (which introduced the season of plenitude) was quite explicitly a secular form of "tribute" (*'auhau*), a tax paid by commoners to their chief and subchiefs. The goods—*waiwai* ("riches")—involved in this tax included barkcloths, loincloths, skirts, fish, dogs and "many other things." They were collected by overseers (*konohiki*) of each subdistrict, who delivered some of them to their own district's subchief and the rest to their tribe's chief, where they were redistributed—some to the chief's gods and their keepers, the rest to members of the chiefly establishment, e.g., the chief's principal wife and other relatives, priests, the chief's "favorites" (*punahele*), warriors, etc.—but none to the commoners (*maka'āinana*) who had produced them (Valeri 1985, 203-4).

The second of the large-scale Makahiki material transactions took place during Lono's circuit and at each of its official halts (at the aforesaid *ahupua'a*). Prior to the procession's arrival, the local overseer collected *ho'okupu* ("offerings") consisting of precious feathers, pigs, chickens, barkcloth and hard-pounded taro, all destined for the tribe's chief and his own gods. If the bearers of Lono's image judged the *ho'okupu* sufficient, a priest accompanying the procession uttered a taboo-lifting prayer and the procession moved on to the next halt, leaving the district's people to celebrate, as described earlier. If not, the god's attendants ordered the district to be plundered until enough *hoʻokupu* had been collected—clearly, a more efficient method of tax-collection than is employed even by the IRS!

The most noteworthy events marking the end of Lono's visit were a spear attack by one of the god's attendants against the chief, the departure of the god himself—but not his wooden image, which was stored in a temple, and a rite for divining the future of the chiefdom's food supplies. The attack against the chief was typically warded off either by the chief himself (who was required by tradition to be a courageous and skillful warrior) or by one of his supporters, thereby permitting him to resume his office (which had been assumed by Lono during his visit). Lono's departure for his otherworldly homeland, *kahiki*, took place in a *waʻa ʻauhau* ("tribute canoe"), an unmanned wickerwork crate filled with food (and one that would eventually sink). And the divination rite was conducted by filling a large-meshed net with all kinds of food and then shaking it so as to make the food drop to the ground. If it did so, abundance would continue; if not, there would be famine.

As a footnote to all the above: when Captain James Cook and his shipmates arrived in the Hawaiian Islands in November 1778, the first non-Polynesians to land there, Cook was perceived by the natives to be Lono, because of the time of his arrival (i.e., near the beginning of the Makahiki), the size of his ships and the marvelous nature of the treasures contained in them, and Cook's obvious role in command of all of them—a perception that became unmistakably manifest by the reverence accorded the Great Navigator through his stay, including the circumstances of his death and the reverent treatment accorded his bones.[187]

PART THREE

THE MAORI

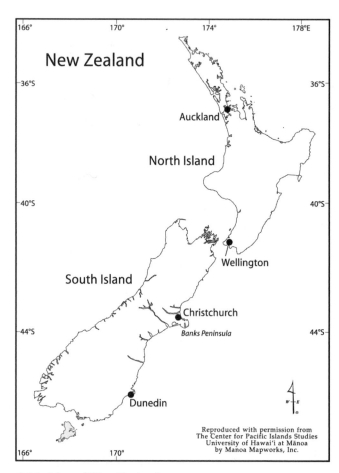

PREFACE

There are at least three reasons for treating the Polynesians of New Zealand, the Maori,[188] separately from those of tropical and subtropical Polynesia. One is New Zealand's climate, which is colder, in some parts very much colder, than on any other islands of Polynesia—a set of conditions that eventuated most significantly in its people's modes of subsistence, many aspects of which differed markedly from those of Polynesians elsewhere. A second is New Zealand's large size (being larger than all other Polynesian islands combined) and its wide variations in physical environments, including climates, which resulted in far wider interregional differences in modes of subsistence, etc., than occurred in any other single Polynesian society. And a third reason for treating the Maori separately is the vast quantity of printed material about them, both descriptive and interpretative. Whereas several societies in tropical (including subtropical) Polynesia have been described, and interpreted, by only one scholar, and several others by no more than three or four, the descriptive literature on the Maori was written, and continues to be written, by scores of individuals, including many Maori, and has been interpreted—and reinterpreted—by many scholars (a process that continues apace, given the increasing number of degree-seeking students of Maori culture in New Zealand's several fine universities).

However, the point of this preface is not only to justify presenting separate chapters about the Polynesians of New Zealand and of their offshoots in the Chatham Islands, the Moriori, but also to issue a caveat about its content. Namely, while the following generalized descriptions about, say, Maori tools may be accurate, and accounts of their various modes of food-getting equally so (that is, when geographically localized), one cannot always be certain about the provenience of some information about social institutions or

24.1. Map of New Zealand

about religious and cosmological concepts (i.e., about whether it is "purely" indigenous or contains elements resulting from Western contact).[189]

PHYSICAL ENVIRONMENT

New Zealand (fig. 24.1) extends north and south some 745 (crow-fly) miles and consists of three major natural regions. The northern region, comprising the northern two-thirds of North Island (except for an extensive area of active volcanism) was temperately warm and, before human settlement, supported a luxuriant semitropical forest, especially in its fertile volcanic soils. The

224

central region, comprising the southern third of North Island and the aforesaid volcanic area along with the northeast coastal area of South Island, was cooler, with some forest growth. The southern region, comprising the rest of South Island, was partly forested, and although it provided some natural food plants was too cold for growing the introduced Polynesian food plants. The terrain of both islands is rugged, including a main north-to-south chain of mountains with peaks of three to six thousand feet in the north and snow-capped ones of up to twelve thousand feet in the south. In the words of Peter Bellwood (whose book *The Polynesians* provides an excellent descriptive summary of the prehistory of Polynesia, including that of New Zealand): "There are perhaps few countries in the world of similar size which have such a degree of environmental varieties, ranging from active volcanoes, high alpine fold mountains, inland lakes and plains, and a highly dissected and varied coastline" (1987, 130).

The only indigenous land mammal was the bat, but there were some two hundred species of birds, including several flightless ones, the largest of which, the *moa* (*Dinornis* spp.), an ostrichlike species, was up to nine feet tall. In addition, the Polynesian settlers found and made use of an abundance of marine animals, including fish, eels, shellfish, fur seals, dolphins and whales.

PREHISTORY

The history of human settlement of New Zealand has been depicted by Europeans in two entirely different ways—the one mythical and legendary, the other archaeological. Leaving aside the Maori's cosmogonic myth of the archipelago's beginning (i.e., as a fish hooked up by the demigod and culture hero Maui—a Polynesia-wide mythic theme), the human settlement of New Zealand was represented in several other Maori myths as having occurred in three episodes. First was its "discovery" in about A.D. 900 (according to number of purported generations) by Kupe, a native of the mythic Hawaiki, who returned home without settling. Then came a number of other voyagers from Eastern Polynesia, who, however, found they had been preceded by a non-Polynesian folk known as the Mouriuri, whose descendants they eventually displaced. Then, in about 1350 (according to European scholars'

rationalizations) there arrived the Great Fleet, an expedition of six canoes (or seven or eight, etc., depending upon the version) from "Hawai'iki" ("identified" as Havai'i [= Rai'atea]), loaded with intending settlers along with their domesticated animals and planting stock. Having landed at different places, they too mingled with the earlier settlers and because of their superior *mana*—"the attribute of a [more] forceful and energetic people" (Best 1924, I: 63)—they came to dominate the earlier settlers. In the words of Peter Buck (who evidently credited the myth with some authenticity), "The Great Migration (*heke*) from Hawai'iki is the most famous event in Maori history, because all the tribes trace their aristocratic lineages back to the so-called "chiefs" of the voyaging canoes which took part in conveying the third and last wave of settlers to New Zealand. It ranks in historical and social importance with the Norman Conquest of English history" (1950, 36).

The social, including political, relevance of those purported events will be touched on below. Meanwhile, present-day scholars—archaeologists, historians and anthropologists—while recognizing the social-political importance of the Great Fleet Myth among nineteenth-century (i.e., postcontact) Maori, have expressed disbelief in its historical authenticity, having discovered it to be a rationalizing synthesis put together by European scholars to provide a coherent framework by which to interpret the prehistory of New Zealand.[190] And while some other migration myths (created by Maori sages mainly in order to justify claims to land) may have had historic foundations, those migrations are now found to have occurred between points along New Zealand's coasts.

Turning to the archaeological version of human settlement, it is the view of most present-day archaeologists that it occurred well after A.D. 800 (Sutton 1994, 244; see also Green 1997, 108) and that it originated in some place or places in Central-Eastern Polynesia (i.e., the Society, southern Cook, and western Austral islands)—the nearest of them about 1,955 crow-fly miles distant and involving a more complex voyage than those undertaken in tropical Polynesia—i.e., "across the trade winds, through a belt of variables to the latitude of prevailing westerlies" (Irwin 1992, 105).[191] A recent find in New Zealand of bones of the "Lapitan" rat (*Rattus exulans*), dated at about A.D. 0, suggests that some canoes may have reached there much earlier—say, from Fiji or even New Caledonia, which is New Zealand's closest inhabited neighbor island (Holdaway 1996)—a possibility that might have lent some credibility to the myth of an earlier settlement but for the circumstance that, so far, no other evidence of such a settlement has been discovered even after decades of extensive and intensive archaeology.

Archaeologists do not—and perhaps cannot—specify the number of expeditions that took part in the colonizing, but in view of the exploratory and migratory zeal manifested by Polynesians elsewhere it is reasonable to conclude that several successful (as well as several unsuccessful) expeditions in the general direction of New Zealand were undertaken over several decades or even centuries, and that at least some of the canoes carried females as well as males, along with all three animal domesticates and planting stock of most or all of the cultivated plants of the homelands. (Much less certain is the possibility that one or more return voyages were ever made between New Zealand and the homelands.)

Although the human colonizers proliferated in their settlements, the only animal migrants to survive and reproduce were dogs and rats—the latter perhaps as stowaways. And of the only cultivated

24.2. Drawing of bracken fern

plants to survive the voyages and transplanting, i.e., taro, yams, sweet potatoes and gourds,[192] only the latter two could be grown south of North Island's far north, and not even those south of South Island's Banks Peninsula (i.e., near the present city of Christchurch). Fortunately, a local fernroot plant (fig. 24.2) was discovered to be edible—its rhizome being somewhat similar to the colonizers' sweet potato in length, though thinner and more fibrous—and came to serve as the major starch supplement to the introduced cultivated plants in the north and, along with the native "cabbage tree," the only substantial source of starchy food in the nonhorticultural south.

In recent decades a host of highly competent archaeologists have made great progress in reconstructing Maori prehistory. (See, for example, summaries by Bellwood 1987; Davidson 1984; Green 1974; Houghton 1980; Leach 1984; Prickett 1982; and Sutton 1990.) However, rather than attempt to summarize the particulars and chronologies of those findings, I shall only list some of the more important factors and (pre) historical processes that led up to the "ethnographic present" (which, as has been often stated, is the focus of this book).

1. To begin with, Maori culture(s), although quite uniform in most cognitive and social-relational respects, was otherwise more diversified than that of any society of tropical Polynesia—the result, mainly, of the archipelago's incomparably larger size and greater geographic diversity, and of what appears to have been the inclination of many early colonizers, accepting the opportunities offered by those geographic circumstances, to separate and move elsewhere rather than remain together in small coastal arrival-place enclaves.

2. The results of those movements into different natural environments were evidenced mainly in food getting, which varied, regionally, from fishing and hunting (of marine animals and, during early centuries, of large flightless birds), plus gathering of wild plants, to heavy dependence upon both horticulture and the gathering of wild plant foods, plus some riverine fishing and occasional rat trapping and bird snaring—with various combinations of the above in between.

3. The dependence on this or that mode of food-getting over the centuries resulted, in several areas, in the destruction of forests or the reduction or total extinction of several species of food ani-

mals (including most of those of the once numerous *moa*).

4. As a result of the above localized reductions in food-getting resources—and of an increase in population beyond an area's stable but limited food-getting resources—many groups were forced or encouraged to expand their areas of swidden or to migrate, either to areas not yet inhabited, thereby leaving some areas uninhabited (including many in South Island), or to some areas already inhabited (thereby leading in some cases either to social amalgamation or warfare and either extinction or further wandering by the losers).

5. In addition to the above kinds of more-or-less permanent movements, most or even all units—including individual households or groups of them—moved residence periodically (i.e., seasonally), in some cases scores of miles, between gardening and fishing areas or between gardening and fernroot areas. Some exchange in basic foods did take place, mainly in the form of outright "gifts"—say, when entertaining guests, or in the form of "gift-exchange." But in addition, other regionally localized goods, including manufactures, were exchanged by barter.

POPULATION

Because of New Zealand's large size and the wide distribution of its native settlements it has been next to impossible to secure even an approximate count of its precontact population. Even "informed" estimates range from 100,000 to 500,000, with some consensus however for 115,000, which gives an overall density of about 1 person per square mile, a figure to be compared with Samoa's 76—and Tikopia's 427! At time of contact over four-fifths of the Maori lived on North Island and in the northern part of South Island, most of the South Island's earlier population having died out or moved northward, as a result of the diminution of that island's food resources.

Based on analysis of archaeologically exposed burials, the average adult age at death at one site was thirty-eight, at another twenty-eight, few of the individuals having lived beyond their fifties. In other words: "few people would survive long enough to become grandparents, . . . and a person over the age of thirty-five or forty would be likely to become a burden on younger relatives" (Davidson 1992, 8).[193] According to the same

source, the Maori were free of infectious diseases and of yaws (which affected many of their tropical cousins). On the other hand, arthritis and spinal degeneration were highly prevalent in persons over age twenty-five (Ibid.).

COSMOLOGY AND RELIGION

Whole books, large parts of other books, and countless articles have been published about Maori cosmology and religion, and the proliferation continues. To begin with, the primary sources for the topics—direct observations by outsiders and innumerable texts of native-language materials—have been subjected to numerous interpretations—and reinterpretations, including some that purport to reveal deepest processes of Maori "thought." And indeed they may, at least the thought of some Maori in some places. What follows in this section, however, concerns the more explicit and widespread features of cosmology and the more evident and widespread elements of religious practice.

At the outset it can be said that Maori cosmogonies differed in detail from place to place,[194] but from what I have read about them, most if not all of them broadly resembled those of some other Polynesians in several fundamental ways. Those beliefs, expressed in sequential or generational (i.e., procreational) form, usually began with a Void and proceeded down through a list of metaphorical entities (e.g., Night, Root, Growth) to a male Sky Being (Rangi) and a female Earth Being (Papa), who then begat many offspring, one of whom forced them apart from their embrace (thereby admitting Light and Space) and all of whom set about to create (i.e., beget) numerous other entities: minor gods, animals, plants, the Ocean, etc., and which, as will be mentioned, then went on to add some of themselves to the pantheon.

Among the most notable sons of Rangi and Papa were Tane, Rongo, Tangaroa, Tu, Haumea and Whiro, each of whom possessed authority over one or another domain of importance to humans: Tane over forests (including their birds); Rongo over horticulture (especially over sweet potatoes) and peace; Tangaroa over ocean (including fish and reptiles); Tu over war and its attendant features, including anger and bravery and the eating of enemies killed or captured in war (the first of whom was offered as sacrifice to this god before being eaten); Haumea over uncultivated plants, especially fernroot; and Whiro over the underworld. As will be recalled, many if not most other Polynesian cosmogonies also contained such "departmental" gods, the major ones with names cognate with the Maori ones and who in several cases presided over identical domains.

Mention was made in chapter 8 of beliefs in some (tropical Polynesian) societies about a Supreme God, Io or Kio, said by some to have created all other gods, etc. A similar belief was held by some Maori, but, according to Buck, only by a few sages, who kept that knowledge and its associated cult practices, if any, largely to themselves. Also, as mentioned earlier, some critics have objected that the Io complex, in New Zealand and elsewhere, was "invented" after contact, and incorporated some doctrines of Christianity. In any case, in some New Zealand versions of the belief Io seems to have been, or become, otiose—i.e., to have taken no further interest or action in human affairs.

As elsewhere in Polynesia the gods of the Maori were thought of as being usually incorporeal and invisible but capable of manifesting themselves in certain particular, and characteristic, natural phenomena—e.g., one in rainbows, another in meteors, another in lizards, etc. Such phenomena or creatures, labeled *aria*, were construed and appropriately feared or revered when seen. Also, when requested, some gods were capable of resting temporarily in certain natural objects, such as the braided lock of hair of a deified ancestor, or more commonly in carved stone figures and manmade "god-sticks." (Such sticks were about twelve inches long with a rounded end carved to resemble a human head.) And as elsewhere in Polynesia, certain gods were wont to rest in—to "possess"—some particular individuals (called "canoes of the god") for longer or shorter periods in order to communicate their judgments or wishes to humans. Also, there were in most (or all?) communities one or more material objects, natural or manmade, set aside for priests for communing with gods. Such shrines (*tuahu*) varied in form from natural stone outcrops to manmade heaps of stones or earth to wooden boxes containing some symbol of a particular god—a very far cry from the elaborate shrines—temples—found in many tropical Polynesian societies. Most Maori shrines also differed from some of the latter in having

been located in secluded spots well away from human habitations.

And finally—a feature that has evoked a wide range of scholarly interpretation—in many places in New Zealand a community's communal latrine was held to be also a sacred shrine, a threshold between the sphere of gods (therefore *tapu*) and that of humans (therefore largely *noa*). The most noteworthy rite carried out there consisted of biting the low horizontal beam on which a user placed his feet when squatting to excrete, an act said to have released the biter's state of *tapu*-ness and returned him to *noa*-ness. (For a detailed elucidation of this peculiarly Maori custom see Hanson and Hanson 1983, 77–86.)

Like all other Polynesians the Maori communicated with their gods by prayer, sometimes supported by obligatory or voluntary offerings. The prayers (*karakia*), composed of precisely worded formulae, varied greatly in length and in purpose. As elsewhere in Polynesia their effectiveness was thought to depend upon word-perfect delivery—which again raises the (unanswerable) question of their "dynamics"—i.e., to what extent was their efficacy dependent upon the response of the addressee gods or upon some potency of the formulae themselves?[195]

Offerings accompanied prayers—or vice versa—on many kinds of occasions: to placate or thank or seek help from gods. The most common kind of offering was food, a token amount of which was given as "first fruits" upon, say, harvesting sweet potatoes or catching fish or snaring rats or birds. Similarly, part of the first enemy slain in war was given to the war god, Tu, as a thanks offering; and on some occasions a (war captive) slave was offered before battle to solicit Tu's assistance.

As in several other Polynesian societies the Maori used fire, water, earth and stone in some of their religious rites. Earth and stone were sometimes heaped into piles to serve as temporary shrines—which acquired additional *mana* by inclusion of stones from one already established (a practice parallel to the Tahitian one of incorporating a stone from a "parental" temple into an offshoot). Stones from established, *tapu* buildings were also used in the bases of new, prestigious buildings (Anne Salmond, pers. com.). Water was used to remove *noa* on some occasions, or *tapu* in others, and fire was sometimes used to add *mana*.

This leads up to the question of what meaning(s) the Maori attached to those important, but polysemous, Polynesia-wide morphemes: *mana, tapu* and *noa.*

As will be recalled, the most common intelligible meanings attached to *mana* here or there in tropical Polynesia were (1) "godliness"—that constituent of never-human gods that was transmitted to their human offspring and then transmitted by them to their descendants by sexual reproduction; (2) those characteristics of some humans, imparted by gods in ways other than sexual reproduction, which conduced to their being outstandingly efficacious in some manifest ways; and (3) the adjective used to characterize those humans or objects or places or animals once *mana*-ized or customarily visited by one or another relatively powerful god: e.g., temples, images and other receptacles, human mediums, etc.; and (4) in some Polynesian societies the word *mana* was also used to characterize persons who had achieved superior status—in war making, in leadership, in knowledge, etc.—largely (and manifestly) on their own (although some scholars would doubtless argue that no such achievements were considered, by Polynesians, to have occurred without some godly intervention).

My reading (of mainly secondary sources) indicates that the Maori—most or all?—used the word *mana* in all the above meanings, including especially the one given in (4). And in Williams' authoritative *Maori Dictionary* the word carries the additional meanings of "authority, control, influence, prestige, power, . . . effectual, authoritative, having influence or power, and to be effectual, be avenged, take effect, binding" (1975, 172).[196]

Turning to *tapu*, as in tropical Polynesia the Maori used the word adjectively to signify some type of "restriction" that derived from something with god-associated *mana*: e.g., a person, a place, an object, a practice, etc. But in addition the word was sometimes used substantively, in some cases parallel to nominal forms of *mana*. Moreover, I have the impression that for the Maori *tapu* applied to many more places, objects and situations than it did for most other Polynesians.

For the Maori the word *noa* also had the Polynesia-wide adjectival meaning of being free from, or opposite to, and in some cases counteractive to, *tapu*. Thus, while in several other Polynesian societies cooking was done by either males or females, depending upon circumstances, for the Maori it was done mainly by *noa* persons (i.e., females and captive males), and cooked food was actively detrimental to some places and activities. (For example, the presence of cooked food in a forest was believed to destroy the forest's god-given *tapu*, thereby banishing its birds. Or in some contexts, the presence of women rendered an otherwise *tapu* place or object *noa*. (For example, an important house was highly *tapu* when under construction but when finished was rendered *noa*—fit for ordinary human use—by a woman stepping over the threshold (Hanson and Hanson 1983, 86–87).[197]

Finally, as in several other Polynesian societies specific measures were taken among the Maori to train some individuals, usually upper-class ones, in matters considered *tapu*—this in addition to the training of youths in more secular occupations.

TOOLS

Like other Polynesians the Maori looked to gods to assist them in satisfying their wants for food, shelter and other things, but relied mainly upon their own efforts to do so. Also, like all other Polynesians they observed a sexual division of labor, which, however, was less strict than in some other Polynesian societies—a situation doubtless influenced by their more-than-average frontierlike existence. Moreover, they differed from some other Polynesian peoples in two other division-of-labor ways: while their social elites were in general less divorced from "work" than in most of those societies—owing perhaps to the smaller size of their subsistence-work units and the smaller amounts of their food "surpluses," some Maori nevertheless owned truly enthralled "slaves" (i.e., war captives) to perform the more menial subsistence tasks.

Concerning the human body as a "tool," it is reasonable to suggest—though no longer possible to prove—that Maori men and women were on the average stronger and hardier than those of several other Polynesian societies,[198] a result, perhaps, of their more invigorating climates and their seasonal migrations, and for males their commitment to, readiness for, and frequent engagement in warfare. (For example, even their dances of "welcome" included and extolled strength and agility. And I can find no evidence of a high evaluation of corpulence, or of corpulence-promoting practices, such as prevailed in some tropical Polynesian societies.) As for their dexterities—their proficiencies in using tools—subsequent pages will provide information on that point, but some preliminary judgment may be formed on the basis of their carvings in wood and bone and stone—which in my opinion had no peer anywhere in tropical Polynesia, even prior to the introduction of Western tools.

Turning now to the primary extrabodily tools, the Maori, like all other Polynesians—and indeed like all other peoples everywhere—made use of many natural unprocessed materials: leaves, sticks, sand, resins, stones, shell, bone, teeth, etc., but the focus here is on their primary fabricated tools—i.e., the ones used for cutting, chipping, gouging and drilling: their adzes, axes, chisels and gouges, all of stone. In the absence of bamboo and in the minimal use of shell, even most soft-object cutting was done with stone flakes or fabricated stone tools. The overall absence of bamboo, and for many communities the unavailability of shell, were offset by the abundance of toolmaking stone—including basalt, andesite, obsidian, argillite and nephrite (greenstone), the latter having been particularly useful and valuable because of its fine grain and evidently "pleasing" colors (and therefore its hard and sharp cutting edge and its use for ornaments).

CORDAGE AND CONTAINERS

In the absence of coconuts and pandanus, the Maori—doubtless after much experimentation—chose several indigenous plants for making cordage, principally the leaves of the native "cabbage tree" (*Cordyline australis*, a close relative of the tropical *ti*), and the (misnamed) native "flax" (*Phormium tenans*), which was in fact stronger and more durable than the analogous tropical materials. Similarly with mats and baskets—i.e., after experimenting, probably, with a local palm leaf the Maori chose other stronger local materials, particularly the so-called "flax," but continued, mainly, to use (pre-New Zealand) homeland plaiting techniques in fabricating the finished articles. With regard to containers in general, one notable exception—to the "local materials:homeland techniques" formula—was the gourd (*Laginaria vulgaris*), a homeland plant successfully introduced by the colonizers, whose immature

fruit was a valued food and whose mature fruit, the gourd, served as a multiuse container.

WOOD

In addition to the many other kinds of native plant products made use of by the Maori was the wood from trees in New Zealand's extensive forests (some of which, at time of contact, had been considerably thinned, largely by the burning done to clear land for horticulture and fernroot collecting. But even then those forests were far more extensive and contained a far greater variety of usable woods than any in tropical Polynesia—usable for the fabrication of many kinds of objects, including tools, containers, houses, and the largest one-piece canoe hulls made in Polynesia.

CLOTHING

Other tools and craftworks will be mentioned later on in connection with the purposes they were used for, but before that something needs mentioning about Maori clothing—garments that represented a very large change from those of the Maori's homelands. It will be recalled that the latter consisted of loincloths (*maro*) for males and kilts (*pareu*) for females, supplemented on occasion with cloaks or ponchos. In the homeland high islands most such garments were of barkcloth, beaten from the inner bark of certain trees—mainly the paper mulberry; in those atolls where such trees did not grow, most garments were made of shredded coconut leaflets and plaited pandanus leaves. It may be assumed that the Maori colonizers also wore such garments, and it is certain that some of them carried along planting stock of the paper mulberry. Moreover, they succeeded, at least in the northernmost settlements, to grow and make use of a few of those plants, but elsewhere, where that plant would not grow, a shift took place to garments made of finely twined "flax," garments that were thicker, stronger and more durable. And in addition to wearing the traditional loincloths and kilts, the early settlers turned to making and wearing thicker and longer capes and cloaks, some of sealskin, for protection against New Zealand's colder climates.[199]

PLANT FOOD

Most if not all of the Polynesian colonizers of New Zealand had originated in east Central

Polynesia, and at least some of their canoes carried cargoes containing planting stock of some or all types of their homeland plants, along with one or two or all three of their domesticated animals. It is not yet known whether representatives of all of their homeland plants and animals had actually reached New Zealand, but on present evidence only a few of them did so and managed to survive transplanting, due to the rigors of the voyages and New Zealand's nontropical environments. Moreover, only sweet potatoes, *ti* and gourds remained cultivable south of the North Island's northern half, and not even sweet potatoes were cultivable in the southern half of South Island.

Notwithstanding such environmental restraints—which might have overcome a less sturdy and less enterprising people—those Polynesian colonizers succeeded in establishing settlements down to New Zealand's southernmost point—an accomplishment made possible by the archipelago's natural food resources.

The most important of those resources turned out to be plentiful supplies of a wide assortment of edible wild plants and animals. Beginning with the former: the colonizers were already aware of the edibility of certain of their homelands' more or less wild-growing plants, including especially the starchy roots of arrowroot and *ti*. Hence they were, evidently, quick to discover the edibility of several native New Zealand plants—most important the starchy rhizome[200] of the bracken fern (*Pteridium esculentum*), which was to become, and remain, the major source of starchy food for Maori throughout most of New Zealand north of the Banks Peninsula, even in places where their introduced food plants were successfully cultivated. For, while its flavor and texture were considered inferior to that of the introduced food tubers, and its processing more laborious (i.e., soaking, then roasting, and then pounding to separate its starch from its inedible fibers), it grew naturally and prolifically and could be harvested, for eating or storage, year-round. This was in contrast to sweet potatoes, which required laborious ground preparation and planting, and in New Zealand had short growing and harvesting seasons. Moreover, once harvested and dried the rhizomes of the fern could be easily and safely stored for year-round consumption—in contrast to the difficulties included in the storage of sweet potatoes.

Other indigenous (i.e., wild) and edible plants eaten here or there included the roots of the so-called "cabbage tree" (*Cordyline australis*, a relative of the tropical *ti*), the roots of several other ferns, the leaves of a few plants and the berries of many. The roots of the cabbage tree and of the black tree fern (*Cyathea medullaris*) were of particular importance in areas where the sweet potato or bracken fern did not grow—e.g., in the southern part of South Island.

The only homeland food plants to survive transplanting in New Zealand were *ti* (*Cordyline terminalis*), taro (*Colocasia esculentum*), yams (*Dioscorea* spp.), gourds (*Lagenaria siceraria*) and sweet potatoes (*Ipomoea batatas*). Of these the *ti*, which required a very long growing season, was restricted to the few frost-free areas of northern North Island. The growing seasons of gourds, taro and yams were even shorter—i.e., six, seven and eight months, respectively, but long enough to restrict their growth to limited parts of North Island. It was only the sweet potato, with a growing season of five months, that was hardy enough for more widespread cultivation, but even it could not survive south of South Island's Banks Peninsula, and in many areas north of there its growth was vulnerable to seasonal climatic vicissitudes. In other words, even in the most favorable areas, horticulture could not provide enough, year-round, of a starchy staple, hence the Maori were obliged to turn to the gathering of wild plant foods, including especially fernroot.

Kumara, the Maori name for sweet potato (cognate with Tahitian *'umara*, Hawaiian *'uala*, etc.), was their most favored plant food and was cultivated wherever it could be grown, despite the labor required in growing it and in storing it for postharvest consumption and future planting. In most places garden sites had to be prepared for cultivation by clearing them of rocks and by burning off existing vegetation (which, however, also served to enrich the soil), and in some places by grubbing up wild-growing roots. In addition, some soils had to be lightened and aerated by turning them, or even by adding sand and gravel. The tools used for those and other gardening operations consisted of short wooden spade-shaped implements, wooden pick-axe–shaped soil looseners (made from a forked tree branch) and long wooden digging sticks with or without a footrest. In most places the plants were planted in regularly spaced intervals and rows, and gardens were laid out in rectangular plots—some of them bordered by rocks (which had been removed when clearing the site) or by reed fences (which served purposely as shelter from high winds). Harvesting had to be done punctually upon maturing in order to prevent rotting or frosting, and great care taken to preserve the harvested tubers from the same perils—their storage having been done in solidly built semisubterranean huts (a most significant Maori invention, which was without parallels among other Polynesians).

Yams required a longer growing period than *kumara*, which limited their growth to warmer areas, but were otherwise cultivated and stored in ways similar to those used for *kumara*. Taro had a growing period similar to that of yams, but required moister soils and had to be eaten, or transplanted, shortly after harvest.

The only other homeland plant that the Maori succeeded in transplanting, the gourd, was cultivated mainly for use as a container, but its immature fruit was sometimes eaten when other vegetables were in short supply (Leach 1984, 66).

In retrospect, the pioneering Maori are entitled to much admiration for their success in adjusting their traditional, tropical-based methods of obtaining plant foods to New Zealand's unfamiliar and in many areas harshly inhospitable climates.[201] At the same time, it can be noted that their methods of cultivation or collecting—including overburning and overuse—served to ravage large areas of erstwhile employable vegetation and soils. Moreover, the erosion resulting from those actions also resulted, in some places, in silting up fish-bearing streams. All of this eventually impelled many of the Maori's principal food-producing units—i.e., households—to move seasonally within ever-widening areas, and in many places to abandon large areas altogether (McGlone 1983).

FOWLING

One of the many wondrous—and in this case surely gratifying—sights that greeted the pioneer colonizers of New Zealand was that of numerous varieties and quantities of birds, including especially the large, flightless, and in the beginning unapprehensive *moa* (*Dinornis* spp.) (fig. 24.3), which ranged in height up to nine feet. Before their nearly total extinction, they constituted a large and important part of the Maori's food

24.3. Reconstruction of four species of New Zealand *moa* bird

supply, especially in the southern half of South Island, where a large proportion of the early colonizers had settled—mainly, perhaps, because of the presence of *moa* (Anderson 1989). And while most species of *moa*, and about twenty other species of flying birds, died out or were killed off during the first five or six centuries of Maori occupation, there remained enough others to provide many, mainly inland, Maori with some flesh to supplement their largely vegetable diets—which leads to a description of how they went about obtaining them.

Bird hunting was practiced, occasionally, in several societies of tropical Polynesia, but rarely only for food. In fact, where it was a highly institutionalized practice, as in Samoa and Tonga, it was engaged in mainly for sport and by upper-class men. In New Zealand it was engaged in mostly for food and by persons of all ranks. There were several methods for obtaining birds, one of the most noteworthy and most widespread having been by snaring—by attaching a loop snare to a fabricated wooden perch in such a way that the waiting fowler could pull it fast around the legs of any bird that settled on the perch (i.e., to eat berries). Thereupon the fowler, who was usually seated on a platform high up in the tree, pulled another cord to detach the perch, which with the captured bird fell to the ground. The trees used for this purpose—i.e., those known for attracting birds—were individually owned and were protected from poaching by harsh sanctions. Also, there were several community-enforced sanctions against anyone, including a tree's owner, snaring out of season (e.g., during the nesting period or before fledglings were able to fly). And, as happened in most institutionalized food-getting activities, especially those involving chance, bird snaring was imbued with religious beliefs and practices. For example, since birds were the creations and wards of specific gods—in most cases of Tane, god of forests—prayers had to be offered for permission to capture them. And since bird snaring was a "sacred" activity, the fowlers themselves were subject to many restrictions while engaged in it. Moreover, while fowling was engaged in mainly for food—and one that was a greatly appreciated supplement to the monotony of starchy tubers—it was evidently an exciting and enjoyable activity, and the individuals who excelled in it, the ones snaring the most birds during the brief fowling season, were rewarded with community-wide praise (but in many cases were allowed to eat only the remnants of their own catches!). After being displayed on a community's common (its *marae*), the birds were plucked and cooked. And while some of them were eaten forthwith, most of them were preserved for future eating by packing them in gourd containers and covering them with liquid fat. As such they remained edible for months, and were either served as delicacies at feasts or were presented to notable visitors as valuable gifts.

Another noteworthy method of catching birds was by netting. This method was used especially in the south for catching mutton birds (*Puffiinis* spp.). These birds flew daily between their inland nesting and breeding areas and their coastal feeding areas. On ridges along their routes, where they flew lower to the ground, nets were set up that succeeded in catching large numbers of them.[202]

For the sake of brevity the following sections about specific food-getting activities will focus mainly on tangible tools and techniques. However, bear in mind that all such activities were embedded in mythical explanations of their origins and were accompanied by verbal and other actions aimed at securing supernatural assistance for success in them and at avoiding supernatural taboos surrounding them.

RAT CATCHING

The native rat (*Kiore maori; Mus exulans*) reached New Zealand in the colonists' canoes—perhaps as stowaways. Unlike their homeland relatives, which infested human settlements, those arriving in New Zealand went to live mostly in the forests, where they not only increased greatly in numbers but became fat, seasonally, on the plentiful supplies of berries and nuts. When that season occurred—being known by many familiar signs—nearby Maori in large numbers took to the forests to capture the little animals, whose flesh was a favored supplement to the usual vegetable fare. The method of capture was by pit or spring traps, which were placed along known "rat runs"—narrow paths made by the rats themselves by their "innumerable traversings of the route they [had] selected in order to reach a feeding ground" (Best 1977, 364). After being captured and killed, the little animals were skinned, grilled and either eaten forthwith or preserved for future eating in their own fat, as was done with birds. Known rat runs were greatly prized and by custom were exploited only by persons who owned the land on which they were located, unauthorized use of them having been fiercely resented, and when known the culprits punished by the owners.

SEALING

"Archaeological analysis has demonstrated that seal hunting was a major activity and seal flesh a significant component of the diet from the time of first human settlement about 800 years ago. . . . Seal hunting gradually declined and disappeared from the northern part of the country about 400–500 years ago but continued throughout the prehistoric sequence in the south." This statement by the prehistorian Ian Smith (1996, 675) prefaces the most recent reconstruction of that important aspect of Maori life as it prevailed in the extreme southern parts of New Zealand in the early contact era. At that time seals were taken in two entirely different ways: by opportunistic killing of individual animals found beached on the shore and—much more productively—by organized sealing expeditions to remote rookeries. Reports are that the animals were killed by clubbing their snouts, after which their flesh was detached from the bones and either cooked or smoked and stored in their own fat in bags made of kelp—a method said to keep the flesh edible for up to two years (Ibid., 677). From archaeological evidence it appears that many if not most of the southernmost Maori who remained in that area after extinction of the *moa* came to depend very heavily on seals and other marine animals, including an occasional whale.

24.4. Maori fishing group

FISHING

The coastal waters of New Zealand abounded with fish and shellfish, as did its lakes, rivers and streams. And while many of those creatures were familiar to the colonizers and were caught in familiar homeland ways, others were unfamiliar or inhabited unfamiliar surroundings, thereby requiring invention of new tools and techniques. For example, the absence of tidal lagoons—the waters having been too cold for the formation of coral reefs—discouraged the homeland practice of narcotizing fish. Similarly, lack of coral blocks disinclined the Maori to construct weirs along the coast—instead of which they built them in inland streams to catch freshwater fish, especially eels and lampreys. In fact, the larger sizes of some of New Zealand's rivers and lakes encouraged the invention and use of freshwater techniques, including especially weirs, to an extent greater than elsewhere in Polynesia. Other innovative adjustments included the use of seines in place of the homeland leaf sweeps, for large-scale netting, and the substitution of "flax" for homeland fibers. One such seine seen by Captain Cook was estimated to be "5 fathoms deep . . . [and] not less than 300 or 400 fathoms long" (Firth 1959, 197). And no less important was the practice of sun-drying fish, which served to preserve them for months, in contrast to the homeland smoke-drying practice, which preserved them for at most only a few days. Otherwise, the colonizers and their descendants also continued to fish in familiar homeland ways—i.e., with nets, traps, hooks and lines, trolling, and dredging—although in many instances with slightly different kinds of equipment and techniques, in adaptation to local materials and environments. (For details see Best 1924; Buck 1950; Downes 1918; and Firth 1959).

DOGS

As mentioned earlier, dogs were the only ones of the three types of domestic animals of tropical Polynesia to survive colonization in New Zealand, and by the time of Western contact there were few of them left.

The Maori used dogs in several ways. Their flesh was a culinary favorite, their skins were joined together to make (highly prized) cloaks and

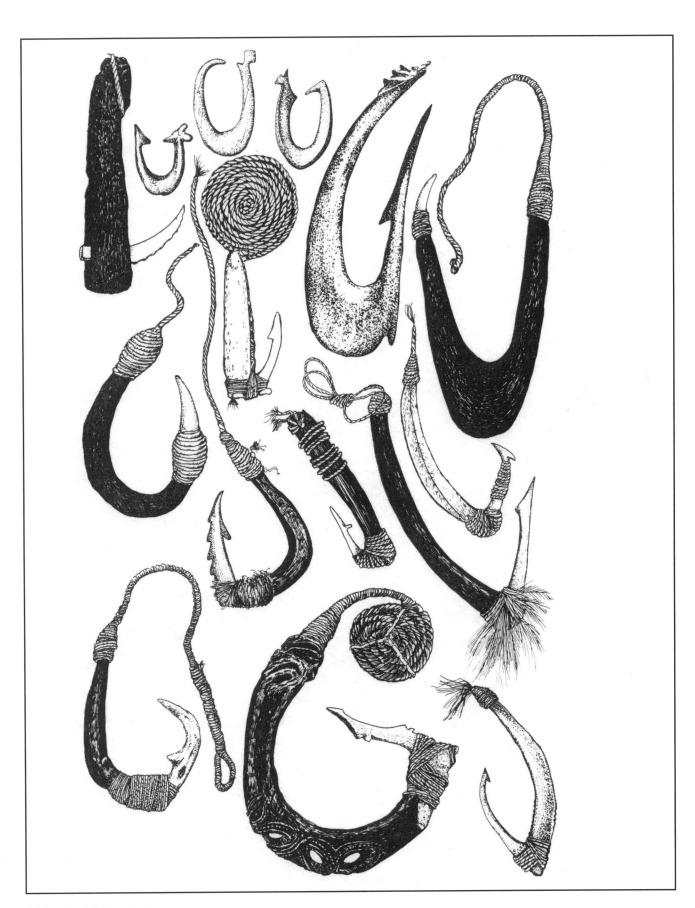

24.5. Maori fishing implements

capes, and tufts of their hair were added to flaxen clothing for decoration. Also, they were sometimes offered as sacrifices to gods (in lieu of humans), their hearts alone having been offered and the rest of them eaten by the sacrificers themselves. What is not reported in sources known to me is who among the Maori were privileged to eat dog flesh and how often they did so.

COOKING

As noted earlier some animal foods were cooked by grilling—either for immediate eating or before preservation. But most cooking was done in earth ovens over hot stones, as was customary also in tropical Polynesia (where most foods were dry-baked, whereas in New Zealand food was often steam-baked, by means of sprinkling water over the food before covering it with mats and earth (Buck 1950, 107; Leach 1984). Another, more gustatory, difference between tropical and New Zealand cooking was the latter's paucity of puddinglike dishes—a consequence, in part, of the absence of coconuts (i.e., of coconut cream).

Finally, with respect to the foregoing pages on Maori food-getting activities, the reader is urged to bear in mind the wide differences among Maori communities in such activities—differences based originally on dissimilarities in natural environments and widened over time by localized innovations. In no other Polynesian society were there such wide localized differences. Even in the Marquesan Archipelago, where distances between islands ranged up to sixty miles, the natural environments were about the same on every island—as were the kinds of food eaten and the methods of getting them. And even among the populated islands of the Hawaiian Archipelago, which were spread out along an arch four hundred miles long and which contained mountains up to nearly three miles high, the same kinds of foods and modes of food getting were somewhat similar on every island—although communities on each of the larger islands differed from one another in modes of food getting according to location (e.g., coastal versus inland, [wet] windward versus [dry] leeward sides). In sharp contrast, some inland Maori communities subsisted entirely by horticulture, fowling and rat trapping, while farther south, other inlanders depended upon wild fern rhizomes and freshwater fishing—or migrated seasonally between inland and coast. Also, coastal residence

itself, permanent or seasonal, did not permit or encourage the same kinds of food getting everywhere, there having been wide differences between fishing in the north and marine animal hunting in the south. Moreover, despite several systems of active and extensive exchange, including in some cases, food, a community's location in this or that natural environment not only placed restraints on and opportunities for its modes of food getting, but influenced its size and residential density as well.

CANNIBALISM

Present-day ethnic minorities tend to be sensitive to charges of cannibalism on the part of their ancestors, but there is undeniable evidence that eighteenth-century and early nineteenth-century Maori engaged in it on occasion—and not only for revenge or for magical reasons but because of an appetite for human flesh as well. With regard to appetite, the anthropologist Peter Vayda has presented convincing proof that cannibalism was sometimes resorted to during warfare—noting that warriors engaged in attacks on distant communities, and therefore, usually short of provisions, would relieve their underlying hunger as well as their fondness for human flesh by eating their victims on the spot, or if the latter were too numerous for that, to transport them home, dead or alive, for immediate or future feasting (Vayda 1960, 120ff).

In another synthesis of early reports, this one by Sir Peter Buck (who demonstrated great pride in his maternal Maori heritage and cannot be accused of denigrating it), wrote that "The absence of pigs and the limited supply of dog's flesh may have been additional factors inducing the Maori to satisfy their hunger for meat with human flesh. Sometimes slaves or other persons were killed and baked on special occasions such as the tattooing of a high chief's daughter, a chiefly marriage, or the funeral of a high chief" (1950, 102). And from Raymond Firth, himself a New Zealander and an admirer of the Maori: "There was a distinct liking for human flesh. If a slave was killed by his master for any offense he was not wasted, but was taken off to the ovens for cooking purposes. As a kindly thought various joints might be sent round to friends and neighbors and were much appreciated. After a victorious raid, cannibal orgies took place and often lasted for several days" (1959, 148). However, Firth goes on to say that cannibalism was "too sporadic and irregular a business to be looked to as a means of supplying in any great measure the need [want?] for flesh food"—a need/want, one can add, which for coastal people and for inlanders living near lakes and rivers, was provided by fish or marine mammals, and for other inlanders not given to migrating seasonally to the coast, by birds and rats.

BUILDINGS

At time of contact the Maori had several kinds of buildings: sleeping-houses (including larger-than-average ones that served also for community-wide meetings), cookhouses, storehouses or storage racks—and in some communities fortifications (*pa*) of several types. The *pa* will be described later; we begin here with houses used mainly for sleeping.

When the colonizers reached New Zealand they encountered a climate significantly cooler and rainier than that of their homelands, especially in winter. As mentioned earlier the Polynesian colonizers of Easter Island had also been greeted with temperatures that ranged between 73 and 63 degrees Fahrenheit—i.e., seven degrees below the lower averages of their East Polynesia homeland(s). Compared with that, the colonizers of New Zealand met with, and evidently adjusted to, winter temperatures as low as 52 degrees Fahrenheit in the north to 42 degrees Fahrenheit in the south (the mean June temperature of the city of Dunedin)—i.e., some fourteen or more degrees colder than the coldest average winter temperatures of their tropical homelands. Outdoors, that adjustment was made with clothing (see above); indoors (literally: Maori sleeping-houses did have a door), by construction of weatherproof buildings warmed by hearth fires.

Sleeping-houses were rectangular or round in floor plan, like their homeland models, but differed from them, mainly, in having thicker end walls with fewer openings, and, in most of them, sunken floors. They also differed from their homeland models in thatch materials (i.e., local grasses and leaves and bark as substitutes for (unavailable) coconut and pandanus leaves) and in some details of construction. (For details see Buck 1950.)

Whare puni ("house-sleep") were of two types. Type 1 were smaller than Type 2 and were

24.6. The inside of a Maori settlement

24.7. A view in New Zealand

24.8. Typical Maori dwelling

24.9. Maori council house

framed with undressed timber, having been seldom more than twenty feet long, ten feet wide and six feet high. Type 2 averaged considerably larger and were better made of dressed timbers, some of which were "decoratively" carved. Both types, however, had sunken floors—from a few inches to one or two feet deep, along with external ditches for drainage. Both types also had a door opening of stoop or crawl size, an even smaller front window (i.e., for letting out smoke), and a relatively deep front porch (which was covered by both roof and side walls). Both types of sleeping-houses also contained hearths—for heating, not for cooking. And in both types the floors were covered with rushes, on which mats were placed for sleeping.

The Type 2 houses (*whare whakairo*, "house-carved") found in some communities were more than sixty feet long, with ornately carved posts, both center and side, along with carved barge boards (see figure 24.9). Such buildings, usually the sleeping-houses for the community's headman, served as assembly places and for distinguished guests.

Storehouses (fig. 24.10) were of various types,

differing in form according to items stored. The simplest were simple elevated platforms, for temporary storage of newly harvested crops or fish. Next were roofed huts used for preserved foods and for household equipment; they were raised on piles for protection against rats, and some of them also had elaborately carved posts and barge boards.[203] Much more distinctive were the arrangements for storing garden crops. As noted earlier, sweet potatoes, taro and yams produced only one crop a year, and to preserve the harvests for year-round consumption and next year's planting, measures had to be taken to keep the tubers from freezing or rotting during the winter months. For sweet potatoes that was accomplished by storing them in underground pits protected by wooden and earth-covered shelters. (As will be recalled, in tropical Polynesia pit storage was also used for "storing" breadfruit—but to foster preservation by fermentation, not to protect it from the cold.) There is no record of how yams and taro were stored in New Zealand (Anne Salmond, pers. com.). And although the Maori did not ferment-store sweet potatoes they did so with berries, in pits.

24.10. Maori storehouse

WATERCRAFT

The earliest Europeans to visit New Zealand saw a few single outrigger and double-hulled canoes, but by the end of the eighteenth century those canoes were no longer in service, leaving in use only single-hulled (nonoutrigger) canoes and a few rafts. The canoes were of three types: small undecorated dugouts, for use on rivers and lakes; larger (up to about forty-six feet long) one-piece dugouts for fishing and travel in coastal waters; and—true masterworks of shipwright and carving skills—war canoes up to one hundred feet long and carrying up to sixty paddlers, along with their fuglemen.

Thanks to New Zealand's huge trees even some of the largest hulls were fashioned out of single tree trunks. Most river and lake canoes consisted of a single dugout hull. To the larger hull of a seagoing fishing and travel canoe was added a separate bowpiece along with a washboard and gunwale strakes. Washboards and gunwale strakes were also added to the dugouts of war canoes, together with a long bow piece and a long, gracefully upward curving and elaborately carved stern piece, some of them (red) painted and decorated with feathers. Not even the canoes of the Marquesans matched the amount and intricacy of the carving lavished on Maori war canoes.

Maori canoe paddles also were unique among those of Polynesia, having had a long, thin, lanceolate blade and a somewhat shorter handle that joined the blade at a slight angle, thereby giving greater drive to the stroke. Since the canoe hulls were seamless except for the joins between hull and strakes, it is possible that they required less bailing; nevertheless they did carry bailers, of wood, some of them elaborately carved. Also, like larger canoes elsewhere in Polynesia they were outfitted with steering paddles, which were usually larger and straighter than those used for paddling. And finally, many of their larger seagoing canoes, both fishing-traveling and fighting, were equipped with one or more sails, which were made of matting, were narrowly triangular in shape, and were attached, permanently, acute point downward, to masts and bowsprits.

Maori canoe paddling was first described by Joseph Banks, in 1770: "I have seen 15 paddles of a side in one of their Canoes move with immensely quick strokes and at the same time as much Justness as if the movers were animated by one

Soul: not the fraction of a second could be observed between the dipping and raising [of] any two of them, the Canoe all the While moving with incredible swiftness . . . " (Banks 1770, II: 11).

Besides canoes the only watercraft in use by the Maori at time of contact were small rafts and floats made of bundles of dried "flax" or bullrush, used for crossing rivers, and wooden ones with outriggers, used for fishing.[204]

GAMES

Maori children played rope skipping (two rope swingers, one skipper), swinging (from a vine hanging from a tree branch), hoop rolling,[205] tobogganing (down a hill slope, seated on leaves or a wooden plank), stilt walking or tripping, and top spinning. Other "diversions," including cat's cradle and draughts, were engaged in by both children and adults.

Most of the games played mainly or only by persons past "childhood" (as the Maori defined that life stage), were competitive—as was the case throughout tropical Polynesia as well. They included running, long leap and jumping (including vaulting), and wrestling—boxing having been engaged in "seriously" only in actual quarrels. The Maori also engaged in various aquatic sports—including diving, swim racing and canoe racing. Those living along some coasts also practiced surf riding on boards or in small canoes, although not as engrossingly as in Hawai'i. In addition, like most other Polynesians, they threw darts and stones, competitively, but in their case by catapult. Even the making of cat's cradles was at times done competitively—two persons having vied to test which one could complete a particular pattern first. Certain other games were designed to test skill in riddle solving, memorization and chesslike calculations.

DANCE AND MUSIC

The most noteworthy of Maori dances were *haka* and *poi*, the former performed by men, the latter once performed by both men and women but eventually by women only. In the *poi* a troop of women performed arm and body movements while twirling a *poi*, a ball, to the accompaniment of singing and in ways described by Peter Buck (who had personally witnessed most other forms of Polynesian dancing) as "the most graceful of all Polynesian dancing" (1950, 244). As for the *haka*, the best known dance of males, it consisted of "rhythmically shouted chants of defiance accompanied by aggressive, stylized movements of hands and feet" (Metge 1976, 335) and by ferocious facial expressions, including protruding tongue and glaring eyes. Although designed (perhaps?) in connection with warfare, it had become also the standard way of welcoming notable visitors![206]

Maori musical (sound-making?) instruments consisted of (wooden) flutes, (wooden) *putorino* (a combination flute-bugle-megaphone), mouth-resonated bows, Jew's harps, bone castanets, tapped whale ribs, whirred discs (for accompanying incantations) and various kinds of bull-roarers (Kaeppler and Love 1998, 932–33).

Singing accompanied many of their activities and for many purposes,[207] and was performed mainly in unison. Early Western visitors reported it to be "mournful and monotonous," and while their actual melodies have since then "disappeared," they are in general described as "kept within narrow ranges," with movement only "stepwise," and their melodic patterns as having "returned repeatedly to a drone" (Te Puoho Katene, in Kaeppler and Love 1998).

WARFARE

Warfare (*taua*) among precontact Maori was frequent, pervasive, small scale—and sometimes exterminative. After the introduction of Western muskets, which were acquired in very large numbers, warfare among Maori continued to be pervasive, etc., but was often larger in scale. Also, although territorial conquest and occupation was infrequent during both eras it became more frequent during the musket era. The following summary, however, focuses on the premusket era and begins with a list of the causes of warfare.[208]

To begin with, it needs noting that in most cases the warring units consisted of the adult male members of a single tribal form of *hapu*—a residentially localized and politically autonomous social unit whose core members claimed, and could corroborate, descent from the same ancestor. As will be described in a later section, the label *hapu* was also applied to common-descent units of various generational depths, shallow or deep, but present reference is to the tribal variant, whose members numbered "several hundred." As in tropical Polynesia, the most frequent and compelling proximate reason (*take*) leading to warfare

was revenge—to avenge real or imagined wrongs against members of one's tribal *hapu*, including homicide (visible, or by suspected sorcery), poaching, infringements of *tapu*, insults to one's chief, interference with the bones of an ancestor, and loss in a previous conflict with the opposing *hapu*. The latter was an especially weighty cause: survivors—if any—of a tribal *hapu* defeated in one round of warfare were sure to seek revenge as soon as they were able to recoup, even after one or more generations. Unprovoked territorial conquest also now and then occurred, mainly in the more densely populated horticultural north, for in most other regions there was enough uninhabited land for a *hapu* to expand into or move to without fighting. As for engaging in warfare for pleasurable excitement, that may indeed have served to encourage participation but is unlikely to have initiated it. Likewise, although an individual's fighting skills and manifested courageous actions in battle did in fact bring him praise, and single him out as a respected *toa* (warrior)[209] there seem to have been very few instances of ambition for that status having served, principally, to lead a whole tribal *hapu* to war.

There was, however, one other motive that played at least a supplementary role in war making, one that was more characteristic of the Maori than of other Polynesian people, namely, the appetite for human flesh.

Turning next to weapons, those of the Maori were few in type (compared with those of, say, Hawai'i, the Marquesas and Tonga), having consisted only of wooden spears—used mainly for thrusting, along with long and short clubs. The spears, of lengths five feet and more, had one end for striking, the other for stabbing. The clubs—made of stone or bone or wood, and used for close-in fighting—had spatulate, sharp-edged business ends; some of those made of greenstone were elaborately carved and came to be highly prized heirlooms. Spears and rocks were sometimes thrown, but Maori fighting was mostly close-in—and very fierce. As was the case with all other Polynesians, the Maori had no shields; in fighting some of them wore thicker-than-ordinary clothing for armor, but many wore only kilts or fought naked. In fact, the most tangible kind of defensive measure undertaken was the building of forts.

The Maori resorted to fort building more than

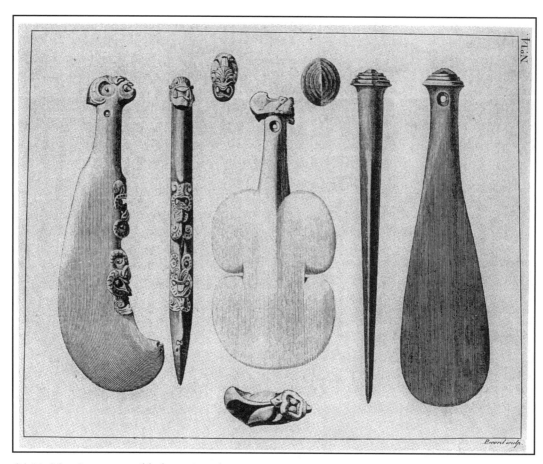

24.11. Maori *patu patu* (bludgeons) used as weapons

24.12. Armed Maori warrior in typical dress

24.13. Portrait of a Maori

any other Polynesians—a consequence, doubtless, of their more frequent wars, especially in the more densely populated north.[210] The word *pa* was applied to settlements that were in some way fortified, in distinction to *kainga*, those that were not. *Pa* were usually located on hilltops, ridges and headlands, or in swamps or on islets—i.e., more easily defended places fortified by ditches or ramparts or palisades, or all three. In some cases they enclosed some or all of a community's dwellings; in others the dwellings were located outside, and the *pa* resorted to only in times of attack.

Applying the classification proposed earlier in this book, Maori warfare consisted mostly of "raids"; "brawls" doubtless did occur occasionally but "open battles" (i.e., forewarned encounters between more or less balanced forces on open ground) took place mostly (or only?) after European contact, and then only rarely and in the thickly settled north. The most frequent kind of raiding was a secret attack against a whole settlement, *pa* or *kainga*, by the adult males of a single tribal *hapu*—i.e., a force of less—in some cases many less—than a few hundred. (According to one computation of 16 *hapu*, the average fighting force was 159 (Vayda 1960, 42). Occasionally, two or more *hapu* joined forces to raid the same objective, but even then they remained separate groups—so separate that occasionally one of them would stop fighting and go home. In Vayda's judgment, however, a one-*hapu* force, large or small, made for effective fighting inasmuch as nearly all of its members were kinsmen and therefore more likely to support one another. On the other hand, in keeping with the Maori's wonted egalitarian relationships at home (at least, among nonslave men), some reports say that they lacked commanding leadership and coordination in fighting. Yet other eyewitness accounts of actual engagements tell of forces having been divided for specific purposes—such as storming a fort from different directions, making diversionary mock attacks, setting up ambuscades for pursuing forces, etc. As for the actual fighting, except for some defensive spear and rock throwing it was done mostly close-in and man to man.

In some cases a raid turned into a siege, against which many forts were provisioned either permanently or prior to a known impending attack, but most sieges were short-lived because of the lack of the attackers' food, and ended either in their quick victory or their dispirited return home.

But rather than cite details of some reasonably documented fights, I refer the reader to Vayda's fine compilation, and turn to some generalizations about their outcomes.

During fighting the aim was not just to render one's individual opponent helpless but to kill him. And when fighting was over, those of the defeated side unable to escape—including men, women and children—were usually either killed on the spot and either cooked and eaten forthwith[211] or taken home for eating or led home captive for later eating or to serve as slaves. (In this connection, in the reasoning of a slave's kinfolk he (or she) was ipso facto "dead.") As noted earlier, except in the relatively densely populated north, the victors rarely took "permanent" possession of their opponents' lands; instead, they destroyed their dwellings, crops and those material possessions they did not carry away.

It is a noteworthy feature of Maori society that few wars ended in truce or in war-ending "peace."[212] One reason for that was the universally held value that one aggressive action required a similar counteraction and that the near-defeated would invariably seek revenge, either by mounting a (secret) raid or by overt acts of treachery—that "value" having been a particular example of the pervasive and powerfully motivating social-relational principle of *utu*—i.e., "equivalent response."

Finally, some words about the singular Maori institution of *muru* ("to plunder"), which, along with direct supernatural punishment or magic or public opinion or chiefly disfavor, was a common way of penalizing infractions of socially sanctioned rules by members of the same community or of communities linked normally by ties of peace. Such infractions included homicide, adultery, damage to crops, and poaching. (They also included "allowing" oneself to be injured or by "allowing" a close relative to die—of which more below.) When such an infraction became known and widely enough condemned, a *taua muru* ("warlike plunder") was organized, and with feigned (?) ferocity the plunderers proceeded to the home of the infractor and seized or destroyed all of his material goods: dwellings, storehouses, stores, tools, clothing and heirlooms—even digging up his crops and killing one or more of his slaves (if any).[213] Moreover, most victims of *muru*

24.14. Maori war canoe bidding defiance

24.15. A fortified Maori settlement

are reported to have accepted their fate with "good grace"—even, in some cases, to have viewed them as an honor, . . . "as showing that he must be a person of some importance" (Best 1924, I: 359).

Not all such *taua muru* ended so quiescently. Especially when raiders and infractor belonged to different communities, the latter sometimes mobilized his neighbors in defense, thereby converting the *muru* into a real *taua* (war)—and eventually into a continuing feud (Ballara 1976, 490).

LIFE CYCLE

Like other Polynesians the Maori distinguished between an individual's body and his or her *wairua* (spirit), and held that the spirit survived the death of the body and unless deliberately or accidentally extirpated (i.e., by gods) could continue existing indefinitely. Moreover, Maori ideas about other components of an individual, both palpable and nonpalpable, resembled those of other Polynesians, as did their ideas and practices about the sacrosanct nature of the head and the magical powers resting in human genitalia, both male and female.

Turning to the course of a Maori's life, according to Peter Buck: "It is . . . evident from the recorded native literature that the Maori were well aware of the main facts in the physiology of human reproduction" (1950, 363)—a statement, it will be recalled, which could also be made about most or all other Polynesian peoples (disregarding some beliefs held here or there about multiple paternity). Like other Polynesians the Maori practiced magical measures to promote conception, but the only measure I know of used to prevent it was physical—i.e., coitus interruptus. As for voluntary abortion, the only custom I have come across that was peculiarly Maori—and uniquely cunning—had to do with gods: namely, if one of them was angered by a pregnant woman for infraction of some *tapu* it killed her fetus—which led some women desiring miscarriage to flout a *tapu* intentionally (Best 1924, II: 5).

To avoid unnecessary prolongation of this section about a Maori's life course, from birth to afterlife, I will list only those aspects of it that differed significantly from life courses in most or all Polynesian societies elsewhere. This is not to say that specific methods of, for example, weaning were the same everywhere: far from it! What is a fact, however, is that all or most Polynesian peoples, including the Maori, engaged in practices to energize an infant to wean. Or, although the Maori conception of kinship "closeness" differed somewhat from those of some other Polynesian peoples, all of them, including the Maori (but excepting highest-rank Hawaiians) proscribed marriage between "close" consanguines, both matri- and patrilateral. While acknowledging that my selection of "significant" may differ from that of other writers regarding Maori differences in this domain, I nevertheless propose the following features.

1. Although several Polynesian peoples practiced rites to dedicate infants or young children to one or another god—for particular service to or guardianship by that god—in some Maori communities most young males were dedicated to either Rongo, principal god of horticulture, or to Tu, principal god of warfare, which determined whether the youthful dedicatees would be trained specifically for horticulture or for warfare—although virtually all of the males of such communities engaged in both when need arose.

2. Speaking of which, while in all or most Polynesian societies their males learned some lore—legendary, mythical and magico-religious—and while a few Polynesian peoples institutionalized such training to some degree, the Maori had proceeded perhaps further than any of them in developing specialized schools of learning" (*whare wananga*, "houses of occult lore") mainly for upper-class youths.

3. Focusing again on the life stage of "youth," certainly one of the most significant and distinctive characteristics of Maori culture was the absence of the otherwise pan-Polynesian practice of supercision—an absence that has been profusely speculated about but never persuasively explained. Another, perhaps not unrelated Maori peculiarity (but not an altogether unique one) was the practice of beginning tattooing *after* the life stage of "youth." And still another characteristic of Maori youth culture—which though not so distinctive is nevertheless noteworthy—was the apparent absence of approval for corpulence or light pigmentation as measures of female beauty (i.e., sexual attractiveness)—perhaps because of the relative paucity of fattening foods in Maori diets and women's relatively more physically demanding work.

4. Moving forward to "maturity"—characterized by marriage[214] and having offspring—there appears to have been nothing about the Maori in this life stage that differentiated them significantly from their peers in many other Polynesian societies—i.e., they continued to engage fully in subsistence activities (having been relieved of much child care by stay-at-home grandparents), and in the case of some males they exercised most of the leadership in their suprafamilial social groups, including "civil" governance and warfare.

5. As for the life stage of "old age"—which, it has been said, was reached earlier by women than by men, but in both cases no later than their forties, perhaps because of their unremitting heavy labor—both male and female elders appear to have been treated with respect (as was the case in most but not all other Polynesian societies as well, Tahiti having been an outstanding exception). And in line with many Maori's relatively deep interest in mythical, legendary and other kinds of knowledge, their sages—most of them elderly—were even venerated.

6. We turn now to the final stage of a Maori's existence, to the disintegration of body and release of the spirit, keeping in mind that the wide geographic spread among Maori settlements had inevitably resulted in regional differences in culture, especially in this domain.

The most widespread method for disposing of a corpse was to bury it until the soft parts were decomposed, then to exhume the bones for final disposition, preferably in the deceased's home community, either by burial or by deposit in a tree or cave (care having been taken in some cases to hide them from enemies)—all such practices having occurred in several other Polynesian societies as well. The common Maori practice of family members' keeping one or more bones with them occurred also elsewhere, but their occasional practice of retaining whole (and preserved) heads—bones, hair, skin and all—of some important personages, both friend and foe (the former to honor and cherish, the latter to spit on and revile), may have been distinctive.

Except in one or two features, most Maori funeral practices resembled those of many or most Polynesian peoples elsewhere—e.g., in stylized forms of weeping and self-laceration, in eulogies and in funeral gifts to bereaved relatives (which when made by visiting delegations were expected to be reciprocated when one of them died). The most noteworthy exceptions to most other Polynesian funerals consisted of the (occasional) slaying of one of a deceased's war-captive slaves—not as a sacrifice to the deceased's god, but to serve the deceased on his journey to the afterlife. (For more on death customs see Oppenheim 1973.)

One other Maori practice that I believe to be unique, not only in Polynesia but, perhaps, in human societies elsewhere, was the funeral version of the Maori-wide custom of *muru*. As described earlier, a *muru* was a raid carried out by a party that believed itself to have been injured in one or another way. In it the injured party and his fellows raided the guilty party and forcibly destroyed much or all of the latter's belongings—his house, his tools, his heirlooms, etc. A Westerner can understand the rationale of such punishment exacted upon a person who has broken one of a community's "laws." What is less comprehensible is the circumstance that a man was sometimes *muru*-ed when he himself became injured—the Maori rationale having been that he had thereby deprived his community of use of his full services. Even less justifiable in Western eyes was the practice of *muru*-raiding a deceased's close relatives, on the grounds that they had "allowed" him to die. Nevertheless, as mentioned earlier, despite the material losses suffered by the victims of a *muru*, it is reported that they felt some satisfaction in being important enough to have been singled out for such a dramatic exhibition of public interest!

The wide scatter of many Maori communities or the hostility that prevailed among many of them allowed for the development of wide differences in beliefs about an after-death realm and a human spirit's experience in it. And while the Maori, like most other Polynesians, referred to it, vaguely, as Hawaiki, or the Po (in contrast to the this-life and place of the Ao), they differed from region to region in several other details. One of the most widespread beliefs was that all ghosts (i.e., the spirits of deceased humans) were to be feared, hence among other incantations performed at funerals were some more or less polite invitations for them to leave *and stay away*. That fear, however, did not deter a deceased's relatives from requesting his or her help now and then. (In this connection, it is reported that individuals were especially fearful of the ghosts of relatives whose bodies they had shared in eating!) Another widespread Maori belief was that ghosts traveled to the afterlife realm by leaping into that realm from New Zealand's northernmost cape (in contrast to the widespread belief of tropical Polynesians in a westernmost point of departure).

Another widespread Maori belief, that all ghosts journeyed to the (or a) postlife realm fairly soon after death, is of course contrary to the equally widespread one that many of them remained indefinitely near their earthly abodes. Not to worry! Like most other humans, the Maori were capable of living, comfortably, with what Westerners might consider to be contradictory beliefs.

Beliefs about the nature of the postlife realm varied regionally: for example, that there was a single postlife underground realm; that there was an Upperworld as well as an Underworld—the former for upper-class persons, the latter for commoners; etc. There was, however, widespread agreement that a person's ghost was not punished for his or her behavior during life. Indeed, in the view of one of their most perspicacious observers, the Maori were not only generally fatalistic but were little concerned with their fates and little interested in the nature of the afterlife—except for the behavior of those ghosts likely to affect them in the (current) world.

With this necessarily brief summary of some peculiarities of Maori beliefs and practices concerning the life course of individuals, we turn to the more obscure ones concerning their social relations.

SOCIAL UNITS

Before attempting to describe the types of social units that made up Maori society it may be useful to list some of the more influential factors that served to shape and to separate some of them.

First was New Zealand's exceedingly large size relative to other Polynesian archipelagoes and the wide diversity and dispersion of its potential food-getting resources. The former permitted and perhaps encouraged widespread human expansion; the latter led to regional differences in techniques of food getting—and consequently in population densities and movements.

Second was the physical-psychological character of most individual Maori, especially males. For example, they were on the average young and

hardy and physically active—their life spans having been short, with little of it spent in senile inactivity—and, unlike some other Polynesians they seem to have had no aesthetic preference for obesity and no apparent respect for "dignified" immobility.

Third were certain beliefs and values brought with them from their East Polynesia homelands. One was the principle of (qualified) bilaterality—of valuing kin ties through both parents (although, in most regions, placing somewhat more value on ties through the father). One basis of that bilaterality was, probably, the belief (i.e., knowledge?) that something of both parents went into the conceiving of a child. (Or it may have been the other way round—i.e., the fact of bilaterality may have fostered the belief.) In either case, corollary to that belief (I propose) was another one, to wit, that entities inherited from both parents included a measure of "godliness"— derived originally from each parent's primal god-ancestor. (Another facet of that belief, that the largest quota of the godliness of both parents passed to their firstborn, was institutionalized in the value attached to seniority. Or perhaps that too was the other way round.[215]

As will be recalled, it was the belief in many if not most Polynesian societies that some godliness was also acquired by some humans in ways other than by procreation (perhaps, for example, by means of direct "implant" by some god)—a circumstance recognizable by an individual's achievement in leadership or in skill in some highly valued profession or craft, etc. And while this additional feature of the godliness belief was held by several other Polynesian peoples, the Maori tended to admire and defer to such "implanted" individuals more than most.

Another influential value brought with them from their homelands was the pan-Polynesian principle of "equivalent response" (utu)—and not only with respect to the exchange of material objects but of actions as well, both helpful and harmful (including homicide). As just noted, this principle of conduct prevailed throughout Polynesia, but perhaps nowhere more so than among the Maori.

One more factor instrumental in shaping Maori social organization was belief in myths about the origin of their larger common-descent units. As noted earlier, after Western contact several of those, in many respects disparate, myths were combined and rationalized by some Western scholars into a unified "Great New Zealand Fleet Myth," which was deliberately composed in order "to provide a coherent framework by which to interpret the prehistory of New Zealand" (Simmons 1976, 316). Among other purposes, that myth, along with inferences from it and from other "rationalizations," served to provide a comprehensive schema for encompassing all "true" Maori (i.e., those descended from the Great Fleet pioneers of 1350) into a single cognatic structure—and one which, until a few decades ago, came to be widely accepted, including by many Maori, as historically authentic.[216] According to that schema, precontact Maori society was divided into thirty to forty or more *iwi* ("bones"), which were labeled "tribes" by some writers and which were subdivided into *hapu* ("pregnant," "conceived"), labeled by some writers "subtribes" or "clans," and which were themselves subdivided into *whanau* ("birth")—i.e., "extended families." In this schema an *iwi* was composed of all persons descended, through males or females, from one or another of the members of one or another of the legendary canoes in the Great Fleet; a *hapu* was composed of all persons descended from an *iwi* ancestor about eight to ten generations back; and a *whanau* of a two- to three-generation–deep family division of a *hapu*. In addition—according to the Great Fleet Myth reconstruction—there were even larger units called *waka* ("canoe"), loose confederations of *iwi*, composed of all the *iwi* whose founders were members of one of the Great Fleet canoes. In other words, the Great Fleet Myth postulated a structure of Maori society based solely on the criterion of ambilineal common descent—a structure that included even *waka*, since, by extending the reasoning behind the schema, all the members of any mythic Great Fleet canoe would likely have been interrelated by ties of common descent.

All well and good, and up to a point a schema that contains a thread of authenticity, since the principle of common descent did undoubtedly play a very important role in the formation of actual historical social units, both groups and categories. However, there were other factors involved in the formation of those units, as the following summary will outline.[217]

During and for some decades after first Western contacts Maori society was in fact divided into two types of social units: Type 1, based largely on common (ambilineal) descent (plus some affines from elsewhere) along with residential proximity and some corporate ownership and some collective action; Type 2, based exclusively on common (ambilineal) descent plus some corporate ownership and only occasional collective action, but not necessarily residential proximity. In many instances the two types of memberships overlapped, as will be mentioned, but for purposes of analysis they will be described separately— beginning with Type 1.

The smallest and most vital Type 1 social unit was the *whanau*, which in most cases consisted of an extended family—of grandparent(s), their unmarried sons and daughters, their married sons and wives and children, plus, in some cases, other relatives or one or more war-captive slaves)—all residing together in one dwelling or in two or more contiguous ones. Marital residence having been mostly virilocal, only the core members of most *whanau*—i.e., grandfather, unmarried sons and daughters, and married sons and their children—would have been related by close ties of common descent, although the wives of the above, along with other relatives in residence, were in most cases doubtless related to those core members by some, more distant, cognatic ties.

Using "vital" to characterize the *whanau* is not an exaggeration ("vital: necessary to existence, essential," etc., *Funk and Wagnalls Collegiate Dictionary*), inasmuch as *whanau* provided, through collective action, most of their members' material needs and wants—in food, shelter, and clothing. Also, each *whanau*, or at least its core members, owned full rights, or uncontested provisional use-rights, in the sites of their dwellings and in the lands and waters in which they gardened, collected, fished and hunted. And in cases in which their dwelling sites—but not necessarily their gardens and forest areas, etc.— were parts of larger, multi-*whanau* (residential) communities, it was usual for each *whanau*'s dwellings to be separated by visible boundaries of some sort.

The numerical size of *whanau* varied, from as few as five persons to (in one recorded case) ninety-two—the average (it may be inferred) having been twenty to forty. Beyond that number, one of its males—typically a younger married brother—

usually moved away and established a unit that in time became a separate *whanau*. And in time the branches of many *whanau* increased to the point that they constituted what was called a *hapu*, herein labeled a Type 1 or "tribal" *hapu*, to distinguish it from a Type 2 or "kin" *hapu*, the type of social unit made up entirely of persons of common descent—of which more below.

Tribal *hapu* were the society's most important "political" units (in terms that will be described). The nucleus of each of them consisted of a number of *whanau*, some of whose core members traced common descent from an ancestor about five to ten generations back and whose name the *hapu* typically bore (e.g., Ngati X, "descendants of X"). According to most accounts, tribal *hapu* were composed of "several hundred" members. Some tribal *hapu* were domiciled—at least part of each year—in a single community—others in two or more neighboring ones. In perhaps most cases each tribal *hapu*, or branch thereof, constituted a separate and relatively "nucleated" community (called a *kainga* if unfortified, *pa* if fortified).[218] In other places two or more tribal *hapu* (or branches thereof) dwelt alongside one or more different tribal *hapu* (or branches thereof). But even when two or more of them were domiciled in a single community, the houses of each of them occupied a separate and often physically boundaried—fenced, or palisaded—neighborhood. (Be it noted, however, that the other areas associated with a tribal *hapu*—its members' gardens, bird-snaring trees, fernroot beds, fishing areas, etc.—were often interspersed among those of the members of other tribal *hapu*.)

According to one leading authority on Maori society, both precontact and modern: "When a [tribe-type] *hapu* grew too large for effective functioning, some of its members broke away under the leadership of one of the chief's sons or younger brothers and established themselves independently, either as part of the original territory or on land acquired by conquest or occupation, sooner or later acquiring a new name. Regarding their origin [however], minor [branch] *hapu* formed in this way often joined forces with the original one for large-scale undertakings" (Metge 1976, 6; see also Ballara 1998, 164–65).

"Tribal-*hapu* were the society's largest type of corporate and functionally cohesive collectivity: more important species of property, such as a war-canoe, a meeting-house, a large eel weir, were regarded as property of the whole tribal-*hapu* and were used by the members as a body. All the land surrounding the [settlement], incorporating, of course, the [use] rights of individuals and of *whanau*, was under the [residual] ownership of this group, while important tasks involving considerable labour power saw a muster of all its members. At large tribal feasts, too, and on similar occasions of ceremony the [tribal-] *hapu* functioned as a body" (Firth 1929, 139; but see Ballara 1998, 179). Also, as noted earlier, such *hapu* were the society's principal, and largely autonomous, units in warfare, the whole manpower of a *hapu* having been mobilized—or asked to mobilize!—to conduct raids or in defense against attacks or encroachments by outsiders.

Granted that the whole membership of a tribal *hapu* may on occasion have acted collectively in, say, feast giving and war making, I am uncertain about ownership of the properties identified with such a *hapu*. Was it the tribal *hapu* as a whole, including inmarrying spouses and other "outsider" relatives? Or only those members of the *hapu*'s core common-descent *hapu*? This distinction may strike some readers as trivial hairsplitting, but it relates to the larger question concerning the relative importance of common descent versus residential contiguity in the formation of Maori corporate units. Also, I am uncertain about accuracy of the above statements regarding land tenure and collective activity in cases where two or more tribal *hapu*, or branches of different ones, occupied the same *kainga* or *pa*, a situation that some accounts seem to imply. But then, Maori society was so widely and in some areas so thinly spread over such a variety of physical environments that generalizations about its social groupings must be very broad, and in some respects qualified, to apply.

Most marriages took place between members of the same tribal *hapu*—an arrangement encouraged by residential proximity and in some cases by desire to keep property rights intact. However, some marriages did occur between members of separate tribal *hapu*, including those arranged for economic or political purposes. When inter-*hapu* marriages did occur, their offspring and subsequent descendants could claim membership, with its attendant rights, in the tribal *hapu* of both parents—although, as with membership in a kin *hapu*, that membership lapsed (became "cold") if it was not validated by active participation in the affairs of either of them, including some residence there.

Reverting to the Maori kin *hapu*, the Type 2 social unit made up exclusively of persons of common descent, an individual could and doubtless sometimes did claim membership in different ones of his potential kin *hapu* in order to satisfy particular wants. For example, he could identify with all other descendants of a certain ancestor in order to obtain fishing rights in their corporately owned eel weir, or with all other descendants of a more remote ancestor in order to obtain fowling rights in their corporately owned part of a forest—provided that both such claims had not become "cold" (in Maori words) through disuse (Salmond 1983; Webster 1975).

Next in order of encompassment were *iwi* ("bones"), which many writers have labeled "tribes," but which in precontact times were in reality loose—in some cases very loose—confederations of adjacent tribal *hapu*, their collective action having consisted mainly of occasional feasts and, sometimes, in banding together, wholly or in part, to defend the territory of one or more of their component tribal *hapu*, which, however, not infrequently fought among themselves. (Indeed, there were cases in which different branches of a single tribal *hapu* were affiliated with different *iwi*.) Moreover, the composition of some *iwi* changed over time, through addition of a previously separate tribal *hapu* or defection or extermination of a member one.

As noted earlier, according to the Great Fleet Myth schema, the founding ancestor of an *iwi* had been one or another member of one or another of the legendary Great Fleet canoes, whose name in many cases became that of the *iwi* (e.g., Ngati Z, "descendants of Z"). At time of contact there were about fifty *iwi*, and despite their looseness in structure their members are described as having expressed strong sentimental ties to them—a carryover, perhaps, of a Maori's veneration of the *iwi*, the "bones," of his ancestors (Salmond 1983, 351). Another reason for that tie may have been a Maori's attachment to the wide landscape contained within an *iwi*'s boundaries, which were wider than any single *hapu*'s. And still another reason for at least postcontact Maori to have emphasized attachment to an *iwi* was the unit's enlarged postcontact role in political affairs, including territorial conquest under more centralized and more aggressive leadership.

Finally, and encompassing all the above units, were *waka* ("canoe"), described as "loose confederations" of *iwi*, whose founding ancestors (according to the Great Fleet Myth) had shared passage in a particular one of the mythical colonizing canoes. In the opinion of most writers a *waka* had no economic function and its constituent *iwi* did not scruple to wage war against one another, but its members did nevertheless "recognize"—and idealize—their bond of union, as was exemplified after the (postcontact) death of one high-ranking member of the Arawa *waka* "whose body had to be carried home for burial by a circuitous route, in order that the honored dead might pass to his last resting place on no other land but [that of] his own 'canoe'" (Firth 1959, 116)—an episode that also signifies that the lands of a *waka*'s *iwi* were not necessarily contiguous.

Unlike most other writers on Maori social organization Ballara has drawn attention to the patchwork quality of its social units, e.g., of two or more tribal *hapu* having occupied the same community, of a tribal *hapu*'s branches having been scattered and in some cases domiciled in communities alongside branches of other tribal *hapu*, of a *whanau*'s land holdings—gardens, fishing locations, etc.—having been located in areas within the holdings of the *whanau* of other tribal *hapu*, etc. All of this seems to emphasize the small sizes of the Maori's more durable functional social groups and the fluidity of their collectivity into larger ones—despite (or because of?) the otherwise unifying potential of their common-descent ideology.

RANK AND AUTHORITY

Another cause for uncertainty about Maori social relationships lies in the inconsistency with which English words have been used to label certain of their offices. Beginning with the word "chief," the reader is confronted with a plethora of them: "minor chiefs," "chiefs of secondary rank," "high chiefs," "supreme chiefs," and simply "chiefs." Further obfuscating the matter is some writers' reference to the "several chiefs of a tribe," without differentiating their hierarchichal relationships, if any. Another source of confusion

24.16. Maori chief

24.17. Portrait of the Maori chief Kahouri

lies with differences in which certain native status-labels, such as *ariki* and *rangatira,* are defined. With my ignorance of the Maori language and my meager sampling of the vast Maori literature I can offer only tentative conclusions about this topic—which, however, are corroborated somewhat by knowledge about similar matters in other Polynesian societies.

Beginning with the (institutionalized) hierarchy of status in the types of social units just described, the principal distinction to be made is between those based on "seniority" and those based on "authority." (In Polynesian contexts, "seniority" refers to birth order among siblings and their respective descendants—with highest status reserved for the firstborn of a line of first-borns, qualified somewhat by a bias in favor of males. And in the terminology of this book, "authority" means the ability to compel someone to do something, by threat or actual use of insti-tutionalized sanctions, including physical force.) Among the Maori (as among many or most other Polynesian peoples) the most "senior" (in the above sense) of the core clan members of most

tribal *hapu* bore the title of *ariki*; as such he (sometimes she) enjoyed greatest influence over a unit's religious matters and, if he displayed quali-ties of secular leadership, held most authority[219] as well—i.e., he was the unit's "chief," as the office is defined in this book. (A person became *ariki* of a tribal *hapu* upon death of its incumbent *ariki* but became and remained its chief only if the unit's more influential members judged him to possess the requisite "chiefly" qualifications—which, according to one leading scholar, included decisiveness, foresight, initiative, and ability (Firth 1957a, 107). Lacking these, Firth added, "the leadership of the tribe [i.e., tribal *hapu*] would pass over him and be invested in his younger brother, if capable, or failing him in the nearest male cousin, as a rule patrilineal, but in default, of matrilineal connection, most fitted to command. But in religious and ceremonial affairs the *ariki* still played his part" (Ibid.).[220]

Elsewhere in his text Firth noted that to main-tain his position a (tribal) chief also needed more than an average amount of wealth, with which to grant "frequent hospitality to travelers, relatives, and visitors of note," adding that "a reputation for liberality was greatly sought after, and conversely, a name for meanness and parsimony was a social stigma of the worst kind" (132). Moreover, the text adds, that wealth was not (as in some Polynesian societies) obtained by forced "tribute" but by "presents" and by "the labour of himself, his wives, slaves, and immediate attendants" (134). In addition, while most chiefs had larger dwellings, and enjoyed richer than average diets, few of them were accorded "exaggerated" forms of respect. "No commoner crouched or made obeisance before a chief, nor were any special titles or terms of respect used in addressing him in ordinary conversation," his special position having been indicated by "the weight of his opinion when expressed at public gatherings, his trained proficiency as an orator, his knowledge of genealogies, proverbs, and songs, his assumption of leadership in war and in economic undertakings, the greater amount of ceremonial pertaining to his birth, marriage, and death, and his observance of a much stricter system of *tapu*."[221] (107). (To a reader skeptical of human perfection, among Polynesians and peoples elsewhere, the above characterization seems more ideal than real—but the ideal it expresses does differ greatly from that attributed to chieftainship in many other Polynesian societies.) More realistically, Firth adds that a Maori chief did not have a "personal claim" in all the lands within his tribe's borders" (377). He did, however, have a claim to those lands inherited from his own ancestors. And although he exercised some (?) control over disposal of the remainder, he (unlike the chiefs of many other Polynesian tribes) "received no material benefit therefrom" except in the form of "presents," not of "tribute" (Ibid.).

Such was the position of the chief—*ariki* or non-*ariki*—of a tribal *hapu*. What, if any, additional role was played by the so-called "chief" of an *iwi*—presumably but not certainly the chief of the *iwi*'s "senior" tribal *hapu* (if there were such), whom some writers label a "supreme chief"—cannot have been exceptionally "supreme," for, although he may have presided over *iwi*-wide festivities and initiated *iwi*-wide actions against other *iwi*, he seems not to have had the authority to compel all of his *iwi*'s constituent tribal *hapu* to join in.[222]

Descending to headship of the society's small-est and "lowest," but in many ways most vital social unit, the *whanau*, the office was labeled *kaumatua* (the general name for "adult") and its incumbent was, presumably, the nonsenile senior of the *whanau*'s core family. And, because of a *whanau*'s never-ending life-sustaining activities, the role of *kaumatua* must have been an engrossing job. This puts in mind that the chiefs of tribal *hapu* were, doubtless, also *kaumatua* of their *whanau* and as such were required to play at least supervisory roles in their *whanau* as well.

SOCIAL STRATIFICATION

All authorities are agreed that there was an underclass in Maori society consisting of "slaves" (i.e., war captives, *taureka* or *taurekareka*, which also meant "scoundrel"), persons having been reduced to that status by capture in war.[223] However, authorities on Maori society disagree somewhat on class stratification among the "free." Some authorities have delineated a two-class system, others a three-class system, and at least one writer, the peerless Elsdon Best, concluded that there was only one—having remarked that during his long and close contacts with Maori from several parts of New Zealand he had never met one who would admit to being "lower class" (Best 1924, II: 346).

One cause for those differences of opinion was a lack of clear-cut behavioral rules that served to define and separate the so-called "classes"—as, for example prevailed in Tahiti, where legitimized marriage between upper- and lower-class persons was proscribed, or as in Hawai'i, where lower-class persons were required to treat upper-class ones with numerous and sometimes exaggerated forms of respect.

Another cause for the opinion differences was indistinction between the two types of statuses involved in class stratification: between those based solely on birth (and initially on birth order) and those based on birth plus other factors, such as leadership and expertise.

A third cause for the differences in opinion doubtless lay in the facts themselves—i.e., the wide differences that prevailed among the Maori: in population density and in size of community and tribe (differences that were surely reflected in social stratification). Moreover, such regional dissimilarities in precontact time were likely to have increased during the early postcontact era, when most of the data on stratification was recorded, and when Maori society was undergoing sweeping changes in geographic distribution, economics and politics.

In view of the above circumstances it is perhaps safest to conclude that in precontact times nonslave Maori were divided into, at most, two social classes: an upper class of "aristocrats" (*rangatira*), including incumbents of the *ariki* office, and a lower class of "commoners" (*tutua, ware*)—with however little if any difference between aristocrats and commoners in terms of their interaction (except for everyone's more or less respectful and obedient behavior toward his own *ariki*). According to this classification: "Those who could trace their descent back to the ancestor of their *hapu* [presumably, their tribal *hapu*] through older and preferably male siblings in each generation (i.e., through senior lines) were recognized as *rangatira* aristocrats. Those who derived from junior lines or whose forebears had lost status through failure or enslavement were reckoned as *tutua* or *ware* (commoners)" (Metge 1989, 78). And Metge, a leading authority on Maori society, went on to say: "Commoners could always claim to be aristocrats because they were related to the chief [presumably the chief "chief"] by descent from the same ancestor, and also by marriage, some aristocrats [having taken] women of lower rank as secondary wives" [224] (Ibid.).

Unlike the distinction between aristocrats and commoners, that between both of them and slaves was in many respects sharp. As noted earlier, anyone captured in warfare became a slave regardless of his or her previous status. Some slaves were redeemed by their relatives and a few came to exercise important roles—while remaining *noa*—in their "host" tribal *hapu*. (Anne Salmond, pers. com.). But most of them became, in effect, nonpersons. Some female slaves served as concubines ("secondary wives") of their masters, but most male slaves performed menial tasks such as cooking and bearing burdens (which were also performed by nonslave females), but were considered too *noa* (in this context, "degrading") for nonslave males. Otherwise, it is reported (in Firth 1959, 110) that slaves were "well fed and

housed," and "the relations between them and their masters were easy and pleasant"—until, that is, "they were called upon for a human sacrifice or to provide a relish for a feast."

It is unusual—some would say, unfair—to end this chapter on the Maori by reporting on their cannibalism (a practice which by most Western values is considered savagely ghoulish, to say the least). Most writings on the Maori, as on most other Polynesians, end on a note of admiration, even laudation, for their many accomplishments—as well they should. The attentive reader of this chapter will doubtless feel the same admiration, with regard to the Maori's many successes in adjusting themselves to wholly new and often arduous environments. Nevertheless, a balanced view of Maori culture, and of all other Polynesian cultures, requires attention both to the "good" and the "bad"—as the final chapter in this book will seek to establish.

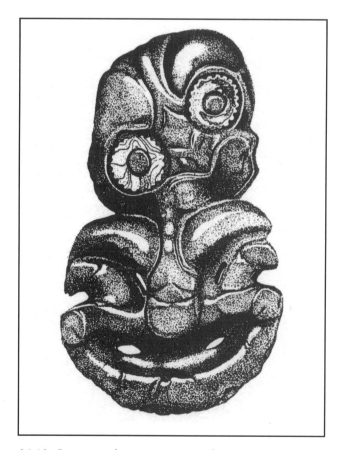

24.18. Greenstone breast ornament (*tiki*)

25

MORIORI

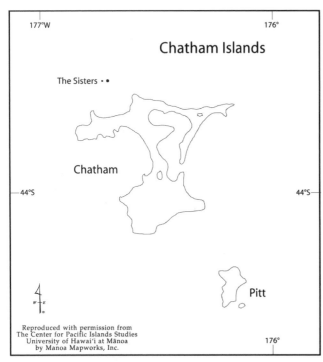

25.1 Chatham Islands

The Chatham Islands lie about 540 miles due east of the New Zealand City of Christchurch. The principal island, Rekohua (renamed Chatham), has an area of about 347 square miles, of which 72 are occupied by a shallow lagoon. Next in size is Rangiavuria (renamed Pitt), about 24 square miles in area. The archipelago also included other smaller islands and rocky reefs, but only Chatham and Pitt were permanently occupied. All the islands are emergent parts of a submarine ridge and are largely volcanic in origin, being topographically rugged, with cliffs, flats, peat bogs, sand beaches, etc. Their climate, which is influenced mainly by strong westerly winds (the Roaring Forties) and the convergence of cold water from the south and warm currents from the north, includes "almost incessant wind . . . , near-constant cloud cover, low sunshine hours, wet winters, and humid summers" (King 1989, 17).

Mean maximum temperatures range from 64 degrees Fahrenheit in summer to 51 degrees Fahrenheit in winter, mean minimum ones from 50 degrees Fahrenheit in summer to 40 degrees Fahrenheit in winter, with rainfall averaging about forty inches a year—not your Hollywood version of a Polynesian Paradise! On the other hand, the islands and their waters were home to or gathering places for numerous kinds and quantities of birds, marine mammals, fish and shellfish, and their soils provided many useful plants—for food, clothing and shelter.

Such were the islands when their first human inhabitants arrived about A.D 1200–1300 (according to archaeologists' consensus). And while they were windier, mistier, and much smaller than their settlers' homeland, their temperature and rainfall and many of their potentially useful natural resources were similar. It is firmly established that the pioneer settlers of the Chathams, the ancestors of the people now known as Moriori, originated in New Zealand, their language having been a dialectical variant of Maori and their tools and weapons closely similar to those of the Archaic phase of Maori cultural history. But unlike the pioneer settlers of New Zealand, whose migration voyages, from Eastern Polynesia, were at least fourteen hundred crow-fly miles longer—and likely undertaken deliberately for discovery and colonization—the one or more pioneer voyages to the Chathams were probably accidental, i.e., trading or resettlement expeditions along the eastern coast of New Zealand that were blown off course and carried by the westerly winds and currents that prevailed in those waters.

The islands were "rediscovered" in 1791 by crew members of HMS *Chatham*, one of the two ships of Vancouver's expedition, which, along with successive "invasions" by both Westerners and other Maori were to change most of the culture developed locally by the Moriori before it had been examined and recorded by competent, on-the-spot observers. Some aspects of the pre-(Western) contact culture—e.g., tools and weapons, boats, subsistence techniques, religious beliefs and practices—have since been reconstructed by archival research, by twentieth-century interrogation of aged native survivors and, more recently, by skillful and perspicacious archaeological research,[225] but information concerning precontact social relations is sketchy and fated to remain so.

The first disastrous impacts were made by crews of the numerous Western sealer and whaler vessels that visited Chatham waters between 1809 and 1838 and that virtually exterminated their once large population of seals, thereby eliminating the Moriori's principal supply of animal food and clothing. In addition to which, the rats, cats and dogs introduced by the sealers and other early Outsiders killed or drove away many of the food-supplying birds. Also, the diseases introduced by the Outsiders killed off scores of Moriori and afflicted many of the rest of them with disabling diseases. Nevertheless, and despite the presence among them of several Western settlers, much of the Moriori's way of life remained intact (e.g., in the absence of Christian missionaries their religious beliefs and practices did not change). That surviving way of life was, however, almost completely destroyed by an invasion of fellow Polynesians.

In 1835 two shiploads of some nine hundred musket-armed Maori from the south of North Island (near the present city of Wellington) set out to colonize the Chathams, having been given to believe that they were resource rich and there for the taking. (By that time, and abetted by an endless supply of muskets, obtained from Westerners in exchange for flax, wars of conquest had become epidemic among Maori tribes.) Upon landing they spread out over Chatham Island, "taking" land by walking over it and either killing (and usually eating) or enslaving the Moriori—the latter, despite their superior numbers and at least equal physical strength, having offered no physical resistance, in conformance with their age-old morality-based prohibition of warfare (see below). Of the some 1,663 Moriori believed to have been alive at that time, 118 men and 108 women were killed—along with an uncounted number of children.[226] By 1862 another 1,336 had died as a result

of starvation, back-breaking enforced toil, beatings, sexual abuse, their Maori masters' appetites for human flesh—and "despair," leaving a total of 101 more or less alive but bereft of their former way of life. No wonder, then, that by the time interested, knowledgeable—and sympathetic—inquirers sought information about their precontact social relations they had to depend on the memories of a few aged survivors (instead of, for example, the large quantity of eyewitness accounts available to students of indigenous [New Zealand] Maori culture).

Summarizing what is credibly recorded about the Moriori's precontact culture, I begin with food getting.

Although the Chatham Islands were suitable for growing sweet potatoes (some varieties having been grown there after contact), the ancestors of the Moriori either did not have seed stock with them on their colonizing voyage(s)—which is understandable if those voyages had been accidental—or they had abandoned horticulture sometime after arrival—perhaps because of the abundance of wild foods. Among the latter were several familiar homeland (i.e., New Zealand) plants, particularly fernroot, the kernel nuts of the *karaka* tree (*Corynocarpus laevigata*), the pith of the *nikau* palm (*Robalostylis sapida*), and seaweed. Of the numerous species of birds found on the islands, wood pigeons, rails and ducks were the most sought after—especially ducks, which congregated by the thousands on Chatham Island's large lagoon. However, the bulk of the people's animal foods came from the sea and included fish, shellfish, sea lions, seals and whales. Seals, especially, were a staple, and before Westerners had hunted them to extinction thousands of them used the islands as breeding grounds. As for whales, pods of the small blackfish, or "pilot," species occasionally stranded themselves on the beaches, where they were thankfully received as gifts from sea gods. The abundance of the above animal foods more than compensated the Moriori for absence of dogs and rats (which their Maori ancestors were accustomed to eat).

The principal garments of the Moriori were capes, and sometimes loincloths, both made of seal skins or flax matting. And speaking of body coverings, for reasons that can only be guessed at the contact-era Moriori did not engage in tattooing.[227]

Except for the absence of pile-built food-storage buildings, Moriori houses were of the same general types as those of the Maori: small lean-to circular huts for shelter during summer food-collection camping, and larger rectangular buildings for the colder months—the latter having had small adjacent cooking sheds (which were off-limits to men). The dwellings were semisubterranean and without vertical side walls, presumably for better weatherproofing, and the fronts of them were made of wooden slabs.

More distinctive were Moriori watercraft, which though shaped something like a broad-beam canoe were in fact rafts—an adjustment to the islands' lack of trees of sufficient size and quality for building Maori-type dugout hulls. The rafts varied considerably in size but were all constructed in the same way, namely, by attaching bundles of flax or kelp to a cratelike wooden frame, which allowed water to pass through but provided enough buoyancy and stability to keep it afloat in the islands' generally rough seas. Lacking sails, the rafts were propelled by rowing or (stern) sculling—not, interesting to note, by paddling.

According to much later recollections by survivors, at time of first Western contact the Moriori numbered about two thousand, thereby constituting a population density of about five persons per square mile. Analysis of skeletal materials from burials reveals a life expectancy of about twenty-two years—but which, discounting a very high rate of infant mortality, would have extended the average age at death to sometime in the thirties. Of course, as Michael King adds, "[Some] individuals lived longer—but not much longer. The few forty-year-olds would have been venerable elders" (1989, 35).

Putting together small bits of evidence: the Moriori lived in extended-family groups (*whanaunga*) that ranged in size from ten to fifty persons and that in all likelihood were similar to Maori *whanau* in many important ways. And according to other bits of evidence, the Moriori were divided into seven territorially distinct "tribes" (*tua imi*), which appear to have been closely similar to Maori tribal *hapu*: they bore similar names (e.g., Edchi or Eti, corresponding with Maori Ngati or Ati), and were "ruled" by Ieriki, who were "heaven-born" (i.e., godliness endowed) hereditary chiefs. There was, however, one crucial difference between Maori and Moriori tribes during that era—i.e. the latter did not engage in intertribal warfare, a trait that, according to legend, began when an individual named Nunuku-whenua, having become mentally sickened by bloodshed (and the prospect of subsequent cannibalism) during a fight between two tribes, pushed between their ranks and ordered them to cease. Whereupon they did so, and upon further orders from the peacemaker burned their weapons, embraced one another (nose to nose), and agreed never to make war or eat human flesh again—all in obedience to Nunuku and in fear of his curse: "May your bowels rot the day you disobey."[228]

In any case, however factual the legend, or whatever the true cause of this remarkable society-wide abolition, at time of Western contact and thereafter angry differences between men were resolved by individual combat, with wooden staves, until blood was drawn. This was, altogether, a highly meritorious renouncement, which distinguished the Moriori not only from most other Polynesians but from most other human peoples as well, but one that led, eventually, to their near extinction at the hands of their Maori (distant) cousins, for whom warfare continued for decades to be a fundamental part of life.

26

EPILOGUE

What is the purpose, beyond idle curiosity, of learning about the lives of the Early Polynesians? Not that idle curiosity is an insufficient reason; for the Polynesians were a remarkable branch of humankind, who though isolated from the high civilizations of the East and West for thousands of years had, with only Stone Age tools and without mechanical navigational devices, succeeded in discovering scores of islands spread over an ocean area about the size of the mainland United States, centuries before any other peoples elsewhere had ventured more than a few hundred miles beyond their shores, and had—again with only Stone Age tools—succeeded in colonizing a very wide variety of physical environments, some of them exceedingly limited in life-sustaining resources. Aside from idle curiosity, however, there are several good reasons, humanistic and scientific, for learning about the Early Polynesians.

One, specifically humanistic, reason has to do with the historical effects that Westerners' "discovery" of Polynesia had upon the West—namely, how their observations about the Polynesians and their natural surroundings served to stimulate and provide substance for the Western sciences of geography, biology, and ethnology, and for the Romantic Movements in fine arts and social philosophy.[229]

Another, more specifically "scientific," purpose served by studying Polynesian cultures has to do with the lessons to be learned from them about human behavior in general by comparing their several historically related cultures to learn, for example, the extent to which their behaviors were shaped by their genes, to what extent by their cultures—such as the correlation, if any, between their methods of horticulture and their settlement patterns, or their religious beliefs and their political organizations, or their methods of child training and their kinship relations—or, more comprehensively, what kinds of institutions served to promote such "desirable" (albeit not altogether likely) situations as "peace," "equality," and "prosperity," as against "war," "inequality," and "poverty." [230] I share the view of many social scientists that sufficient conclusions about such matters cannot be obtained from study of any one or any randomly selected few of the thousands of mankind's cultures—that in order for conclusions to be as accurate and representative as possible the comparisons must include data from a wide variety of cultures, including those stereotyped as "primitive." Moreover, the accuracy of the conclusions is enhanced to the degree that the comparisons are "controlled"; that is to say, that the phenomena being compared, in this case the cultures, include as few variables as possible—that they are alike in many more ways than they differ. Thus, little if anything of scientific accuracy can be discovered about the causes of, say, suicide—or thievery, or infant mortality, or religious dogmatism or altruism, etc.—by comparing their incidence and their social and economic contexts in, say, a nineteenth-century village in New England and an eighteenth-century one in Italy or China. On the other hand, there is much to be learned by seeking causes of many cultural phenomena by comparing their differences and their social-economic contexts in two or more Early Polynesian societies, because of the many cultural practices and beliefs their peoples shared. And even more can be learned about such causes if the units compared were of about the same size—e.g., single communities in Tahiti, Samoa, and New Zealand.

As the reader will have concluded, the present book has not focused on those humanistic and scientific aspects of Early Polynesian societies, but in closing it some paragraphs will be devoted to evaluating their members' beliefs and practices in terms of certain standards regarded by many Westerners to be essential for the continued existence of any human society.

During the sixteenth through nineteenth centuries Westerners characterized themselves—along with ancient Greeks, Romans and a few other ancient and imperial Oriental peoples—as "civilized" and all others as "barbaric," or downright "primitive." (Some Westerners, mainly intellectuals—influenced by the reports of explorers and navigators, softened that judgment about some of the latter by labeling them *noble savages*," an appellation that was applied especially to Tahitians. However, for many, perhaps most, Westerners that older characterization of some peoples as "primitives" has persisted—although modified somewhat by calling some of their customs "quaint" or "picturesque," because, perhaps, they were no longer considered "dangerous.")

Then, beginning about seven decades ago, some social scientists, including anthropologists, declared that, technology and literacy aside, no people's culture was superior to any other—a position that was influenced by the increasing political liberalism of those intellectuals and reinforced by their own and others' field studies among "primitives" (which often resulted in sympathetic attachment to "their" natives).

But after a time, some other social scientists, persuaded perhaps in part by the Holocaust, sought to temper that doctrine of "absolute" cultural relativity by advocating that some cultures were indeed "better" than others in ways besides technology and literacy, and proposed criteria for evaluating them in terms of those ways. Some of their criteria resembled those of biological evolutionists when evaluating the behaviors of an animal species with respect to their effect upon that species' survival—an approach, as summarized in Lorenz (1966) and Storr (1968), that, when applied to human cultures, asked, "How effectively does a culture, viewed as an instrument, ensure the continuity of its adherents' existence as a distinct society?"

One of the most comprehensive and systematic approaches to this question is titled "The Functional Prerequisites of a Society" (Aberle et al. 1950), whose authors begin by listing the four conditions that in their view could terminate the existence of a society and the nine ways by which it could thrive.

The four "terminating" situations are (1) "the biological extinction or dispersion of the members," (2) the "apathy" of most of its members—i.e., "the cessation of individual motivation," (3) "the war of all against all," and (4) "the absorption of the society into another society."

A review of what is known about Polynesian societies suggests that some of them had indeed ceased to exist because of "biological extinction"—e.g., those small bands of colonists (i.e., the nuclei of future societies) that had been lost at sea or had died of starvation on desert islands. Moreover, at least one society, the Mor_iori, had been nearly extinguished and the remainder absorbed, as slaves, by Maori adventurers. And although a "war of all against all" had extinguished large segments of some societies (e.g., Rangiroa, Maori, Mangaia), those societies themselves had survived. As for "apathy": I know of no case in which that situation had been deep and extensive enough to cause the disunity of a whole society, although in at least one case large numbers of Hawaiians had forsaken their homes and their family responsibilities and gone "on the road" (Sahlins 1992).

Turning to the "functional prerequisites" for maintaining a society in "good health," the authors of the study list nine:

(1) "Provision for adequate relationship to the environment and for sexual recruitment." I judge that Polynesian societies were effective on both counts. They exhibited remarkable ability for obtaining enough food and shelter in a number of different and in many cases austere environments. And their rules regarding sexual activity were flexible enough to ensure population replacement whatever the society's size.

(2) "Role differentiation and role assignment." In this "condition" Polynesian societies were more than adequate. Nearly all roles were very clearly defined, and most of them were assigned by birth—the rest having been reached and occupied by well-known and widely sanctioned means.

(3) "Communication" (i.e., "No society, however simple, can exist without shared, learned, symbolic modes of communication"). In some Polynesian societies a few different words were used when addressing equals or superiors, but such differences were universally known. Also, in a few large and widely spread societies there had developed several local differences in vocabulary, but rarely to a degree that can be labeled "dialects." Moreover, all Polynesian languages

were alike enough for speakers of one of them to converse in another within a fairly short time.

(4) "Shared cognitive orientation." As previously noted, in the largest societies there were numerous differences, among individuals and between locales, about cosmogony and cosmology and religious practice, but not enough to create the kinds of religious or philosophical or ethical fissions that divide some societies elsewhere.

(5) "A shared, articulated set of goals." To begin with, the "goals" of all Polynesian peoples seem to have been limited to those of the Ao, the mortal everyday world—i.e., generally speaking, individuals did not act in ways aimed at securing a desirable existence in the afterlife, in the Po. (Indeed, with a very few possible exceptions Polynesian religious beliefs contained no promises of rewards or punishments in the afterlife for this or that kind of this-life behavior.) As for this-life goals, it can be assumed that everyone—like most humans elsewhere—wished for plenty of food, bodily comfort, satisfying sex (for those still able), some public esteem and occasional diversions. For most Polynesians those goals were obtainable, having been assured at birth by (a) a generally fruitful subsistence economy (except, of course, in times of famine, or in periodically unfruitful places such as Mangareva and in Mangaia's unproductive zones; (b) adequate housing and clothing, even on Easter Island and New Zealand; (c) a sufficiently flexible regime of sexual choice; (d) opportunities for gaining public esteem through expertise in a number of activities; and an ideology that did not favor "work for work's sake" nor disfavor repose and pleasurable diversion. In addition, most persons appear to have cherished, and experienced, living in familial surroundings and among large numbers of supportive relatives. Even Hawai'i's underclass (i.e., *kauwā*) had enough to eat, etc., as did Maori slaves—except of course when they themselves became food for others. For some Polynesians, however, "enough" meant "more" than was readily available: more food delicacies, more public esteem, etc.—and especially more authority over other persons. And while competition for some positions of high esteem provoked envy and enmity, and rivalry for high authority often involved destructive conflict, such competition and its outcomes were within the bounds of convention.

(6) "The normative regulation of means"—in other words, society-sanctioned rules for attaining its common goals. To begin with, belief was that the only rules that gods enforced—typically by death or physical injury or failed crops or shipwrecks, etc.—were those in support of their own personal interests. Similarly, for rules concerning behavior among humans, it was in most cases left to the individual to enforce those affecting his own interests. For example, tribe chiefs, clan seniors, and community headmen themselves customarily enforced rules affecting their own authorities and privileges; families customarily punished the injurer of one of their own members; husbands customarily killed or maimed their wives' seducers or rapists; etc. There were here and there institutions that resembled courts of law—such as the *fono* of Samoa, the Council of Elders of Pukapuka, and the *muru* parties of the Maori. Also, numerous tribemates sometimes cooperated to curb or even replace or kill a chief who was thought to exceed his authority and privileges. But otherwise, an infraction of even tribe-wide norms was not usually punished by tribe-wide action (except when a chief mobilized his tribe on behalf of his own personal interests).

(7) "The regulation of affective expression"—i.e., regulation of emotions, such as violence-producing anger, overt display of disrespect toward persons of authority, and excessive expression of sexual desire as exemplified in rape and incest (as locally defined). As just noted, while such "expressions" were counter to tribe- or society-wide norms (except when directed against a tribe's enemies), their regulation was usually undertaken only by the individual, and his close supporters, injured in some way by those "expressions."

(8) "Socialization"—i.e., "How effective do [Polynesians'] cultures ensure that every individual will acquire a working knowledge of the behaviors and attitudes relevant to his roles?" Except for some periods devoted to "play," nearly all Polynesians spent their early years with adults—observing, imitating, and being instructed by the latter in their various everyday activities—surely, a more direct and effective way of learning about those activities than being taught about them, formally and secondhand, in schools. As for the formal schooling—mainly in priestcraft and chronicling—that took place in a few societies, that involved only a handful of "students"

and prepared them specifically for highly specialized jobs.

(9) "The effective control of affective behavior." This "condition" is similar to those of both (6) and (7) and requires no further comment here.

From the above, one must conclude that Early Polynesian cultures, viewed as "instruments," were largely effective in ensuring the continuity of their peoples' societies. However, what is only indirectly dealt with in the above method of evaluation is the nonphysiological well-being of the individuals making up those societies.

As just noted, the basic physiological needs of most individual Polynesians seem to have been fairly well satisfied. The same was true of their nonphysiological (i.e., psychological) wants—which were of course shaped by an ideology of ascriptive hierarchy and of male superiority, that ideology having been flexible enough to allow a few men to rise in the hierarchy by personal achievement. It was also flexible enough to allow a number of women to overcome some of their ascribed disabilities and rise to positions of political influence. Nevertheless, given the institution of slavery (which existed in only a few societies), the almost insurmountable inequalities of females (found in most societies), the class-based discriminations (found in nearly all of them), and the outright tyrannies (practiced in many of them), such flexibility fell far short of the ideal of "the supreme worth and equality and moral responsibility of each and every individual" that is enshrined in the ideologies of some Western democracies—but not altogether common in their practices! However, it is unlikely that any Polynesian could have known about or felt deprived of the individual rights enshrined in any other ideology but that of his own society's.[231] Moreover, it is unlikely that the Polynesians, as a people, would have survived, proliferated, and spread out so widely without a certain amount of ascribed or achieved social inequality among adult males: the evident success of so many of their widespread colonizations could in all probability not have been attained without some form of institutionalized leadership.

NOTES

1. I.e., *575* crow-fly miles; because of contrary winds the actual distance traveled by the canoes would have been considerably longer (Irwin 1992, 66–68). NOTE WELL that all distances, on land and sea, given in this book will be in statute miles (i.e., one mile = 5,280 feet), and all other measures (e.g., lengths, breadths, heights, depths, weights, etc.) in the English system of feet, inches, and pounds. This departure from the more "scientific" metric system is done reluctantly, but for the convenience of nonscientist readers, for whom the book is written.

2. Ethnic: "of, belonging to, or distinctive of a particular racial, cultural, or language division of mankind" (Funk and Wagnalls *Standard College Dictionary*, text ed.).

3. For a critique of these labels see Green 1991.

4. The best of which, in English, are Archey 1979; Bellwood 1987; Buck 1938b; Goldman 1970; E.S.C. Handy 1927; Howard and Borofsky 1989; Jennings 1979; Kirch 1984; Luomala 1951; Sahlins 1958; and Suggs 1960.

5. To reconstruct the cultures as they were "at or soon after" Western contacts is at least the aim of parts Two and Three—an aim that is, however, difficult if not impossible to achieve in some instances, inasmuch as some of the cultures were competently studied only decades after contact.

6. For an authoritative and highly readable synopsis of human evolution in general see William Howells' *Getting Here* (1993).

7. For more recent (and highly technical) findings on this issue see articles by John F. Relethford and by Gregory J. Adcock et al. in *Proceedings of the National Academy of Sciences of the United States of America*, vol. 98, no. 2, January 16, 2001.

8. Needless to say, archaeologists differ somewhat concerning this and subsequent dates listed in this chapter—a characteristic of even the best practitioners of the profession! Such differences, however, do not distort the succession of the events being outlined, or the "about whens" they happened. For a recent summary of those events see Irwin 1992 and several reviews of that work in Green et al. 1998.

9. Many linguists have replaced "Papuan" with non-Austronesian" (usually shortened to "NAN") in recognition of the assumed historical diversity of those languages.

10. Similarly, during roughly the same era, one or more other groups of Oceanic speakers ventured forth from the Solomons and successfully reached the uninhabited Gilbert or Marshall Islands or both—which were even further from their starting points than were the voyages to Fiji. From those landfalls the descendants of some of them ventured westward and colonized the eastern and central Carolines (the western Carolines and the Marianas having been colonized, probably earlier, by Malayo-Polynesian speakers from the southern Philippines and northern Celebes).

11. For a discussion of this topic, including some opposing views, see Spriggs 1997 and Yen 1998.

12. For a comprehensive report on these findings see Kirch 1997.

13. The authors of a 1993 genetic study of prehistoric bones found in Fiji and Polynesia have stated that the more recent of them (from Tonga, Makatea, Hawai'i, New Zealand and the Chatham Islands), which have been dated at 700 to 300 B.P. (Before Present), contain an Asia-specific DNA characteristic, whereas the oldest of them (from Fiji, Tonga and Samoa), dated at 2,700 to 2,200 B.P., do not, thereby leading to their conclusion that the original migrations to the region contained few if any of what I call "Mongoloid" genes. However, as the authors of this study caution, the bone samples they used were too small, and perhaps contaminated by handling, to permit irrefutable proof of the truth of their "findings" (Hagelberg and Clegg 1993).

14. In due course the Lapitans remaining in Fiji mixed, physically and culturally, with the later, darker-skinned immigrants, thereby engendering another distinctive physical type and culture. But that is another story, told elsewhere (e.g., Frost 1979; Sahlins 1962; and summarized in Oliver 1989b and c).

15. Here and throughout this book the letter ' in native words represents the glottal stop, a true consonant found in all Polynesian languages. The same sound occurs in spoken English, as, for example, before the second "oh" in the exclamation "oh-oh!," and in some individuals' pronunciation of, say, "bottle" (i.e., "bo'ul"); in neither case, however, is the sound phonemic—i.e., meaningfully significant, as it is in Polynesian speech.

16. For a cautionary view about assigning meanings to a reconstructed proto-Polynesian word for nonmaterial phenomena see Sutton 1996.

17. As this book was being prepared for publication,

there appeared a large volume authored by Patrick Kirch and Roger Green titled *Hawaiki: Ancestral Polynesia* (Cambridge University Press), which examines with critical acumen the glosses of some 620 Proto-Polynesian (PPN) lexical reconstructions achieved by them and other scholars and representing all domains of culture—material, social, and ideological, thereby producing a greatly enlarged and enriched picture of early Polynesian life. This remarkable accomplishment, produced by combining archaeology (the authors' primary profession) with linguistics and comparative ethnography, provides a solid foundation for research concerning the continuities and transformations experienced by the thirty or so Polynesian peoples since their survival in or dispersal from the Polynesian homeland.

18. They had also discovered and made attempts to colonize twelve other so-called "Mystery Islands" within the triangle—including Necker, Pitcairn and Fanning—as evidenced by material remains of their presence there, but had either moved on or died out there by European times.

19. The "how" and "when" matters discussed in this chapter are most comprehensively, and recently, treated in Irwin 1992 and by reviews thereof in Davidson et al. 1997. See also Green 1998.

20. These judgments about paddling are based on experiments with an eighteenth-century–type Hawaiian canoe, but are doubtless relevant to the performance of their ancient forerunners.

21. Population figures—most of them rough estimates and all of them recent—for the Outlier islands are given in Bayard's monograph and are reproduced in chapter 6.

22. "Wave" theory was also proposed in some early writings about the anatomical characterizations of the Polynesians, as will be noted in chapter 6.

23. One question concerning the "fairly soon" hypothesis of dispersal is Had those colonizers already "become" Polynesians before setting out or were they culturally still Lapitans?—a question that is not as quibbling, ethnologically, as it may appear.

24. Namely, from north to south: Nukuoro, Kapingamarangi, Nuguria, Takuu, Nukumanu, Ontong Java, Sikaiana, Rennell, Bellona, Pileni, Taumako, Tikopia, Anuta, Emae, Mele, Fila, West Uvea, Aniwa and West Futuna.

25. Words are said to be "cognate" if they are derived from the same "ancestral" form—thus, English "father" is cognate with German "vater" (both clearly derived from ancestral Old English "faeder"), but not with, say, Tahitian "metua tane" (parent-male), Tahitian being an Austronesian language, totally unrelated to English and German and other Indo-European languages.

26. Leaving aside their initial, patently mythical ancestors, the lengthiest and most detailed—and perhaps most authentic—genealogies are those of Tonga's chiefly dynasties, as recorded by Elizabeth Bott in her *Tongan Society At the Time of Captain Cook's Visits* (1982).

27. For the sake of brevity the word "tropical" will henceforth be used to include "subtropical" Polynesia as well.

28. These and other climatic conditions listed here prevail not only now but likely have done so in tropical Polynesia throughout the period of settlement there. For more detailed discussions of both winds and currents see Irwin 1992 and Finney 1994b.

29. One notable physiographic effect of the trade-wind pattern is in coral formation, which tends to be more prolific along leeward—i.e., more protected—shores. Also, the dominance of such winds, especially when accompanied by rain, has shaped most high islands by sculpturing steeper slopes on their windward sides.

30. For a record of recent damages to Polynesian islands from high winds, tsunami, earthquakes and volcanic action see Hamnett n.d.

31. For a readable summary of the entire topic see Kay 1980.

32. This classification, in Papy 1954, applies particularly to the Society Islands; it goes without saying that no two archipelagoes contain identical types of vegetation zones.

33. Speaking of compass points, while they were referred to in connection with the sources of winds and, in some instances, with the location of distant places, most locational specifications were in terms of an object or a person being *makai* ("toward the sea," "farther seaward") or being *mauka* ("toward the land," "farther inland").

34. The most heated present-day controversy about such numbers concerns the Hawaiian Islands, for which estimates range from 200,000, the figure proposed by the Hawai'i state demographer, R. C. Schmitt (1968, 1971) and widely favored by archaeologists, to 1,000,000, the figure argued for by the historian D. E. Stannard (1990)—in order, perhaps, to emphasize the cataclysmic effects of Western contact upon Hawaiians, who at their first systematic census, of 1831-2, numbered only about 124,049.

35. Reference here is to the technological measures, such as irrigation, undertaken by some peoples to increase the productivity of limited areas of land.

36. As for example in a public proclamation by a chief's principal spokesman: "For the man who sleeps

with his wife, and who ejaculates, let him beget only two children, one a boy and one a girl—the boy for obtaining coconuts the girl for keeping the water bottle (i.e., those along with the father and mother being enough for maintaining a family). But if a man persists in begetting more than the two there will be not enough coconuts and other resources to feed them, so that they will end up by stealing nuts etc. from others" (Firth 1967, 263–76).

37. For details concerning this method see Clark 1979; Crowley 1992; and Pawley 1996. See also Biggs 1994 for some caveats regarding its use.

38. For other examples of Polynesian mythic themes see Kaeppler 1987.

39. The *Kumulipo* has been "recovered," translated, edited and interpreted by several scholars. The version summarized here, the Kalākaua Text, is that of Martha Beckwith, a noted folklorist who devoted many years to its preparation. Another, more recent, more comprehensive, and pictorially illustrated version of the chant, along with a translation, is that of the eminent historian Rubellite Kawena Johnson, who adds many descriptive and interpretative enlargements and contextualizes the chant in wide-ranging descriptions of Hawaiian natural history—altogether, a gem of a publication.

40. For some other types of (poetically expressed) cosmogonies see chapter 8.

41. Fischer's study, representing years of research, includes a detailed account of the history of the controversy and an analysis of the surviving tablets. It does not merely "suggest" but convincingly argues that the *rongorongo* script was an invention by Easter Islanders in imitation of European writing.

42. According to the ethnographer of the Kunimaipa people of New Guinea, when they were asked to describe the abode of spirits the reply was, "I don't know, I've never been there—have you?" Or when asked what supernatural punishment occurred to survivors who did not pay proper ritual respect to a dead human's bones, a common reply was, "How would I know? Bones don't talk" (McArthur 2000).

43. "Respective" because of evidence that each Polynesian people's cosmology contained some features that were distinctive, along with some that were shared by many or all—the latter being the main subject matter of this chapter.

44. Examples of the (imagined) nature of that something follow.

45. I am also reluctant to use the word "supernatural," because, although most of the beings Polynesians placed in this category were believed to be super (i.e., superior in power, etc.) to most humans, all except the

otiose (i.e., withdrawn) ones were very much constituents of their everyday lives. Nor can the phrase "immaterial being" be used to describe all of them; for, as noted below, I am uncertain whether such and such a god was thought to "control," say, a volcano or "was" that volcano.

46. As will be mentioned in Part Three, some early reports on Maori (New Zealand) cosmologies contain references to a god named Io (which also meant "core"), who was said to have been "supreme," the creator of all other gods, etc., but whose identity and characteristics were known only to a few "highest" priests, who kept their knowledge—and their associated cult practices—secret from all other persons. Similar examples of "secret" cultism have been "discovered" by Western writers in a few other Polynesian societies, but critics are skeptical of their authenticity as wholly precontact concepts.

47. As noted earlier, Polynesia-wide stories about Maui have been brought together in a delightful book by Katherine Luomala (1949).

48. While word-perfect delivery may have been necessary in order to please the addressee god, it is also possible that the words themselves, correctly delivered, were "magical"—i.e., that they themselves were believed to bring about the desired effects: a possibility that can no longer be tested.

49. Albeit, gods themselves were believed to behave, now and then, in "improper" ways, including flagrant incest.

50. In many if not most societies the title of *ariki*—or some cognate thereof—was applied to its most eminent firstborns, namely the seniors of its largest or most venerable or most politically ascendant clans.

51. In one documented case in Tahiti a "possessed" commoner succeeded in gaining enough of a following to pose a threat not only to the orthodox priesthood but to his tribal chief as well—an analogue to some of the evangelistic leaders of twentieth-century America.

52. For recent reviews of the various explications of these words see Keesing 1984 and Shore 1989.

53. In conversations with twentieth-century Tahitians (see Oliver 1981) they sometimes referred to certain contemporary politicians and bureaucrats as *mea mana* (i.e., "powerful")—without, I think, implying that their "power" was to any degree "divine." This suggests that ancient Polynesians, or at least ancient Tahitians, might also have used the word *mana* in that nonreligious sense.

54. For these and other Polynesian tools and their manufacture the reader is referred to the many books on material culture written by Peter Buck.

55. The few sherds found recently in the southern Cook Islands appear to have been of Tongan manufacture (Irwin 1992, 76).

56. The only peoples in pre-Western Oceania who practiced "true" (i.e. loom) weaving were in the Caroline Islands, to which the craft had diffused from the Indonesian Archipelago.

57. Buck describes one highly valued Hawaiian needle as having been made from the shinbone of an expert fisherman, who was without hair on his limbs: "As fish were said to be attracted by the bones of such individuals, he was slain to provide material for fishing implements" (Buck 1957, 292).

58. The standardizing function of the gage, named *afa* in several Polynesian languages, was extended metaphorically to other activities, as illustrated by the Samoan phrase "When all the opinions are made from the same *afa*, that matter is settled" (Buck 1930, 270).

59. For more on Hawaiian and Tahitian featherwork see Rose 1978. And for excellent color reproductions of some Hawaiian and Tahitian befeathered objects—and for other kinds of Polynesian artifacts as well, see Kaeppler 1978.

60. For an excellent account of Hawaiian barkcloth decoration—in fact, of all Hawaiian uses of plants, see Abbott 1992.

61. The fact that they had intrinsic value, for clothing, bedding, etc., and were not exchangeable for all other kinds of objects and services, makes them fall short of what some economists call "true money"—but even in Western money-based societies "there are some things that money can't buy."

62. As someone once said, "Primitive art is what we [Westerners] call 'art' done by people we call 'primitive.'" Except for their lack of writing and of metal tools, the Polynesians cannot be stereotyped as "primitive"—but the comment is otherwise apposite.

63. This taxonomy is of course "etic" (i.e., nonnative, Outsider), being that of Western art historians using Western principles of aesthetic classification. It would be appropriate to report how ancient Polynesians described and classified the visual aspects of their sculptures, but known records of such information do not exist. Even Ralph Linton's pioneer study of Marquesan views on the subject (1941) was made more than a century after full-scale Westernization had commenced.

64. The literature on tropical Polynesians' "embellishments" (i.e., in Western terms their "Art") is rich. For a guide to such literature see Kaeppler 1989. Their "markings" on people's bodies were especially numerous and varied, as will be described.

65. An example of token pudency is reported by Ralph Linton: "Even when [Marquesans were] entirely nude the Marquesan sense of modesty required that the head of the penis should be covered. The foreskin, which was split but not removed in the native form of circumcision [i.e., supercision], was drawn over it and confined by a ligature" (1923, 416).

66. In the Marquesas, where the whole of a male's body was sometimes tattooed, the phrase "completely covered with tattoo" is compounded of a word meaning "to cry a long time," and a word meaning "a wound that inspires horror" (W. C. Handy 1922, 23).

67. I have consulted specific local descriptions of tattooing in Buck (1930 for Samoa, 1938a for Mangareva, and 1944 for Cook Islands); Burrows (1936 for Futuna, 1937 for Uvea); Emory (1946 for Hawai'i); W. C. Handy (1922 for Marquesas); Linton (1923 for Marquesas); Metraux (1940 for Easter Island); Oliver (1974 for Tahiti); and Roth (1905 for Tahiti and 1906 for Tonga). Most of the above, on tattooing, is excellently summarized by R.W. Sparks in his unpublished "Polynesian Tattooing: the Techniques, Iconography, Patronage, Profession, and Esthetics" (1965), which is deposited in the Hamilton Library of the University of Hawai'i. In what follows I have drawn extensively on Sparks's manuscript, and wish to acknowledge with many thanks my debt to him and to the Graduate School Council for permission to utilize it.

68. For a minutely detailed description of tattooing implements, see the publications of Peter Buck, listed in the Bibliography.

69. A different technique, used in Tokelau and in the Ellis Islands (now known as Tuvalu), and probably derived from Micronesia, consisted of first painting the design on the skin and then tapping it into the skin.

70. For a detailed study of Marquesan tattoo designs see Handy 1922; Steinen 1925; and Garanger 1998.

71. Maori (i.e., New Zealand) tattooing was also distinctive in some respects, as will be described in Part Three.

72. For authoritative summaries concerning the origin and distribution of this and other Pacific, including Polynesian, food plants, see Yen 1998.

73. "A range of disciplines also support a dual origin for . . . the South American bottle gourd (*Lagenaria siceraria*) in the Pacific. One by Europeans from the west, [and] as far east as Fiji and western Polynesia, the other from the east, during the 11-12 centuries A.D. and thence to New Zealand." Roger Green, *JPS* 109 (2): 191-97. Although the bottle gourd was cultivated by several Polynesian peoples for use as a container, in a few places, including New Zealand, it served also as a food.

74. This distinction, first characterized by the French ethnobotanist J. Barrau (1965), has been adopted and amplified by the archaeologist P. V. Kirch (1984).

75. There were, however, some exceptions—for example in Tahiti it was claimed that occasionally a boar became "possessed" by a war god, which converted it into a demonic creature capable of consuming a chief and all his people (Oliver 1974, 273).

76. In Hawai'i the name given to the basic (but not the smallest) official land division was *ahupua'a*, literally "altar-pig," the platform at a division's boundaries on which the division's land rent was placed for collection by agents of its owner-chief.

77. For more on the distribution of dogs see Buck 1938b/1959 and Titcomb 1969.

78. A similar practice prevailed in Hawai'i, as reported in Titcomb 1969, 3–4.

79. Included in Honolulu's Bishop Museum is a collection of leg ornaments, worn by dancers, containing the canine teeth of 2,346 dogs (Buck 1957, 3).

80. Native rats did not long survive the postcontact introduction of cats or were superseded by less "domesticated" breeds from Westerners' ships.

81. It should be recalled that references in this chapter are to tropical Polynesia and do not include New Zealand, whose freshwater faunal resources were more numerous and diverse.

82. The Micronesians of the Gilbert Islands (now Kiribati) topped this method by allowing an octopus to embrace them fully before being hoisted by rope to the surface, where the octopus was then killed. I know of no similar Polynesian practice, but consider the Mangaians' arm-capturing one a close runner-up in potential suicide!

83. See Nordhoff 1930 for a gripping account of recent but seemingly "traditional" Tahitian offshore fishing; or see Oliver 1974 for a résumé of that account. Nordhoff, the coauthor of the fictional *Bounty* trilogy, lived in Tahiti, where he himself became an expert fisherman.

84. In central and peripheral tropical Polynesia, where pottery was lacking (except in the earliest phases of settlement), fishhooks, because of their durability and their relatively frequent changes in shape, have become for archaeologists one of the best diagnostics for classifying phases of cultural change.

85. Only recently has Western science become cognizant of the meteorological and oceanographic events associated with the noncyclic but recurrent El Niño. Whether any Polynesians recognized and made allowances for that complex of phenomena is doubtful.

86. Some temples identified in the literature as "fishermen's" may also have been utilized by nonguildsmen, i.e., by ordinary fishermen for the purpose of supplicating and thank-offering specialized "fishing gods"—a matter which, however, is not clear.

87. Earlier than Firth's stay there the Tikopians had deliberately exterminated—and doubtless eaten—their pigs, because of the animals' inroads on garden produce. For a detailed description of each of the Tikopians' food recipes, see Firth 1936, 103–10.

88. Predictably, Western missionaries and other moralists succeeded in eliminating kava imbibing in many Polynesian societies (thereby unwittingly encouraging the substitution of alcohol), and even where they did not—for example, in Samoa and Tonga—the chewing of the root was replaced by the more "hygienic" method of pulverizing it by mortar and pestle.

89. In using these terms I do not propose to perpetuate them into the already overloaded glossary of anthropological jargon, and promise not to use them outside of this book!

90. The credibility of this account is perhaps (?) strengthened by the fact that Buck himself was half-Polynesian and not given to disparaging his ethnic "cousins," nor prone to be taken in by any of their cock-and-bull inventions—which, in my experience, many present-day Polynesians delight in telling to credulous non-Polynesians.

91. And for detailed information on religious buildings and other material remains, see Jennings 1979.

92. Buck's richly detailed account of the material aspects of such proceedings are too lengthy to quote or even paraphrase here, but merit reading by anyone interested in more than this introductory text.

93. The narrowness of the hulls may have derived from the (hypothesized) circumstance that their prototypes consisted mainly of dugouts, rather than of planks, and that the available trees used in their construction were not thick enough to ensure balancing.

94. One expert prefers to label this element a "yard" rather than a "mast"; hence canoes of this category would be "mastless" (Lewis 1975). Not to worry! In the domain of Polynesian and other Oceanic watercraft there are as many schemes of classification as there are writers on the subject.

95. Conjecture is that the Type Two (i.e., Fijian) arrangement had diffused to Fiji from Micronesia—but that is another story.

96. Confirmation of this practice is given in reports that potential victims scarred in this way were unaccept-

able for human sacrifice—another example of the "contagious" nonsanctity (*noa*) quality of females.

97. Speaking of spouses, and hence the effect of marriage upon an adult's sexual activities, responses to acts of adultery differed not only from individual to individual (as they doubtless do in every human society), but from society to society as well—a difference in this respect having prevailed between those of eastern and western Polynesia.

98. Not however in Tonga, where according to Gifford: "the female attendants upon the daughter of a chief did not allow her to eat too much. This *tapu* was enforced to prevent the overdevelopment of her abdominal region" (1929, 129).

99. For an insightful review of these and other aspects of fattening practices, see Shore 1989.

100. A notable exception (which, as they say, "goes to prove the rule") was the practice in some societies of engaging an older, "experienced," woman to initiate a boy in how to copulate.

101. James's article, just cited, provides a fine description and insightful analysis of the postcontact institutionalization of male effeminacy in Tonga, plus a persuasive argument that such *fakafine* ("men who do women's work") were not only tolerated but respected because of their ability to make fine mats—mat making having been a woman's craft and fine mats the Tongans' most valued "currency."

102. Nor is much guidance contained in Huizinga's classic *Homo Ludens*, which purports to extend the "play element" to law, warfare, poetry, art, etc.

103. For a detailed description and keen analysis of one such match see Raymond Firth's "A Dart Match in Tikopia," in *Oceania*, Vol. I, no. 1.

104. As stated in *Surfing: The Sport of Hawaiian Kings* (Finney and Houston 1966): "The use of a strong board to aid in swimming or for riding the waves . . . wouldn't be too great a step for a water-oriented people. And the step from there to a more organized form of the sport isn't hard to imagine." (4) Much of this chapter's information on surfing is taken from this excellent little book, which calls attention to the pre–nineteenth-century existence of surfboarding not only in other regions of the Pacific but in West Africa as well.

105. After a few decades of Western contact, surfing in Hawai'i nearly ceased, but interest and participation in it was revived at the beginning of the twentieth century and has been growing ever since.

106. For further descriptions of Polynesian dancing the reader is referred to *Australia and the Pacific Islands*, vol. 9 of *The Garland Encyclopedia of World Music*, edited by A. L. Kaeppler and J. W. Love, a 1,088-page richly illustrated collection of articles on the music and dance, both "traditional" and modern, of every indigenous people in the area about whom professionally qualified scholars have studied.

107. Scientifically, it would be useful to attempt to account for this and other cases of uneven trait distribution, but such is not possible in a survey such as the present one.

108. Readers interested in such matters are referred to the following sample: Helen Roberts (1926) and Elizabeth Tatar (1982) on Hawai'i, Jacob Love (1979) and Richard Moyle (1972) on Samoa, Richard Moyle (1987) on Tonga, Mervyn McLean (in Firth 1990) on Tikopia, Edwin Burrows (1933) on the Tuamotus and (1945) on East Uvea and East Futuna, and several articles by other writers in the *International Encyclopedia of World Music*, referred to earlier.

109. For a fuller description of Tahitian theatricals see Oliver 1974, 339–43.

110. It was due in part to this practice that Western visitors often overestimated the sizes of native populations. That is, during their circuits of some islands, usually by ship, and in making estimates of the numbers of persons seen at each stop, they often encountered, and counted, many individuals two or more times.

111. As will be amplified in chapter 21, our definition of "tribe" is a territorially bounded social group composed of one or more communities under overall authority of a chief, or combination of chiefs, who was (or were) under the political authority of no one else anywhere.

112. There were however situations in which "en masse" did not mean every member of the enemy unit—when, for example, a member of one warring unit would, by convention, spare the life of a relative belonging to the enemy unit.

113. Needless to say, any classification of human behaviors—including the present one—is more or less arbitrary. The present one is proposed only for the purpose of economy of presentation, while recognizing that the typology could be made much finer-grained to fit the actual shapes of Polynesian military conflicts. The Polynesians themselves had many words for what they considered "types" of military conflict, but their words applied more to tactics than to the larger-scale classes of behavior here.

114. It has been proposed that such voyages were made by Tongan colonists residing in Fiji, which, if so, would have shortened the voyages somewhat.

115. Examples of such actions include Boraborans'

conquest of Raiatea (Oliver 1974), and Hawai'i Islanders' campaigns against Maui (Kamakau 1961, 85).

116. For a second- or third-hand account of a large-scale Hawaiian battle of conquest see Kamakau 1961, 85.

117. In Hawai'i, however, chiefs themselves were supposed to lead their forces in battle. In fact, in Hawai'i expertise in fighting was, ideally, one of the prime characteristics of chiefs.

118. In the Marquesas, however, where such restrictions were especially severe, it was reported that "women could prevent war by uttering a curse on the road over which the warriors would have to pass, [declaring] 'The road leading to battle is my pudendum.' If warriors passed over [that] road it was believed that they would surely be massacred" (E.S.C. Handy 1923, 135).

119. This inventory is very brief, and its glosses much simplified, out of necessity—i.e., because of the need for brevity and generalization in a book of this kind. In some Polynesian cultures the makeup of an individual's non-palpable anatomy was believed to be considerably more complex. And, needless to say, the translations—or glosses—given here are in some respects oversimplified. Nevertheless, they are the closest I am able to manage in general terms.

120. One exception to this belief was that of the Tikopians, who held that the role of a child's mother in procreation was limited to providing a receptacle for the semen, etc., of the child's father and a "shelter house" for the developing fetus.

121. The anthropologist E. W. Gifford collected about 3,000 different names in use among the 23,750 Tongans during his stay there in 1920: an indication of Tongan inventiveness—and of that observer's attention to detail!

122. Not an altogether satisfactory translation, but the nearest I can propose.

123. One partial exception occurred on Pukapuka, where all persons born during the same standardized period were assigned to the age cohort of the first one born in that period—the cohort being named for that person. Thereby the whole population was divided into numerous, sequentially arranged age grades of cohorts, whose members advanced one grade up the series upon the founding of each new grade (Beaglehole and Beaglehole 1938, 233).

124. One reported exception to this characterization was the pariah status occupied by Hawaiians known as kauwā. See below.

125. This is a practice that calls to mind a proposition that was advanced in anthropology's heady "Culture and Personality" era of the thirties and forties and that derived a person's personality from the extent to which an infant was confined (by narrow cradling and tight-binding swaddling) or left unconfined, etc.

126. The kind of "harm" referred to here seems to have been inflicted in part upon the sufferer's stomach—i.e., by ingested food that had been in contact, directly or indirectly, with the source of the godliness. Evidence for this includes reports that the father of a highly ranked child—i.e., one with much godliness—had to be fed by others, his own hands being "infected" by having directly touched his child. However, this interpretation is probably not exhaustive: the question of how Polynesian "religious" processes were perceived to "work" does not have a simple explain-all answer.

127. Another question raised by Tahitians' amo'a rites, and by similar rites elsewhere, has to do with godliness itself: did the rites supposedly reduce that godliness to the point of reducing its harmfulness? Or did they serve only to insulate it, without reducing its "amount" and efficacy? While favoring the second answer, I must add that the question—the distinction—may have been quite meaningless to the Tahitians themselves.

128. There are several other detailed studies, made in recent decades, about intrafamily relationships, but all of them concern peoples far along the (rocky and socially modifying) road to Westernization.

129. In early reports about Hawaiians some youths are described as having shunned most productive work, having depended upon their fathers for food; that however seems to have been a situation peculiar to Hawai'i.

130. For example, in present-day Tahitian, ta'ata pa'ari means, roughly, "person-adult." And in the mid–nineteenth-century Davies Tahitian and English Dictionary the adjectival meanings given for pa'ari were "wise, knowing, skillful, cunning; mature, old, ripe [as a fruit]—and hard." It can be assumed, not unreasonably, that such adjectives were also considered characteristic of adults [i.e., maturity] in pre-European times.

131. One exception to this was on Pukapuka, as described in note 123.

132. Pietrusewsky and Douglas 1994.

133. In case the reader objects to the repetitive use of quotation marks around "old" (and "youth" and "mature"), be reminded that such adjectives refer to cultural and not necessarily chronological measures of age.

134. In the preceding account I have used the word "spirit" to designate that entity both before and after its associated body had died. In some societies a lexical distinction was made between the two—i.e., between "spirit" (or "soul") and "ghost," but because that distinction

was not universal (in Polynesia) I will ignore it and continue to use only "spirit."

135. Not, however, in Tonga, where, according to one early and longtime Western visitor, commoners lacked a "spirit," and therefore left no entity to survive their death. (But see Gifford 1929, 109.)

136. For a learned compilation of several Polynesian eschatologies the reader is referred to Handy's classic work *Polynesian Religion*.

137. I enter this caveat because of the possibility that the "simplicity" of the eschatologies attributed to some peoples may have been due to superficial reporting and not to the native doctrines themselves.

138. "Pool-sharing" is the label applied here to the type of transaction in which, normatively, all able members of a group contributed appropriate kinds and amounts of goods and services to a common "pool" and took from it for personal use appropriate kinds and amounts of the same—"appropriate" being culturally defined in terms of criteria such as age, gender, authority status, etc. (To paraphrase a well-known maxim: "from each according to his [culturally defined] abilities; to each according to his [culturally defined] needs.")

139. Or, in a few cases, mostly in the Marquesas, of a wife and her two or more "husbands."

140. For a discussion of explanations of this so-called "universal incest taboo" see Murdock 1949.

141. Also, some myths and legends of those and a few other Polynesian peoples contain episodes of male gods having had sexual intercourse with their daughters—some such episodes having produced the first humans.

142. As noted above, in Hawaiian society marriage between "close" consanguines was prescribed for upper-class persons and proscribed for commoners, in both cases for "supernatural" reasons—but then Hawai'i was not unique among human societies in having different rules for upper- and lower-class persons.

143. In one delicious but unconfirmed report some cunning young women, no longer virginal, used chicken blood to circumvent the test.

144. In most scholarly writings on the subject, the term "status" is defined as including obligations as well as rights, but the obligation aspect of "status" will be only touched on here.

145. Patterns concerning child custody were too varied and circumstantial to attempt to describe in this introductory text.

146. Notable exceptions to this are the works of Firth

and Feinberg, whose subjects were living in the twentieth century but whose lives were largely un-Westernized.

147. All that changed in the twentieth century, when several anthropologists, stimulated by Watsonian and other psychologies, carried out intensive field studies on child socialization, including parent:child relations—as summarized by James and June Ritchie (in Howard and Borofsky 1989). All such studies, however, were made on twentieth-century Polynesians. And while some of the behaviors described may well have been continuities from ancient times, there is not enough certainty about that to include them here.

148. As to which preceded which—the coresidence or the terminology—it is no longer possible to know.

149. In the Polynesian societies studied by anthropologists during the mid- and late 1900s, the numbers of such adoptions ranged from 25 to 90 percent of all births (Howard and Kirkpatrick 1989, 75)—which suggests but does not conclusively prove that similar percentages applied to earlier Polynesia as well.

150. For studies of adoption in twentieth-century Polynesian societies see Beaglehole and Beaglehole 1938; Feinberg 1981b; and articles in Brady 1974; and Carroll 1970.

151. As rationalized in some societies, it was the first-born who "opened the path" by which subsequent offspring emerged.

152. "Most" but not all. In Tikopia, for example, there was a single term for both a male's sister and a female's brother—i.e., *kave*, which meant "sibling of opposite sex."

153. One noteworthy exception (in eastern Polynesia) occurred in Hawai'i, where among the upper grades of the upper class, firstborn females often achieved positions of political influence—so much so that they, rather than their brothers, figured in aristocratic pedigrees.

154. For additional, and possibly "deeper" discussions of gender relations in general, and brother-sister relations in particular, see Linnekin 1990; Ortner 1981; Schoeffel 1978; and Shore 1989.

155. Other labels used in the literature include "descent units," "descent lines," "lineages" and "ramages." I use the older label because it has more resonance for the nonspecialist reader (to whom this book is addressed).

156. In Hawai'i some individuals were believed to have been sired by two men—a circumstance which, however, does not negate the definition of clanship herein used, since clanship had become nearly defunct there.

157. For a discerning discussion of kin assimilation, including a Polynesia-wide survey of this matter, see Feinberg 1981, 171–97.

158. For the sake of precision and clarity a terminological distinction is made herein between the offices of "clan senior" and "tribe chief"—although there were many individuals throughout Polynesia who were both. Also, throughout this book "aristocrat" will be applied to persons standing in close enough relationship to the senior of an upper-class clan or the chief of a powerful tribe to share some of the same entitlements as they (e.g., respect behaviors, obedience in certain matters, etc.). In some societies the entitlements were extended only to such a senior's or chief's offspring and high-ranking spouse(s), in others to a wide circle of their kinfolk as well. (In Samoa, for example, in the words of Irving Goldman: "[T]he title of ali'i (aristocrat) has become as common and about as meaningful as 'colonel' in Kentucky" (1970, 262).

159. For an excellent study of the growth, branching and coalescing of clans, see Ottino's study (1970) of Rangiroa, an atoll in the Tuamotus.

160. One exception to this form of ownership prevailed on Anuta Island, where subclans (patongia) of the society's clans (kaimanga) held full ownership rights in the plots of land usually used by them.

161. The Samoa-wide grading of the titles of all its clans was, despite their rivalries, based on the myth that all of their members were descended from the same creator-god, Tangaloa.

162. In 1865 the reigning secular chief of the tribe (which by then had become known as a "kingdom") reclaimed religious (by that time, Christian) authority as well—an arrangement, patterned after that of Great Britain, that has continued ever since.

163. Here as in some other Polynesian societies it was considered beneath the dignity of a high-ranking clan senior to engage in public speaking—i.e., in reciting genealogies, in exhorting assemblies, etc. Instead, such functions were performed by genealogists and official spokesmen, permitting their seniors to remain silent and sessile in Buddha-like composure (a posture that was in conformity with and which doubtless contributed to the obesity of many of them).

164. Circumstances similar to this prevailed also on the Outlier Islands of Rennell and Bellona with respect to their (otherwise) patrilineal clans (Elbert and Monborg 1955).

165. By Ernest and Pearl Beaglehole, on whose monograph (1938) this résumé is based.

166. For this and other reasons, the ethnographer Julia Hecht, who studied Pukapuka in 1972, labeled the units "burial lineages."

167. By "referential" is meant that such terms were used mainly to refer to a relationship—and only occasionally, and somewhat formally, to address the specific relative (i.e., when speaking to him or her). In a few Polynesian societies those also served as generic terms of address, but in most of them a person used one of a kinsman's personal names when addressing him or her.

168. This fact has been particularly, and consummately, established by Richard Feinberg, who in his study of Anuta (1981) not only documents the "conduct" component of "kinship" in that small Outlier society, but summarizes its occurrence in several other Polynesian societies as well.

169. This caveat applies also to my proposals about "godliness," which, it may be recalled, is the identification and translation of what I myself think to be the "substance" believed by some Polynesian peoples to be shared by persons of common descent. In extenuation, however, my notion about "godliness" is much narrower and more specific than what some writers about Polynesia identify as "kinship."

170. To flesh out this necessarily brief discussion of Polynesian "kinship," the reader is referred to the following studies: Brady 1976; Carroll 1970; Feinberg 1981 a and b; Firth 1951; Goldman 1970; Hanson 1970; Howard and Kirkpatrick 1989; Huntsman and Hooper 1996; Oliver 1974. And for lists of the basic kin (referential) terms of several Polynesian societies see the appendix in Goldman 1970.

171. Most of the nucleated villages now found throughout Polynesia were created after Western contact, and due largely to missionary or colonial administration influence.

172. Except in Hawai'i and Tonga, where—as previously noted—clans (as herein defined) existed only among persons of upper-class status.

173. Most of Samoa's nucleated communities—villages—were tightly organized and semiautonomous, having consisted of three or four village-wide groups: a governing council (fono) made up of the seniors (matai) of its resident clans, an aumaga (a group of its untitled males, who carried out village work projects), in some villages an aualama (a group of the wives of its titled men), and a group made up of its other wives and older girls, the female counterpart of the aumaga. In addition (as was noted earlier), many villages included a taupo (its "official" virgin), and an official orator (tulafale)—a matai who served also as the fono's executive officer (thereby relieving its principal matai of active (i.e., unseemly) functions, such as debating and haranguing.

174. Like "clan," the word "tribe" has been used by countless writers and with a wide range of meanings, but still retains enough of a familiar core of them; its usage will avoid ambiguity, in this book at least, if held to the definition given here. Similarly with the word "chief," which herein will be the label applied only to the office of the sovereign ruler of a tribe, and which differs from the corresponding offices of clan senior and community headman. In many writings about Polynesia, "chief" is used undiscriminatingly—e.g., for clan senior, for community headman, and for a chief's close kinfolk—with consequent loss of clarity. With respect to the latter, in this book the word "chiefly" is used, as distinct from "aristocratic" and "upper class"—although in most cases persons who were "chiefly" were also "aristocratic" and members of the "upper class."

175. For a résumé of Tongan traditions regarding their political history see Bott 1982 and Goldman 1970.

176. That statue, although larger than average, was only one of over six hundred on the island. Moreover, Easter Islanders numbered no more than about seven thousand persons, who were divided into many tribes, suggesting that the number of men engaged in carving, moving and erecting the statue may have been no more than about two hundred to three hundred.

177. One influential writer (Marcus 1982) prefers "kingly" to "sacred" and "populist" to "secular" for reasons that may be cogent for some societies but that would require lengthier explication than is appropriate in this introductory text.

178. So much so that their dynastic founders were, in retrospect, believed to have been alien, and supernatural, Outsiders—or in the words of one writer, "Stranger-Kings" (Sahlins 1987B).

179. Intratribal because "wrongs" against members of another tribe did not count as such.

180. A distinction is in order here between personal "wrongs" against a chief's property or authority (i.e., treason), and violations, witting or unwitting, of his sanctity-derived taboos—it being acknowledged, however, that such distinctions cannot always be drawn.

181. Too little has been published about Polynesians' rare matriclans to conclude anything about their stratification, if any.

182. Earlier but more piecemeal attempts to account for stratification differences among Polynesian societies include those of Edwin Burrows, E.S.C. Handy, Ralph Piddington, and Robert Williamson. (See Bibliography.)

183. In Hawai'i commoners were indeed "landless" in terms of full, residual, or more or less secure provisional tenure, and may have been so in Mangareva and Tonga as well, but not in Tahiti, where all but war refugees had at least some secure provisional use rights in some land.

184. This section is based mainly on Métraux 1940.

185. This section is based mainly on Oliver 1974.

186. The most comprehensive and detailed review of the material summarized in this section is Valerio Valeri's *Kingship and Sacrifice.*

187. The description and analysis of this momentous episode is best covered by Marshall Sahlins in his *Historical Metaphors and Mythical Realities.* The identification of Cook as Lono, as described by Sahlins, has been challenged, most notably—and I believe unsuccessfully—by the Sri Lankan scholar Gananath Obeyeskere, in his book *The Apotheosis of Captain Cook.* For a discussion of the controversy see Borofsky 1997.

188. Maori means "native" or "not foreign." Cognates of the word include *maoli* (in Hawaiian), *ma'ohi* (in Tahitian), *ma'oi* (in Mangarevan), etc. For some reason or other the word has served to label in Western languages only those Polynesians of New Zealand.

189. This chapter owes much of its up-to-dateness to its scrutiny by Anne Salmond (see Bibliography), whose knowledge of the Maori, both contemporary and historic, is likely unsurpassed in comprehensiveness—and in some matters in depth as well.

190. One scholar whose research contributed to this finding was H. D. Simmons, in his book *The Great New Zealand Myth* (1976). Another contributing scholar is Angela Ballara, whose book *Iwi* (1998) provides not only an account of the individuals and events responsible for the myth's formulation but detailed analyses of the historically documented nature and postcontact transformations of Maori social institutions.

191. For a thorough survey of such colonizing see Sutton 1994.

192. As in tropical Polynesia the gourd was grown mainly for use as containers, but before ripening, and hardening, was sometimes used as a food supplement.

193. The undocumentable but persuasive judgments of some early European settlers indicate that several Maori they knew lived to much older ages than those inferred from the burials (Anne Salmond, pers. com.).

194. Those Maori residing inland, near or within forests and more dependent upon forest products (e.g., birds, rats, berries) gave more prominence in their cosmogonies to Tane, the principal god of forests and birds, than to Tangaroa, principal god of ocean and fish, who featured more prominently in the cosmogonies of coastal

dwellers. Be it noted however that this is a proposition I have not attempted to document!

195. For a readable discussion of this question and of other features of Maori prayers see Buck 1950, 489–590.

196. For particulars about these and other Maori meanings of *mana* see Best 1924, I: 386–90. Be it noted also that in Maori "thinking" some of the above forms of *mana* once acquired could also be lost—the exception, I suppose, having been the kind described in (1).

197. For further discussion over these and other important concepts see Johansen, Hanson and Hanson, and Salmond (1989).

198. According to Joseph Banks, who accompanied Cook on his first voyage: "The men are of the size of the larger European, stout, clean Limnd and active [,] fleshy but never fat as the lazy inhabitants of the South Sea Isles are, vigorous, nimble and at the same time Clever in all their exercises" (Beaglehole 1962, II: 11).

199. For more on clothing, including description of the elaborate decorations of some garments, see Buck 1926 and S. M. Mead 1969.

200. A rhizome is a subsoil rootlike plant stem, having roots from its lower surface and shoots or leaves from its upper surface.

201. For more detailed accounts of Maori horticulture see Best 1925, which was reprinted in 1976; Buck 1950; and Leach 1984.

202. For more on fowling see Anderson 1989; Best 1942, reprinted in 1977; Buck 1949; and Downes 1978.

203. For more on carvings see the several works of S. M. Mead listed in the Bibliography.

204. Information used in composing this section was taken from Bathgate 1969; Best 1924; Buck 1950; Hornell 1936; and Beaglehole 1962, II.

205. In an adult version of hoop rolling, the tattooed skin of a slain enemy was stretched over the hoop "and trundled between two jeering groups to satisfy their hate for the deceased" (Buck 1950, 246).

206. For more on Maori dance see Karetu 1993; and articles in Kaeppler and Love 1998, 944–47.

207. These included laments for various situations: love songs, lullabies, soliloquies, gossip mongering, peacemaking, recitations of ancient events, taunts, etc. (Te Ahukaramu Charles Royal, in Kaeppler and Love 1998, 939–40). And for Maori music in general see McLean 1996.

208. This section is based mostly on Peter Vayda's comprehensive and well documented *Maori Warfare*, supplemented by Ballara 1976.

209. In her glossary of key Maori words Joan Metge defines *toa* as "Adj. male of animals; brave; boisterous, rough, stormy; a brave man, warrior; bravery, roughness of sea. In duplicative form, *totoa*, impetuous, fierce; boisterous, stormy, reckless" (1976, 347).

210. Peter Bellwood, citing Irwin, writes that up to 1985 the remains of some 5,500 forts had been identified in New Zealand, most of them in the northern half of North Island. And by that date no precontact ones had been found beyond the range of sweet potato cultivation (1987, 150).

211. One more or less "reasonable" explanation for eating slain or captured enemies on the spot was simple hunger—due to the fact that raiding parties were seldom well provisioned; but that "simple hunger" was doubtless increased by the abiding appetite for human flesh. In this connection, records exist of some captives having been saved by women or by "chiefly" intervention from being eaten.

212. Some truces were sought to be ratified by marriages or exchanges of feasting and gifts. In fact there were official peacemakers employed in the process. It is not recorded how many of such efforts actually ended in more or less permanent truce (Anne Salmond, pers. com.).

213. "It will be noted that bloodshed was not a normal feature of a *taua muru*, always excepting slaves, who if caught were destroyed in the same spirit that houses were burned, with the added advantage that their carcasses provided *kinacki* (relish) to the victory feast that usually followed" (Ballara 1976, 491-92).

214. For particulars on Maori marriage see Biggs 1960.

215. As proposed earlier: While it is in keeping with the Polynesia-wide belief that all or most humans had descended originally from one or another god, and therefore contained some godliness—the amount having diminished with birth order—for most members of any society that amount was so small as to have had little, or even no, social significance. (I add "most" because of my uncertainty about native beliefs about the origins of such under- or outcaste persons as the Hawaiian *kauwā* and Tongan commoners.

216. In addition to Simmons' work, just cited, the most detailed account of the composing of the Great New Zealand Myth is contained in Angela Ballara's outstanding book *Iwi* (1998), which also describes the subsequent unraveling of many aspects of it.

217. In this summary, which draws much on Ballara's

Iwi and on Salmond (1991), use will be made of labels defined, and applied, earlier in this book—a practice that in several cases will differ from usages well established in the Maori literature, but which is adopted in order to make this description conformable to those in Part Two.

218. The term *pa* was used both for a wholly fortified *kainga* and for a fortified section of it—i.e., for the part used as a sanctuary when the *kainga* was under attack.

219. Or in native terms, *mana*, which though containing a component of godliness (as defined earlier in this book), could also be transferred or delegated to someone less "godly," or could be acquired by, say, political or martial superiority.

220. As in most other Polynesian societies, many Maori tribes and clans (i.e., tribal *hapu* and kin *hapu*) also included other offices, such as seer, war leader, and expert in one or another subsistence activity or craft. Most of those offices were acquired by achievement but some by a combination of inheritance ratified by achievement.

221. There were, however, some (Ariki) chiefs in some areas who were believed to be so imbued with *mana* that they were carried about on litters (as was also the case in Tahiti) or were seated on high platforms or on house roofs (Anne Salmond, pers. com.)—presumably because of the contagious effect that would result from their feet touching the ground.

222. This situation evidently changed after Western contact, when some chiefs obtained guns, and thereby emboldened, set out upon unprovoked and often successful wars of conquest, which served not only to increase their appetites for more and wider authority but in some cases to satisfy them.

223. There is evidence that the offspring of a (war prisoner) slave and a nonslave was ipso facto "free," but I have not discovered any clear evidence on the class-status of the offspring of two slaves.

224. This reference to "secondary" wives suggests that "aristocrats" did indeed marry, "primarily," only women of their own class—as many of them certainly did, both for political purposes and for godliness-associated eugenic reasons as well.

225. Skinner 1923; King 1989; Sutton 1980; and Shand 1911. The very readable book by King is comprehensive and also traces the histories of the handful of Moriori survivors up to the present.

226. Concerning this episode the distinguished New Zealand ethnologist—and Maori apologist!—H. D. Skinner wrote (presumably seriously): "Anyone who has carefully scrutinized the evidence must conclude that the commonly accepted verdict of unmitigated barbarity on the part of the Maori conquerors is not justified. A contest in which [only!] two hundred [sic] out of a population of sixteen hundred [Moriori] were killed does not, judged by European standards, constitute exceptional ferocity."

227. Possible reasons were that they had left New Zealand before tattooing became widespread there; that their numbers were not large enough to encourage the use of "tribal" marks of identification; or that the absence of warfare among them (see below) served to minimize emphasis on such signs of, among other things, male ferocity.

228. Although between that time and the arrival of the 1835 Maori invasion they had, however, killed individual Maori who had landed on their shores (Anne Salmond, pers. com.).

229. For an excellent account of those influences upon the fine arts, see Bernard Smith, *European Vision and the South Pacific: 1768–1850*, and *Imagining the Pacific: In the Wake of the Cook Voyages*.

230. "Not altogether likely" because of, among other things, geographic differences in the amounts and distributions of natural life-sustaining resources, deep-seated differences in cultural patterns of enculturation, and—least alterable—genetic differences among individuals in intellectual capacity and "aggressive" drive.

231. A situation that was to change when outsiders, mainly Westerners, arrived and introduced different ideologies and tools, etc., that have transformed many of the beliefs, values and practices of most of the peoples described in this book.

BIBLIOGRAPHY

Abbott, I. A. 1991. Polynesian uses of sea-weed. In *Islands, plants and Polynesians: An introduction to Polynesian ethnobotany*, edited by P. A. Cox and S. A. Banack, 135–46. Portland, Oregon: Dioscorides Press.

———. 1992. La'au *Hawai'i: Traditional Hawaiian uses of plants*. Honolulu: Bernice Pauahi Bishop Museum Press.

Aberle, D. F. et al. 1950. The functional pre-requisites of a society. *Ethos* 60 (2).

Adams, H. 1901. *Memoirs of Ari'i Taimai*. Paris: privately printed.

Adcock, G. J., et al. 2001. Mitochondrial DNA sequences in ancient Australians: Implications for modern human origins. *Proceedings of the National Academy of Sciences* 98:2.

Alexander, W. D. 1893. Specimens of ancient Tahitian poetry. *Journal of the Polynesian Society* 2:55–59.

Allen, J. 1984. In search of the Lapita homeland: Reconstructing the prehistory of the Bismarck Archipelago. *Journal of Pacific History* 19 (4):186–201.

Allen, J., and C. Gosden., eds. 1991. *Report of the Lapita Homeland Project*. Occasional Papers in Prehistory 20. Canberra: Australian National University.

Allen, T. 1991. *European explorers and Marquesan tattooing*. Honolulu: Hardy Marks Publications.

Anderson, A. 1980. Towards an explanation of protohistoric social organization and settlement patterns amongst Southern Ngai Taku. *New Zealand Journal of Archaeology* 2:3–23.

———. 1989. *Prodigious birds: Moas and moa-hunting in prehistoric New Zealand*. Cambridge: Cambridge University Press.

———. 1997. *Welcome to strangers: An ethnohistory of Southern Maori*. Dunedin: Otago University Press.

Anderson, J. C. 1934. *Maori music: With its Polynesian background*. Polynesian Society Memoir 10. New Plymouth: Avery.

Anell, B. 1957. The Polynesian cities of refuge. In *Orientalia suecana*, vol. 5, edited by Uppsala, 189–210.

Arago, J. 1822. *Promenade autour du monde*. Paris: Leblanc.

———. 1825. *Promenade autour du monde pendant les années 1817-1820 sur les corvettes du roi L'Uranie et La Physicienne*. Paris: Leblanc.

Archey, G. 1966. Polynesia; Polynesian cultures. *Encyclopedia of world art*. Vol. 11. New York: McGraw-Hill Book Company.

Ballara, A. 1976. The role of warfare in Maori society in the early contact period. *Journal of the Polynesian Society* 85 (4):487–506.

———. 1998. Iwi: *The dynamics of tribal organisation from circa 1769 to circa 1845*. Wellington: Victoria University Press.

Barrau, J. 1965. *L'humide et le sec:* An essay on ethnobiological adaptation to contrasted environments in the Indo-Pacific area. *Journal of the Polynesian Society* 74:329-46.

Barrow, T. 1956. Maori decorative carving: An outline. *Journal of the Polynesian Society* 65:305.

———. 1985. *An illustrated guide to Maori art*. Honolulu: University of Hawai'i Press.

Barthel, T., ed. 1971. Precontact writing in Oceania. In *Linguistics in Oceania: 1165–1168*, edited by T. Sebeok. The Hague: Mouton.

Bathgate, M. A. 1969. Maori river and ocean-going craft in Southern New Zealand. *Journal of the Polynesian Society* 78 (3):344–77.

Bayard, D. T. 1976. The cultural relationships of the Polynesian outliers. In *Otago University Studies in Prehistoric Archaeology 9*.

Beaglehole, E. 1957. *Social change in the South Pacific: Rarotonga and Aitutaki.* London: Allen and Unwin.

Beaglehole, E. and Pearl. 1938. *Ethnology of Pukapuka.* Honolulu: Bernice Pauahi Bishop Museum Bulletin 150.

Beaglehole, J. C. 1962. *The* Endeavour *journal of Joseph Banks: 1768-1771.* Sydney: Angus and Robertson.

———, ed. 1955–1967. *The journals of Captain James Cook on his voyages of discovery.* 3 vols. Cambridge: Cambridge University Press.

Bechtol, C. 1962. Sailing characteristics of oceanic canoes. *Supplement to Journal of Polynesian Studies* 71:98–101.

Beckwith, M. W. 1932. *Kepolino's traditions of Hawaii.* Honolulu: Bernice Pauahi Bishop Museum Press.

———. 1944. Polynesian story composition. *Journal of the Polynesian Society* 53:177–203.

———. 1951. *The* kumulipo: *A Hawaiian creation chant.* Chicago: University of Chicago Press.

Beechey, F. W. 1831. *Narrative of a voyage to the Pacific and Beering's Strait.* 2 vols. London: Colburn and Bentley.

Bellwood, P. 1979. *Man's conquest of the Pacific: The prehistory of Southeast Asia and Oceania.* New York: Oxford University Press.

———.1987. *The Polynesians: Prehistory of an island people.* Rev. ed. London: Thames and Hudson.

Bennett, W. C. 1931. *Archaeology of Kauai.* Honolulu: Bernice Pauahi Bishop Museum Bulletin 80.

Best, E. 1924. *The Maori.* Vol. 2. Polynesian Society Memoir 5. New Plymouth: Avery.

———. 1942. *Forest lore of the Maori.* Polynesian Society Memoir 18. New Plymouth: Avery.

———. 1977. *Forest lore of the Maori.* Wellington: Government Printer.

Biggs, B. 1960. *Maori marriage.* Polynesian Society Memoir 1. New Plymouth: Avery.

———. 1972. Implications of linguistic subgrouping, with special reference to Polynesia. In *Studies in oceanic cultural history*, edited by R. C. Green and M. Kelly. Honolulu: Bernice Pauahi Bishop Museum Studies in Oceanic Cultural History 3.

———. 1990. *English-Maori, Maori-English Dictionary.* Auckland: Auckland University Press.

———. 1994. Does Maori have a closest relative? In *The origins of the first New Zealanders*, edited by D. G. Sutton. Auckland: Auckland University Press.

Bing, S. et al. 2000. Polynesian origins: Insights from the Y chromosome. *Proceedings of the National Academy of Sciences of the United States of America* 97 (15): 8193–8746.

Blust, R. 1978. *The proto-oceanic palatals.* Polynesian Society Memoir 43. New Plymouth: Avery.

Borofsky, R. 1997. Cook, Lono, Obeyesekere, and Sahlins. *Current Anthropology* 38:255.

Bott, E. 1982. *Tongan society at the time of Captain Cook's visit.* Polynesian Society Memoir 44. New Plymouth: Avery.

Bougainville, L. A. de. 1772. *A voyage round the world, 1766–1769.* Translated by J. R. Forster. London: Nourse and Davies.

Brady, I., ed. 1976. *Transactions in kinship: Adoption and fosterage in Oceania.* Association for Social Anthropology in Oceania Monograph 4. Honolulu: University of Hawai'i Press.

Brewis, L. et al. 1990. Modeling the prehistoric Maori population. *Journal of Physical Anthropology* 81:343–56.

Bryan, E. H., Jr. 1941. *American Polynesia: Coral islands of the Central Pacific.* Honolulu: Tongg Publishing Company.

Buck, P. (Te Rangi Hiroa). 1926. *The evolution of Maori clothing*. Polynesian Society Memoir 7. New Plymouth: Avery.

———. 1930. *Samoan material culture*. Honolulu: Bernice Pauahi Bishop Museum Bulletin 75.

———. 1932. *Ethnology of Tongareva*. Honolulu: Bernice Pauahi Bishop Museum Bulletin 92.

———. 1934. *Mangaian society*. Honolulu: Bernice Pauahi Bishop Museum Bulletin 122.

———. 1938A. *Ethnology of Mangareva*. Honolulu: Bernice Pauahi Bishop Museum Bulletin 157.

———. 1938B. *Vikings of the sunrise*. New York: F. A. Stokes Co.

———. 1943. The feather cloak of Tahiti. *Journal of the Polynesian Society* 52 (1): 12–15.

———. 1944. *Arts and crafts of the Cook Islands*. Honolulu: Bernice Pauahi Bishop Museum Bulletin 179.

———. 1950. *The coming of the Maori*. 2d ed. Wellington: Whitcombe and Tombs.

———. 1957. *Arts and crafts of Hawaii*. Honolulu: Bernice Pauahi Bishop Museum Special Publication 45.

———. 1959. *Vikings of the Pacific*. Chicago: University of Chicago Press.

Buhler, A., T. Barrow, and C. P. Mountford. 1962. *Oceania and Australia: The art of the South Seas*. London: Methuen.

Burrows, E. 1933. *Native music of the Tuamotus*. Honolulu: Bernice Pauahi Bishop Museum Bulletin 109.

———. 1934. Polynesian part singing. *Zeitschrift fur Vergleichende Musik Wissenschaft* 2:69–76.

———. 1937. *Ethnology of Uvea (Wallis Island)*. Honolulu: Bernice Pauahi Bishop Museum Bulletin 145.

———. 1939A. Breed and border in Polynesia. *American Anthropologist* 41:1–21.

———. 1939B. *Western Polynesia: A study in cultural differentiation*. Gothenberg: Ethnological Studies 7.

———. 1940. Culture areas in Polynesia. *Journal of the Polynesian Society* 49:349–63.

———. 1945. *Songs of* Uvea *and* Futuna. Honolulu: Bernice Pauahi Bishop Museum Bulletin 183.

Burton-Bradley, B. G. 1972. Betel-chewing. In *Encyclopedia of Papua and New Guinea*. Melbourne: Melbourne University Press.

Carrington, H., ed. 1948. *The discovery of Tahiti: The journal of George Robertson*. London: Folio Press.

Carroll, V., ed. 1970. *Adoption in Eastern Oceania*. Association of Social Anthropology in Oceania Monograph 1. Honolulu: University of Hawai'i Press.

Churchill, W. 1917. *Club types of nuclear Polynesia*. Washington, D.C.: Carnegie Institute Publication 255.

Clark, R. 1979. Language. In *The prehistory of Polynesia*, edited by J. D. Jennings, 244–70. Cambridge: Cambridge University Press.

Cleave, P. 1983. Tribal and state-like political formation in New Zealand Maori society, 1750–1900. *Journal of the Polynesian Society* 92:51–92.

Connor, J. 1983. A descriptive classification of Maori fabrics, cordage, plaiting, etc. *Journal of the Polynesian Society* 92:189–214.

Cook, J. 1777. *A voyage towards the South Pole and round the world, performed in His Majesty's ships the resolution and adventure, in the years 1772, 1773, 1774, and 1775*. 2 vols. London: W. Strahan and T. C. Cadell.

Cook, J. and J. K. 1784. *A voyage to the Pacific Ocean . . . in the years 1776, 1777, 1778, 1779, and 1780*. 3 vols. London: W. Strahan and T. C. Cadell.

Cordy, R. 1981. *A study of prehistoric change: The development of complex societies in the Hawaiian Islands*. New York: Academic Press.

———. 2000. *Exalted sits the chief: The ancient history of Hawai'i Island*. Honolulu: Mutual Publishing.

Corney, B. G., ed. 1913–1918. *The quest and occupation of Tahiti by emissaries of Spain during the years 1772–1776*. 3 vols. London: Cambridge University Press.

Coutts, P. J. F. 1971. Greenstone: The prehistoric exploitation of . . . from Anita Bay, Milford Sound. *Journal of the Polynesian Society* 80:42–73.

Cox, J. H., with E. Stasack. 1970. *Hawaiian petroglyphs*. Honolulu: Bernice Pauahi Bishop Museum Special Publication 70.

Cox, J. H., and W. H. Davenport. 1974. *Hawaiian sculpture*. Honolulu: University of Hawai'i Press.

Cox, P. A. 1991. Polynesian herbal medicine. In *Islands, plants and Polynesians: An introduction to Polynesian ethnobotany*, edited by P. A. Cox and S. A. Banack, 197–98. Portland, Oregon: Dioscorides Press.

Cox, P. A., and S. A. Banack, eds. 1991. *Islands, plants and Polynesians: An introduction to Polynesian ethnobotany*. Portland, Oregon: Dioscorides Press.

Crocombe, R. G. 1964. *Land tenure in the Cook Islands*. London: Oxford University Press.

Crowley, T. 1992. *An introduction to historical linguistics*. Oxford: Oxford University Press.

Cumberland, K. B. 1949. New Zealand about 1780. *Geographical Review* 39:401–24.

———. 1962. *Western Samoa: Land, life and agriculture in tropical Polynesia*. Edited by Fox et al. Christchurch: Whitcombe and Tombs.

Danielsson, B. 1956a. *Love in the South Seas*. London: Allen and Unwin.

———. 1956b. *Work and life in Raroia (Tuamotus)*. London: Macmillan.

Darlington, P. J. 1957. *Zoogeography: The geographical distribution of animals*. New York: Wiley.

Daugherty, J. 1979. *Polynesian warfare and fortifications*. Auckland: Master's thesis, University of Auckland.

Davenport, W. H. 1959. Non-unilinear descent and descent groups. *American Anthropologist* 61:557–72.

———. 1994. Pi'o: *An inquiry into the marriage of brothers and sisters and other close relations in old Hawaii*. Philadelphia: University of Pennsylvania Publications in Anthropology 5.

Davidson, J. 1983. Maori prehistory: The state of the art. *Journal of the Polynesian Society* 92:291–308.

———. 1984. *The prehistory of New Zealand*. Auckland: Longman Paul.

———. 1992. The Polynesian Foundation. In *The Oxford history of New Zealand*, 2d ed., edited by Geoffrey W. Rice, 3–67. Auckland: Oxford University Press.

Davidson, J. et al. 1996. *Oceanic culture history: Essays in honour of Roger Green*. Dunedin: New Zealand Journal of Archaeology Special Publication.

Davies, J. 1851. *A Tahitian and English dictionary*. Tahiti: London Missionary Society Press.

———. 1961. *The history of the Tahitian mission, 1799–1830*. Edited by C. W. Newbury. Cambridge: Cambridge University Press.

Davis, R. I., and J. F. Brown. 1999. *Kava (Piper methysticum) in the South Seas*. Canberra: Australian Centre for Agricultural Research.

Dempwolff, O. 1934–1938. *Vergleichende lautlehre des Austronesischen Wortschatzes. Zeitschrift für Eingeborenen-Sprachen*. Berlin: Reimer.

Dening, G. M. 1962. The geographical knowledge of the Polynesians and the nature of inter-island contact. In *Polynesian navigation: A symposium on Andrew Sharp's theory of accidental voyages*, edited by J. Golson, 102–53. Wellington: Supplement to Journal of the Polynesian Society.

———. 1980. *Islands and beaches: Discourse on a silent land, Marquesas 1774–1880*. Melbourne: Melbourne University Press.

Domeny de Rienzi, G. 1836–38. *Océanie, ou cinquième partie du monde*. 3 vols. Paris: Firmin.

Downes, T. W. 1918. Notes on eels and eel weirs. *New Zealand Institute* 50:296–316.

———. 1928. Bird snaring etc. in the Whanganui River District. *Journal of the Polynesian Society* 37:1–29.

Duff, R. 1950. *The moa-hunter period of Maori culture.* Wellington: Government Printer.

———. 1959. Neolithic adzes of eastern Polynesia. In *Anthropology in the South Seas*, edited by J. D. Freeman and W. Geddes. New Plymouth: Avery.

Elbert, S. H. 1970. *Spoken Hawaiian.* Honolulu: University of Hawai'i Press.

Elbert, S. H., and T. Monberg. 1965. *From the two canoes: Oral traditions of Rennell and Bellona.* Honolulu and Copenhagen: University of Hawai'i Press and Danish Natural History Press.

Ellis, W. 1782. *An authentic narrative of a voyage performed by Captain Cook and Captain Clerke in His Majesty's ships in Resolution and Discovery.* 2 vols. London: Robinson et al.

Ellis, W. 1829. *Polynesian researches.* 2 vols. London: Fisher et al.

———. 1969. *Polynesian researches: Hawaii.* Rutland, Vermont: Tuttle.

Ember, M. 1959. The non-unilinear descent groups in Samoa. *American Anthropologist* 61:573-577.

———. 1962. Political authority and the structure of kinship in aboriginal Samoa. *American Anthropologist* 64:964–71.

Emerson, N. 1909. *Unwritten literature of Hawaii: The sacred songs of the hula.* Washington, D.C.: Bureau of American Ethnology Bulletin 38.

Emory, K. P. 1933. *Stone remains in the Society Islands.* Honolulu: Bernice Pauahi Bishop Museum Bulletin 116.

———. 1946. *Hawaiian tattooing.* Honolulu: Bernice Pauahi Bishop Museum.

———. 1965. *Kapingamarangi, social and religious life of a Polynesian atoll.* Honolulu: Bishop Museum Bulletin 228.

———. 1972. Easter Island's position in the prehistory of Polynesia. *Journal of the Polynesian Society* 81:57–69.

Feinberg, R. 1981a. Anuta: *Social structure of a Polynesian island.* Honolulu: Institute for Polynesian Studies in cooperation with Danish National Museum.

———. 1981b. What is Polynesian kinship all about? *Ethnology* 20:115–31.

Finney, B. 1959. Fa'ahe'a, l'ancien sport de Tahiti. *Bulletin de la Société des Études Océaniennes* 11:53–56.

———. 1964. Notes on bond-friendship in Tahiti. *Journal of the Polynesian Society* 73:431–35.

———. 1977. Voyaging canoes and the settlement of Polynesia. *Science* 196:1277–85.

———. 1979. Hokule'a: *The way to Tahiti.* New York: Dodd, Mead.

———. 1994a. Polynesian-South American round trip voyages. *Rapa Nui Journal.*

———. 1994b. *Voyage of rediscovery.* Berkeley: University of California Press.

Finney, B., and J. D. Houston. 1966. *Surfing: The sport of Hawaiian kings.* Rutland, Vermont: Tuttle.

Firth, R. 1929. *Primitive economics of the New Zealand Maori.* New York: E. P. Dutton.

———. 1930. A dart match in Tikopia. *Oceania* 1:64-96.

———. 1930-1. Totemism in Polynesia. *Oceania* 1: 291-321, 377-398.

———. 1936. *We, the Tikopia.* London: Allen and Unwin.

———. 1940. The analysis of *mana*, an empirical approach. *Journal of the Polynesian Society* 49:483–512.

———. 1954. Anuta and Tikopia: Symbiotic elements in social organization. *Journal of the Polynesian Society* 63: 87–131.

———. 1957a. A note on descent groups in Polynesia. *Man* 57 (2): 4-8.

———. 1957b. *We, the Tikopia.* 2d. ed. London: Allen and Unwin.

———. 1959. *Economics of the New Zealand Maori.* 2d ed. Wellington: Government Printer.

———. 1961. *History and traditions of Tikopia.* Wellington: The Polynesian Society.

———. 1963. *Bilateral descent groups.* London: Journal of the Royal

Anthropological Institute Occasional Paper 15.

———. 1967. *The work of the gods in Tikopia.* London: Athlone Press.

———. 1973a. The sacredness of Tikopia chiefs. In *Politics and leadership: A comparative perspective*, edited by W. A. Snack and P. S. Cohen, 139–68. Oxford: Clarendon Press.

———. 1973b. Tikopia art and society. In *Primitive art and society*, edited by A. Forge. New York: Oxford University Press.

Firth, R., with Mervyn McLean. 1990. *Tikopia songs: Poetic and musical art of a Polynesian people of the Solomon Islands.* Cambridge: Cambridge University Press.

Fischer, H. 1974a. *Bau und Spieltechnik.* Baden-Baden: V. Koerner.

———. 1974b. *Schallgeräte in Ozeanien.* Baden-Baden: V. Koerner.

Fischer, S. R. 1997. Rongorongo: *The Easter Island script: History, tradition and texts.* Oxford: Clarenden Press.

Fornander, A. 1916. *Fornander collection of Hawaiian antiquities and folklore.* Edited by T. Thrum. Honolulu: Bernice Pauahi Bishop Museum Memoirs 4, 5, 6.

Forster, G. 1777. *A voyage round the world in His Brittanic Majesty's sloop,* Resolution. 2 vols. London: B. White et al.

Freeman, J. D. 1983. *Margaret Mead and Samoa: The making and unmaking of an anthropological myth.* Cambridge: Harvard University Press.

Freeman, J. D., and W. Geddes, eds. 1959. *Anthropology in the South Seas.* New Plymouth: Avery.

Frost, E. L. 1979. Fiji. In *The prehistory of Polynesia*, edited by J. D. Jennings. Cambridge: Harvard University Press.

Garanger, J. 1967. *Archaeology of the Society Islands.* Honolulu: Bernice Pauahi Bishop Museum Press.

Gassner, J. S., trans. 1969. *Voyages and adventures of La Perouse.* Honolulu: University of Hawai'i Press.

Gathercole, P., A. L. Kaeppler, and D. Newton. 1979. *The art of the Pacific.* Washington D.C.: National Gallery of Art.

Gathercole, P. et al. 1979. Changing attitudes in the study of Maori carvings. In *Exploring the visual art of Oceania*, edited by S. M. Mead. Honolulu: University of Hawai'i Press.

Gell, A. 1993. *Wrapping in images: Tattooing in Polynesia.* Oxford Studies in the Anthropology of Cultural Forms. New York: Oxford University Press.

Geraghty, P. 1983. *The history of the Fijian language.* Honolulu: Oceanic Linguistics Special Publication 19.

Gifford, E. W. 1929. *Tongan society.* Honolulu: Bernice Pauahi Bishop Museum Bulletin 61.

Gill, W. W. 1876. *Life in the southern isles.* London: Religious Tract Society.

———. 1880. *Historical sketches of savage life in Polynesia.* Wellington: Government Printer.

———. 1894. *From darkness to light in Polynesia.* London: Religious Tract Society.

Gilson, R. P. 1963. Samoan descent groups: A structural outline. *Journal of the Polynesian Society* 72:372–77.

Goldman, I. 1960. The evolution of Polynesian societies. In *Culture in history*, edited by S. Diamond. New York: Columbia University Press.

———. 1970. *Ancient Polynesian society.* Chicago: University of Chicago Press.

Goldwater, Robert et al. 1969. *Art of Oceania, Africa, and the Americas from the Museum of Primitive Art, New York.* England: Curwin Press.

Golson, J. 1959. Culture change in prehistoric New Zealand. In *Anthropology and the South Seas*, edited by J. D. Freeman and W. Geddes. New Plymouth: Avery.

———. 1965. Some considerations of the role of theory in New Zealand archaeology. *New Zealand Archaeological Association Newsletter* 8:79–92.

Golson, J., ed. 1962. *Polynesian navigation:*

A symposium on Andrew Sharp's theory of accidental voyages. Wellington: Supplement to *Journal of the Polynesian Society.*

Goodenough, Ward. 1955. A problem in Malayo-Polynesian social organization. *American Anthropology* 57:71–83.

Gosden, C. 1991. Learning about Lapita in the Bismarck Archipelago. In *Report of the Lapita Homeland Project*, edited by J. Allen and C. Gosdon, Occasional Papers in Prehistory 20, 260–68. Canberra: Australian National University.

Grace, G. 1959. The position of the Polynesian languages within the Austronesian (Malayo-Polynesian) language family. Baltimore: International Journal of American Linguistics Memoir 16.

———. 1966A. Linguistic subgrouping within Polynesia: The implications for prehistoric settlement. *Journal of the Polynesian Society* 75:6-38.

———. 1966B. *Austronesian lexicostatistical classification.* Carbondale, Illinois: Oceanic Linguistics Special Publication 1.

Green, R. C. 1966. Linguistic subgrouping within Polynesia: The implications for prehistoric settlement. *Journal of the Polynesian Society* 75:6-38.

———. 1967. The immediate origins of the Polynesians. In *Polynesian culture history: Essays in honor of Kenneth P. Emory*, edited by Highland et al. Honolulu: Bernice Pauahi Bishop Museum Special Publications 56.

———. 1974. *Adaptation and change in Maori culture.* The Hague: Junk.

———. 1989. Lapita people: An introductory context for skeletal materials associated with pottery of this cultural complex. *Records of the Australian Museum* 41:207–13.

———. 1991. Near and remote Oceania: Disestablishing "Melanesia" in culture. In *Man and a half: Essays in Pacific anthropology and ethnobiology in honour of Ralph Bulmer*, edited by A. K. Pawley, 491–502. Auckland: The Polynesian Society.

———. 1993. Tropical Polynesian prehistory: Where are we now? In *A community of culture: People and culture of the Pacific*, edited by M. Spriggs et al., 218–38. Occasional Papers in Prehistory 21. Canberra: Australian National University.

———. 1998. *Rapa nui* origins prior to European contact: The view from Eastern Polynesia. In *Easter Island and East Polynesian Prehistory*, edited by P. V. Casanova, 218–38. Santiago: Universidad de Chile, Instituto de Estudios Isla de Pascua.

———. 2000. A range of disciplines support a dual origin for the bottle gourd in the Pacific. *Journal of the Polynesian Society* 109 (2):191-97.

Green, R. C., and M. Kelly, eds. 1972. *Studies in Oceanic culture history.* Honolulu: Bishop Museum Studies in Oceanic Culture History 3.

Green, R. C., and M. M. Creswell, eds. 1976. *Southeast Solomon Islands cultural history: A preliminary report.* Wellington: Bulletin of the Royal Society of New Zealand 11.

Greiner, R. 1923. *Polynesian decorative designs.* Honolulu: Bernice Pauahi Bishop Museum Bulletin 7.

Groube, L. M. 1967. Models in prehistory: A consideration of the New Zealand evidence. *Archaeology and Physical Anthropology in Oceania* 2:1–27.

———. 1971. Tonga, Lapita pottery, and Polynesian origins. *Journal of the Polynesian Society* 80:278–316.

Guiart, J. 1963. *The arts of the South Pacific.* New York: Golden Press.

Gunson, N. 1964. Great women and friendship contract rites in pre-Christian Tahiti. *Journal of the Polynesian Society* 73:53–69.

Guy, J. 1985. On a fragment of the Tahual Tablet. *Journal of the Polynesian Society* 94:367–88.

Hagelberg, E., and J. B. Clegg. 1993. Genetic polymorphisms in prehistoric Pacific Islanders determined by analysis of ancient bone DNA. *Proceedings of the Royal Society of New Zealand*, 163–70.

Hamnett, M. P, n.d. *National disaster mitigation in Pacific Island countries.* Honolulu: South Pacific Disaster Reduction Programme.

Handy, E. S. C. 1923. *The native culture in the Marquesas.* Honolulu: Bernice Pauahi Bishop Museum Bulletin 9.

———. 1927. *Polynesian religion.* Honolulu: Bernice Pauahi Bishop Museum Bulletin 3.

———. 1930. *History and culture in the Society Islands.* Honolulu: Bernice Pauahi Bishop Museum Bulletin 79.

———. 1951–52. The Hawaiian family system. *Journal of the Polynesian Society* 60–61.

Handy, E. S. C., and M. K. Pukui. 1958. *The Polynesian family system in Ka-ʻu, Hawaii.* Wellington: The Polynesian Society.

———. 1972. *The Polynesian family system in Ka-ʻu, Hawaii.* Rutland, Vermont: Tuttle.

Handy, W. C. 1922. *Tattooing in the Marquesas Islands.* Honolulu: Bernice Pauahi Bishop Museum Bulletin 1.

———. 1927. *Handicrafts of the Society Islands.* Honolulu: Bernice Pauahi Bishop Museum Bulletin 42.

———. 1938. *L'Art des Marquisas.* Paris: Les Editiones d'art et d'histoire.

Hanson, F. A. 1970. *Rapan lifeways: Society and history on a Polynesian island.* Boston: Little Brown.

———. 1987. Polynesian religions: An overview. In *Encyclopedia of religions*, edited by M. Eliade, 423–32. New York: MacMillan.

———. 1989. The making of the Maori: Culture invention and its logic. *American Anthropologist* 91.

Hanson, F. A., and L. Hanson. 1983. *Counterpoint in Maori culture.* London: Routledge and Kegan Paul.

Harlow, R. B. 1979. Regional variation in Maori. *New Zealand Journal of Anthropology* 5:123–38.

———. 1994. Maori dialectology and the settlement of New Zealand. In *The origins of the first New Zealanders*, edited by D. G. Sutton. Auckland: Auckland University Press.

Harry, R. R. 1953. *Ichthyological field data on Raroia Atoll, Tuamotu Archipelago.* Washington D.C.: Atoll Research Bulletin 18.

Hawkesworth, J. 1773. *An account of the voyages undertaken by His Present Majesty for making discoveries in the Southern Hemisphere.* 3 vols. London: W. Strahan and T. Cadell.

Hecht, J. 1977. The culture of gender in Pukapuka: Male, female and the *mayaki-tanga* (sacred maid). *Journal of the Polynesian Society* 86:103–206.

———. 1981. The cultural contexts of siblingship in Pukapuka. In *Siblingship in Oceania: Studies in the meaning of kin relations*, edited by M. Marshall. Lanham, Maryland: University Press of America.

Henry, T. 1928. *Ancient Tahiti.* Honolulu: Bernice Pauahi Bishop Museum Bulletin 48.

Hertzberg, M. S. et al. 1989. Mitochondrical DNA markers and Polynesian prehistory. In *Mitochondrical DNA variation in past and present Pacific populations*, edited by M. S. Stoneking. Pullman: University of Washington Press.

Heuer, B. N. 1969. Maori women in tribal family and tribal life. *Journal of the Polynesian Society* 78:448–94.

Heyerdahl, T. 1952. *American Indians in the Pacific: The theory behind the* Kon-Tiki *Expedition.* London: Allen and Unwin.

Highland, G. A. et al., eds. 1967. *Polynesian culture history: Essays in honor of Kenneth P. Emory.* Honolulu: Bernice Pauahi Bishop Museum Special Publications 56.

Hill, A. V. S., and S. W. Sargeanson, eds. 1989. *The colonization of the Pacific: A genetic trail.* Oxford: Clarendon Press.

Hogbin, H. I. 1930. The social organisation of Ontong Java. *Oceania* 2:398–425.

———. 1931. A note on Rennell Island. *Oceania* 2:174–78.

———. 1934. *Law and order in Polynesia: A study of primitive legal institutions.* New York: Harcourt Brace.

Hollyman, J., and A. Pawley, eds. 1981. *Studies in Pacific languages and cultures in honour of Bruce Biggs.* Auckland: Linguistic Society of New Zealand.

Holmes, L. D. 1979. The kava complies in Oceania. *New Pacific* 4:30–33.

Hornell, J. 1936. *The canoes of Polynesia, Fiji, and Micronesia.* Honolulu: Bernice Pauahi Bishop Museum Special Publication 27.

Houghton, P. 1980. *The first New Zealanders.* Auckland: Hodder and Stoughton.

———. 1989. Watom: The people. *Records of the Australian Museum* 41:223–33.

———. 1990. The adaptive significance of Polynesian body form. *Annals of Human Biology* 17:19–32.

———. 1996. Dead on arrival: A stimulation of survival in neolithic Pacific voyages. In *Oceanic culture history: Essays in honour of Roger Green,* edited by Davidson et al. Dunedin: New Zealand Journal of Archaeology Special Publication.

Howard, A. 1967. Polynesian origins and migrations: A review of two centuries of speculation and theory. In *Polynesian culture history: Essays in honor of Kenneth P. Emory,* edited by G. A. Highland et al., 45–102. Honolulu: Bernice Pauahi Bishop Museum Special Publications 56.

Howard, A., ed. 1971. *Polynesia: Readings on a culture area.* Scranton: Chandler Publishing Co.

Howard, A. et al. 1970. Traditional and modern adoption patterns in Hawaii. In *Adoption in Eastern Oceania,* edited by V. Carroll. Association of Social Anthropology in Oceania Monograph 1. Honolulu: University of Hawai'i Press.

Howard, A., and R. Borofsky, eds. 1989. *Developments in Polynesian ethnology.* Honolulu: University of Hawai'i Press.

Howard, A., and J. Kirkpatrick. 1989. Social organization. In *Developments in Polynesian ethnology,* edited by A. Howard and R. Borofsky, 47–94. Honolulu: University of Hawai'i Press.

Howells, W. W. 1973. *The Pacific Islanders.* London: Weidenfeld and Nicolson.

———. 1979. Physical anthropology. In *The prehistory of Polynesia,* edited by J. D. Jennings. Cambridge: Harvard University Press.

———. 1993. *Getting here: The story of human evolution.* Washington D.C.: The Compass Press.

Huntsman, J. 1981. Butterfly collecting in a swamp: Suggestions for studying oral narratives as creative art. *Journal of the Polynesian Society* 90:209–18.

Huntsman, J., and A. Hooper. 1996. Tokelau: *A historical ethnography.* Auckland: Auckland University Press.

Irwin, G. J. 1992. *The prehistoric exploration and colonization of the Pacific.* Cambridge: Cambridge University Press.

James, K. E. 1994. Effeminate males and changes in the construction of gender in Tonga. *Pacific Studies* 17 (2):39–69.

Jennings, J. D., ed. 1979. *The prehistory of Polynesia.* Cambridge: Harvard University Press.

Johansen, J. P. 1954. *The Maori and his religion in its non-ritualistic aspects.* Copenhagen: Munksgaard.

Johnson, R. K. 1981. *Kumulipo.* Honolulu: Topgallant Publishing Co.

Joppien, R., and B. Smith. 1985-1988. *The art of Captain Cook's voyages.* 4 vols. New Haven and Oxford: Oxford University Press and Yale University Press with the Australian Academy of Humanities.

Kaeppler, A. 1971. Eighteenth century Tonga: New interpretations of Tongan society and material culture at the time of Captain Cook. *Man* 6:204–20.

———. 1978a. *Artificial curiosities.* Honolulu: Bishop Museum Special Publication 65.

———. 1978b. Exchange patterns in goods and spouses: Fiji, Tonga, and Samoa. *Mankind* 11:246–52.

———. 1978c. Melody, drone, and decoration: Underlying structures and surface manifestations in Tongan art and society.

In *Art in society*, edited by M. Greenhalgh and V. Megaw, 261–74. London: Duckworth.

———. 1979. A survey of Polynesian art, with selected reinterpretations. In *Exploring the visual art of Oceania*, edited by S. M. Mead, 180–91. Honolulu: University of Hawai'i Press.

———. 1983. *Polynesian dance: With a selection for contemporary performances*. Honolulu: Alpha Delta Kappa.

———. 1987. Polynesian mythic themes. In *Encyclopedia of religions*. Vol. 11. Edited by M. Eliade, 432–35. New York: Macmillan.

———. 1988. Hawaiian tattoo: A conjunction of genealogy and aesthetics. In *Marks of civilization*, edited by A. Rubin, 157–70. Los Angeles: Museum of Cultural History.

———. 1989. Art and aesthetics. In *Developments in Polynesian ethnology*, edited by A. Howard and R. Borofsky. Honolulu: University of Hawai'i Press.

Kaeppler, A., and J. W. Love. 1998. Australia and the Pacific Islands. *Garland encyclopedia of world music*. Vol. 9. New York and London: Garland Publishing, Inc.

Kamakau, S. M. *Ruling chiefs of Hawaii*. Honolulu: Kamehameha Schools Press.

———. 1964. Ka Po'e Kahiko *(The people of old)*. Honolulu: Bishop Museum Special Publication 51.

———. 1992. *Ruling chiefs of Hawaii*. Rev. ed. Honolulu: Kamehameha Schools Press.

Karetu, T. S. 1993. *Haka*. Wellington: Reed.

Kawharu, I. H. 1984. Maori sociology: A commentary. *Journal of the Polynesian Society* 93:231–46.

Kay, E. A. 1980. *Little worlds of the Pacific: An essay on Pacific Basin biogeography*. Honolulu: University of Hawaii Harold L. Lyon Arboretum Lecture 9.

Kay, P. 1963. Tahitian fosterage and the form of ethnographic models. *American Anthropologist* 63:1027–44.

Kelly, K. M. 1996. The end of the trail. In *Oceanic culture history: Essays in honour of Roger Green*, edited by Davidson et al. Dunedin: New Zealand Journal of Archaeology Special Publication.

Kikuchi, W. K. 1976. Prehistoric Hawaiian fishponds. *Science* 193:295–99.

King, M. 1989. *Moriori: A people rediscovered*. Auckland: Viking.

Kirch, P. V. 1979. Archaeology and the evolution of Polynesian culture. *Archaeology* 32 (5):44–52.

———. 1984. *The evolution of the Polynesian chiefdoms*. Cambridge: Cambridge University Press.

———. 1985. *Feathered gods and fishhooks: An introduction to Hawaiian archaeology and prehistory*. Honolulu: University of Hawai'i Press.

———. 1986. Rethinking East Polynesian prehistory. *Journal of the Polynesian Society* 95:9–40.

———. 1990A. The evolution of socio-political complexity in prehistoric Hawaii. *Journal of World Prehistory* 4:311–45.

———. 1990B. Monumental architecture and power in Polynesian chiefdoms: A comparison of Tonga and Hawaii. *World Archaeology* 22:206–22.

———. 1991. Polynesian agricultural systems. In *Islands, plants and Polynesians: An introduction to Polynesian ethnobotany*, edited by P. A. Cox and S. A. Banack, 113–34. Portland, Oregon: Dioscorides Press.

———. 1992. *The archaeology of history*. Vol. 2 of *Anahulu: The anthropology of history in the Kingdom of Hawaii*. Chicago: University of Chicago Press.

———. 1997. *The Lapita peoples: Ancestors of the oceanic world*. Cambridge, Mass: Blackwell.

Kirch, P. V., and T. S. Dye. 1979. Ethno-archaeology and the development of Polynesian fishing strategies. *Journal of the Polynesian Society* 88:53–76.

Kirch, P. V., and D. Lepofsky. 1993. Polynesian irrigation: Archaeological and linguistic evidence for origins and development. *Asian Perspectives* 32 (2).

Kirch, P. V., and D. E. Yen. 1982. *Tikopia:*

The prehistory and ecology of a Polynesian outlier. Honolulu: Bernice Pauahi Bishop Museum Bulletin 238.

Kirtley, B. F. 1971. *A motif-index of traditional Polynesian narratives*. Honolulu: University of Hawai'i Press.

Koch, G. 1966. The Polynesian-Micronesian culture boundary. In *Abstracts of Papers*. Canberra: 11th Pacific Science Congress 9.

Kooijiman, S. 1972. *Tapa in Polynesia*. Honolulu: Bernice Pauahi Bishop Museum Bulletin 234.

Koskinen, A. A. 1960. *Ariki the first-born*. Helsinki: Folklore Fellows Communication 181.

Krusenstern, A. J., trans. 1968. *Voyage round the world, 1803–1806*. New York: Da Capo Press.

Kuschel, G. 1975. *Biogeography and ecology in New Zealand*. The Hague: Junk.

Lamb, W. K., ed. 1984. *The voyage of George Vancouver: 1791–1795*. 4 vols. London: The Hakluyt Society.

Langsdorffs, G. H. von. 1812. *Bemerkungen auf einer Reise um die Welt: Nebst ausfuhrlicher Erklarung*. 2 vols. Frankfurt am Mayn: Friedrich Wilmans.

La Perouse, J.-F. 1980. *Voyage autour du Monde sur L'Astrolabe et La Boussole, 1785–1788*. Paris: F. Maspero.

Layton, B. 1984. Alienation rights in traditional Maori society: A reconsideration. *Journal of the Polynesian Society* 93:345–98. (Commentary by Alan Ward in *Journal of the Polynesian Society* 95: 259–62.)

Leach, H. 1984. *1000 years of gardening in New Zealand*. Wellington: Reed.

Lebot, V. 1991. Kava (*Piper methysticum Forst, f.*): The Polynesian dispersal of an Oceanian plant. In *Islands, plants and Polynesians: An introduction to Polynesian ethnobotany*, edited by P. A. Cox and S. A. Banack. Portland, Oregon: Dioscorides Press.

Lee, G., and E. Stasack. 1999. *Spirit of place: The petroglyphs of Hawaii*. Los Usos, California: Easter Island Foundation: Bearsville and Cloud Mountain Press.

Leenhardt, M. 1950. *Arts of the oceanic peoples*. London: Thames and Hudson.

Levison, M., R. G. Ward, and J. H. Webb. 1973. *The settlement of Polynesia: A computer simulation*. Minneapolis: University of Minnesota Press.

Levy, R. I. 1970. Tahitian adoption as a psychological message. In *Adoption in Eastern Oceania*, edited by V. Carroll. Association of Social Anthropology in Oceania Monograph 1. Honolulu: University of Hawai'i Press.

Lewis, D. 1972. *We, the navigators: The ancient art of landfinding in the Pacific*. Honolulu: University of Hawai'i Press.

Lieber, M. D. 1970. Adoption in Kapingamarangi. In *Adoption in Eastern Oceania*, edited by V. Carroll. Association of Social Anthropology in Oceania Monograph 1. Honolulu: University of Hawai'i Press.

Linnekin, J. 1990. *Sacred queens and women of consequence: Rank, gender, and colonialism in the Hawaiian Islands*. Ann Arbor: University of Michigan Press.

Linton, R. 1923. *The material culture of the Marquesas Islands*. Honolulu: Bernice Pauahi Bishop Museum Memoir 8 (5).

———. 1939. Marquesan culture. In *The individual and his society*, edited by A. Kardiner, 138–96. New York: Columbia University Press.

———. 1941. Primitive art. *Kenyon Review* 3:321–24.

Linton, R., and P. Wingert. 1946. *Arts of the South Seas*. New York: Museum of Modern Art.

Love, J. W. 1991. *Samoan variations: Essays on the nature of traditional oral arts*. In *Harvard dissertations in folklore and oral tradition*. Edited by A. B. Lord. New York and London: Garland.

Luomala, K. 1949. *Maui-of-a-thousand-tricks: His Oceanic and European biographers*. Honolulu: Bernice Pauahi Bishop Museum Bulletin 198.

———. 1951. The menehune of Polynesia.

Honolulu: Bernice Pauahi Bishop
Museum Bulletin 203.

———. 1955. *Voices on the wind: Polynesian myths and chants*. Honolulu: Bishop Museum Press.

McArthur, A. M. 2000. *The curbing of anarchy in Kunimaipa society*. Sydney: Oceania Monograph 49.

McArthur, N. 1968. Island populations of the Pacific. Canberra: Australian National University Press.

McCall, G. 1981. Traditions and survival on Easter Island. Honolulu: University of Hawai'i Press.

McGlone, M. S. 1983. Polynesian deforestation of New Zealand: A preliminary synthesis. *Archaeology and Physical Anthropology in Oceania* 18:11-25.

McKern, W. C. 1929. *Archaeology of Tonga*. Honolulu: Bernice Pauahi Bishop Museum Bulletin: 60.

McLean, M. 1979. *An annotated bibliography of Oceanic music and dance*. Wellington: The Polynesia Society.

———. 1990. Tikopia songs. In *Tikopia songs: Poetic and musical art of a Polynesian people of the Solomon Islands*, by R. Firth. Cambridge: Cambridge University Press.

McLean, M., ed. 1996. *Maori music*. Auckland: Auckland University Press.

McLean, M., and M. Orbell. 1979. *Traditional songs of the Maori*. Auckland: Auckland University Press.

Malo, D. 1951. *Hawaiian antiquities*. 2d ed. Translated from Hawaiian by N. B. Emerson in 1898. Honolulu: Bernice Pauahi Bishop Museum Special Publications.

Maning, F. M. 1945. *Old New Zealand*. Christchurch Whitcombe & Tombes.

Marck, J. 1996. The first-order anthropomorphic gods of Polynesia. *Journal of the Polynesian Society* 105:217-58.

Marcus, G. E. 1980. *The nobility and the chiefly tradition in the modern kingdom of Tonga*. Wellington: The Polynesia Society Memoir 42.

Mariner, W. 1817. *An account of the natives of the Tonga Islands*. 2 vols. London: J. Martin.

Marshall, D. S. 1962. *Island of passion: Ralivavae*. London: Allen and Unwin.

Marshall, D. S., and C. F. Snow. 1956. An evaluation of Polynesian craniology. *American Journal of Physical Anthropology* 14:405-27.

Marshall, D. S., and R. C. Suggs. 1971. *Human sexual behavior: Variations in the ethnographic spectrum*. New York: Basic Books.

Marshall, M., ed. 1981. *Siblingship in Oceania: Studies in the meaning of kin relations*. Lanham, Maryland: University Press of America.

Marshall, M., and J. L. Caughay, eds. 1989. *Culture, kin, and cognition in Oceania: Essays in honor of Ward Goodenough*. New York: American Anthropological Association Special Publication.

Marshall, P. 1927. *Geology of Mangaia*. Honolulu: Bernice Pauahi Bishop Museum Bulletin 36.

Mead, M. 1928. The role of the individual in Samoan culture. *Journal of the Royal Anthropological Institute* 58:481–95.

———. 1930. *Social Organization of Manu'a*. Honolulu: Bernice Pauahi Bishop Museum Bulletin 76.

Mead, S. M. 1969. *Traditional Maori clothing*. Wellington: Reed.

———. 1975. Origins of Maori art. *Oceania* 45:173–211.

———. 1995. *The art of Maori carving*. Wellington: Reed.

Mead, S. M., ed. 1979. *Exploring the visual art of Oceania*. Honolulu: University of Hawai'i Press.

———. 1984. *The Maori: Maori art from New Zealand collections*. New York: Harry Abrams.

Mead, S. M., with B. Kernot. 1983. *Art and artists in Oceania*. Palmerston North: Dunmore Press.

Melton, T. et al. 1995. Polynesian genetic affinities with Southeast Asian populations as identified by mtDNA analysis. *American Journal of Human Genetics*

57:403-414.

Melton, T. et al. 1998. Genetic evidence for the proto-Austronesian homeland in Asia: mtDNA and nuclear DNA variation in Taiwanese aboriginal tribes. *American Journal of Human Genetics* 63:1807–23.

Melville, H. n.d. *Typee.* New York: Dodd, Mead and Co.

Merrill, E. D. 1945. *Plant life of the Pacific world.* New York: MacMillan.

Metge, J. 1976. *The Maoris of New Zealand.* Rev. ed. London: Routledge and Kegan Paul.

———. 1989. *Te reo o te harakeke:* Conceptions of the *whaanau. Journal of the Polynesian Society* 99:55–92.

Métraux, A. 1937. The kings of Easter Island. *Journal of the Polynesian Society* 46:41–62.

———. 1940. *Ethnology of Easter Island.* Honolulu: Bernice Pauahi Bishop Museum Bulletin 160.

———. 1971. *Ethnology of Easter Island.* New York: Kraus Reprint.

Michels, J. W. 1973. *Dating methods in archaeology.* New York: Seminar Press.

Milke, W. 1958. Zur inneren Gliederung und geschichtlichen Stellung der ozeanisch-austronesischen Sprachen. *Zeitschrift für Ethnologie* 82:58–62.

———. 1964. *Oceanic kinship terms.* Honolulu: East-West Center.

Moerenhout, J. A. 1837. *Voyages aux îles du Grand Océan.* 2 vols. Paris: A. Bertrand.

Monberg, T. 1991. *Bellona Island beliefs and rituals.* Honolulu: University of Hawai'i Press.

Montgomery, J., ed. 1831. *Journal of voyages and travels by the Rev. Daniel Tyerman and George Bennet, esq.* 3 vols. Boston: Crocker and Brewster.

Morrison, J. 1935. *The journal of James Morrison, Boatswain's mate of the bounty.* Edited by O. Ritter. London: Golden Cockerel Press.

Moyle, R. 1972. *Samoan song types.* Nedlands: University of West Australia Press.

———. 1987. *Tongan music.* Auckland: Auckland University Press.

Mühlmann, W. E. 1938. *Staatsbildung und amphiktyonien in Polynesien.* Stuttgart: Verlag Strecker und Schroeder.

———. 1955. *Arioi und mamaia: Studien zur kulturkunde.* Vol. 14. Wiesbaden: Franz Steiner Verlag.

Mulloy, W. 1970. A speculative reconstruction of techniques of carving, transporting, and erecting Easter Island statues. *Archaeology and Physical Anthropology in Oceania* 5:1–23.

Murai, M. et al. 1958. *Some tropical Pacific foods.* Honolulu: University of Hawai'i Press.

Murdock, G. P. 1949. *Social structure.* New York: MacMillan.

Newbury, C., ed. 1961. *The history of the Tahitian mission, 1799–1830, written by John Davies.* Cambridge: Cambridge University Press.

Nordhoff, C. 1930. Notes on off-shore fishing of the Society Islands. *Journal of the Polynesian Society* 39:137–73; 221–62.

Noricks, J. S. 1983. Unrestricted cognatic descent and corporateness on Niutao, a Polynesian island of Tuvalu. *American Ethnologist* 10:571–84.

Obeyesekere, G. 1992. *The apotheosis of Captain Cook: European mythmaking in the Pacific.* Princeton: Princeton University Press.

Oliver, D. 1974. *Ancient Tahitian society.* 3 vols. Honolulu: University of Hawai'i Press.

———. 1981. *Two Tahitian villages: A study in comparisons.* La'ie, Hawaii: Institute for Polynesian Studies, Brigham Young University.

———. 1988. *Return to Tahiti: Bligh's second breadfruit voyage.* Melbourne and Honolulu: Melbourne University Press and University of Hawai'i Press.

———. 1989a. *Native cultures of the Pacific Islands.* Honolulu: University of Hawai'i Press.

———. 1989b. *Oceania: Native cultures of Australia and the Pacific Islands.*

Honolulu: University of Hawai'i Press.

———. 1989C. *The Pacific Islands*. 3d ed. Honolulu: University of Hawai'i Press.

———. 2001. Becoming "old" in Polynesia. *Bulletin de la Société des Études Océaniennes*. (forthcoming)

Oppenheim, R. S. 1973. *Maori death customs*. Wellington: Reed.

Orsmond, J. M. n.d. Tahitian texts on Arioi, War, etc. Sydney: Mitchell Library.

Ortner, S. 1981. Gender and sexuality in hierarchical societies: The case of Polynesia and some comparative implications. In *Sexual meanings*, edited by S. Ortner and H. Whitehead. Cambridge: Cambridge University Press.

Ottino, P. 1967. *Early 'ati of the Western Tuamotus*. Honolulu: Bishop Museum Special Publication 56.

———. 1970. Adoption on Rangiroa Atoll, Tuamotu Archipelago. In *Adoption in Eastern Oceania*, edited by V. Carroll. Association of Social Anthropology in Oceania Monograph 1. Honolulu: University of Hawai'i Press.

———. 1972. *Rangiroa: Parenté étendue*. Paris: Cujas.

Panoff, M. 1965. La terminologie de la parenté en Polynesie: Essai d'analyse formelle. *L'Homme* 3:60–87.

Papy, H. R. 1954. *Tahiti et les îles voisines*. 2 vols. Toulouse: Les Artisans de l'Imprimerie Douladoure.

Parkinson, S. 1773. *A journal of a voyage to the South Seas, on His Majesty's ship* Endeavour. *Faithfully transcribed from the papers of the late Sydney Parkinson*. London: printed for Stanfield Parkinson.

Pawley, A. K. 1966. Polynesian languages: A subgrouping based on shared innovations in morphology. *Journal of the Polynesian Society* 75:39–64.

———. 1967. The relationships of Polynesian outlier languages. *Journal of the Polynesian Society* 76:259–98.

———. 1972. On the internal relationships of Eastern oceanic languages. In *Studies in oceanic culture history*, edited by R. C. Green and M. Kelly. Honolulu: Bernice Pauahi Bishop Museum.

———. 1974. Austronesian languages. In *Encyclopedia Brittanica*, 15th ed.

———. 1981. Melanesian diversity and Polynesian homogeneity: A unified explanation for language. In *Studies in Pacific languages and cultures in honour of Bruce Biggs*, edited by J. Hollyman and A. Pawley. Auckland: Linguistic Society of New Zealand.

———. 1991. On the Polynesian subgroup as a problem for Irwin's continuous settlement hypothesis. In *Man and a half: Essays in Pacific anthropology and ethnobiology in honour of Ralph Bulmer*, edited by A. K. Pawley, 387–410. Auckland: The Polynesian Society.

———. 1996. On the Polynesian subgroup as a problem for Irwin's continuous settlement hypothesis. In *Oceanic culture history: Essays in honour of Roger Green*, edited by J. Davidson et al., 387–410. Dunedin: New Zealand Journal of Archeology, special publication.

Pawley, A. K., ed. 1991. *Man and a half: Essays in Pacific anthropology and ethnobiology in honour of Ralph Bulmer*. Auckland: The Polynesian Society.

Pawley, A. K., and R. Green. 1971. Lexical evidence for the proto-Polynesian homeland. *Te Reo* 14:1–35.

———. 1975. Dating the dispersal of the Oceanic languages. *Oceanic Linguistics* 12:1–67.

Pawley, A. K. and M. D. Ross. 1993. Austronesian historical linguistics and culture history. *Annual Review of Anthropology* 22:425-59.

Pietrusewsky, M. 1989a. A Lapita-associated skeleton from Natunuku, Fiji. *Records of the Australian Museum* 41:297–325.

———. 1989b. A study of skeletal and dental remains from Watom Island and comparisons with other La Pita people. *Records of the Australian Museum* 41:235–92.

———. 1996. The physical anthropology of Polynesians: A review of some cranial and skeletal studies. In *Oceanic culture history: Essays in honour of Roger Green*, edited by J. Davidson et al., 343–53. Dunedin: New Zealand Journal of Archaeology Special Publication.

Pietrusewsky, M., and M. T. Douglas. 1994. An osteological assessment of health and disease in precontact and historic (1778) Hawaii. In *In the wake of contact*, edited by C. S. Larson and G. R. Milner, 179–196. New York: Wiley-Liss.

Prickett, N., ed. 1982. *The first thousand years: Regional perspectives in New Zealand archaeology*. Palmerston North: New Zealand Archaeological Association.

Pukui, M. 1942. Hawaiian beliefs and customs during birth, infancy, and childhood. *Bernice Pauahi Bishop Museum Occasional Papers* 16:357–81.

Pukui, M., and S. H. Elbert. 1957. *Hawaiian dictionary*. Honolulu: University of Hawai'i Press.

Pukui, M. et al. 1972–79. Nana i ke kumu (*Look to the source*). 2 vols. Honolulu: Queen Lili'uokalani Children's Center.

Radcliffe-Brown, A. R. 1924. The mother's brother in South Africa. *South African Journal of Science* 21:542–75.

Ragone, D. 1991. Ethnobotany of breadfruit in Polynesia. In *Islands, plants and Polynesians: An introduction to Polynesian ethnobotany*, edited by P. A. Cox and S. A. Banack. Portland, Oregon: Discorides Press.

Ray-Lescure, P. 1946. Le chien en Polynesie. *Bulletin de la Société des Études Océaniennes* 77:266–72.

Redd, A. J. et al. 1995. Evolutionary history of the CUII/t RNA (Lys) intergenic 9 base pair deletion in human mitochondrial DNAs from the Pacific. *Molecular Biology and Evolution* 12:604–15.

Relethford, J. H. 2001. Ancient DNA and the origins of modern humans. *Proceedings of the National Academy of Sciences* 98:2.

Richards, M. et al. 1998. MtDNA suggests Polynesian origins in Eastern Indonesia. *American Journal of Human Genetics* 63:1234–36.

Rienzi, G. L. de. 1836–38. *Océanie, ou cinquième partie du Monde*. Paris: Firmin Didot Freres.

Ritchie, J. et al. 1989. Socialization and character development. In *Developments in Polynesian ethnology*, edited by A. Howard and R. Borofsky, 95–136. Honolulu: University of Hawai'i Press.

Roberts, H. 1926. *Ancient Hawaiian music*. Honolulu: Bernice Pauahi Bishop Museum Bulletin 29.

Rolett, B. V. 1993. Marquesan prehistory and the origin of East Polynesian society. *Journal de la Société des Océanistes* 96:29–47.

Rose, R. 1978. *Symbols of sovereignty*. Pacific Anthropological Records 28. Honolulu: Bernice Pauahi Bishop Museum Department of Anthropology.

Sahlins, M. 1958. *Social stratification in Polynesia*. Seattle: University of Washington Press.

———. 1961. The segmentary lineage: An organization of predatory expansion. *American Anthropologist* 63:322-45.

———. 1962. *Moala: Culture and nature on a Fijian island*. Ann Arbor: University of Michigan Press.

———. 1981a. *Historical metaphors and mythical realities: Structure in the early history of the Sandwich Island Kingdom*. Ann Arbor: University of Michigan Press.

———. 1981b. The stranger-king: Dumezil among the Fijians. *Journal of Pacific History* 16:107–32.

———. 1992. *Historical ethnography*. Vol. 1 of *Anahulu: The anthropology of history in the Kingdom of Hawaii*. Chicago: University of Chicago Press.

———. 1995. *How "natives" think: About Captain Cook, for example*. Chicago: University of Chicago Press.

St. Cartonail, K. 1997. *The art of Tonga*. Nelson, New Zealand: Craig Potton Publishing.

Salmond, A. 1978. *Te ao tawhito*: A semantic approach to the traditional Maori cosmos. *Journal of the Polynesian Society* 87:5–28.

―――. 1983. The study of traditional Maori society: The state of the art. *Journal of the Polynesian Society* 92:309–32.

―――. 1989. Tribal words, tribal worlds: The translatability of *tayu* and *mana*. In *Culture, kin, and cognition in Oceania: Essays in honor of Ward Goodenough*, edited by M. Marshall and J. L. Caughy, 55–78. Washington, D.C.: American Anthropological Association Special Publication.

―――. 1991a. *Tipuna*—ancestors: Aspects of Maori cognatic descent. In *Man and a half: Essays in Pacific anthropology and ethnobiology in honour of Ralph Bulmer*, edited by A. K. Pawley. Auckland: The Polynesian Society.

―――. 1991b. *Two worlds: First meetings between Maori and Europeans, 1642–1771*. Auckland: Viking.

―――. 1997. *Between worlds: Early exchanges between Maori and Europeans, 1773–1815*. New York: Viking.

Sanchez, A. 1998. *(Homo) sexualité hawai-iene: l'aikané et la société*. Bulletin de la Société des Études Océaniennes 279–80, 105–23.

Scaglion, R., and K. A. Soto. 1994. *A prehistoric introduction of the sweet potato in New Guinea*. Honolulu: Association of Social Anthropology in Oceania Monograph 15.

Schmitt, R. C. 1968. *Demographic statistics of Hawaii, 1778–1965*. Honolulu: University of Hawai'i Press.

―――. 1971. New estimates of the pre-censal population of Hawaii. *Journal of the Polynesian Society* 80:237–73.

―――. 1973. *The missionary censuses of Hawaii*. Honolulu: Bernice Pauahi Bishop Museum Pacific Anthropological Records 20.

Schoeffel, P. 1978. *Gender, status and power in Samoa*. Canberra: Anthropology 1 (2): 69–81.

Schwimmer, E. G. 1966. *The world of the Maori*. Wellington: Reed.

―――. 1978. Lévi-Strauss and Maori social structure. *Anthropologica* 20:201–22.

―――. 1990. The Maori *hapu*: A quantitative model. *Journal of the Polynesian Society* 99:297–318.

Shand, A. 1911. *The Moriori people of the Chatham Islands: Their history and traditions*. Wellington: Polynesian Society Memoir 2.

Shapiro, H. L. 1943. *Physical differentiation in Polynesia*. Cambridge, Mass.: Papers of the Peabody Museum 20

Sharp, A. 1956. *Ancient voyagers in the Pacific*. Wellington: Polynesian Society Memoir 32.

Sharp, A., ed. 1970. *The Journal of Jacob Roggeveen*. Oxford: Oxford University Press.

Shawcross, K. 1967. Fern root and the total scheme of 18th century Maori food production in agricultural areas. *Journal of the Polynesian Society* 76:330–52.

Shawcross, F. W. 1970. Ethnographic economics and the study of population in prehistoric New Zealand through archaeology. *Mankind* 7:279–91.

Shirres, M. F. 1982. Tavu. *Journal of the Polynesian Society* 9:7–28.

Shore, B. 1982. *Salalilua: A Samoan mystery*. New York: Columbia University Press.

―――. 1989. *Mana* and *tapu*. In *Developments in Polynesian ethnology*, edited by A. Howard and R. Borofsky. Honolulu: University of Hawai'i Press.

Shutler, R., Jr., and J. Marck. 1975. On the dispersal of the Austronesian horticulturalists. *Archaeology and Physical Anthropology in Oceania* 10:81–113.

Simmons, D. R. 1969. Economic change in New Zealand prehistory. *Journal of the Polynesian Society* 78:3-34.

―――. 1976. *The great New Zealand myth*. Wellington: Reed.

Sinclair, K. 1988. *A history of New Zealand*. New York: Penguin.

Sinoto, Y. H. 1979a. Excavations on Huahine, French Polynesia. *Pacific Studies* 3:1-40.

―――. 1979b. The Marquesas. In *The pre-*

history of Polynesia, edited by J. D. Jennings. Cambridge: Harvard University Press.

Skinner, H. D. 1921. Culture areas. *Journal of the Polynesian Society* 30:71–79.

———. 1923. *The Morioris of Chatham Islands*. Honolulu: Bernice Pauahi Bishop Museum Memoir 9 (1).

Skinner, H. D., and W. C. Baucke. 1928. *The Morioris*. Honolulu: Bernice Pauahi Bishop Museum Memoir 5.

Smith, B. 1960. *European vision and the South Pacific, 1768–1850*. Polynesian Center Memoir 40. Oxford: Clarendon Press.

———. 1992. *Imagining the Pacific in the wake of the Cook voyages*. Melbourne: Melbourne University Press.

Smith, I. 1989. Maori impact on the marine megafauna. *New Zealand Archaeological Association Monograph* 17:76–108.

———. 1996. Historical documents, archaeology and 19th century seal hunting in New Zealand. In *Oceanic culture history: Essays in honour of Roger Green*, edited by J. Davidson et al., 675–85. Dunedin: New Zealand Journal of Anthology Special Publication.

Smith, J. 1974. *Tapu* removal in Maori religion. Wellington: Polynesian Society Memoir 40.

Söderstrom, J. 1939. *A sparrman's ethnographical collection from James Cook's 2nd expedition (1772–1775)*. Stokholm: Bokforlags Aktiebolatet Thule.

Sparks, R. 1955. Polynesian tattooing: The techniques, iconography, patronage, profession and esthetics. Honolulu: Master's thesis, University of Hawai'i.

Spriggs, M. 1984. The Lapita cultural complex. *Journal of Pacific History* 19:202–23.

———. 1990. Dating the Lapita culture: Another view. In *Proceedings of the LaPita Design Workshop*. Canberra: Australian National University.

———. 1997. *The Island Melanesians*. Oxford: Blackwell.

Spriggs, M. et al. 1993. A community of culture: People and culture of the Pacific. *Occasional Papers in Prehistory* 21. Canberra: Australian National University.

Stannard, D. E. 1989. *Before the Horror: The population of Hawai'i on the eve of the Western contact*. Honolulu: Social Sciences Research Center, University of Hawai'i.

Steinen, Karl von den. 1925–28. *Die Marquesaner und ihre kunst*. 3 vol. Berlin: Reimer.

Stimson, J. F. 1928. Tahitian names for the nights of the moon. *Journal of the Polynesian Society* 37:326–37.

———. 1933a. *The cult of Kiho-tumu*. Honolulu: Bernice Pauahi Bishop Museum Bulletin 111.

———. 1933b. *Tuamotuan religion*. Honolulu: Bernice Pauahi Bishop Museum Bulletin 103.

———. 1934. *Legends of Maui and Tahaki*. Honolulu: Bernice Pauahi Bishop Museum Bulletin 127.

Stokes, J. F. G. 1930. Ethnology of Rapa. Honolulu: Unpublished ms., Bernice Pauahi Bishop Museum.

Stolpe, Hjalmar. 1899. *Über die Tatowirung der Oster-Insulaner*. Dresden: Abhandlungen und Berichte des K. Zoologisches und Anthropologisch-Ethnographisches Museum.

Stoneking, M., and A. C. Wilson. 1989. Mitochondrial DNA. In *The colonization of the Pacific: A genetic trail*, edited by A. Hill and S. W. Sergjeanson 215–45. Oxford: Clarendon Press.

Suggs, R. C. 1960. *The island civilizations of Polynesia*. New York: Mentor.

Sutton, D. G. 1980. A culture history of the Chatham Islands. *Journal of the Polynesian Society* 89:67–94.

———. 1996. Historical linguistics and Pacific archaeology. In *Oceanic culture history: Essays in honour of Roger Green*, edited by J. Davidson et al. Dunedin: New Zealand Journal of Archaeology Special publication.

Sutton, D. G., ed. 1989. *Saying so doesn't make it so: Papers in honour of B. Foss Leach*. Auckland: New Zealand Archeological Association Monograph 17.

———. 1990. Organisation and ontology: The origins of the northern Maori chiefdoms, New Zealand. *Man* 25:667–92.

———. 1994. *The origins of the first New Zealanders*. Auckland: Auckland University Press.

Sykes, B. C. et al. 1995. The origins of the Polynesians: An interpretation from mitochondrial lineage analysis. *American Journal of Human Genetics* 57:1463–75.

Tatar, E. 1982. *Nineteenth century Hawaiian chants*. Honolulu: Bernice Pauahi Bishop Museum Anthropological Records 33.

Tiffany, S. W. and W. W. 1975. The cognatic descent groups in contemporary Samoa. *Man* 10:430–47.

Tiffany, S. W. et al. 1978. Optation, cognatic descent and redistribution in Samoa. *Ethnology* 17 (4):367–90.

Tischner, H., and F. Hewicker. 1954. *Oceanic art*. London: Thames and Hudson.

Titcomb, M. 1948. Kava in Hawaii. *Journal of the Polynesian Society* 57:105–71.

———. 1969. *Dog and man in the ancient Pacific*. Honolulu: Bernice Pauahi Bishop Museum Special Publication 69.

Turnbull, J. 1813. *A voyage round the world, in the years 1800, 1801, 1802, 1803 and 1804*. 2d ed. London: A. Maxwell.

Turner, G. 1861. *Nineteen years in Polynesia*. London: J. Snow.

———. 1884. *Samoa: A hundred years ago and long before*. London: MacMillan.

Valeri, V. 1985. *Kingship and sacrifice: Ritual and society in ancient Hawaii*. Translated by Paula Wissing. Chicago: University of Chicago Press.

Vancouver, G. See Lamb.

Vayda, A. P. 1960. *Maori warfare*. Wellington: Polynesian Society Monograph 2.

Von Sydow, E. 1921. *Exotische Kunst Afrika und Oceanien*. Leipzig: Klinknauft und Bierman.

Walch, D. B. 1967. The historical development of the Hawaiian alphabet. *Journal of the Polynesian Society* 76:353–66.

Ward, R. G., J. W. Webb, and M. Levison. 1976. The settlement of the Polynesian outliers: A computer simulation. In *Pacific Navigation and Voyaging*, edited by B. R. Finney. Wellington: Polynesian Society Memoir 39.

Ward, R. G., and M. Brookfield. 1992. The dispersal of the coconut: Did it float or was it carried to Panama? *Journal of Biogeography* 19:467–80.

Wardwell, A. 1967. *The sculpture of Polynesia*. Chicago: The Art Institute of Chicago.

Watling, D. 1982. *Birds of Fiji, Tonga and Samoa*. Wellington: Milwood Press.

Webster, S. 1975. Cognatic descent groups and the contemporary Maori. *Journal of the Polynesian Society* 84: 121–52.

Whistler, W. A. 1991. Polynesian plant introductions. In *Islands, plants and Polynesians: An introduction to Polynesian ethnobotany*, edited by P. A. Cox and S. A. Banack. Portland, Oregon: Dioscorides Press.

White, R. G. 1967. Onomastically induced word replacement in Tahitian. In *Polynesian culture history: Essays in honor of Kenneth P. Emory*, edited by Highland et al. Honolulu: Bernice Pauahi Bishop Museum Special Publications 56.

Whitmore, T. C. 1981. *Wallace's line and plate tectonics*. Oxford: Clarendon Press.

Wiens, H. J. 1962. *Atoll environment and ecology*. New Haven: Yale University Press.

Wilder, G. P. 1928. *The breadfruit of Tahiti*. Honolulu: Bernice Pauahi Bishop Museum Bulletin 50.

Williams, H. W. 1975. *A dictionary of the Maori language*. 7th ed. Wellington: Government Printer.

Williams, J. 1837. *A narrative of missionary enterprises in the South Sea islands*. New York: D. Appleton and Co.

Williams, W. 1985. Sex and shamanism: The making of the Hawaiian *mahu. The Advocate* 48–49.

Williamson, R. W. 1933. *Religious and cosmic beliefs of Central Polynesia*. 2 vols. Cambridge: Cambridge University Press.

Wilson, J. 1799. *A missionary voyage to the Southern Pacific Ocean*. London: Chapman.

Wright, O. 1955. *Translation of extracts from Dumont d'Urville: Voyage au Pol Sud et dans Océanie sur les corvettes L'Astrolabe et La Zelée etc*. Wellington: Reed.

Yen, D. 1961. The adaptation of the *kumara* by the New Zealand Maori. *Journal of the Polynesian Society* 70:338–48.

———. 1973. The origins of Oceanic agriculture. *Archaeology and Physical Anthropology in Oceania* 1.

———. 1974. *The sweet potato and Oceania*. Honolulu: Bernice Pauahi Bishop Museum Bulletin 236.

———. 1980. The Southeast Asian foundations of oceanic agriculture: A reassessment. *Journal de la Société des Océanistes* 36 (66–67): 140–47.

———. 1985. Wild plants and domestication in Pacific Islands. In *Recent advances in Indo-Pacific Prehistory*, edited by V. N. Misra and P. Bellwood. Oxford: Oxford University Press.

———. 1991. Polynesian cultigens and cultivars: The question of origins. *In Islands, plants, and Polynesians: An introduction to Polynesian ethnobotany*, edited by P. A. Cox and S. A. Banack. Portland, Oregon: Dioscorides Press.

———. 1994. *South Pacific indigenous nuts*. Canberra: Australian Centre for International Agricultural Research.

———. 1998. Subsistence to commerce in Pacific agriculture: Some four thousand years of plant exchange. In *Plants for food and medicine*, edited by H. D. V. Prendergast et al., 161–83. Kew: Royal Botanic Gardens.

Yen, D., and J. Gordon, eds. 1973. *Anuta: A Polynesian outlier in the Solomon Islands*. Honolulu: Department of Anthropology, Bernice Pauahi Bishop Museum.

INDEX

Numbers in bold type indicate illustrations.

sleeping-houses, 104–10

slingstones, 146–47

slit gongs, 141

"social category," defined, 178

"social class," 126–27

"social group," defined, 178

social stratification, 209–12, 252–53

social units, 247–50, 256

societies, 214–21

society, prerequisites for
functional, 258–60
terminating, 258

sound-making instruments, 141–43, 241
variety of, 143

"span" (of clan) 191

spears, 146

spells (magical), 40

spirit (of human), 157

"status," defined, 181–82

sterility, 159

stilt-walking, 134

stratification, social, 209–11, 252–53

"Stratified" societies, 211

sugarcane 10, 79

suicide, 172

Sunda, Sundanoid, 7–10

supercision, 166–67

surfing, 136–37

sweet potato, 78–79, 77

swimming, 132

T

Tahaa, 204

Tahiti
afterlife, 176–77
archery in, 135
boxing in, 133–34
breadfruit in, 74–75
cannibalism, assimilative, 102
canoes, **114, 118,** 119, **152**
clan succession in, 194

clothing, 63–66

dancing, **139**

death in, **173, 174**

dogs in, 82

drama, 143–44

drum, **141**

eating described, 97–98

feathers in, 58

fishing, 85, 86, 87, 90, 91–92, 93

friendship in, 201

gods, 43, 44, 46, 48

homosexuality in, 130–31

house type, **105**

infanticide, 161

infants, seclusion of high-ranking, 165–66

kava in, 99

Mahaite *marae,* 206

migration to Hawai'i, 213

mourners in, **174**

multisired children, 158

music, 138

name avoidance in, 40–41

names, personal, 162

naval battle described, 151

"noble savages," 258

old age in, 171

'Oro cult, 215–18

points of daylight, 30

Pomare II, 185, **203**

population, 32, 33, 34

rafts, 123

sexual behavior in, 124, 125–26, 129, 130–31

slingstones, 146

social stratification, 210, 211–12

strong teeth, 53

surfing in, 137

voyaging to/from Hawai'i, 17–18

woman of, **205**

women, authority of, 171

word meanings, 51–52

wrestling in, 133

Taiwan, 8, 10

Tangaloa, 112

defined, 202
stratification of, 210
trumpets, 142
tsunami, 28
Tuamotu Archipelago, 54, **105**, 117, **118**, 258
Tupaia, 19
turmeric, 65, 79
Tutuila. *See* Samoa
Tuvalu. *See* Ellis Islands

u

uncles and aunts, relations with, 167
uniforms (war), 148

v

virginity testing, 164, 180
volcanism, 25–27
voyaging, 1, 10–11, 15–19

w

warfare, 145–55, 241–45, 256
causes of, 145–46
defensive measures, 148
open battles, 150–52
raiding, 150

refuge from, 148
religious aspects of, 154–55
sieges, 152
social aspects of, 152–54
tactics, 151
types of, 148–52
weapons used in, 146–48, **147**, 154
water, as a tool, 54
watercraft, 114–23, 240, 256. *See also* canoes, rafts
proto-Polynesian words for, 114
"wave" theory of colonization, 19, 213
weaning, 165
West Futuna, 34
West Uvea, 34
"wet" vs. "dry" cultivation, 79
wet-nursing, 165
whistles, 142
Wilson, James, 130–31
wind sound instruments, 141–42
winds, 15, 17–18, 27–28, 30; map of, **27**
work sheds, 160
wrestling, 133

y

yam, 78–79, **77**
youth, 125, 168–69
"youth" houses, 110

3M